Frommer's 96

OFFICIAL G...

Atl...a

AND THE

Olympic Summer Games

by Rena Bulkin

Macmillan • USA

ABOUT THE AUTHOR

Rena Bulkin began her travel writing career in 1964 when she set out for Europe in search of adventure. She found it writing about hotels and restaurants for the *New York Times* International Edition. She has since authored dozens of magazine articles and 15 travel guides to far-flung destinations.

MACMILLAN TRAVEL

A Simon & Schuster Macmillan Company
1633 Broadway
New York, NY 10019

ISBN 0-02-860702-3
ISSN 1047-7888

Editor: Lisa Renaud
Map Editor: Douglas Stallings
Design by Michele Laseau
Digital cartography by Jim Moore and Ortelius Design

SPECIAL SALES

Bulk purchases (10+ copies) of Frommer's Travel Guides are available to corporations at special discounts. The Special Sales Department can produce custom editions to be used as premiums and/or for sales promotion to suit individual needs. Existing editions can be produced with custom cover imprints such as corporate logos. For more informa-tion write to: Special Sales, Simon & Schuster, 8th floor, 1633 Broadway, New York, NY 10019.

Manufactured in the United States of America

Contents

List of Maps

AN INVITATION TO THE READER

In researching this book, we discovered many wonderful places—hotels, restaurants, shops, and more. We're sure you'll find others. Please tell us about them, so we can share the information with your fellow travelers in upcoming editions. If you were disappointed with a recommendation, we'd love to know that too. Please write to:

Rena Bulkin
Frommer's Atlanta '96
Macmillan Travel
1633 Broadway
New York, NY 10019

AN ADDITIONAL NOTE

Please be advised that travel information is subject to change at any time—and this is especially true of prices. We therefore suggest that you write or call ahead for confirmation when making your travel plans. The authors, editors, and publisher cannot be held responsible for the experiences of readers while traveling. Your safety is important to us, however, so we encourage you to stay alert and be aware of your surroundings. Keep a close eye on cameras, purses, and wallets, all favorite targets of thieves and pickpockets.

WHAT THE SYMBOLS MEAN

✪ Frommer's Favorites

Hotels, restaurants, attractions, and entertainment you should not miss.

ⓢ Super-Special Values

Hotels and restaurants that offer great value for your money.

The following abbreviations are used for credit cards:

AE	American Express	EU	Eurocard
CB	Carte Blanche	JCB	Japan Credit Bank
DC	Diners Club	MC	MasterCard
DISC	Discover	V	Visa
ER	enRoute		

Introducing Atlanta

They call it the Big A, the capital of the New South, and the International Gateway City—all names evocative of Atlanta's dynamism, dash, and spirit. This ever-expanding city—the 13th largest metropolitan area in the United States—teems with energy. Its downtown area is an architecture showplace of glittering glass skyscrapers, appropriate to the city's role as the South's major marketplace and its hub of finance, communications, and transportation.

This is the home of the world's largest airport. It's one of the nation's top meeting and convention cities—headquarters for hundreds of businesses, including Coca-Cola (never ask for a Pepsi here), Delta Air Lines, UPS, Holiday Inn, Ritz-Carlton, Georgia-Pacific, and Turner Broadcasting. It is the major shopping center of the Southeast region; home to 29 colleges and universities; and a crossroads where three interstate highways converge. The city hosted the Democratic National Convention in 1988 and Super Bowl XXVIII in 1994. And as we go to press, it is gearing up for the biggest event of them all, the 1996 Olympic Games.

Atlanta is also called the Dogwood City, for this bustling metropolis is a very southern city of magnolias and colonnaded white mansions. Every spring (and spring here can begin in February), the city blossoms with delicate pink dogwood buds, fragrant honeysuckle and yellow jasmine, and beautiful pink, white, and red azaleas. Drive a few miles out of the metropolitan area and you'll find yourself in verdant countryside.

Big-city Atlanta celebrates holidays with small-town exuberance. Annual events include chili and barbecue cookoffs, traditional Fourth of July picnics and parades, and Christmas chestnut roasts. The city's patron saint is *Gone With the Wind* author Margaret Mitchell (the book comes up almost on a daily basis), and history—especially Civil War history—is venerated. And while it's extremely dynamic, this is also a leisurely city where people are never in so much of a rush that they dispense with southern graciousness and hospitality. Atlanta is consistently ranked as one of the best places in the country to live—a sentiment that any resident will enthusiastically confirm.

To this appealing mix of urban sophistication and southern gentility add a vibrant cultural scene, with a growing theater community; major art and science museums; a well-regarded symphony; big-league sports; a culinary spectrum that ranges from fried chicken 'n' biscuits

The Atlanta Region

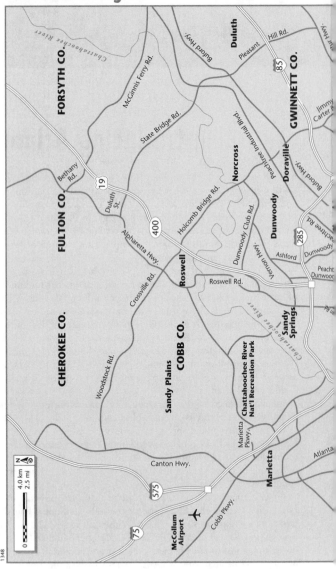

to beluga caviar; hot nightlife; and a delightfully temperate climate (except for those steamy summers).

Add further a clean and safe state-of-the-art urban mass-transportation system and visitor attractions that run the gamut from legacies of the Confederacy to black heritage sites (Martin Luther King, Jr., was born and is buried here), and from historic homes to the futuristic SciTrek Museum. And you might not expect it, but Atlanta also

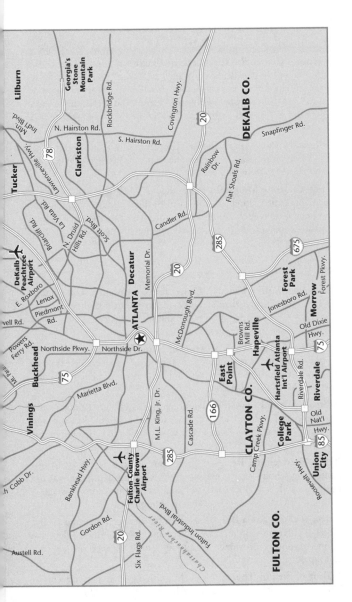

has some surprising things to offer: theme parks, a presidential library (Jimmy Carter's, of course), a magnificent botanical garden and conservatory, and a winery that's a replica of a 16th-century French château. And then there's Georgia's Stone Mountain Park, one of the nation's most gorgeous parks and the third most-visited paid tourist attraction in the United States (after Disneyworld and Disneyland); it's a lovely setting for all kinds of recreational activities.

1 Frommer's Favorite Atlanta Experiences

Afternoon Tea at the Ritz-Carlton Buckhead   It's served in the lovely mahogany-paneled lobby lounge, where an oak-log fire crackles in the hearth and a classical pianist provides soothing background music. Fresh-baked scones with fruit preserves and Devonshire cream, finger sandwiches, and English tea bread and tarts accompany pots of your favorite tea.

A Chastain Park Amphitheatre Concert   Big-name entertainers perform under the stars, and everyone brings elaborate picnic fare. It's always a great evening.

Georgia's Stone Mountain Park   Spend a leisurely day seeing the sights, including lunch or bountiful buffet Sunday brunch at the Evergreen Conference Center and Resort. You can also choose from an array of activities—golf, tennis, swimming, biking, hiking, boating, and more.

Yellow River Wildlife Game Ranch   A totally satisfying encounter of the four-legged kind. Bring a picnic lunch.

The Martin Luther King, Jr. Center for Nonviolent Social Change
It's a very moving experience to view videos of Martin Luther King, Jr., delivering his most stirring sermons and speeches, including "I Have a Dream" from the March on Washington.

Time Travel at Fernbank Museum of Natural History   Travel back 15 billion years and experience the "Big Bang" that heralded the formation of the universe! The museum's stunning architecture is also notable. IMAX films here, too.

A Stroll Around Oakland Cemetery   This 88-acre cemetery is a peaceful place, and its Victorian graves are of aesthetic, historic, and symbolic interest. The guided tour is recommended. Bring a picnic lunch.

Relax, Rejuvenate, Renew   Treat yourself to a day of luxurious pampering—body wraps, massage, facials, and much more—at the posh Spa Sydell in Buckhead. For couples, a same-room massage—followed by champagne—is a romantic option.

Tapas at the Segovia Bar   The plush bar of the Occidental Grand Hotel—with seating in intimate alcoves and elegantly draped floor-to-ceiling windows—provides a sumptuous setting for afternoon sherries and tapas.

A Tour of the Fox Theatre   This Moorish-Egyptian palace exemplifies the glamorous movie-theater architecture of the 1920s, complete with onion domes, minarets, and a twinkling starlit sky over the auditorium. Once again, take the tour.

Japanese Breakfast   Ever started your day with roasted seaweed, grilled salmon, and rice? The classically elegant Kamogawa in the Nikko Hotel (designed by temple craftsmen from Kyoto) offers a serene setting for this traditional morning meal; the cedar-paneled dining room overlooks a Japanese rock garden and waterfalls.

2   Atlanta Past & Present

It is most fitting that Atlanta in the 1990s is an international gateway/transportation hub. The city was conceived as a rail crossroads for travel north, south, east, and west, and its role as a strategic junction has always figured largely in its destiny. It all began with a peach tree.

THE STANDING PEACHTREE

Today, just about everything in Atlanta is called "Peachtree" something, but the first Peachtree reference was in 1782 when explorers discovered a Cherokee village on the Chattahoochee River called Standing Peachtree. Since peach trees are not native to the region, some historians maintain the village was actually named for a towering "pitch" tree (a resinous pine). Nevertheless, the Indian village became the location of Fort Peachtree, a tiny frontier outpost, during the War of 1812; a Peachtree Road connecting Fort Peachtree to Fort Daniel (in Gwinnett County) was completed by 1813.

In 1826, surveyors first suggested this area of Georgia as a practical spot for a railroad connecting the state with northern markets. This was not yet the heyday of railroads, and the report was more or less ignored for a decade. But in 1837, the state legislature approved an act establishing the Western & Atlantic Railroad here. Today a marker known as Zero Milepost in Underground Atlanta marks the W & A Railroad site around which a city grew. The new town was unimaginatively dubbed "Terminus." But future governor Alexander H. Stephens, visiting what was still dense forest in 1839, predicted that "a magnificent inland city will at no distant date be built here."

THE TRAIL OF TEARS

One aspect of the city's inception, however, was far from "magnificent." In the early 1800s, most of Georgia was still Native American territory. White settlers coveted the Cherokee and Creek lands they needed to expedite the railroad and further expand their settlements. To keep the peace, native leaders throughout the 1820s signed numerous treaties ceding millions of acres. They adopted a democratic form of government similar to the white man's, complete with a constitution

Dateline

- **1782** Explorers discover Cherokee village of Standing Peachtree.
- **1820s** Cherokee and Creek leaders cede millions of acres to white settlers in hopes of keeping peace.
- **1837** The town, newly named Terminus, is selected as site of railroad terminus connecting Georgia with the Tennessee River. The same year, 17,000 Native Americans are forced to march westward on a "Trail of Tears."
- **1843** Terminus is renamed Marthasville.
- **1845** The first locomotive chugs into town; the city is renamed Atlanta.
- **1851** Georgia secedes from the Union, Civil War begins, and Atlanta becomes a major Confederate supply depot and medical center.
- **1864** Union forces under General William Tecumseh Sherman burn Atlanta.

continues

- **1865** Civil War ends.
- **1877** Atlanta becomes the permanent capital of Georgia.
- **1886** Newspaper editor Henry Grady inspires readers with vision of a "New South." John S. Pemberton introduces Coca-Cola.
- **1888** Atlanta adopts the symbol of a phoenix rising from the ashes for its official seal.
- **1900** Atlanta University professor W. E. B. Du Bois founds the NAACP.
- **1904** Piedmont Park designed.
- **1917** Fire destroys 73 square blocks of the city.
- **1929** Atlanta's first airport opens; Delta Air Lines takes to the skies and becomes Atlanta's home carrier.
- **1936** Margaret Mitchell's blockbuster novel, *Gone With the Wind,* is published.

continues

and supreme court; erected schools and shops; built farms; and accepted Christianity. But the white frontierspeople cared little whether the Native Americans adapted—they wanted them to leave.

With President Andrew Jackson's support, Congress passed a bill in 1830 forcing all southern tribes to move to lands hundreds of miles away on the other side of the Mississippi River. When the U.S. Supreme Court ruled against the order, Jackson ignored their ruling and backed the Georgia settlers. In 1832, the state gave away Cherokee farms in a land lottery; the white settlers assumed control over the land at gunpoint. The issue culminated in 1837, when 17,000 Native Americans were rounded up by federal soldiers, herded into camps, and forced on a cruel westward march called the "Trail of Tears." Some 4,000 died on the 800-mile journey to Oklahoma, and even those who survived suffered bitterly from cold, hunger, and disease.

Terminus and its surroundings were now firmly in the hands of the white settlers.

A CITY GROWS

Terminus soon began its evolution from a sleepy rural hamlet to a thriving city, a meeting point of major rail lines. In 1843, the town was renamed Marthasville, for exgovernor Wilson Lumpkin's daughter Martha. No one in Marthasville took note in 1844 when a 23-year-old army lieutenant, William Tecumseh Sherman, was stationed for two months in their area, but the knowledge he gained of local geography would vitally affect the city's history two decades later. The first locomotive, the *Kentucky,* chugged into town in 1845, and shortly thereafter the name Marthasville was deemed too provincial for a burgeoning metropolis. J. Edgar Thomson, the railroad's chief engineer, suggested Atlanta (a feminized form of Atlantic).

In 1848, the newly incorporated city held its first mayoral election, an event marked by dozens of street brawls. Moses W. Formwalt, a maker of stills and member of the Free and Rowdy party, was elected over temperance candidate John Norcross. But if Atlanta was a bit of a wild frontier town, it also had civic pride. An 1849 newspaper overstated things poetically:

Atlanta, the greatest spot in all the nation,
The greatest place for legislation,
Or any other occupation—
The very center of creation.

STORM CLOUDS GATHER: ANTEBELLUM ATLANTA

By the middle of the 19th century, the 31-state nation was in the throes of a westward expansion and the institution of slavery was a major issue of the day. In his 1858 debate with Stephen Douglas, Abraham Lincoln declared, "This government cannot endure permanently half slave and half free." A year later it was obvious that only a war would resolve the issue. In 1861 (a year that began dramatically in Atlanta—with an earthquake), Georgia legislators voted for secession and joined the Confederacy. In peacetime, the railroads had fashioned Atlanta into a center of commerce, known as the Gate City. In wartime, this transportation hub would emerge as a major Confederate military post and supply center—the vital link between Confederate forces in Tennessee and Virginia. Federal forces early on saw the city's destruction as essential to Northern victory.

On a lighter note, Atlanta made the following ridiculous bid to become the capital of the Confederacy: "The city has good railroad connections, is free from yellow fever, and can supply the most wholesome foods and, as for 'goobers,' an indispensable article for a Southern legislator, we have them all the time." The lure of plentiful peanuts notwithstanding, the Confederacy chose Richmond, Virginia, as its capital.

A CITY BURNS

Atlanta was not only a major Southern supply depot, it was also the medical center of the Confederacy. Throughout the city, buildings were hastily converted into makeshift hospitals and clinics, and trains pulled into town daily to disgorge sick and wounded soldiers. By 1862, close to 4,000 soldiers were convalescing here, and the medical crisis was further aggravated by a smallpox epidemic. That same year, Union spy James J. Andrews and a group of Northern soldiers disguised as civilians seized a locomotive called the *General,* with the aim of blocking supply lines by destroying tracks and bridges behind them. A

- **1939** The movie version of *Gone With the Wind* premiers in Atlanta.
- **1952** The city of Atlanta incorporates surrounding areas, increasing its population by 100,000 and its size from 37 to 118 square miles.
- **1960** Sit-ins and boycotts protesting segregation begin. The million-square-foot Merchandise Mart is erected.
- **1961** Ivan Allen, Jr., defeats segregationist Lester Maddox in mayoral election. Atlanta's public schools and the Georgia Institute of Technology are peacefully desegregated.
- **1964** Atlanta native Martin Luther King, Jr., wins Nobel Peace Prize. The Beatles perform at Atlanta Stadium.
- **1965** 106 civic and cultural leaders die in plane crash at Orly Airport in Paris; Atlanta–Fulton County Stadium is built.

continues

- **1966** Baseball's Braves move from Milwaukee and the Falcons become a new NFL expansion team.
- **1968** Martin Luther King, Jr., is assassinated in Memphis.
- **1974** Atlanta's first black mayor, Maynard Jackson, is inaugurated. Atlanta Brave Hank Aaron hits his record-breaking 715th home run.
- **1976** Georgian Jimmy Carter elected president. Georgia World Congress Center, the nation's largest single-floor exhibit space, is completed.
- **1979** MARTA rapid-transit train system opens.
- **1980** New Hartsfield International Airport dedicated.
- **1983** Martin Luther King, Jr.'s birthday becomes national holiday.
- **1988** Atlanta hosts Democratic National Convention.
- **1989** Underground Atlanta opens with great fanfare.

continues

wild train chase ensued, and the raiders were caught and punished (most, including Andrews, were executed). The episode came to be known as "the Great Locomotive Chase," one of the stirring stories of the Civil War and the subject of two subsequent movies. The *General* is today on view at the Big Shanty Museum in Kennesaw.

The locomotive chase was an Atlanta victory, but the Northern desire to destroy the Confederacy's supply link remained intact. In 1864, General Ulysses S. Grant ordered Major General William T. Sherman to "move against Johnston's army to break it up, and get into the interior of the enemy's country as far as you can, inflicting all the damage you can against their resources." Georgians had great faith that the able and experienced General Joseph E. Johnston, whom they called "Old Joe," would repel the Yankees. As Sherman's Georgia campaign got under way, an overly optimistic editorial in the *Intelligencer* scoffed at the notion of Federal conquest, claiming "we have no fear of the results, for General Johnston and his great and invincible satellites are working out the problem of battle and victory at the great chess board at the front." Johnston himself was not as sanguine. Sherman had 100,000 men to his 60,000, and the Union troops were better armed. By July, Sherman was forcing the Confederate troops back, and Atlanta's fall seemed a foregone conclusion; Johnston informed Confederate President Jefferson Davis that he was outnumbered almost two to one and was in a defensive position. His candid assessment was not appreciated, and Davis removed him from command, replacing him with the pugnacious 32-year-old General John Bell Hood. The change of leadership only further demoralized the ranks, and Sherman openly rejoiced when he heard the news.

Some disgruntled Confederate soldiers deserted. Hood abandoned the defensive tactics of Johnston, aggressively assaulting his opponent. His policy cost thousands of troops and gained nothing. In the Battle of Peachtree Creek on July 20, 1864, Union casualties totaled 1,710, Confederate, 4,796. Throughout the summer, the city suffered a full-scale artillery assault. Over 8,000 Confederates perished in the Battle of Atlanta on July 22, while Union deaths totaled just 3,722. And after hours of fierce fighting on July

28, the Confederates had lost another 5,000 men, the Federals, 600. The Yankees further paralyzed the city by ripping up train rails, heating them over huge bonfires, and twisting them around trees into useless spirals of mangled iron that came to be known as "Sherman's neckties." The most devastating bombardment came on August 9— "that red day . . . when all the fires of hell, and all the thunders of the universe seemed to be blazing and roaring over Atlanta."

By September 1, when Hood's troops pulled out of the area, first setting fire to vast stores of ammunition (and anything else that might benefit the Yankees), the town was in turmoil. Its roads were crowded with evacuees, its hospitals, hotels, and private residences flooded with wounded men. Crime and looting were rife, and food was almost unavailable; the price of a ham-and-eggs breakfast with coffee soared to $25! Rooftops were ripped off houses and buildings, there were huge craters in the streets, and many civilians were dead. The railroads were in Sherman's hands. On September 2, Mayor James M. Calhoun, carrying a white flag to the nearest Federal unit, officially surrendered the city. The U.S. Army entered and occupied Atlanta, raising the Stars and Stripes at city hall for the first time in four years. Claiming he needed the city for military purposes, Sherman ordered all residents to evacuate. Atlantans piled their household goods on wagons and, abandoning their homes and businesses, became refugees. Before departing Atlanta in November, Union troops leveled railroad facilities and burned the city, leaving it a wasteland—defunct as a military center and practically uninhabitable. The Yankees marched out of the city to the music of "The Battle Hymn of the Republic."

In January 1865, there was $1.64 in the treasury, the railroad system was destroyed, and most of the city was burned to the ground.

A CITY REBUILDS

Slowly, exiled citizens began to trickle back into Atlanta. Confederate money was worthless. At the inauguration of his second term in 1865, Lincoln pledged "malice toward none, charity for all"—but after his

■ 1994 Atlanta hosts Super Bowl XXVIII and gears up for the 1996 Olympic Games with the opening of the 70,500-seat Georgia Dome and Centennial Olympic Park.

■ 1996 The world's greatest amateur athletes arrive for the Olympic Games.

The terminus of that railroad will never be anything more than an eating house.   —James M. Calhoun, 1836
                              (Calhoun later became mayor of Atlanta)

Atlanta lies . . . diamond like, in the very center of Georgia, yea, of the South, rough and unpolished . . . in the eyes of jealousy and prejudice, but destined . . . to becoming a bright and glittering jewel in the diadem of Southern cities.
                              —Luther J. Glenn, Atlanta mayor, 1858 inaugural address

No one goes anywhere without passing through Atlanta.
> —Francis C. Lawley, *London Times* reporter, 1861

I want to say to General Sherman, who is an able man . . . though some people think he is kind of careless about fire, that from the ashes he left us in 1864 we have raised a brave and beautiful city; that we have caught the sunshine in our homes and built therein not one ignoble prejudice or memory.
> —Henry Grady, *Atlanta Constitution* editor, 1886

---

assassination later that year, this policy was replaced with one of harsh Republican vengeance. It wasn't until 1876 that Federal troops were withdrawn and Atlanta was freed from military occupation. Still, the city was making a remarkable recovery. Like the ever-resilient Scarlett O'Hara ("It takes more than Yankees or a burning to keep me down"), Atlanta rolled up its sleeves and began rebuilding. A Northern newspaper reported, "From all this ruin and devastation a new city is springing up . . . the streets are alive from morning till night with drays and carts and hand-barrows and wagons . . . with loads of lumber and loads of brick. . . ."

In postwar years, Atlanta was filled with carpetbaggers and adventurers hoping to turn a quick buck, and with them came gambling houses, brothels, and saloons. But the city also boasted hundreds of new stores and businesses, churches, schools, banks, hotels, theaters, and a new newspaper, the *Atlanta Constitution.* Blacks chartered Atlanta University in 1867, today the world's largest predominantly black institution of higher learning. Moreover, the railroads were operative once again. Newspaper editor Henry Grady inspired readers with his vision of an industrialized and culturally advanced "New South." He was Atlanta's biggest civic booster. A new constitution in 1877 made Atlanta the permanent capital of the state of Georgia. Two years later, General Sherman visited the city he had destroyed and was welcomed with a ball and, lest he get any funny ideas, a grand military review.

In 1886 a new headache cure was introduced to the city—a syrup made from the cocoa leaf and the kola nut that would eventually become the world's most renowned beverage, Coca-Cola. Atlanta adopted the symbol of a phoenix rising from the ashes for its official seal in 1888 and, the following year, dedicated the gold-domed state capitol and opened a zoo in Grant Park. Piedmont Park was built in 1904 as the site of the Cotton States and International Exposition—a $2.5 million world's fair–like extravaganza with entertainments ranging from Buffalo Bill and His Wild West Show to international villages. Former slave Booker T. Washington gave a landmark address, and John Philip Sousa composed the "King Cotton March" to mark the event.

THE TWENTIETH CENTURY

At the turn of the century, Atlanta's population was 90,000, a figure that more than doubled two decades later. Though a massive fire destroyed almost 2,000 buildings in 1917, the city was on a course of

Centennial Olympic Park

Designed as "a landscape quilt in the city of trees," Centennial Olympic Park will serve as a venue for Olympic celebrations and an inviting greenspace and gathering place for visitors. In close proximity to major Game venues, it occupies 21 acres adjacent to the Georgia World Congress Center. The park is heralded by an Olympic ring–shaped fountain that spills into a reflecting pool flanked by a Centennial-symbolic pair of 100-year-old Georgia oak trees. The fountain is the central focus of a vast paved plaza bordered by 23 flags honoring all the host countries of the Modern Games. Other areas of the park include an 8,000-seat grassy outdoor amphitheater that will be used for nightly superstar concerts during the Olympic Games (and remain as a concert venue after the Games), verdant lawns and gardens planted with native flowers, pedestrian promenades, and pathways of commemorative bricks. At the park's Superstore, visitors will be able to view exhibits about the Games and purchase memorabilia. After the Olympic Games, the park will remain, under state jurisdiction, as a lasting legacy to the 1996 Centennial Olympic Games. An Olympic Games museum is planned for the site.

rapid growth. In 1929, Atlanta opened its first airport on the site of today's Hartsfield International, presaging the growth of a major air-travel industry. The same year, Delta Air Lines took to the skies and became Atlanta's home carrier. Margaret Mitchell's blockbuster Civil War epic *Gone With the Wind,* which went on to become the world's second-best-selling book (after the Bible) and the basis for the biggest-grossing picture of all time, was published in 1936. Louis B. Mayer turned down a chance to make the film version for MGM, because "no Civil War picture ever made a nickel."

A more dire legacy of the Civil War and the institution of slavery was racial strife, and the early years of the 20th century were marked by violent race riots. Atlanta University professor W. E. B. Du Bois founded the NAACP in 1900. In 1939, black cast members were unable to attend the glamorous premiere of *Gone With the Wind* because the theater was segregated. And as late as 1960, segregation in Atlanta (as everywhere in the South) was still firmly entrenched and backed by state law. Unlike much of the South, though, the city has, for the most part, adopted a progressive attitude regarding race relations. Even before the civil rights movement there were black advancements—the hiring of black police officers, the election of a black to the Atlanta Board of Education, the desegregation of a public golf course in 1955, and, in 1959, the desegregation of public transit. Mayor Bill Hartsfield (who held office for almost three decades) called Atlanta "a city too busy to hate." And his successor, Mayor Ivan Allen, Jr., called on Atlantans to face race problems "and seek the answers in an atmosphere of decency and dignity."

Without screaming mobs, Atlanta peacefully desegregated its public schools and the Georgia Institute of Technology in 1961. Atlanta native Dr. Martin Luther King, Jr., headquartered his Southern Christian Leadership Conference here and made Ebenezer Baptist Church, which he co-pastored with his father, a hub of the movement. In 1974 Atlanta inaugurated its first black mayor, Maynard Jackson, and, following a term by another black mayor, Andrew Young, Jackson was re-elected.

In 1966 Atlanta went major league when the Braves and the Falcons came to town. Atlantans went wild in 1974 when Hank Aaron broke Babe Ruth's home-run record here.

THE CITY TODAY

The 1960s saw the beginning of downtown development with the rise of the million-square-foot Merchandise Mart, designed by an innovative young Atlanta architect named John Portman. It became the nucleus for the nationally renowned Peachtree Center complex. Portman's futuristic design for the downtown Hyatt Regency (1967) introduced a towering atrium-lobby concept that revolutionized hotel architecture in America. Today Peachtree Center—a 13-city-block "pedestrian village"— comprises three Portman-designed megahotels, the 5.9-million-square-foot Atlanta Market Center (including the Apparel Mart and the high-tech-oriented INFORUM), 200,000 square feet of retail space, a restaurant row, and six massive office towers, its various elements connected by covered walkways and bridges. This is an open-ended project, still very much in a process of expansion.

MARTA rapid-transit trains began running in 1979. Today just about every part of Atlanta is accessible by bus or subway.

In 1980, a revitalized black neighborhood called Sweet Auburn became a National Historic District, its 10 blocks of notable sites including Martin Luther King, Jr.'s boyhood home, his crypt, the church where he preached, a museum, and the Martin Luther King, Jr. Center for Non-Violent Social Change. It is probably *the* major black history attraction in the country, and in the last several years, it has undergone a major revitalization and restoration.

Media mogul Ted Turner inaugurated CNN here in 1980, following with Superstation TBS, Headline News, and TNT. The High Museum of Art opened its doors in 1983. And in 1989, Underground Atlanta, a retail/restaurant/entertainment complex with a historical theme, garnered national attention.

In the 1990s, when other big cities are struggling to survive, Atlanta continues to soar, with new projects like the $214 million, 70,500-seat Georgia Dome. At presstime, the city is completing preparations for the 1996 Olympic Games (expected to have an overall $5.1 billion economic impact on Georgia from 1991 to 1997) with new hotels, tour packages, and megastadiums. Among the outstanding venues are the Olympic Stadium and the Stone Mountain Tennis Center. An Olympic Village has been erected on the campus of the Georgia Institute of Technology. Downtown, 21-acre Centennial Olympic Park—which will contain an 8,000-seat outdoor amphitheater, lawns, and gardens—is nearing completion as I write; it will be a venue for big-name concerts and Olympic-related festivities. And downtown, Woodruff Park is undergoing a $5 million renovation before the Games.

Atlanta in the nineties remains a forward-looking city that is constantly renewing itself—a dynamic metropolis where the past is honored and the present enthusiastically embraced.

3 Famous Atlantans

Henry Louis "Hank" Aaron   (b. 1934) An outfielder with the Milwaukee (later Atlanta) Braves, Aaron broke Babe Ruth's record in 1974 with his 715th home run, in Atlanta–Fulton County Stadium. He remained cool and dignified in the face of the media frenzy surrounding his pursuit of the record, despite receiving countless death threats and bags of hate mail from bigots who felt that Ruth's achievement should never be surpassed by a black man. He retired in 1976 with 755 homers.

Henry Woodlin Grady   (1850–89) Managing editor of the *Atlanta Constitution,* Grady preached post–Civil War reconciliation, and worked passionately to draw Northern capital and diversified industry to the agrarian South. His name is synonymous with the phrase "The New South."

Joel Chandler Harris   (1848–1908) Called "Georgia's Aesop," he created Uncle Remus, the wise black raconteur of children's fables. His tales of Br'er Rabbit and Br'er Fox were the basis for Disney's delightful animated feature *Song of the South.*

Robert Tyre "Bobby" Jones   (1902–71) Golf's only Grand Slam winner, he was the founder of the Masters Tournament. Jones has been called the world's greatest golfer; he retired from the game in 1930 but his record remains unsurpassed. He also held academic degrees in engineering, law, and English literature.

Martin Luther King, Jr.   (1929–68) Civil rights leader, minister, orator, and Nobel Peace Prize winner, King preached Gandhi's doctrine of passive resistance.

Impressions

It stinks, I don't know why I bother with it, but I've got to have something to do with my time.
—Margaret Mitchell, author of *Gone With the Wind*

Gone With the Wind *is very possibly the greatest American novel.*
—*Publishers Weekly*

We're going to ride these buses desegregated in Atlanta, Georgia, or we're going to ride a chariot in heaven or push a wheelbarrow in hell.
—Rev. William Holmes Borders, civil rights leader, 1957

Margaret Mitchell   (1900–49) Author of the definitive southern blockbuster novel, *Gone With the Wind*. Originally a journalist, Mitchell began writing "the book" in 1926 when a severe ankle injury forced her to give up reporting. *GWTW* is, next to the Bible, the world's best-selling book.

John C. Portman   (b. 1924) Architect/developer who revolutionized hotel design in America with his lofty atrium-lobby concept and almost singlehandedly designed Atlanta's skyline. He has been called "Atlanta's one-man urban-renewal program."

Robert Edward "Ted" Turner III   (b. 1938) Dubbed "the mouth from the South," America's most dynamic media mogul, Ted Turner, owns 24-hour cable news networks CNN and Headline News, along with entertainment networks Superstation TBS and TNT, not to mention a portion of MGM and the Atlanta Braves and Atlanta Hawks. Turner's high-profile wife is actress, activist, and aerobics guru Jane Fonda.

Robert W. Woodruff   (1889–1985) Coca-Cola Company president, philanthropist, and leading Atlanta citizen for over half a century. He put Coca-Cola on the map worldwide; promoted civil rights; and gave over $400 million to Atlanta educational, artistic, civil, and medical projects such as Emory University, the Woodruff Arts Center, and the High Museum.

About the Olympic Games

Since the announcement in 1990 that Atlanta would host the 1996 Olympic Games (July 19 through August 4), the city has been in a frenzy of activity gearing up for the occasion. Much of Atlanta has been spruced up with beautiful new landscaping, several stadiums have been constructed, and almost all of the city's sightseeing attractions have planned special events and exhibits.

Many of the athletic events will take place at venues within the "Olympic Ring"—an imaginary circle, three miles in diameter, centered in downtown Atlanta. Inside the Ring stands the 85,000-seat Olympic Stadium, which will host the opening and closing ceremonies and track and field events (after the Olympic Games, it will become the new home of the Atlanta Braves baseball team). There's also the 72,000-seat Georgia Dome, the 16,400-seat Omni Coliseum, Centennial Olympic Park, Georgia State University, the 52,000-seat Atlanta–Fulton County Stadium, Morris Brown College, Clark Atlanta University, Morehouse College, the Georgia World Congress Center, and the Georgia Tech Aquatic Center and Alexander Memorial Coliseum. Also in the Ring's parameters is the Olympic Village at Georgia Tech, designed to provide housing, dining areas, and practice facilities for participating athletes and officials; after the Olympic Games, its new dorms will be used as student housing.

Other nearby venues include a Tennis Center, Archery Range, and Velodrome at Georgia's Stone Mountain Park, 16 miles east of downtown Atlanta; Georgia International Horse Park, 33 miles east of the Olympic Village in Conyers, Georgia (for equestrian events, mountain biking, and modern pentathlon); and the Wolf Creek Shooting Complex, near Atlanta's Hartsfield International Airport, 21 miles from the Olympic Village.

Sixteen competitions will be held outside the Atlanta metropolitan area. For example, the slalom events of the canoe/kayak category will be held on the Ocoee River in Tennessee at the Georgia border, and yachting competitions will take place off the coast of Savannah, 250 miles southeast of Atlanta. The Games will also extend to Miami and Orlando, Florida; Birmingham, Alabama; and Washington, D.C., for preliminary rounds of soccer.

The 1996 program will be comprised of 26 sports and 37 disciplines. More than 10,000 athletes from almost 200 nations will compete, and a total of 1,933 medals will be awarded.

Some two million visitors are expected to view the various events. If you're planning to attend the Games of the XXVI Olympiad (which, by the way, marks the 100th anniversary of the Modern Olympic Games), I've compiled everything you need to know in this chapter.

1 Information Sources

For up-to-the-minute information, the best source is **The Atlanta Committee for the Olympic Games** (☎ **404/744-1996**). You can call 24 hours a day, seven days a week.

ACOG additionally operates a public-information gallery/gift shop called **The Olympic Experience** (☎ **404/658-1996**) in Underground Atlanta at the corner of Upper Alabama and Peachtree streets. It is open Monday to Saturday 10am to 9:30pm, Sunday noon to 6pm.

The **Welcome South Visitors Center,** on the corner of Spring Street and International Boulevard in downtown Atlanta (☎ **404/ 224-2000**), provides full information about the Olympic Games. It also houses a large Olympic Games merchandise store and a foreign-exchange office. After December 1, 1995, you can buy tickets to Olympic sessions here. This comprehensive facility, which boasts a multilingual staff, offers exhibits and information on all aspects of Atlanta tourism as well as attractions in other southeastern states. It's open 10am to 6pm Monday to Saturday, noon to 6pm Sunday.

The **Atlanta Convention & Visitors Bureau** (☎ **404/222-6688**) can answer your questions regarding hotels, attractions, shopping, and dining.

Cyberspace surfers can access continuously updated facts, figures, photos, illustrations, and video and audio content on the Internet by connecting with the 1996 Olympic Games World-Wide Web server (WWW); just browse to http://www.atlanta.olympic.org. to find the 1996 Olympic Games Home Page.

When in town, check the *Atlanta Journal-Constitution* daily for up-to-the-minute information.

2 Obtaining Tickets

Tickets went on sale in May of 1995 when a vast mail-order program—heralded by widespread national media coverage—was initiated. Ticket Catalogs and order forms are available by sending $5 to: 1996 Olympic Ticket Request Forms, P.O. Box 105153, Atlanta, GA 30348-5153. The $5 fee is automatically deducted from your handling charge. The brochure contains everything ticket-buyers need to organize an ideal Olympic Games itinerary, including descriptions of each sport, number of sessions for each sport, session times, methods of payment, ticket prices, and details on how to fill out your request form. Answers are provided to all of the most commonly asked questions.

Beginning in February 1996, tickets can be bought over the telephone by calling **404/744-1996.** VISA (an official sponsor of the Games) is the only credit card that will be accepted for payment. During the Games themselves, you can buy tickets at box office locations

> ### ❓ Did You Know?
>
> - The first Modern Olympic Games were held on April 6–15, 1896, in Athens, Greece, with 13 nations represented.
> - Eastman Kodak has been an official Olympic sponsor since the first Games in 1896 (the company was founded in 1892).
> - The five-ring Olympic flag represents the five continents: the Americas, Europe, Africa, Asia, and Oceania.
> - Women first competed in the Games in 1900; there were 19 of them, compared to 1,206 men.
> - Swimmer Johnny Weissmuller won five gold medals in 1924 and 1928 and then won fame as Tarzan.
> - General Patton (then a lieutenant) finished fifth in the 1912 pentathlon event. He was the only non-Swede among the top seven finishers.
> - The first Olympic Winter Games were held in 1924 in Chamonix, France.

at all 31 venues as well as Atlanta's Welcome South Visitors Center, and other downtown locations. For details call **404/744-1996.** Tickets may also be available via hotel packages, and can be purchased at the Welcome South Visitors Center beginning in late spring or early summer of 1996.

Note: About 900,000 tickets have been set aside for purchase outside the United States.

ACOG assures me that no one need panic about acquiring tickets, because Olympic Games simply do not sell out—especially the Centennial Olympic Games, which will be the largest in history, offering more tickets than Los Angeles and Barcelona combined. Altogether, ACOG has available an astounding 11 million tickets! In addition 1.2 million Cultural Olympiad/Olympic Arts Festival tickets—spanning 200 performances and 25 exhibitions in more than 30 venues—are available. Even if you arrived in town with no tickets in hand—not that I'm suggesting you do—tickets will very likely still be available to many events. ACOG is pioneering a new ticket sales system that will allow visitors to buy tickets for any event at any venue, and regular updates will be available on site about ticket availability. Large numbers of tickets are purchased by corporate groups—whose members may not all show up to certain events; in such cases, tickets may be available even to major events at the last minute.

HELPFUL HINTS WHEN ORDERING TICKETS

Each Olympic Games session offers the opportunity to see the world's greatest athletes in competition. The hard part is selecting the 10 or 15 you'll attend from the hundreds of possibilities.

1. Keep game times and geographic proximity in mind when making your selections. This will both prevent exhaustion and

The Olympic Ring

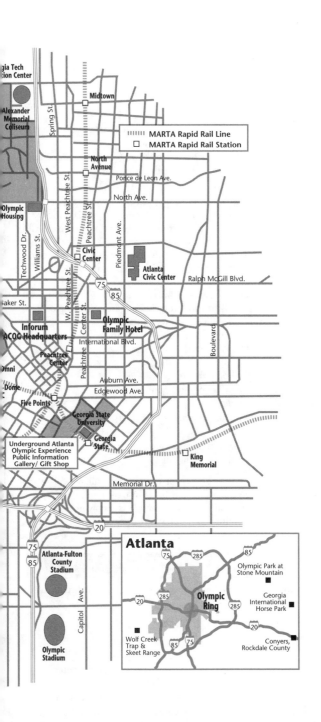

increase the number of sessions you have time to see on a given day. Take advantage of the Olympic Ring—20 sports within walking distance of each other—to request same-day sessions in different spots.

2. Involve all members of your party in choosing the sessions you want to see.

3. To insure that you'll get to see some of the most popular sports, subscribe to early rounds of competition.

4. Choose some sports away from downtown (Stone Mountain and beyond); they make for enjoyable day trips.

TICKET PRICES   Nearly all (95% of) tickets to the 1996 Games are priced at $75 or less, and 75% are priced at $40 or less. The most expensive tickets, to opening and closing ceremonies, are $200 to $600. For other events, ticket prices range from $6 (for preliminary baseball) to $250 (for track and field finals). The average seat costs $39.72, and every sport has at least one session for which tickets are available at or below $25. Only the last session of athletics—and finals for basketball, boxing, diving, artistic gymnastics (including gala), soccer, swimming, tennis, and volleyball—have tickets priced over $75. All ticket prices include transportation costs to and from Atlanta-area venues. Needless to say, there are almost infinite ticket combinations.

To give you an estimate of probable expenditures, I've listed some ticket options for a family of four:

Four tickets to:

One event—baseball preliminary	$24
Two events—gymnastics podium training and basketball preliminary	$80
Three events—diving preliminary, soccer quarterfinal, and athletics final	$360
Three events—gymnastics (artistic) preliminary, tennis quarterfinal, and diving final	$500

TOUGHEST TICKETS   The toughest tickets to come by will be for opening and closing ceremonies and finals in basketball, gymnastics, track and field, boxing, and volleyball. Though you may not get to see the finals, you will definitely have access to earlier rounds.

3 The Events

Olympic events include preliminary, intermediate, and final rounds. All in all, there will be 542 sessions.

Major Event/Sport	Venue
Opening Ceremony	Olympic Stadium
Aquatics	
Diving	Georgia Tech Aquatic Center
Swimming	Georgia Tech Aquatic Center
Synchronized Swimming	Georgia Tech Aquatic Center
Water Polo	Georgia Tech Aquatic Center

MARTA in the Olympic Ring

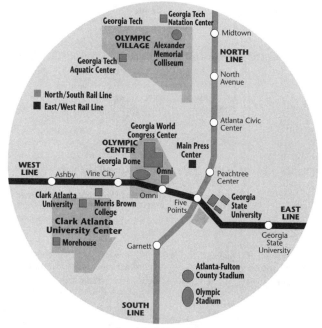

Georgia Tech
Georgia Tech Natation Center
OLYMPIC VILLAGE
Alexander Memorial Coliseum
Georgia Tech Aquatic Center
Midtown
NORTH LINE
North Avenue
Atlanta Civic Center

■ North/South Rail Line
■ East/West Rail Line

Georgia World Congress Center
OLYMPIC CENTER
Main Press Center
Georgia Dome
WEST LINE
Ashby   Vine City   Omni
Peachtree Center
Clark Atlanta University
Morris Brown College
Omni
Five Points
Georgia State University
EAST LINE
Clark Atlanta University Center
Morehouse
Garnett
Georgia State University
Atlanta-Fulton County Stadium
Olympic Stadium
SOUTH LINE

Copyright © 1995 MARTA

Major Event/Sport	Venue
Archery	Stone Mountain Park
Athletics (Track and Field)	Olympic Stadium
Marathons	Throughout Atlanta
Race Walks	Throughout Atlanta
Badminton	Georgia State University
Baseball	Atlanta–Fulton County Stadium
Basketball	Morehouse College/Georgia Dome
Boxing	Georgia Tech Alexander Memorial Coliseum
Canoe/Kayak	
Slalom	Ocoee Whitewater Center, TN
Sprint	Lake Lanier, GA
Cycling	
Mountain Bike	Georgia International Horse Park, Conyers, GA
Road	Atlanta
Track	Stone Mountain Park
Equestrian	Georgia International Horse Park, Conyers, GA
Fencing	Georgia World Congress Center
Field Hockey	Morris Brown College and Clark Atlanta University

Major Event/Sport	Venue
Football (Soccer)	
Semifinals/Finals	Sanford Stadium, Athens, GA
Preliminary/Quarterfinals	Orange Bowl, Miami, FL; Florida Citrus Bowl, Orlando, FL; RFK Memorial Stadium, Washington, D.C.; Legion Field, Birmingham, AL
Gymnastics	
Artistic	Georgia Dome
Rhythmic	University of Georgia
Handball	Georgia World Congress Center/ Georgia Dome
Judo	Georgia World Congress Center
Modern Pentathlon	
Shooting	Wolf Creek Shooting Complex, Wolf Creek, GA
Fencing	Georgia World Congress Center
Swimming	Georgia Tech Aquatic Center
Riding/Running	Georgia International Horse Park, Conyers, GA
Rowing	Lake Lanier, GA
Shooting	Wolf Creek Shooting Complex, Wolf Creek, GA
Softball	Golden Park, Columbus, GA
Table Tennis	Georgia World Congress Center
Tennis	Stone Mountain Park
Volleyball	
Beach	Atlanta Beach at Clayton County International Park (20 miles south of the Olympic Village)
Indoor	Omni Coliseum/University of Georgia
Weightlifting	Georgia World Congress Center
Wrestling	Georgia World Congress Center
Yachting	Wassaw Sound, Savannah, GA
Closing Ceremony	Olympic Stadium

4   Accommodations & Dining

HOTELS   The good news is that a new Georgia law designed to pre-vent hotel price gouging is already in effect, forbidding rate increases above a certain percentage over published 1994 rates. To ensure the availability of rooms, ACOG has, to date, more than 320 officially des-ignated hotels representing 50,975 rooms, in its Host Hotel Network. These include lodgings in greater metropolitan Atlanta, Augusta,

Olympic Venues in the Greater Atlanta Area

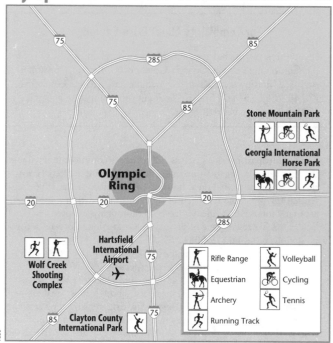

Athens, Columbus, Gainesville, Macon, and Savannah. ACOG's host hotels have committed up to 80% of their rooms to Olympic visitors and agreed to a fair rate structure. To book a room via ACOG, call **404/744-1996** for information.

Now for the problematical aspects: Many of these committed rooms have already been set aside by ACOG for officials and corporate sponsors. Also, participating hotels are alloted four tickets per day, per committed room (one high-demand, three low-demand), which means you may be asked to purchase a package that includes room and tickets. Though this could be a good deal, if you have your heart set on certain events, you'll want to know just what these hotel-package tickets include—and possibly you'll want to obtain accommodations and tickets separately. If you make accommodations on your own, be sure to get written confirmation of your reservation and quoted room rates.

PRIVATE HOMES & APARTMENTS It seems like everyone you meet in Atlanta these days is planning to rent out his or her house or apartment during the Olympic Games (where will they all go, I wonder?). This can be a very viable accommodations option, as many of these homes and apartments will be close to Olympic venues and offer more facilities than a hotel room in the same price range. ACOG is supplementing hotel facilities with a large roster of rooms in private

---

For Complaints About Price-Gouging

If you think you are being overcharged by a hotel during the Olympic Games, contact the Georgia Governor's Office of Consumer Affairs, 2 Martin Luther King, Jr. Dr., Suite 356, Atlanta, GA 30334 (☎ **404/657-7544**). They can check out your complaint, and, if it's valid, help you to get restitution.

---

homes and apartments (as well as full private accommodations) under the auspices of an organization called Private Housing 1996 (PH'96)—the only officially sanctioned housing coordinator for the 1996 Centennial Olympic Games. Each of these accommodations—and there are many thousands of them—has been thoroughly accepted and rated by PH'96. To reserve one of these ACOG-sanctioned private accommodations call **404/455-0081.**

In addition, you'll find numerous classified ads for accommodations in newspapers and magazines (check especially *The New York Times* and big-city publications such as *New York* magazine and *Washingtonian*) as well as in Atlanta newspapers. Though most of these will probably be fine, you do, of course, run risks renting a place sight unseen; to protect yourself get as much written documentation about costs and facilities as possible. *Caveat emptor!* If you have friends or family in Atlanta, they'll also be a good source of information. For additional sources see listings in Chapter 6.

DINING   Many restaurants will be sold out to corporate clients far in advance. And since there will be so much restaurant traffic generated by the Olympic Games, some establishments are planning to ask for reservations backed up by advance payment via credit card in order to prevent no-shows. On the flip side, many restaurants will extend their hours during the Games. Check out Chapter 7 ("Dining"), and begin making your restaurant reservations as soon as possible. It's best to have them all in hand before you leave home. It's hard to predict how difficult it will be getting into restaurants during the Games, and how long lines for seating will be. Eating meals off regular lunch and dinner hours (early or late) may help. If it becomes a major hassle, you might want to consider picnics (you can buy fixings at international food concessions at the various venues) and restaurants and food courts at shopping malls. Hotel restaurants will make it a priority to serve their in-house guests; after you've booked your hotel room, see about making restaurant reservations at the property.

5 Transportation

For the first time in Olympic history, bus and rail transportation to and from Olympic venues will be included in ticket prices, and visitors will be able to board free satellite buses from outer areas. Do plan to use these transportation systems to avoid parking fees, traffic jams, and other hassles.

The city's Metropolitan Atlanta Rapid Transit Authority (MARTA) will operate the Olympic Transportation System—an interconnected network of park-and-ride lots, shuttle buses, and rapid rail cars which will serve all Atlanta-area venues. Newly designed and lighted pedestrian walkways, signage, and interactive information kiosks will enhance the efficiency of this transportation network, and detailed transportation information will be included with your tickets. No venues in the Olympic Ring will have parking for private cars. Visitors can buy one-trip tokens, discounted rolls of tokens, or transit passes (called Transcords) that are accepted in all fare boxes and at all staiton fare gates. Weekend, weekly, and monthly passes are also available. During the Games, MARTA will offer a special 17-day pass.

See the maps on pages 23 and 29 for venues outside the Olympic Ring.

6 The Cultural Olympiad/Olympic Arts Festival

Complementing the Olympic Games is the Cultural Olympiad—a "multi-disciplinary arts and culture festival designed to provide an . . . air of celebration and excitement." Since the fall of 1993, ACOG has been producing one of the most extensive Cultural Olympiads in history, which will culminate with the Olympic Arts Festival.

The Cultural Olympiad has a dual purpose: showcasing the rich and diverse cultural heritage of Atlanta and the South, and simultaneously promoting international understanding by bringing artists and performers from all over the world to Atlanta. In this international vein, it has already presented events ranging from a month-long cultural exchange with Lillehammer, Norway (host city of the 1994 Olympic Winter Games) to Mexican and African festivals in Atlanta. In 1996—especially during the 17 days of the Olympic Games—there will be hundreds of concerts, exhibitions, and performances taking place in downtown Atlanta, many of them in the newly developed Centennial Olympic Park.

Tickets to Olympic Arts Festival events went on sale in the fall of 1995. To find out how to get them in advance of your visit, and to obtain additional information about Olympics-related cultural events, call **404/744-1996** (or 404/546-4099 Telecommunications Device for the Deaf) from a touch-tone phone any time, day or night, for recorded information. If you call between 8am and 5pm Eastern Standard Time, you will be able to connect with a customer service representative.

After you arrive in Atlanta, you can obtain tickets (unless otherwise specified) at box office locations at all 31 Games venues as well as Centennial Olympic Park, Hartsfield International Airport, Atlanta's Welcome South Visitors Center, and other downtown sites. While in town, it's also a good idea to check the newspaper for events listings, which will include numerous happenings at local museums and sightseeing attractions.

Note: At presstime, this events schedule was still subject to change. For an update, call **404/224-1835.**

OLYMPIC PROGRAM   *Schedule is subject to change*

Sport	Venue
Opening Ceremony	Olympic Stadium
Aquatics	
Diving	Georgia Tech Aquatic Center
Swimming	Georgia Tech Aquatic Center
Synchro Swimming	Georgia Tech Aquatic Center
Water Polo	Georgia Tech Aquatic Center
Archery	Stone Mountain Park
Athletics	Olympic Stadium
Marathon	Atlanta (Course to be Determined)
Race Walk	Summerhill/Grant Park Area
Badminton	Georgia State University
Baseball	Atlanta-Fulton County Stadium
Basketball	Georgia Dome/Morehouse College
Boxing	Alexander Memorial Coliseum
Canoe/Kayak	
Slalom	Ocoee Whitewater Center, Tennessee
Sprint	Lake Lanier
Cycling	
Mountain Bike	Georgia International Horse Park
Road	Atlanta
Track	Stone Mountain Park
Equestrian	Georgia International Horse Park
Fencing	Georgia World Congress Center
Football (Soccer)	
Semifinals/Finals	Sanford Stadium, Athens, Georgia
Prelim/Quarterfinals	Birmingham, Alabama/Miami, Florida
Preliminaries	Orlando, Florida/Washington, D.C.
Gymnastics	
Artistic	Georgia Dome
Rhythmic	University of Georgia
Handball	Georgia World Congress Center/Georgia Dome
Hockey	Morris Brown College/Clark Atlanta University
Judo	Georgia World Congress Center
Modern Pentathlon	Multiple Sites
Rowing	Lake Lanier
Shooting	Wolf Creek Shooting Complex
Softball	Golden Park, Columbus, Georgia
Table Tennis	Georgia World Congress Center
Tennis	Stone Mountain Park
Volleyball	
Beach	Atlanta Beach, Clayton County International Park
Indoor	Omni Coliseum/University of Georgia
Weightlifting	Georgia World Congress Center
Wrestling	Georgia World Congress Center
Yachting	Wassaw Sound, Savannah, Georgia
Closing Ceremony	Olympic Stadium

Key   NS = No Spectators   ✪ = Gala Event   TT = Ticketed Training   • = Date(s) of Event

	July													August					
	19	20	21	22	23	24	25	26	27	28	29	30	31	1	2	3	4	**Days**	**Event Finals**
	F	S	Su	M	T	W	Th	F	S	Su	M	T	W	Th	F	S	Su		
	•																	1	0
								•	•	•	•	•	•	•	•			8	4
		•	•	•	•	•	•	•										7	32
												•			•			2	1
		•	•	•	•	•		•	•	•								8	1
										NS	•	•	•	•	•			6	4
								•	•	•	•		•	•	•	•		8	39
										•							•	2	2
								•							•			2	3
						•	•	•	•	•	•	•	•	•				9	5
			•	•	•	•			•	•	•	•		•	•	•	•	12	1
		•	•	•	•	•	•	•	•	•	•	•	•	•	•	•	•	16	2
			•	•	•	•	•	•	•	•			•	•	•	•	•	15	12
							TT	•	•									3	4
												•	•	•	•	•	•	6	12
												•						1	2
			•										•			•		3	4
						•	•	•	•	•								5	8
			•	•	•	•	NS	•	•	•	•		•	•		•	•	13	6
		•	•	•	•	•	•											6	10
										•		•	•	•	•			5	2
		•	•	•	•	•	•		•	•								8/8	0
		•	•	•	•	•	•											6/6	0
		•	•	•	•	•	•			•	•	✪						9	14
														•	•	•	•	4	2
						•	•	•	•	•	•	•	•	•	•	•	•	12	2
		•	•	•	•	•	•	•										7	14
												•						1	1
			•	•	•	•	•	•	•	•								8	14
		•	•	•	•	•	•	•	•									8	15
			•	•	•	•	•	•	•			•	•					9	1
						•	•	•	•	•	•	•	•	•	•			10	4
						•	•	•	•	•	•	•	•	•	•	•	•	12	4
				•	•	•	•	•	•									6	2
		•	•	•	•	•	•	•	•	•	•	•	•	•	•	•	•	16	2
			•	•	•	•	•	•		•	•	•	•					10	10
			•	•	•	•						•	•	•	•			8	20
			•	•	•	•	•	•	•	•	•	•	•					11	10
																	•	1	0

AT&T AMPHITHEATER CONCERTS

A series of 22 concerts under the stars in Centennial Olympic Park will feature 50 international pop acts, with several performers appearing at each concert. Among those already scheduled at presstime were Gloria Estefan, who will kick off her 1996 world tour here; James Brown, the godfather of soul; country stars Travis Tritt, Trisha Yearwood, and Willie Nelson; African funk diva Angelique Kidjo; and Okinawan folk hero Shoukichi Kina.

Some of the special programs include Wei Wei (the reigning superstar of the People's Republic of China) in a "World in Concert" program with Brazil's Gal Costa and Australia's pop Aboriginal group Nomad; the Sounds of Blackness headlining an evening of hot new gospel acts; jazz and pop legends collaborating in a special tribute to Miles Davis; "The Olympic Guitar Summit," which will bring together some of the world's finest rock, jazz, and classical players; and Alison Krauss and others in the "Olympic Bluegrass Festival."

The concerts will be held July 12 through August 3, nightly at 8pm. Ticket prices range from $20 to $125. Call **404/774-1996** for information.

CLASSICAL MUSIC & JAZZ CONCERTS IN SYMPHONY HALL

Symphony Hall in the Woodruff Arts Center will host a series featuring the Atlanta Symphony Orchestra, an Opera Gala, and soloists Itzhak Perlman and Jessye Norman, among other performers. Call 404/774-1996 for information.

Bayerischer Rundfunk (Bavarian Radio Symphony)

One of Germany's oldest and most popular ensembles, led by musical director Lorin Maazel, offers performances on July 16 and 17, both at 8pm. Tickets range from $30 to $60.

Program I: Brahms: Symphony no. 2 in D
              R. Strauss: *Till Eulenspiegel's Merry Pranks*
              R. Strauss: Suite from *Der Rosenkavalier*
Program II: Maazel: music for Violoncello and Orchestra
              Bruckner: Symphony no. 7

The Atlanta Opera

The company will present George and Ira Gershwin's *Of Thee I Sing,* a Pulitzer Prize–winning political satire and the longest-running Broadway musical of the 1930s. Paul Sorvino will appear in the production, which runs July 18 at 8pm and July 19 at 2pm. Tickets are $25 to $60.

The Atlanta Symphony Orchestra with Itzhak Perlman

July 20 at 8pm. Tickets are $35 to $65.

Jeunesses Musicales (World Youth Orchestra)

Former U.S. Ambassador to the U.N. and ACOG Co-Chairman Andrew Young will narrate a premiere performance, conducted by Robert Spano, on July 21 at 2pm. Tickets run $5 to $20.

Debussy: *Iberia*
Alvin Singleton: "Umoja: Each One of Us Counts" (world premiere; text by Rita Dove, former U.S. poet laureate)
Tchaikovsky: Symphony no. 4

Olympic Venues Outside the Atlanta Area

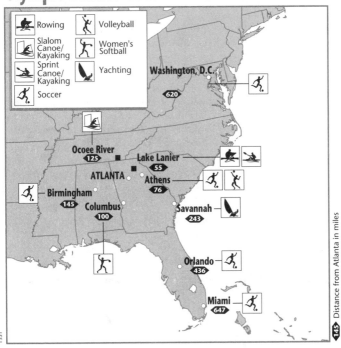

Rowing

Slalom Canoe/Kayaking

Sprint Canoe/Kayaking

Soccer

Volleyball

Women's Softball

Yachting

Washington, D.C. 620

Ocoee River 125

Lake Lanier 55

ATLANTA

Athens 76

Birmingham 145

Columbus 100

Savannah 243

Orlando 436

Miami 647

145 Distance from Atlanta in miles

1351

An Olympic Celebration of Chamber Music

Itzhak Perlman, Frederica von Stade (mezzo-soprano), and Pinchas Zuckerman (violin) are just a few of the renowned soloists joining artistic director Charles Wadsworth on July 22 at 8pm.

Tickets are $35 to $75.

The London Chamber Orchestra, featuring pianist Hae-Jung Kim

An astounding young Korean pianist joins one of Europe's most acclaimed classical ensembles. July 23 at 8pm. Tickets are $25 to $60.

Purcell: Sonata for Trumpet and Strings
Tippett: Variations on a Theme of Corelli
Shostakovich: Piano Concerto no. 1
Elgar: Introduction and Allegro

Atlanta Symphony Youth Orchestra

Jere Flint conducts this noted youth ensemble on July 24 at 2pm. Tickets are $5 to $20.

Eddie Horst: "Journey to Atlanta"
Bernstein: Symphonic Dances from *West Side Story*
Howard Hanson: Symphony no. 2, *Romantic*

Soprano Jessye Norman with the Atlanta Symphony Orchestra

Georgia's best-known international opera star performs July 24 and July 26 at 8pm. Tickets are $35 to $75.

Russian National Orchestra

This new ensemble, which has attracted international attention under the direction of Mikhail Pletnev, performs on July 25 at 8pm. Tickets are $35 to $75.

International Opera Gala

Representing three Olympic Games host countries, Dame Gwyneth Jones (soprano), Agnes Baltsa (mezzo-soprano), and Jose Van Dan (baritone), join with the Atlanta Opera, the Atlanta Symphony Orchestra, and conductor William Fred Scott for a celebration of operatic virtuosity. Saturday, July 27 at 8pm. Tickets are $35 to $75.

Olympic Jazz Summit

Artistic director Wynton Marsalis leads the ultimate all-star jazz band on July 28 and July 29 at 8pm. Tickets are $30 to $75.

Australian Youth Orchestra

This highly acclaimed group visits the South for the first time. July 29 at 2pm. Tickets are $5 to $20.

   Shostakovich: Symphony no. 10
   Haydn: Trumpet Concerto in E-flat

Jerusalem Symphony Orchestra, featuring pianist Yefim Bronfman

This performance celebrates Jerusalem's 3,000th anniversary. July 30 at 8pm. Tickets are $30 to $65.

   Menachem Weisenberg: "In Honor of 3000" (U.S. premiere)
   Brahms: Piano Concerto no. 1
   Prokofiev: Symphony no. 5

Atlanta Symphony Youth Orchestra and Australian Youth Orchestra

The youth ensemble of the 1996 host city joins with its counterpart in the 2000 host country on July 31 at 8pm. Tickets are $5 to $20.

   Stravinsky: Suite from *The Firebird*
   Smetana: "The Moldau" from *Ma Vlast*
   Tchaikovsky: Symphony no. 5

Atlanta Symphony Orchestra and Chorus

Soloists Kallen Esperian (soprano) and Jennifer Larmore (mezzo-soprano) join conductor Yoel Levi in a performance of Mahler's Symphony no. 2, *The Resurrection.* August 1 at 8pm, and August 2 at 2pm. Tickets are $25 to $60.

The Smithsonian Jazz Orchestra

Musical directors David Baker and Gunther Schuller lead the masters of the genre in a tribute to Duke Ellington. August 2 at 8 pm. Tickets are $5 to $20.

OLYMPIC ARTS FESTIVAL DANCE PROGRAMS

Call 404/744-1996 for information on ordering tickets.

Gregor Seyffert and Company

This acclaimed German father-and-son ensemble will perform on July 10 at 8pm and July 11 at 3pm at the 14th Street Playhouse. Tickets are $25.

Miami City Ballet

Under the artistic direction of Edward Villella, the company will perform July 13–14 at 8pm, and July 15 at 3pm at the Atlanta Civic Center. Tickets are $20 to $30.

Alvin Ailey American Dance Theater

Among the world's best known and most eclectic modern dance companies, the Ailey tradition remains strong and vibrant under the artistic direction of Judith Jamison. Performances on July 17–18 at 8pm, on July 19–20 at 3pm at the Atlanta Civic Center. Tickets range from $25 to $35.

Soweto Street Beat Dance Company

Relocated from Soweto, South Africa, in 1992, this Atlanta-based company pays tribute to the new democracy of its homeland with a dazzling world premiere. Expect some surprise special guests. Performances July 20 at 8pm, July 21 at 3pm at the MLKing Chapel. Tickets are $15 to $25.

Dallas Black Dance Theater

Celebrating its 20th-anniversary season in 1996, DBDT is known for its vivid contemporary repertoire based in ethnic, jazz, and spiritual work. July 22 at 8pm, July 23 at 3pm at the MLKing Chapel. Tickets are $15 to $25.

Netherlands Dance Theater

A full-length ballet based on an ancient Japanese fairy tale, set to a driving primal score by Maki Ishii, and performed on traditional Japanese instruments. July 22–23 at 8pm, July 24 at 3pm at the Atlanta Civic Center. Tickets are $20 to $30.

Pilobolus Dance Theater

Celebrating its 25th-anniversary season, this acclaimed troupe will perform on July 24 at 8pm, July 25 at 3pm at the MLKing Chapel. Tickets run from $20 to $30.

Phoenix Dance Company

Young and vibrant, this hip British ensemble combines street dance, graceful athleticism, and polished modern technique. July 26 at 8pm, July 27 at 3pm at the MLKing Chapel. Tickets are $15 to $25.

Ballethnic

This cutting-edge, multinational company performs a world premiere by Irene Tassembedo, who fuses contemporary ballet with traditional African dance. Performances are July 28 at 8pm and July 29 at 3pm at the MLKing Chapel. Tickets are $15 to $25.

Royal Thai Ballet

A masked dance-drama of excerpts from the *Ramakirti*—a traditional Asian epic tale—with traditional costumes, choreography, and instrumental accompaniment. With narrative description in English. July 29 at 8pm, July 30 at 3pm at the Atlanta Civic Center. Tickets are $15 to $25.

Atlanta Ballet: *Drastic Cuts; Dance Technology Project*
America's oldest ballet company presents a world premiere featuring the innovative choreography of Donald Byrd as well as a cutting-edge collaboration with Georgia Tech. Performances August 1–2 at 8pm, August 3 at 3pm at the Atlanta Civic Center. Tickets are $20 to $30.

Karas
Tokyo-based choreographer Saburu Teshigawara and his riveting dancers combine Japanese Buto technique, classical ballet, and modern dance to create *Noiject.* July 27 at 8pm and July 28 at 3pm at the Atlanta Civic Center. Tickets are $20 to $30.

OLYMPIC ARTS FESTIVAL THEATER PROGRAMS
Call 404/744-1996 for information on ordering tickets.

The Royal National Theatre
England's leading theater ensemble, known around the world for its definitive Shakespearean interpretations, unveils to U.S. audiences a new comedy by British playwright Patrick Marber. Performances are July 10–13 at 8pm, and July 13–14 at 3pm at the Alliance Theater. Tickets are $35 and $45.

Theater Emory/Saratoga International Theater Institute
One of America's foremost stage directors, Anne Bogart, and Japan's leading director, Tadashi Suzuki, are redefining and revitalizing contemporary American theater through the New York–based SITI. Their latest tour de force uses contemporary music as the backbone of a series of emotional vignettes called *Short Stories,* staged July 11–13 at 8pm at the Alliance Studio Theater. Tickets are $25.

Actor's Express
The Harvey Milk Show, here revived by its originators, chronicles the election and ultimate assassination of San Francisco's first openly gay political figure. July 12 and 15 at 8pm; July 13–14 and 16 at 3pm at the 14th Street Playhouse Second Stage. Tickets are $25.

Center for Puppetry Arts
For children of all ages, this venue boasts an international reputation for hosting the finest practitioners of the art-form.

Shows recommended for the family:
Topsy-Turvy World (July 12–13)
Kudzu Jack and the Giant (July 15–20)
The Hungry Tiger and Other Tales from China (July 22–27)
Bathtub Pirates (July 29–August 3)
   Performances last one hour and are held Monday through Saturday at 11am and 1pm, Wednesday at 3pm as well. Tickets are $8.

For audiences 12 and over:
Jon Ludwig's *Frankenstein,* running July 12–August 3, Thursday through Saturday at 8pm. Tickets are $20.

Museum: The Muppets in Atlanta Exhibition
Monday through Saturday from 9am to 8pm. Admission is $5 for adults, $4 for children; or free with price of show admission.

Alabama Shakespeare Festival

The largest classical theater in the American South and one of the best-regarded Shakespeare companies in the world presents *Lizard* July 13–16 at 8pm, July 15 at 3pm at the 14th Street Playhouse. Tickets are $25.

Alliance Theater Company

The latest offering by one of America's hottest playwrights, Pearl Cleage, is presented by its 1995 originators as the Alliance Theater Company stages **Blues for an Alabama Sky.** Evening performances are July 18, 20, 23–27, and 30–31, and August 1–2 at 8pm. Afternoon performances are at 3pm on July 19–21, 24, 27–28, and 31, and August 3. Tickets are $25 and $35.

Horizon Theater Company

Adapted from Melissa Faye Green's award-winning novel and presented by Atlanta's premiere contemporary company is *Praying for Sheetrock,* the story of the late coming of civil rights to a small town in coastal Georgia. July 18–20 at 8pm, July 19–21 at 3pm at the 14th Street Playhouse. Tickets are $25.

Seven Stages

Pulitzer Prize–winner Sam Shepard and director Joseph Chaiken have created *On the Edge of the World,* a new work presented by Atlanta's leading producer of new plays. Performances are July 19–20 and 23 at 3pm, July 20–22 at 8pm at the 14th Street Playhouse. Tickets are $25.

Alliance Theater Company

Playwright Alfred Uhry, of *Driving Miss Daisy* fame, is here represented by the world premiere of his newest work, a comedy called *Last Night of Ballyhoo,* set during Christmas 1939 prior to the film debut of *Gone with the Wind.* Mounted by one of the South's finest theater companies on July 20, 21, 24, 27, 28, and 31 and August 3 at 3pm. Evening performances are July 20, 23–27, 30, and August 1–2 at 8pm at the Alliance Theater. Tickets are $25 and $35.

Seven Stages

Poet and playwright Robert Earl Price utilizes the shape and feel of Thelonius Monk's music to create a jazz drama called *Blue Monk,* here presented in its world premiere on July 23–24 at 8pm, on July 25–26 at 3pm at the 14th Street Playhouse Second Stage. Tickets are $25.

ALI

A touching, humorous, and heartwarming solo tour de force that captures the life and times of Olympic gold medalist and three-time world heavyweight champion Muhammed Ali. July 25–27 at 8pm, July 27–28 at 3pm at the 14th Street Playhouse. Tickets are $25.

ART Station

Known for its first-class depictions of contemporary Southern life, this innovative company presents the world premiere of Ferrol Sams' short story *Harmony Ain't Easy,* about a comic marital relationship of 40 years. Staged July 29–30 at 8pm and July 30–August 1 at 3pm at the 14th Street Playhouse Second Stage. Tickets are $25.

Jomandi Productions
Electrifying choreography meets a driving score of jazz, r&b, and hip hop to create a new musical comedy called *Hip II: Birth of the Boom,* featuring Afro Joe and the Doo Wop Orchestra and mounted by one of America's leading African-American theater companies. July 31–August 2 at 8pm, August 2–3 at 3pm at the 14th Street Playhouse. Tickets are $25.

SOUTHERN CROSSROADS

Right in the heart of downtown Atlanta, Southern Crossroads celebrates the American South in a free outdoor festival spanning six acres in Centennial Olympic Park. Food, music, dance, a bustling marketplace, and hundreds of artists and performers from the 12-state region will show international visitors the flavor of the American South.

Highlights include:

Talking Feet: Live bands accompany expert demonstrations in Cajun two-step, hip-hop, western swing, salsa, square dancing, precision clogging, and more. You're welcome to join in!

The South on Record: Elvis's famed Sun Sessions revisited; cooking shows; interviews with well-known Southerners in arts, politics, and religion; and lively entertainment in a special recording/television studio created just for Southern Crossroads.

Byways and Skyways: Learn about art and technology as it has developed in the American South through demonstrations of cutting-edge technology in digital communications, transportation, and other fields, with performances and stories of work, invention, and discovery.

Southern World Music: Trace music of southern origin—rock and roll, jazz, gospel, blues, country—from its roots to its international branches through live performances.

Tastes of the South/Family Picnic: For $1 a taste, you can sample a sumptuous array of southern regional cuisine from traditional to nouveau, from Smithfield Ham to roasted oysters. Decide what you like and buy the full portion, enjoying it in a special picnic area, where long tables accommodate visitors family style. Augmented by strolling a cappella groups, string bands, and bluesmen.

Southern Market: With demonstrations by the South's leading potters, quilt-makers, basket weavers, and others, the Southern Market is the place to buy all things Southern—books, music, videos, crafts, and more.

Southern Celebrations: Spontaneous processions will criss-cross throughout the festival . . . from Mardi Gras parades to American Indian processions.

This free event is coproduced with the Smithsonian Institution and the Southern Arts Federation and runs daily from July 17 to August 4 from noon to midnight.

OLYMPIC ARTS FESTIVAL EXHIBITIONS & SPECIAL PROGRAMS
TICKETED BY THE OLYMPIC ARTS FESTIVAL

Call 404/744-1996 for information on ordering tickets.

The Olympic Woman

This fascinating multimedia exhibition chronicles the history of women in the Modern Olympic Games, from the women who entered the 1900 Paris Olympic Games to the more than 3,000 participants in the 1992 Barcelona Games. Utilizing the latest in exhibition technology, The Olympic Woman brings together Olympic memorabilia, photography, film, and video from collections all over the world.

June 23–July 11: 10am–5pm
July 12–August 4: 10am–7pm
Georgia State University Alumni Hall; $5.
(Start times within each of the three daily sessions will vary and will be on the half hour; for instance, start time for a 10–1 ticket might be 11:30.)

The American South: Past, Present and Future

Gone with the Wind, civil rights, jazz, William Faulkner, cotton farming, barbecue, and much more—this lively exhibition weaves historic and modern photos with artifacts, video, and text to show the rich fabric of the American South's history and culture. Organized by the Atlanta History Center to complement the Southern Crossroads festival in Centennial Olympic Park.

June 29–July 18 and after August 5: call venue for hours and rates (☎ 404/814-4000).
July 19–August 4: 10am–6pm at the Atlanta History Center; $10.
(Price includes admission to other exhibits, historical houses, and gardens.)

Souls Grown Deep: African-American Vernacular Art of the South

A landmark exhibition of over 250 paintings, sculptures, and works on paper by 40 contemporary self-taught artists from the region. These visionary pieces, created in the wake of the Civil Rights Movement, represent the newest wave in contemporary American art.

June 29–July 18; August 4–October 15: call venue for hours and rates (☎ 404/727-4248).
July 19–August 4: 10am–7pm at the Michael C. Carlos Museum at City Hall East; $5.

Thornton Dial: Remembering the Road

A companion exhibition to *Souls Grown Deep,* featuring a comprehensive look at the recent work of this renowned self-taught Southern artist. Organized by the Michael C. Carlos Museum at Emory University.

June 29–July 18; August 4–October 15: call venue for hours and rates (☎ 404/727-4248).
July 19–August 4: 10am–7pm at the Michael C. Carlos Museum at City Hall East; $5.

Rings: Five Passions in World Art

A once-in-a-lifetime artistic experience organized by Atlanta's High Museum of Art and directed by J. Carter Brown, director emeritus of the National Gallery of Art in Washington, D.C. The objects featured in "Rings . . ." embody the Olympic ideals and evoke five universal human emotions: love, anguish, awe, triumph, and joy. More than 100 masterpieces are included, spanning 8,000 years and ranging from Greek bronzes to African figures to favorites by Monet, Rodin, and Picasso.

July 4–August 5: 10am–7pm at the High Museum of Art; $10.

August 5–September 29: call venue for hours and rates (☎ 404/733-4400).

(Start times within each of the three daily sessions will vary and will be on the half hour; for instance, start time for a 10–1 ticket might be 11:30.)

TICKETED BY VENUE OR FREE ADMISSION

Ways of Welcoming: Greeting Rituals from Around the World

Objects and artifacts from around the world that illustrate the incredible variety of international welcoming traditions. Organized by the Atlanta International Museum of Art and Design.

May 24–July 18; August 5–November 8: call venue for hours and rates.

July 19–August 4: 11am–5pm at the Atlanta International Museum of Art and Design (☎ 404/688-2467); $5.

Roland L. Freeman's "I've Known Rivers": A Retrospective Documentary Photography Exhibit on African-American Expressive Culture

A collection of works by one of this country's preeminent photographers exploring three decades of African-American cultural expressions and experience.

June 1–September 30: call venue for hours. Auburn Avenue Research Library of African American Culture and History (☎ 404/730-4001); free.

Public Art Premieres

An exciting array of more than 20 permanent and temporary public art pieces, organized and in most cases commissioned by the Cultural Olympiad in honor of the Centennial Olympic Games. From Siah Armajani's magnificent Centennial Olympic Cauldron to works by international and regional artists, these new sculptures add a welcome dimension to the Atlanta landscape.

Various sites throughout Atlanta.

An International Celebration of Southern Literature

Southern literature, to borrow a phrase from the South's own William Faulkner, has not merely endured, it has prevailed. This conference brings the region's leading authors together with preeminent international scholars—from the United Kingdom to Japan to Africa—to explore new perspectives on the literature and culture of the American South.

June 6–9 at Agnes Scott College. Call 404/224-1835 for complete information.

Muntadas: On Translation

Hosted by the Atlanta College of Art Gallery, this new multimedia installation is Barcelona-born artist Muntadas' latest work, and continues his investigation of power structures and their influence on culture, economics, and politics.

June 7–July 18: call venue for hours (☎ 404/733-5051).
July 19–August 4: 11am–9:30pm at the Atlanta College of Art; free.

Picturing the South, 1863–1996

Using photographic images that span more than a century, this exhibition organized by the High Museum of Art examines the facts, contradictions, and myths that have shaped the South's unique cultural heritage.

June 15–July 3; August 6–September 14: call venue for hours and rates (☎ 404/577-6950).
July 4–August 5: 10am–7pm at the High Museum of Art, Folk Art and Photography Galleries; $5.

The Vision of Ulysses Davis, American Folk Artist

A newly installed permanent exhibition of up to 200 sculptures by one of the last great Southern woodcarvers working in the African tradition.

June 16–July 18 and after August 4: call venue for hours (☎ 912/234-8000).
July 19–August 4: 10am–5pm at the Beach Institute African American Cultural Center/Savannah; free.

Wadsworth Jarrell: A Shared Ideology

An exhibition of new paintings and sculptures created by this important New York–based African-American artist.

June 28–July 18 and August 5–September 28: call venue for hours (☎ 404/817-6981).
July 19–August 4: 8:30am–8pm at City Gallery East; free.

Southeast Artists Exhibition

This provocative exhibition showcases multiple new works by eight vanguard artists—chosen from a field of 800—working in the region.

June 28–July 18 and August 4–25: call venue for hours and rates (☎ 404/688-2500).
July 19–August 3: 10am–6pm at the Nexus Contemporary Art Center; $5.

Beyond Category: The Musical Genius of Duke Ellington

A celebration of the achievements of one of America's greatest composers, featuring objects, original photographs, and manuscripts from the Smithsonian Institution's Duke Ellington Collection.

July 4–August 4: 10am–7pm at the Robert Woodruff Library at Atlanta University Center (☎ 404/522-8980).

California Impressionists

This exhibition focuses on landscape paintings by American painters working in California from 1895 to 1940, selected from the collection of the Irvine Museum of Irvine, California, and organized by the Georgia Museum of Art in Athens.

July 6–September 1: Mon–Sat 9am–5pm, Sun 1–5pm at the Georgia Museum of Art/Athens (☎ 706/542-3255); free.

African-American Culture: An American Experience

A living exhibit focusing on Atlanta's historic Auburn Avenue and the Atlanta University Center includes storytelling, jazz, blues, gospel, rap, and exhibitions. Produced in collaboration with many of Atlanta's leading African-American cultural institutions.

July 19–August 3: Schedule available in Olympic Arts Festival Program Guide, to be published in the summer of 1996.

Centennial Collectibles: OLYMPHIEX '96/Stamps, Coins, and Memorabilia

Occupying more than 90,000 square feet, this will be the largest and most comprehensive gathering of the world's greatest Olympic collection of stamps (OLYMPHIEX'96), coins, and memorabilia in history.

July 19–August 2: 10am–7pm; August 3: 10am–5pm at the Atlanta Apparel Mart; free.

From Rearguard to Vanguard: Selections from the Clark Atlanta University Collection of African-American Art

Marking the reopening of the newly renovated Clark Atlanta University Art Gallery, this exhibition features 30 works from an important and rarely seen collection of art by 20th-century American artists, including Charles White, Jacob Lawrence, Elizabeth Catlett, Henry Ossawa Tanner, and Romare Bearden.

July 19–August 4: 10am–7pm at Clark Atlanta University Art Gallery (☎ 404/880-8000); free.
August 5–September 15: call venue for hours and rates.

Lifting the Veil: Robert S. Duncanson and the Emergence of the African American Artist

Organized by the Washington University Gallery of Art, St. Louis, this exhibition features 55 paintings by an important mid-19th-century African-American landscape painter.

July 19–August 3: 10am–7pm; Clark Atlanta University Art Gallery and Hammonds House (☎ 404/752-8730); $8 (includes admission to "From Rearguard . . .").
August 4–September 15: Call venue for hours and rates.

100 Years of World Cinema

This showing of 100 international landmark films celebrates the 100th anniversary of film with screenings of everything from *Apocalypse Now* to noted foreign films such as Jean Cocteau's 1947 *Beauty and the Beast.* During the Games, the focus will be classic American movies, shown in repertory.

July 19–August 4: call Woodruff Arts Center's Rich Auditorium at the High Museum of Art (☎ 404/733-4570) for schedule.

7   The Paralympic Games

Most of us are in awe of the almost superhuman capabilities of Olympic athletes. Perhaps even more inspiring are the feats of athletic champions with disabilities. On August 16, 1996, 12 days after the close of the 1996 Centennial Olympic Games, the Games of the Xth Paralympiad—celebrating the triumphs and achievements of people with disabilities—will officially begin 10 days of competition. International in scope, it will host some 3,500 athletes from 115 nations participating in 17 sports.

The 115 confirmed nations means the Atlanta Paralympic Games have exceeded the number of countries to compete in the 1968 Olympic Games at Mexico City, where 113 competed. "It is not only a sign of growth, but gives us credibility as a truly worldwide event," said Andy Fleming, president and CEO of the Atlanta Paralympic Organizing Committee. The full-medal sports for the Paralympics are: archery, athletics (track, throwing and jumping, pentathlon, and marathon), basketball, boccia (an Italian game played by athletes with cerebral palsy; its object is to place balls closest to a white target ball on a long alleylike field of play), cycling, equestrian, fencing, goalball (a game played by blind competitors who try to throw balls equipped with bells into their opponents' goal), judo, lawn bowls, powerlifting, football (soccer), shooting, swimming, table tennis, wheelchair tennis, and volleyball. There are also two demonstration sports—racquetball and yachting. The Paralympic Games will include over 700 events—more than twice the number of Olympic events—because Paralympic athletes compete according to degree of disability and functional level, creating additional categories. Events will utilize most of the Olympic Games venues as well as other Atlanta-area locations.

For further information about the Paralympics call **404/588-1996;** to order tickets to Paralympics events call **404/724-2TIX;** to work as a volunteer call **404/724-2VOL.**

3

Planning a Trip to Atlanta

If you're going to a beach resort, there's little need to plan your vacation—you can wing it. But when visiting a city where dozens of sightseeing attractions and activities vie for your time, planning is the key to optimum enjoyment. In the pages that follow, I'll tell you everything you need to know.

1 Information & Money

As soon as you know you're going to Atlanta, write to or call the **Atlanta Convention & Visitors Bureau (ACVB),** 233 Peachtree St. NE, Suite 2000, Atlanta, GA 30303 (☎ **404/222-6688**). They'll send you a copy of *Atlanta Now* (a visitor's guide), a book of discount coupons, a *Metro Atlanta Attractions Guide,* a map, and a two-month calendar of events; they can also advise you on anything from Atlanta's hotel and restaurant scene to the best tour packages available. You can call weekdays between 8:30am and 5:30pm. May 1 through December 25 you can also call a toll free 24-hour number (**800/ATLANTA**) for an informational recording.

In addition, the ACVB publishes the *International Visitors Guide* for foreign tourists; it's available in five languages.

2 When to Go

THE CLIMATE

Atlanta's climate is mostly temperate year round. The city enjoys four distinct seasons, but the variations are less extreme than elsewhere.

It seldom snows much in winter. But be forewarned about the city's humid summer hot spells. Spring and autumn are long seasons, and, in terms of natural beauty and heavenly climate, they're optimum times to visit. Annual rainfall is about 48 inches, and the wettest months are December through April and July.

Atlanta's Average Daytime Temperature and Rainfall

	Jan	Feb	Mar	Apr	May	June	July	Aug	Sept	Oct	Nov	Dec
Temp.°F	45	46	52	60	69	77	79	79	73	63	52	43
Rainfall"	4.4	4.5	5.3	4.4	3.1	3.8	4.7	3.6	3.2	2.4	2.9	4.3

What Things Cost in Atlanta	U.S.$
Taxi from airport to downtown, for one person	$15
Bus from airport to downtown	$8
Double at The Ritz-Carlton Atlanta (very expensive)	$169–$295
Double at Marriott Suites (expensive)	$179
Double at the Comfort Inn downtown (moderate)	$99–$149
Double at Cheshire Motor Inn (inexpensive)	$41–$48
Three-course dinner at the City Grill including wine, tax, and tip (very expensive)	$45 and up
Three-course dinner at Bistango, including wine, tax, and tip (expensive)	$35 and up
Three-course dinner at Kudzu Café, including wine, tax, and tip (moderate)	$25 and up
Three-course dinner at Original Rocky's Brick Oven Italian Restaurant, including wine, tax, and tip (inexpensive)	$17 and up
Theater ticket at the Alliance	$14–$34

ATLANTA CALENDAR OF EVENTS

Note: Some events, such as the Georgia Renaissance Festival, begin in one month and continue for several months thereafter. These are listed in the month of inception. So do look back a few months prior to your visit for ongoing events. Also: To get to the Old Courthouse in Decatur, site of several below-listed events, take MARTA to the Decatur station.

January

- **Martin Luther King Week,** the second week of the month, is a major happening, comprising more than 30 events. It begins with an interfaith service and includes plays, musical tributes, seminars, films, a parade down Peachtree Street to Auburn Avenue, and speeches by notables (including Mrs. Coretta Scott King). There are also concerts by major performers (in past years Kris Kristofferson, Luther Vandross, Stevie Wonder, and the Neville Brothers, among others). For details, contact the King Center (☎ **404/524-1956**).
- **Atlanta Boat Show.** This five-day event at the Georgia World Congress Center is one of the largest inland marine shows in the United States. It features houseboats, yachts, cabin cruisers, saltwater craft, pleasure craft, and more. Admission is $7 for adults, $3 for children 6–12, under 6 free. For details, call **305/531-8410.**

February

- **Cathedral Antiques Show.** For four days in mid-February, 30 to 35 dealers of high-quality antiques display their wares at the

Cathedral of St. Philip, 2744 Peachtree Rd. The merchandise ranges from 18th- and 19th-century furnishings to vintage jewelry and Oriental rugs. A sit-down lunch, served in a genteel setting, is available each day. Admission is $6 per day, or you can attend the preview party for $25 and come back all four days for free. For details, call **404/365-1000.**

- **Southeastern Flower Show.** One of the South's premier gardening events, it takes place in City Hall East (at 675 Ponce de Leon Ave.) for five days, usually including Valentine's Day but sometimes as late as early March. It offers three acres of stunning landscapes and gardens displaying both flowers and vegetables. Other displays might include anything from a bamboo forest to a wildlife refuge. Garden-related products and patio furniture are sold, and there are demonstrations of gardening techniques, photography exhibitions, and events for children. Admission is $10 for adults, with discounts for seniors and children. Proceeds benefit the Atlanta Botanical Garden. For information, call **404/888-5638.**

March

- **Atlanta Home and Garden Show.** This four-day mid-month event at the Georgia World Congress Center emphasizes display gardens and landscaping ideas, and there are seminars on subjects ranging from southern gardens to antique restoration. Admission is $7 for adults, $6 for seniors, $4 for children 7–12, under 7 free. Call **404/998-9800** for details.

- ✪ **St. Patrick's Day Parade.** A major production here, with some 7,000 marchers each year and 150,000 viewers. The mayor and other local politicians attend, and there are sports celebrities, high school bands, clowns, cloggers, drill teams, and bagpipers. The parade culminates near Underground Atlanta with concerts of Irish music, dance, and other festivities. If you want to continue celebrating, head over to **Limerick Junction,** 822 N. Highland Ave. (☎ **404/874-7147**), a cozy pub that provides the requisite green beer, bagpipe players, and Irish fare.

  Where: The parade begins at West Peachtree Street and Ralph McGill Boulevard. **When:** The Saturday closest to St. Patrick's Day. **How:** Just show up. Check the local paper for details.

- **The High Museum Atlanta Wine Auction.** Events begin with a gala wine reception and formal dinner on Friday night. On Saturday, you can discuss wines with prominent winemakers, sample premium wines and gourmet fare prepared by Atlanta's finest chefs, and participate in a silent auction. The event culminates with the auctioning off of great wines, fabulous trips, wine dinners, and artworks. It all takes place the last weekend of the month under a tent at a location determined annually. Proceeds benefit the museum. At this writing, admission to the gala is $225. Tickets for the vintner's reception auction are $100 per couple, $60 per person. Call **404/733-4424** for details.

April

✪ **The Atlanta Dogwood Festival.** Culminating in Piedmont Park on a weekend in mid-April, this environmentally themed spring celebration is a biggie, with several related events taking place the week prior. Activities include concerts, food booths, kite-flying contests, children's activities, a juried arts and crafts show, canine frisbee championships, and Earth Day celebrations featuring presentations by environmental groups—all in Piedmont Park. There's also a display of hot-air balloons.

    Where: Piedmont Park. **When:** Three days in mid-April. **How:** Admission is free. For details, call **404/952-9151** or check the local papers for a full listing of events.

- **Antebellum Jubilee.** Demonstrations of early American/southern arts and crafts, a re-created Civil War encampment, string bands, and concerts on the dulcimer, harp and zither, are all part of this annual celebration at Georgia's Stone Mountain Park the first weekend in April. All festival activities are included in the price of regular admission to the plantation. For details, call **404/498-5702.**

- **The Easter Egg Hunt.** Held on the south lawn of the Old Courthouse in Decatur, with prizes for those who collect the most eggs. Admission is free. For details, call **404/371-8386.**

- **Stone Mountain Village Easter Egg Hunt.** On Saturday morning of Easter weekend, a hunt for painted eggs and candy departs from The Children's Hour, a toy store at 5377 Manor Dr. Prizes include gift certificates for toys. There are separate areas for children ages 2 to 4 and 5 to 7. Admission is free. Call **404/498-1351** for details. The Village also sponsors a "**Breakfast with Bunny**" the Saturday before Easter weekend at the Basket Bakery and Garden Café, 6655 Memorial Dr., at Main Street. Call **404/498-0329** for details.

- **Easter Sunrise Services** are held at the top and the base of Georgia's Stone Mountain at 6am. Park gates open at 4am and the skylift begins operation at 4:30am (though it seems more appropriate to walk up if you're in good shape). For details, call **404/498-5702.**

- **The Run for Restoration,** a 5K race at Oakland Cemetery, takes place mid-month. Proceeds go to cemetery upkeep. Entry fee is $12 prerace, $13 the day of the race. Call **404/688-2107** for details.

- **Lasershow,** also at Stone Mountain Park, is a sight-and-sound spectacular of laser lights and fireworks choreographed to popular, patriotic, country, and classical music. It begins on April weekends (Friday, Saturday, and Sunday nights at 9pm). Admission is free. Beginning in early May through Labor Day, Lasershow can be seen nightly at 9:30pm. For details, call **404/498-5702.**

- **FEBAAC '96 USA** (Festival of Black and African Arts & Culture) will take place April 12 to 22 at sites throughout the city. An international festival and trade expo, it will include art shows, crafts exhibits, workshops, concerts, and varied performances from African diaspora nations. For details, call **404/766-5533.**

- **The Inman Park Festival** takes place the last weekend in April in an Atlanta suburb noted for its gorgeous turn-of-the-century Victorian mansions. Activities include a tour of homes, music (jazz bands, cloggers), an arts-and-crafts festival/flea market, a parade, a Saturday-night street dance, and food vendors. Tickets, available at the festival, are about $10, good for all events both days. To get here take MARTA to the Inman Park station. For more information, call **404/242-4895.**

○ **The Georgia Renaissance Festival Spring Celebration.** This re-creation of a 16th-century English county fair in a 30-acre "village" called Willy Nilly features a juried crafts show with over 100 craftspeople (many of them demonstrating 16th-century skills); continuous entertainment on 10 stages (there are over 100 shows each day); period foods; a birds of prey show; and a cast of costumed characters including jousters, jugglers, storytellers, giant stilt-walkers, minstrels, magicians, choral groups, and knights in shining armor. King Henry VIII and one of his wives oversee the festivities.

  Where: In Fairburn—10 miles south of the airport on I-85, Exit 12. **When:** On eight weekends, from the last Saturday in April through the second Sunday in June (plus Memorial Day). **How:** Purchase tickets at the gate. Admission is $10.95 for adults, $5.25 for ages 6–15, 5 and under free. For details, call **404/964-8575.**

May

- **Blue Sky Concerts** are free performances of jazz, classical, bluegrass, and rock music, held at noon every Wednesday in May on the south lawn of the Old Courthouse in Decatur. Bring a blanket and a picnic lunch. For more information, call **404/371-8386.**

- **Concerts on the Square,** a similar series at the courthouse, takes place every Saturday night in May at 7:30pm. It traditionally opens with a performance by the Dekalb Symphony Orchestra. For details, call **404/371-8386.**

- **The Gardens for Connoisseurs Tour,** proceeds of which go to the Atlanta Botanical Garden, visits outstanding private gardens the weekend of Mother's Day. Tickets are $20 for the entire tour, $5 per garden. For details, call **404/876-5859.**

- **Springfest.** There's good eatin' at this event, which includes the annual BBQ Pork Cookoff and southern food booths. It takes place on a weekend early in May at Georgia's Stone Mountain Park. Continuous live entertainment on three stages (emphasizing folk and country music and featuring some big names, like Lee Roy Parnell, Archer/Park, and Tracy Byrd), the South's largest garage sale, and children's activities, round out the events. All activities are free. For information, call **404/498-5702.**

- **Kingfest International.** This free outdoor internationally themed festival takes place during a weekend in mid-May at the Martin Luther King, Jr. Center. Events include international dance performances, arts and crafts exhibits, foods, concerts, theater, an artist's market, and more. Admission is free. For details, call **404/524-1956.**

- **Midtown Music Festival.** This terrific festival takes place on a weekend in mid-May at a lot on 10th and Peachtree Streets. Events—beginning Friday night—include dozens of concerts on five stages (many of them big-name performers such as James Brown, Al Green, and Joan Baez), a southeastern artist's market, and ethnic food booths from regional restaurants. Kids' activities, too: face painting, special performances, arts and crafts, circus workshops, and more. Admission is $15 for one day, $25 for all three days; free for children under 12 accompanied by an adult. Call **404/798-7785.**
- **Decatur Arts Festival,** a three-day event on the south lawn of the Old Courthouse in Decatur, takes place Memorial Day weekend. It features an art show on the lawn, various juried shows nearby, a garden tour, mimes, jugglers, puppet shows, clowns, children's art activities, great food, and performances by music, dance, and theater groups. The literary arts are celebrated with storytelling, readings, and book signings. A great family outing. For details, call **404/371-8386.**
- **A Taste of the South.** Part of Stone Mountain Park's Memorial Day weekend celebrations, this happening has music, dance, regional foods (everything from collard greens to grits), art, crafts demonstrations, and more. For details, call **404/498-5702.**
- **The Peach Carnival,** another Memorial Day weekend celebration, is a festival of Caribbean arts and culture. It includes reggae and calypso bands, food and crafts booths, and an elaborately costumed parade, complete with stilt-walkers, along Peachtree Street from Woodruff Park to the Atlanta Civic Center. For details call **404/220-0158.**
- **The Atlanta Jazz Festival,** during Memorial Day weekend, features free ongoing concerts in Grant Park (at the main stage next to Cyclorama). The afternoon begins with local performers and goes on to major stars by evening—for example, Wynton Marsalis, Nancy Wilson, Shirley Horn, Cyrus Chestnut, Max Roach, and Sonny Rollins. Arrive early to get a good space, and bring a blanket and a picnic lunch. Some years, there's also a concert (admission is charged) featuring major jazz artists at the Chastain Park Amphitheatre at Powers Ferry Road and Stella Drive. For details on any of the above, call **404/817-6815.**

June

- **The Atlanta Film & Video Festival,** which takes place for two weeks in mid-June at the IMAGE Film/Video Center, 75 Bennett St. NW (and other Atlanta theaters), features about 70 films and videos by some of the country's most important independent media artists. Admission is $6 per film, with discounts available for students and seniors. Call **404/352-4225** for details.
- **Kingfest.** This free outdoor festival takes place during a weekend in mid-June at the Martin Luther King, Jr. Center. Events begin on a Friday evening with a concert by a major artist such as Ahmad Jamal. Saturday is "kids' day," filled with children's activities—

puppet making, pony rides, face painting—and performances by young people. And Sunday is gospel day, presenting premier gospel singers. During the festival, Freedom Plaza is transformed into an artist's market. Admission is free. For details, call **404/524-1956.**

- **The Annual Shakespeare Festival** offers three or four productions between mid-June and mid-August, performed in a 400-seat theater tent at Oglethorpe University, 4484 Peachtree Rd. Preceding the performances, audiences enjoy farcical vignettes on the lawn. Everyone brings a preperformance picnic or arranges in advance to purchase it on the premises. The company, made up of Actors Equity pros for the most part, offers both traditional and innovative Shakespearean productions as well as other classics. A recent season included *Much Ado About Nothing, King Lear,* and *The Country Wife* by William Wycherly. Picnic grounds open at 6:30pm, the preshow begins at 7pm, the actual show at 8pm. Admission is $16 to $20 for adults, $3 less for seniors, $10 to $15 for students. Call for tickets as far in advance as possible, especially for weekend performances (☎ **404/264-0020**). To order a picnic, call **404/396-5361.**

- **The Stone Mountain Village Annual Arts & Crafts Festival** is held on Father's Day weekend. Over 200 southeast craftspeople display their wares in a juried show, local community groups set up fabulous food booths, and entertainment (cloggers, clowns, country music, and more) is offered continually in the Village. For details, call **404/871-4971.** Admission is $1 for adults, free for children under 12.

- **Beach Party.** Decatur's not on the ocean, but that doesn't stop its residents from throwing this bash every year on the Friday closest to June 21 on the south lawn of the Old Courthouse in Decatur. The lawn is covered with sand, plastic palms and volleyball courts are erected, a live band provides music, food and drink are sold, and there are sandcastle-building, hula hoop, and dance contests. For details, call **404/371-8386.**

- **NationsBank Summer Film Festival.** Don't miss this event at the fabulous Fox Theatre. About a dozen films are shown from June through August, mostly on Monday and Thursday nights, and the shows include vintage cartoons, a sing-along organ concert (follow the bouncing ball), and a feature film at just $5.50 per ticket. Coupon books are available at a discount, a good bet for families. For details, call **404/881-2100.**

- **The Gay Pride Parade,** usually the last Sunday in June (though, possibly, it will be scheduled earlier in 1996 so as not to conflict with the Olympics), proceeds from a downtown site (selected annually) to Piedmont Park. The whole month is event-filled (June is National Gay Pride Month), including performances by the Gay Men's Chorus and musical entertainment and an art market in Piedmont Park the weekend of the parade. For details, call **404/662-4533.**

- **The National Black Arts Festival** is a 7- to 10-day affair (even-numbered years only) in late July and early August (in late June/early

July in 1996), with more than 150 events (most of them free) taking place throughout the city. Billed as "a celebration of the works of artists of African descent," it features dozens of events—concerts (including big names like Nancy Wilson and Wynton Marsalis), theater, film, dance, storytelling, poetry readings, performance art, art and folk-art exhibitions, children's activities, African puppet shows, and that's not the half of it. For details, call **404/730-7315.**

July

- **The Asian Cultural Experience.** The Atlanta Botanical Garden celebrates Asian culture during a weekend in early July with demonstrations of crafts such as Chinese calligraphy, ikebana, and origami. Saturday evening features music, dancing, and a dragon parade on the great lawn. Other events might include musical performances, games, children's activities, tai chi demonstrations, Asian art shows, and bonsai exhibits. Admission is included with Garden admission price. For details, call **404/876-5859.**

- **Independence Day** is celebrated at Georgia's Stone Mountain Park's three-day Fantastic Fourth Celebrations—a star-spangled festival of free concerts, sports competitions, patriotic music, clogging, choreographed fireworks displays, and Lasershows. For details, call **404/498-5702.**

  An old-fashioned **Fourth of July Parade,** with more than 100 floats, also takes place in Stone Mountain Village, from Mountain Street at the foot of the west gate of Stone Mountain Park along Main Street through the Village shop area. There are bands, cloggers, baton twirlers, and barbecues, and the shops offer sales. The parade begins at 10am, preceded by a 10K run. There are fireworks in the Village at night. For details, call **404/879-4971.**

  You can celebrate the **Fourth in Decatur.** Festivities begin with a Pied Piper Parade departing at 6pm from the Decatur Baptist Church on Courthouse Square. Decorate yourself, your bicycle, or your car and join in. The parade is followed by a concert at 7:30pm (bring a picnic and blanket) and a great fireworks display. Everything is free. For details, call **404/371-8386.**

  And about 100,000 people gather every July 4th at Underground Atlanta for the **Thunder Over Atlanta** celebration featuring live bands, including big names such as Jefferson Starship. Call **404/523-2311** for details.

- **The World Drum and Dance Summit** features workshops and performances by international drummers and dancers (African, Caribbean, Asian, and others) at an annually selected site. It takes place on a weekend mid-month. Admission is charged to some events; others are free. Call **404/817-6815** for details.

- **Superfest '96** will take place along Auburn Avenue (from Woodruff Park to Howell Street) July 1 through September 7. In addition to live music (blues and fusion), it will include theater presentations by Jomandi Productions, African pavilions, African art and cultural presentations, and a children's village. Auburn Avenue of the 1920s and 1930s will be re-created with vintage cars, period dress, and events such as tea parties and corn roasts.

September

- **The Montreux Atlanta International Music Festival** is a four- to six-day affair (including Labor Day) featuring jazz, blues, gospel, reggae, and zydeco music in Piedmont Park and local theaters. Both regional and internationally known artists perform, and the fun usually includes late-night jam sessions at local hotels. Most events are free. Call **404/817-6815** for details.

- **Blue Sky Concerts and Concerts on the Square.** The fall schedules of these concert series (see May) begin in Decatur. Concert times are the same as above. The final Saturday night concert is all "golden oldies." For details, call **404/371-8386.**

- **The Yellow Daisy Festival** at Georgia's Stone Mountain Park is a vast outdoor arts-and-crafts show (over 400 exhibitors) with musical entertainment, a flower show, great food, storytellers, and puppetry. Taking place in early September, it has been rated the nation's number one arts-and-crafts festival. About 300,000 people attend each year. For details, call **404/498-5702.**

- **Georgia Music Festival.** This statewide celebration of music takes place for a week to 10 days mid-month. Events (many of them free) include jazz, gospel, bluegrass, country, and rock concerts, as well as dancing. Call **404/656-3596** for details.

- ✪ **Arts Festival of Atlanta.** One of the nation's oldest and largest outdoor art events, this contemporary visual and performing arts festival features regional, national, and international artists. Indoor art exhibits are supplemented by a 300-booth outdoor Artist Market. Stages are set up for music, dance, and theater performances. Children's activities are numerous, and food concessions throughout the park offer everything from funnel cakes to fajitas.
    Where: Piedmont Park (plus performances and special exhibits at sites selected annually). **When:** Nine days, beginning the second or third week of September. **How:** All events are free. For details, call **404/885-1125.**

October

- **The Heritage Festival** takes place in early October on the south lawn of Courthouse Square in Decatur. It celebrates the old days with candlemaking, blacksmithing, and other crafts demonstrations; bluegrass music and other entertainment; and food booths. Admission is free. For details, call **404/371-8386.**

- **The American Association of University Women's Annual Book Fair** is a four-day event in Lenox Square Mall in early October. AAUW collects and categorizes over 75,000 used books each year for the fair. All are in good condition, some are valuable, and prices are low. Proceeds go to scholarship for women. Admission is free. Hours are 10am to 9:30pm. Call **404/355-1861** to find out the fair's location in the mall and exact dates.

- **The Miller Lite Chili Cookoff** is held at Georgia's Stone Mountain Park on a weekend day early in the month. You can sample thousands of varieties of chili, Brunswick stew, and corn bread. Entertainment varies each year but will likely include cloggers, country music, jalapeño-eating contests, and other folksy fun. For details, call **404/498-5702.**

- **The Annual Scottish Festival and Highland Games,** held mid-month at Stone Mountain, is a gathering of the clans comprising three days of military tattoos, Highland dancers, pipe and drum concerts, Scottish harping and fiddling, sword dancing, reels, lilts, and athletic events such as the hammer throw and caber toss. For details and admission charges, call **404/634-7402** or **404/396-5728.**

- ✪ **The Georgia Renaissance Fall Festival.** This 16th-century fair is the autumn complement to the spring celebration described above (see April listing for details). All of its offerings are the same, but since it's in October, a haunted house is added to the attractions and shops are geared up for holiday shopping.

  Where: In Fairburn—10 miles south of the airport on I-85, Exit 12. **When:** Five weekends in October and early November. **How:** You can purchase tickets at the gate. Admission is $10.95 for adults, $5.25 for ages 6–15, under 6 free. For details, call **404/964-8575.**

- **Fall Gardening Festival.** Designed to teach people about fall gardening, this one-day mid-month event at the Atlanta Botanical Garden features about 50 nonprofit exhibitors, display gardens, produce competitions, a plant and flower expo, food, music, and children's activities. Admission is free, but a $1 donation is suggested. For details, call **404/876-5859.**

- **Sunday in the Park at Oakland Cemetery.** On an annually selected October Sunday this graveyard party features storytellers, historians, guided tours, a hat contest, a turn-of-the-century concert, and Victorian boutiques. Admission is free. You can reserve a $5 picnic supper. Call **404/688-2107** for details.

November

- **Veteran's Day Parade.** Atlanta mounts an impressive version of this parade each year, on the 11th, with floats, drill teams, marching bands, clowns, color guards, and more. The parade begins at 11am from Lenox Square (in front of the Ritz-Carlton) and proceeds south. For details, call **404/416-0377.**

- **The High Museum Antique Show & Sale,** taking place at an annually selected Buckhead location on a weekend in mid-November, features about 50 exhibitors—outstanding international antique dealers all. In addition, it offers lectures, workshops, a tour of homes rich in decorative arts, and other special events. Admission to the show is $8 per day at the door, $6 with advance purchase. For details, call **404/733-4426.**

- **Holiday Celebrations** in Atlanta kick off with a dazzling array of events at Stone Mountain Park from late November through December 30. A "tree of lights" atop the mountain is visible from miles away; the park's roads offer a stunning display of lights, animated scenes, music, and traditional decorations; and activities include visits with Santa, candlelight plantation tours, carriage rides, holiday sing-along train rides, a special Lasershow, and lots of entertainment. For details, call **404/498-5702.**

- **Stone Mountain Village Candlelight Shopping.** Every Thursday night until 9pm, beginning the first Thursday in November and continuing through Christmas, this charming shopping village is candlelit, and visitors are lured into decorated shops by the aroma of mulling cider. A jolly St. Nick, gaily lighted trees, and carriage rides are part of the fun. It's a delightful way to do your holiday shopping. No admission. Christmas generally is greatly celebrated throughout November and December in the Village, including a **tree lighting** the day after Thanksgiving and many special events. Call **404/879-4971** for details.

- The **Atlanta Christmas Show,** sponsored by the Southern Exposition Management Company (SEMCO) takes place at the Galleria, 2 Galleria Pkwy. About 150 holiday-related crafts booths are set up. Call **404/998-9800** for details.

- **Christmas** is heralded in Atlanta by the **Lighting of the Great Tree** (a traditionally decorated 80-foot pine topped by an eight-foot star) on Thanksgiving night. There are choirs singing Christmas carols. It all takes place at Underground Atlanta at Peachtree Fountains, across from Five Points MARTA station. Arrive early via MARTA; traffic comes to a standstill as hundreds of thousands converge to view the spectacle. For details, call **404/523-2311.**

- The **Fidelity Tree Lighting** takes place in front of the Fidelity Bank at Commerce Drive and Clairmont Avenue in Decatur the last Friday in November. In addition to lighting a 60-foot tree, festivities include caroling, choruses, and food vendors. The fun begins at 7pm. Decatur's seasonal events also feature a **Candlelight Tour of Homes,** a **Bonfire and Christmas Carol Sing-Along** (with a marshmallow roast around a blazing fire), a **Breakfast with Santa** at a local Holiday Inn, and strolling carolers. Call **404/371-8386** for details.

December

- The **Stone Mountain Village Sugarplum Festival** begins with a country buffet breakfast with Santa ($5 per person) and includes carriage rides, special discounts in shops, and entertainment. Call **404/879-4971** for details.

- **Christmas at Callanwolde,** at Callanwolde Fine Arts Center, 980 Briarcliff Rd. NE, is usually held during the first two weeks in December (some years it begins in late November). Noted interior and floral designers decorate the Gothic-Tudor mansion, and shops (sweets, toys, pottery, garden, etc.) are set up in different rooms. Activities also include concerts on a 3,752-pipe Aeolian organ, children's breakfasts with Santa, caroling and hymn singing, and other entertainment. Admission: $8 adults, $6 seniors, $5 children 12 and under. For details, call **404/872-5338.**

- **Country Christmas.** The Atlanta Botanical Garden throws this fete on the first Sunday in December. The garden is beautifully decorated, and highlights of the afternoon include carolers, bell ringers, children's theater, entertainers, chestnuts roasting on an open fire, pony rides, cranberry and popcorn stringing, and strolling mimes, musicians, and magicians. Christmas crafts like wreath making are demonstrated, and you can shop for handcrafted gifts and homemade baked goods. Refreshments include mulled wine and cider. And, of course there's a giant tree. Admission is free the day of the fete. For details, call **404/876-5859.**

- ✪ **Egleston Children's Christmas Parade and Festival of Trees.** Both of these events raise money for Egleston Children's Hospital. The parade is a major to-do with award-winning bands, lavish holiday-themed floats, helium-balloon comic characters, Santa Claus, carolers, clowns, and costumed storybook and Disney characters. The parade kicks off the nine-day Festival of Trees for which Atlanta artists, interior designers, florists, and corporations innovatively decorate and donate trees, wreaths, and Christmas vignettes that are exhibited and auctioned off. The festival also features musical performances, children's activities, an antique carousel, the "pink pig" monorail ride, ice-skating demonstrations, and an international area of heritage displays from 28 countries.

  Where: The parade proceeds from Marietta and Spring Streets to West Peachtree Street and Ralph McGill Boulevard. The Festival of Trees takes place at the Georgia World Congress Center, 285 International Blvd. **When:** The parade begins at 10:30am the first Saturday in December; the nine-day festival follows. **How:** For details on the parade, call **404/264-9348** or check the local papers. Admission to the Festival of Trees is $8 for adults, $5 for seniors and children 2–12, under 2 free. For details, call **404/325-NOEL.**

- **The Peach Bowl Game.** Some time between Christmas and New Year's (occasionally in early January) at the Georgia Dome. Call **404/223-9200** for information, **404/249-6400** to charge tickets.

- **New Year's Eve.** The Big Peach that rings in Atlanta's New Year is dropped at the stroke of midnight from the 138-foot light tower at Underground Atlanta. But festivities begin earlier (about 8pm) with live music for dancing in the streets (it progresses from '60s tunes through the '90s), a pyrotechnic display and laser show, balloons, and a marching band. Some 250,000 revelers converge on the complex for this event. Several on-premises nightclubs offer dinner/party packages. Call **404/523-2311** for details.

3   Tips for Travelers with Disabilities, Seniors, Gay Travelers & Families

A free newspaper called *Creative Loafing,* available at over 3,000 locations around town (hotels, restaurants, shops, MARTA stations, etc.), lists numerous events each issue and has special sections for "Gay and

Lesbian Activities" and "Singles." For a free copy prior to your visit call **800/950-5623.**

FOR TRAVELERS WITH DISABILITIES   **Accessible Journeys** (☎ **610/521-0339** or 800/TINGLES) and **Flying Wheels Travel** (☎ **507/451-5005** or 800/535-6790) offer tours for people with physical disabilities. **The Guided Tour Inc.** (☎ **215/782-1370**) has tours for people with physical or mental disabilities, visual impairments, and who are elderly.

Recommended books: A publisher called **Twin Peaks Press,** Box 129, Vancouver, WA 98666 (☎ **360/694-2462**), specializes in books for people with disabilities. Write for their *Disability Bookshop Catalog,* enclosing $4.

Some nationwide resources: Mobility International USA, P.O. Box 10767, Eugene, OR 97440 (☎ **503/343-1284**), offers accessibility information and has many interesting travel programs for travelers with disabilities. They also publish a quarterly newsletter called *Over the Rainbow* ($15 per year to subscribe). Help (accessibility information and more) is also available from the **Travel Information Service** (☎ **215/456-9600**) and the **Society for the Advancement of Travel for the Handicapped** (SATH), 347 Fifth Ave., Suite 610, New York, NY 10016 (☎ **212/447-7284**).

Amtrak (☎ **800/USA-RAIL**) provides redcap service, wheelchair assistance, and special seats at most major stations with 72 hours' notice. People with disabilities are also entitled to a 25% discount on one-way regular coach fares. Disabled children ages 2 to 15 can also get a 50% discount on already discounted one-way disabled adult fares. Documentation from a doctor or an ID card proving your disability is required. For an additional charge, Amtrak also offers wheelchair-accessible sleeping accommodations on long-distance trains, and service dogs are permissible and travel free of charge. Write for a free booklet called *Amtrak's America* from Amtrak Distribution Center, P.O. Box 7717, Itasca, IL 60143, which has a section detailing services for passengers with disabilities.

Greyhound (☎ **800/752-4841**) allows a disabled person to travel with a companion for a single fare and, if you call 48 hours in advance, they will arrange help along the way.

FOR SENIORS   Always carry some form of photo ID so that you can take advantage of discounts wherever they're offered. And it never hurts to ask.

If you haven't already done so, consider joining the **American Association of Retired Persons** (AARP), 601 E St. NW, Washington, DC 20049 (☎ **202/434-2277**). Annual membership costs $8 per person or per couple. You must be at least 50 to join. Membership entitles you to many discounts. Write to Purchase Privilege Program, AARP Fulfillment, 601 E St. NW, Washington, DC 20049, to receive AARP's Purchase Privilege brochure—a free list of hotels, motels, and car-rental firms nationwide that offer discounts to AARP members.

Elderhostel is a national organization that offers low-priced educational programs for people over 55 (your nonspouse companion must be at least 50). Programs are generally a week long, and prices average about $325 per person, including room, board, and classes. For information on programs in Atlanta call or write Elderhostel headquarters, 75 Federal St., Boston, MA 02110-1941 (☎ **617/426-7788**) and ask for a free U.S. catalog.

Amtrak (☎ **800/**USA-RAIL) offers a 15% discount off the lowest available coach fare (with certain travel restrictions) to people 62 or over.

Greyhound also offers discounted fares for senior citizens. Call your local Greyhound office for details.

FOR GAY MEN & LESBIANS   Atlanta has a large gay community and you can access it via a free magazine called *Etcetera Magazine,* like *Creative Loafing* (see above) available in front of MARTA stops and in some shops, bars, and restaurants. If you'd like a copy in advance of your trip, send $2 for a current issue to P.O. Box 8916, Atlanta, GA 30306. Or, when you arrive call **404/525-3821** to find out where you can pick up an issue near your hotel. You can also call that number for information on gay resources in town ("we call ourselves the gay 411," an *Etcetera* representative assured me).

Another free gay publication is *Southern Voice.* Call **404/876-1819** for a free issue, a distribution point near your hotel, or, once again, information on gay resources in Atlanta.

FOR FAMILIES   Careful planning makes all the difference between a successful, enjoyable vacation and one that ends with exhausted, irritable parents and cranky kids. Here are just a few hints to help:

Get the Kids Involved   Let them, if they're old enough, write to tourist offices for information and color brochures. If you're driving, give them a map on which they can outline the route. Let them help decide your sightseeing itinerary.

Packing   Although your home may be toddler-proof, hotel accommodations are not. Bring blank plugs to cover outlets and whatever else is necessary.

En Route   Carry a few simple games to relieve the tedium of traveling. A few snacks will also help and save money. If you're using public transportation (Amtrak, airlines, bus), always inquire about discounted fares for children.

Accommodations   Children under 12, and in many cases even older, stay free in their parents' rooms in most hotels. Look for establishments that have pools and other recreational facilities. Reserve equipment such as cribs and playpens in advance.

4 Getting There

BY PLANE

Hartsfield Atlanta International Airport, 10 miles south of downtown, is the world's largest and second-busiest airport and transfer hub.

Delta Air Lines, (☎ 800/221-1212 for reservations and flight information), which is based at Hartsfield, is the major carrier to Atlanta, connecting it to pretty much the entire country as well as 32 countries internationally. It carries 80% of the air passengers who come into Atlanta, serves 23 European cities, and is the official airline of the 1996 Olympic Games. Other major carriers include America West(☎ 800/235-9292), American (☎ 800/433-7300), British Airways (☎ 800/247-9297), Continental (☎ 800/732-6887), Kiwi (☎ 800/538-5494), KLM (☎ 800/374-7747), Northwest (☎ 800/225-2525), Swissair (☎ 800/221-4750), TWA (☎ 800/221-2000), United (☎ 800/241-6522), USAir (☎ 800/428-4322), and ValuJet(☎ 800/825-8538).

Generally, the least expensive fares (except for specially promoted discount fares announced in newspaper travel sections) are advance-purchase fares that involve certain restrictions. For example, in addition to paying for your ticket 3 to 21 days in advance of your trip, you may have to leave or return on certain days, stay a maximum or minimum number of days, and so on. Also, advance-purchase fares are often nonrefundable. Nonetheless, the restrictions are usually within the framework of one's vacation plans. The further in advance you reserve, the better your options, since sometimes there are a limited number of seats sold at discounted rates.

When you reserve, be sure to inquire about money-saving packages that include hotel accommodations, car rentals, tours, and other like expenses, with your airfare.

GETTING DOWNTOWN FROM THE AIRPORT   Hartsfield Atlanta International Airport is just 10 miles south of downtown. It's a well-planned airport, with ample parking space (and low parking charges), retail shops, facilities for the handicapped, and banking and currency-exchange facilities.

There are several options for getting from the airport to your hotel. The cheapest, if your luggage is manageable, is to take Atlanta's subway (MARTA), which has a stop right in the airport. The fare is just $1.25. Almost all hotels are very close to MARTA rail stations. It should take you about half an hour to reach downtown.

A taxi from the airport to a downtown hotel costs $15 for one passenger, $8 each for two or more. The ride should take about half an hour. To midtown and Buckhead hotels, the fare is $25 for one passenger, $26 for two, $9 each for three or more.

Atlanta Airport Shuttle Vans (☎ **404/524-3400** or 800/842-2770) operate between the airport and most downtown, midtown, and Buckhead hotels. They depart from the Delta baggage claim/ground transportation area in the South Terminal. You can catch one about every 15 minutes in either direction from 7am to 11pm seven days a week. To downtown and midtown locations, cost is $8 one-way, $14 round-trip; children under 5 ride free. To Buckhead locations, cost is $12 one-way, $20 round-trip, free for children under 5. Some properties further afield are also served. It's a very well-organized system, with destinations clearly marked and helpful attendants on hand. Call **404/768-7600** or 800/277-1165 for information about transport to suburban locations. When you leave Atlanta, check with your hotel desk about departure times; for some hotels, reservations are required a day in advance.

If you're renting a car at the airport, it's easy to drive to your hotel. The airport is bordered by I-75 and I-85, which converge as you head toward downtown. I-285, known as the Perimeter because it rings the city, is also accessible from the airport.

BY TRAIN

Amtrak operates the *Crescent* daily between Atlanta and New York, with stops in Washington, D.C., Philadelphia, and other intermediate points. Three times a week, the *Crescent* also goes beyond Atlanta to many points south, terminating in New Orleans. And other Amtrak trains connect with most of the country. To find out if your city connects via rail with Atlanta, call **800/USA-RAIL.**

Like the airlines, **Amtrak** offers several discount fares, and though not all are based on advance purchase, you may increase your options by reserving early. At this writing, **regular round-trip coach fares and discount fares** are as follows between Atlanta and these cities.

	Full Fare	Discount Fare
Boston–Atlanta	$318	$166
Chicago–Atlanta	$342	$178
Los Angeles–Atlanta	$494	$254
Miami–Atlanta	$506	$178
New Orleans–Atlanta	$190	$102
New York–Atlanta	$294	$154

Call **Amtrak's Great American Vacations** (☎ **800/321-8684**) to inquire about money-saving packages that include hotel accommodation and attractions tickets with your train fare. **Amtrak** trains arrive in Atlanta at 1688 Peachtree St, just off I-85. From this very central location, you can take a taxi to your hotel or to the nearest MARTA station (Arts Center). For information, call **404/881-3060** or 800/USA-RAIL.

BY BUS

Greyhound buses (☎ **404/584-1728** or 800/231-2222 for reservations and information) connect the entire country with Atlanta. The bus terminal is in the heart of downtown Atlanta at 81 International Blvd., at Williams Street. The Peachtree Center MARTA station is about two blocks away, and taxis are available.

The fare structure on buses is complex and not always based on distance traveled. The good news is that when you call Greyhound, they'll always give you the lowest-fare options. Once again, advance-purchase fares booked 3 to 21 days prior to travel represent big savings.

BY CAR

Three major interstate highways (I-20, I-75, and I-85) converge near the center of downtown Atlanta. For car-rental information, see "Getting Around" in Chapter 5.

4

For Foreign Visitors

Although American fads and fashions have spread across Europe and other parts of the world so that America may seem like familiar territory before your arrival, there are still many peculiarities and uniquely American situations that any foreign visitor will encounter.

1 Preparing for Your Trip

ENTRY REQUIREMENTS

DOCUMENT REGULATIONS   Canadian citizens may enter the U.S. without visas; they need only proof of residence.

Citizens of the U.K., New Zealand, Japan, and most western European countries traveling on valid passports may not need a visa for fewer than 90 days of holiday or business travel to the U.S., providing that they hold a round-trip or return ticket and enter the U.S. on an airline or cruise line participating in the visa waiver program.

(Note that citizens of these visa-exempt countries who first enter the U.S. may then visit Mexico, Canada, Bermuda, and/or the Caribbean islands and then reenter the U.S., by any mode of transportation, without needing a visa. Further information is available from any U.S. embassy or consulate.)

Citizens of countries other than those stipulated above, including citizens of Australia, must have two documents:

- a valid **passport,** with an expiration date at least six months later than the scheduled end of the visit to the U.S.; and
- a **tourist visa,** available without charge from the nearest U.S. consulate. To obtain a visa, the traveler must submit a completed application form (either in person or by mail) with a 1 1/2-inch square photo and demonstrate binding ties to a residence abroad.

Usually you can obtain a visa at once or within 24 hours, but it may take longer during the summer rush from June to August. If you cannot go in person, contact the nearest U.S. embassy or consulate for directions on applying by mail. Your travel agent or airline office may also be able to provide you with visa applications and instructions. The U.S. consulate or embassy that issues your visa will determine whether you will be issued a multiple- or single-entry visa and any restrictions regarding the length of your stay.

MEDICAL REQUIREMENTS   No inoculations are needed to enter the United States unless you are coming from, or have stopped over in, areas known to be suffering from epidemics, particularly cholera or yellow fever.

If you have a disease requiring treatment with medications containing narcotics or drugs requiring a syringe, carry a valid signed prescription from your physician to allay any suspicions that you are smuggling drugs.

CUSTOMS REQUIREMENTS   Every adult visitor may bring in free of duty: one liter of wine or hard liquor; 200 cigarettes or 100 cigars (but no cigars from Cuba) or three pounds of smoking tobacco; $100 worth of gifts. These exemptions are offered to travelers who spend at least 72 hours in the United States and who have not claimed them within the preceding six months. It is altogether forbidden to bring into the country foodstuffs (particularly cheese, fruit, cooked meats, and canned goods) and plants (vegetables, seeds, tropical plants, and so on). Foreign tourists may bring in or take out up to $10,000 in U.S. or foreign currency with no formalities; larger sums must be declared to Customs on entering or leaving.

INSURANCE

There is no national health system in the United States. Because the cost of medical care is extremely high, we strongly advise every traveler to secure health coverage before setting out.

You may want to take out a comprehensive travel policy that covers (for a relatively low premium) sickness or injury costs (medical, surgical, and hospital); loss or theft of your baggage; trip-cancellation costs; guarantee of bail in case you are arrested; costs of accident, repatriation, or death. Such packages (for example, "Europe Assistance" in Europe) are sold by automobile clubs at attractive rates, as well as by insurance companies and travel agencies.

MONEY

CURRENCY & EXCHANGE   The U.S. monetary system has a decimal base: one American **dollar** ($1) = 100 **cents** (100¢).

Dollar bills commonly come in $1 ("a buck"), $5, $10, $20, $50, and $100 denominations (the last two are not welcome when paying for small purchases and are not accepted in taxis or at subway ticket booths). There are also $2 bills (seldom encountered).

There are six denominations of coins: 1¢ (one cent or "penny"), 5¢ (five cents or "a nickel"), 10¢ (ten cents or "a dime"), 25¢ (twenty-five cents or "a quarter"), 50¢ (fifty cents or "a half dollar"), and the rare $1 piece.

TRAVELER'S CHECKS   Traveler's checks denominated in U.S. dollars are readily accepted at most hotels, motels, restaurants, and large stores. But the best place to change traveler's checks is at a bank. Do not bring traveler's checks denominated in other currencies.

CREDIT CARDS   The method of payment most widely used is the credit card. VISA (BarclayCard in Britain) is an official sponsor of the

Olympic Games and is the only credit card accepted for ticket payment. Other cards commonly used in the United States include Mastercard (EuroCard in Europe, Access in Britain, Chargex in Canada), American Express, Diners Club, Discover, and Carte Blanche. You can save yourself trouble by using "plastic money" rather than cash or traveler's checks in most hotels, motels, restaurants, and retail stores (a growing number of food and liquor stores now accept credit cards). You must have a credit card to rent a car. It can also be used as proof of identity (often carrying more weight than a passport), or as a "cash card," enabling you to draw money from banks that accept them.

Note: The "foreign-exchange bureaus" so common in Europe are rare even at airports in the United States, and nonexistent outside major cities. Try to avoid having to change foreign money, or traveler's checks denominated other than in U.S. dollars, at a small-town bank, or even a branch in a big city; in fact, leave any currency other than U.S. dollars at home—it may prove more nuisance to you than it's worth.

SAFETY

GENERAL   While tourist areas are generally safe, crime is on the increase everywhere, and U.S. urban areas tend to be less safe than those in Europe or Japan. Visitors should always stay alert. This is particularly true of large U.S. cities. Ask the tourist office if you're in doubt about which neighborhoods are safe. Avoid deserted areas, especially at night.

Remember also that hotels are open to the public, and in a large hotel, security may not be able to screen everyone entering. Always lock your room door—don't assume that once inside your hotel you are automatically safe and no longer need be aware of your surroundings.

DRIVING   Safety while driving is particularly important. Question your rental agency about personal safety, or ask for a brochure of traveler safety tips when you pick up your car. Obtain written directions, or a map with the route marked in red, from the agency showing how to get to your destination. And, if possible, arrive and depart during daylight hours.

Recently more and more crime has involved cars and drivers. If you drive off a highway into a doubtful neighborhood, leave the area as quickly as possible. If you have an accident, even on the highway, stay in your car with the doors locked until you assess the situation or until the police arrive. If you are bumped from behind on the street or are involved in a minor accident with no injuries and the situation appears to be suspicious, motion to the other driver to follow you. *Never* get out of your car in such situations. Go directly to the nearest police precinct, well-lighted service station, or all-night store.

If you see someone on the road who indicates a need for help, do *not* stop. Take note of the location, drive on to a well-lighted area, and telephone the police by dialing **911.**

Park in well-lighted, well-traveled areas if possible. Always keep your car doors locked, whether attended or unattended. Look around you before you get out of your car, and never leave any packages or valuables in sight. If someone attempts to rob you or steal your car, do *not* try to resist the thief/carjacker—report the incident to the police department immediately.

2   Getting To & Around the U.S.

Travelers from overseas can take advantage of the **APEX (Advance Purchase Excursion) fares** offered by all the major U.S. and European carriers. Flying to Atlanta from about 30 European cities, **Delta** offers daily nonstop flights to Atlanta from London, Manchester, Paris, Frankfurt, Zurich, Shannon, Madrid, and Barcelona. **British Airways** (☎ **0345 222111** in the UK) flies daily from London. **KLM** has direct service four days a week from Amsterdam (☎ **020 4747 747**). For Canadian travelers, **Air Canada** provides daily nonstop service to Atlanta from Toronto (☎ **800/268-7240**) and Montréal as of July 4, 1995 (☎ **800/361-8620**).

Some large American airlines (for example, TWA, American Airlines, Northwest, United, and Delta) offer travelers on their transatlantic or transpacific flights special discount tickets under the name **Visit USA,** allowing travel between any U.S. destinations at minimum rates. They are not on sale in the United States, and must, therefore, be purchased before you leave your foreign point of departure. This system is the best, easiest, and fastest way to see the United States at low cost. You should obtain information well in advance from your travel agent or the office of the airline concerned, since the conditions attached to these discount tickets can be changed without advance notice.

The visitor arriving by air, no matter what the port of entry, should cultivate patience and resignation before setting foot on U.S. soil. Getting through Immigration control may take as long as two hours on some days, especially summer weekends. Add the time it takes to clear Customs and you'll see that you should make very generous allowance for delay in planning connections between international and domestic flights—an average of two to three hours at least.

In contrast, travelers arriving by car or by rail from Canada will find border-crossing formalities streamlined to the vanishing point. And air travelers from Canada, Bermuda, and some places in the Caribbean can sometimes go through Customs and Immigration at the point of departure, which is much quicker and less painful.

For further information about travel to Atlanta, see "Getting There" in Chapter 3.

International visitors can also buy a **USA Railpass,** good for 15 or 30 days of unlimited travel on Amtrak. The pass is available through many foreign travel agents. Prices in 1995 for a 15-day pass are $229 off-peak, $340 peak; a 30-day pass costs $339 off-peak, $425 peak. (With a foreign passport, you can also buy passes at some Amtrak offices in the U.S., including locations in San Francisco, Los Angeles, Chicago, New York, Miami, Boston, and Washington, D.C.) Reservations are generally required and should be made for each part of your trip as early as possible.

Visitors should also be aware of the limitations of long-distance rail travel in the U.S. With a few notable exceptions (for instance, the

Northeast Corridor line between Boston and Washington, D.C.), service is rarely up to European standards: delays are common, routes are limited and often infrequently served, and fares are rarely significantly lower than discount airfares. Thus, cross-country train travel should be approached with caution.

Although ticket prices for short bus trips between cities are often the most economical form of public transit, at this writing, bus passes are priced slightly higher than similar train passes. **Greyhound,** the sole nationwide bus line, offers an **Ameripass** for unlimited travel for 7 days (for $259), 15 days ($459), and 30 days (for $559). Bus travel in the United States can be both slow and uncomfortable, so this option is not for everyone.

FAST FACTS: For the Foreign Traveler

Automobile Organizations   Auto clubs will supply maps, suggested routes, guidebooks, accident and bail-bond insurance, and emergency road service. The major auto club in the United States, with 983 offices nationwide, is the American Automobile Association (AAA). Members of some foreign auto clubs have reciprocal arrangements with the AAA and enjoy its services at no change. If you belong to an auto club, inquire about AAA reciprocity before you leave. The AAA can provide you with an International Driving Permit validating your foreign license. You may be able to join the AAA even if you are not a member of a reciprocal club. To inquire, call **800/222-4357.** In addition, some automobile rental agencies now provide these services, so you should inquire about their availability when you rent your car.

Automobile Rentals   To rent a car you need a major credit card. A valid driver's license is required, and you usually need to be at least 25. Some companies do rent to younger people but add a daily surcharge. Be sure to return your car with the same amount of gas you started out with; rental companies charge excessive prices for gasoline. All of the major car rental companies are represented in Atlanta. Atlanta Rent-A-Car (☎ **404/763-1160**) offers particularly low prices.

Business Hours   Offices are usually open Monday through Friday from 9am to 5pm. Banks are open Monday through Friday from 9am to 3 or 4pm, and sometimes on Saturday mornings. Hundreds of automated teller machines located throughout Atlanta offer 24-hour withdrawal with international ATM cards. Post offices are usually open Monday through Friday from 8:30am to 5pm and on Saturday from 8:30am to noon. Shops are generally open from 10am to 5 or 6pm. Those in malls tend to stay open late, to about 9pm Monday through Saturday and until 5 or 6pm on Sunday. Museum days and hours of operation vary.

Climate   See "When to Go" in Chapter 3.

Currency   See "Money" in "Preparing for Your Trip," earlier in this chapter.

Currency Exchange   You will find currency exchange services in major airports with international service. Elsewhere, they may be quite difficult to come by. A very reliable choice is Thomas Cook Currency Services, Inc., which has been in business since 1841 and offers a wide range of services. They also sell commission-free foreign and U.S. traveler's checks, drafts, and wire transfers; they also do check collections (including Eurochecks). Their rates are competitive and service excellent. They maintain several offices in New York City: on Fifth Avenue (☎ **212/757-6915**), at the JFK Airport International Arrivals Terminal (☎ **718/656-8444**), and at La Guardia Airport in the Delta terminal (☎ **718/533-0784**).

In Atlanta there's a Thomas Cook foreign exchange office at the Welcome South Visitors Center, downtown at the corner of Spring Street and International Boulevard (☎ **404/224-2000**). It's open Monday through Saturday from 10am to 6pm, and Sunday from noon to 6pm.

Drinking Laws   See "Liquor Laws" in "Fast Facts: Atlanta," Chapter 5.

Electricity   The United States uses 110–120 volts, 60 cycles, compared to 220–240 volts, 50 cycles, as in most of Europe. In addition to a 100-volt converter, small appliances of non-American manufacture, such as hairdryers or shavers, will require a plug adapter, with two flat, parallel pins.

Embassies and Consulates   All embassies are located in the national capital, Washington, D.C.; some consulates are located in major cities, and most nations have a mission to the United Nations in New York City. Foreign visitors can obtain telephone numbers for their embassies and consulates by calling "Information" in Washington, D.C. (☎ **202/555-1212**).

Nations with official consulates in Atlanta include: Canadian Consulate General, Suite 400, South Tower, One CNN Center, Atlanta, GA 30303 (☎ **404/577-1512**); Consulate of France, 285 Peachtree Center Ave., Suite 2800, Atlanta, GA 30303 (☎ **404/522-4226**); Consulate General of the Federal Republic of Germany, Marquis Two Tower Suite 901, 285 Peachtree Center Ave. NE, Atlanta, GA 30303 (☎ **404/659-4760**); British Consulate General, 245 Peachtree Center Ave., Marquis One Tower, Suite 2700, Atlanta, GA 30303 (☎ **404/527-5762**); and Consulate General of Japan, 100 Colony Sq., Suite 2000, Atlanta, GA 30361 (☎ **404/892-2700**). For complete information, contact the Atlanta Chamber of Commerce, International Dept., P.O. Box 1740, Atlanta, GA 30301 (☎ **404/586-8470**).

Emergencies   In all major cities (including Atlanta), you can call the police, an ambulance, or the fire department through the single emergency telephone number **911.** Another useful way of reporting an emergency is to call the telephone-company operator by dialing **0.**

See also listing for the Travelers Aid Society in Chapter 5 under "Visitor Information."

Gasoline (Petrol)   One U.S. gallon equals 3.75 liters, while 1.2 U.S. gallons equals one Imperial gallon. You'll notice there are several grades (and price levels) of gasoline available at most gas stations. And you'll also notice that their names change from company to company. The unleaded ones with the highest octane are the most expensive (most rental cars take the least expensive "regular" unleaded) and leaded gas is the least expensive, but only older cars can take this any more, so check if you're not sure.

Holidays   On the following legal national holidays, banks, government offices, post offices, and many stores, restaurants, and museums are closed:

> January 1 (New Year's Day)
> Third Monday in January (Martin Luther King Day)
> Third Monday in February (Presidents Day,
>   Washington's Birthday)
> Last Monday in May (Memorial Day)
> July 4 (Independence Day)
> First Monday in September (Labor Day)
> Second Monday in October (Columbus Day)
> November 11 (Veterans Day/Armistice Day)
> Last Thursday in November (Thanksgiving Day)
> December 25 (Christmas)
> Finally, the Tuesday following the first Monday in
>   November is Election Day, and is a legal holiday
>   in presidential-election years.

Information   Write or call the Atlanta Convention & Visitors Bureau (ACVB), 233 Peachtree St. NE, Suite 2000, Atlanta, GA 30303 (☎ **404/222-6688**) for a free copy of its *International Visitors Guide*. It's available in English, French, German, Japanese, and Spanish. See also "Visitor Information" in Chapter 5.

Languages   Major hotels may have multilingual employees. Unless your language is very obscure, they can usually supply a translator on request.

Legal Aid   The foreign tourist, unless positively identified as a member of the Mafia or of a drug ring, will probably never become involved with the American legal system. If you are pulled up for a minor infraction (for example, of the highway code, such as speeding), never attempt to pay the fine directly to a police officer; you may wind up arrested on the much more serious charge of attempted bribery. Pay fines by mail, or directly into the hands of the clerk of the court. If accused of a more serious offense, it's wise to say and do nothing before consulting a lawyer. Under U.S. law, an arrested person is allowed one telephone call to a party of his or her choice. Call your embassy or consulate.

Mail   If you want your mail to follow you on your vacation and you aren't sure of your address, your mail can be sent to you, in your name, c/o General Delivery at the main post office of the city or region where you expect to be. The addressee must pick it up in person and produce proof of identity (driver's license, credit card, passport, etc.).

Generally to be found at intersections, mailboxes are blue with a red-and-white stripe and carry the inscription U.S. MAIL. If your mail is addressed to a U.S. destination, don't forget to add the five-figure postal code, or ZIP (Zone Improvement Plan) Code, after the two-letter abbreviation of the state to which the mail is addressed (CA for California, FL for Florida, NY for New York, and so on).

Multilingual Visitor Assistance   Under the auspices of the Georgia Council for International Visitors is a language bank of about 45 languages. If you need a translator, interpreter, or tour guide who speaks your language, call **404/873-6170.** The office is open Monday to Friday from 9am to 5pm.

The Welcome South Visitors Center (see "Visitor Information" in Chapter 5) has a multilingual staff.

Newspapers and Magazines   With a few exceptions, such as the *New York Times, USA Today,* the *Wall Street Journal,* and the *Christian Science Monitor,* daily newspapers in the United States are local, not national.

There are also innumerable newsweeklies like *Newsweek, Time,* and *U.S. News & World Report,* as well as specialized periodicals, such as the monthly magazines devoted to a single city. In Atlanta, the major daily is the *Atlanta Journal-Constitution.* The city magazine is called *Atlanta.* Also informative is *Creative Loafing,* a free publication you'll see in stores, restaurants, and other places around town.

The airmail editions of foreign newspapers and magazines are on sale only belatedly, and only at airports and international bookstores in the largest cities.

Radio and Television   Audiovisual media, with four coast-to-coast networks—ABC, CBS, NBC, and FOX—plus the Public Broadcasting System (PBS) and the cable network CNN, play a major part in American life. In the big cities, televiewers have a choice of about a dozen channels (including the UHF channels), most of them transmitting 24 hours a day, without counting the pay-TV channels showing recent movies or sports events. In smaller communities, the choice may be limited to four TV channels (there are 1,200 in the entire country), and a half dozen local radio stations (there are 6,500 in all), each broadcasting a particular kind of music—classical, country, jazz, pop, or gospel—punctuated by news broadcasts and frequent commercials.

Safety   See "Safety" in "Preparing for Your Trip," earlier in this chapter.

Taxes   In the United States there is no VAT (Value-Added Tax) or other indirect tax at a national level. Every state, and each city in it, has the right to levy its own local tax on all purchases, including hotel and restaurant checks, airline tickets, and so on. In Atlanta hotel tax is 13%. That includes room tax (7%) and sales tax (6%).

Telephone, Telegraph, and Telex   The telephone system in the U.S. is run by private corporations, so rates, especially for long distance service, can vary widely—even on calls made from public telephones. AT&T (an official sponsor of the Olympic Games) offers reliable, competitive rates. Other dependable long-distance companies include Sprint and MCI. Local calls in the U.S. usually cost 25¢.

Generally, hotel surcharges on long-distance and local calls are astronomical. You are usually better off using a public pay telephone, which you will find clearly marked in most public buildings and private establishments as well as on the street. Outside metropolitan areas, public telephones are more difficult to find. Stores and gas stations are your best bet.

Most long-distance and international calls can be dialed directly from any phone. For calls to Canada and other parts of the U.S., dial 1 followed by the area code and the seven-digit number. For international calls, dial 011 followed by the country code, city code, and the telephone number of the person you wish to call.

For reversed-charge or collect calls, and for person-to-person calls, dial 0 (zero, *not* the letter "O") followed by the area code and number you want; an operator will then come on the line, and you should specify that you are calling collect, or person-to-person, or both. If your operator-assisted call is international, ask for the overseas operator.

For local directory assistance ("information"), dial **411;** for long-distance information, dial 1, then the appropriate area code and **555-1212.**

Like the telephone system, telegraph and telex services are provided by private corporations like ITT, MCI, and above all, Western Union, the most important. You can bring your telegram to the nearest Western Union office (there are hundreds across the country), or dictate it over the phone (a toll-free call, **800/325-6000**). You can also telegraph money, or have it telegraphed to you, very quickly over the Western Union system.

Telephone Directory   There are two kinds of telephone directories available to you. The general directory is the so-called White Pages, in which private and business subscribers are listed in alphabetical order. The inside front cover lists the emergency number for police, fire, and ambulance, and other vital numbers (like the Coast Guard, poison-control center, crime-victims hotline, and so on). The first few pages are devoted to community-service numbers, including a guide to long-distance and international calling, complete with country codes and area codes.

The second directory, printed on yellow paper (hence its name, Yellow Pages), lists all local services, businesses, and industries by type of activity, with an index at the back. The listings cover not only such obvious items as automobile repairs by make of car, or drugstores (pharmacies), often by geographical location, but also restaurants by type of cuisine and geographical location, bookstores by special subject and/or language, places of worship by religious denomination, and other information that the tourist might otherwise not readily find. The Yellow Pages also include city plans or detailed area maps, often showing postal ZIP Codes and public transportation routes.

Time   The United States is divided into four time zones (six, if Alaska and Hawaii are included). From east to west, these are: eastern standard time (EST), central standard time (CST), mountain standard time (MST), Pacific standard time (PST), Alaska standard time (AST), and Hawaii standard time (HST). Always keep changing time zones in mind if you are traveling (or even telephoning) long distances in the United States. For example, noon in New York City (EST) is 11am in Chicago (CST), 10am in Denver (MST), 9am in Los Angeles (PST), 8am in Anchorage (AST), and 7am in Honolulu (HST).

Atlanta observes eastern standard time.

"Daylight saving time" is in effect from the last Sunday in April through the last Saturday in October (actually, the change is made at 2am on Sunday) except in Arizona, Hawaii, part of Indiana, and Puerto Rico. Daylight saving time moves the clock one hour ahead of standard time.

Tipping   This is part of the American way of life, on the principle that you must expect to pay for any service you get. Here are some rules of thumb:

> Bartenders: 10%–15%.
> Bellhops: at least 50¢ per piece; $2–$3 for a lot of baggage.
> Cab drivers: 15% of the fare.
> Cafeterias, fast-food restaurants: no tip.
> Chambermaids: $1 a day.
> Checkroom attendants (restaurants, theaters): $1 per garment.
> Cinemas, movies, theaters: no tip.
> Doormen (hotels or restaurants): not obligatory.
> Gas-station attendants: no tip.
> Hairdressers: 15%–20%.
> Redcaps (airport and railroad station): at least 50¢ per piece, $2–$3 for a lot of baggage.
> Restaurants, nightclubs: 15%–20% of the check.
> Sleeping-car porters: $2–$3 per night to your attendant.
> Valet parking attendants: $1.

Toilets   Foreign visitors often complain that public toilets are hard to find in most U.S. cities. True, there are none on the streets, but the visitor can usually find one in a bar, restaurant, hotel, museum, department store, or service station—and it will probably be clean (although the last-mentioned sometimes leaves much to be desired). The cleanliness of toilets at railroad stations and bus depots may be more open to question, and some public places are equipped with pay toilets, which require you to insert one or more coins into a slot on the door before it will open.

THE AMERICAN SYSTEM OF MEASUREMENTS

Length

1 inch (in.)	=	2.54 cm					
1 foot (ft.)	=	12 in.	=	30.48 cm	=	.305 mi.	
1 yard (yd.)	=	3 ft.			=	.915 mi.	
1 mile (mi.)	=	5,280 ft.					= 1.609 km

To convert miles to kilometers, multiply the number of miles by 1.61 (for example, 50 mi. × 1.61 = 80.5km). Note that this conversion can be used to convert speeds from miles per hour (m.p.h.) to kilometers per hour (km/h).
To convert kilometers to miles, multiply the number of kilometers by .62 (for example, 25km × .62 = 15.5 mi.). Note that this same conversion can be used to convert speeds from kilometers per hour to miles per hour.

Capacity

1 fluid ounce (fl. oz.)			=	.03 liters		
1 pint (pt.)	=	16 fl. oz.	=	.47 liters		
1 quart (qt.)	=	2 pints	=	.94 liters		
1 gallon (gal.)	=	4 quarts	=	3.79 liters	=	.83 Imperial gal

To convert U.S. gallons to liters, multiply the number of gallons by 3.79 (example, 12 gal. × 3.79 = 45.58 liters.)
To convert U.S. gallons to Imperial gallons, multiply the number of U.S. gallons by .83 (example, 12 U.S. gal. × .83 = 9.95 Imperial gal.).
To convert liters to U.S. gallons, multiply the number of liters by .26 (example, 50 liters × .26 = 13 U.S. gal.).
To convert Imperial gallons to U.S. gallons, multiply the number of Imperial gallons by 1.2 (example, 8 Imperial gal. × 1.2 = 9.6 U.S. gal.).

Weight

1 ounce (oz.)			=	28.35 g			
1 pound (lb.)	=	16 oz.	=	453.6 g	=	.45 kg	
1 ton			=	2,000 lb.	=	907 kg	= .91 metric tons

To convert pounds to kilograms, multiply the number of pounds by .45 (example, 90 lb. × .45 = 40.5 kg).
To convert kilograms to pounds, multiply the number of kilos by 2.2 (example, 75 kg × 2.2 = 165 lb.).

Area

1 acre			=	.41 ha		
1 square mile	=	640 acres	=	259 ha	=	2.6 km²

To convert acres to heactares, multiply the number of acres by .41 (example, 40 acres × .41 = 16.4 ha).

To convert square miles to square kiometers, multiply the number of square miles by 2.6 (example, 80 sq. mi. × 26 = 208 km²).

To convert hectares to acres, multiply the number of hectares by 2.47 (example, 20 ha × 2.47 = 49.4 acres).

To convert square kilometers to square miles, multiply the number of square kilometers by .39 (example, 150 km² × .39 = 58.5 sq. mi.).

Temperature

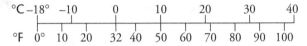

To convert degrees Farenheit to degrees Celsius, subtract 32 from °F, multiply by 5, then divide by 9 (example, 85°F − 32 × $^5/_9$ = 29.4°C).

To convert degrees Celsius to degrees Fahrenheit, multiply °C by 9, divide by 5, and add 32 (example, 20°C × $^9/_5$ + 32 = 68°F).

5

Getting to Know Atlanta

Atlanta is a fairly compact city rather than a sprawling metropolis. After a few days in town, you'll know your way around.

1 Orientation

VISITOR INFORMATION

For information about hotels, restaurants, and attractions, contact the **Atlanta Convention & Visitors Bureau (ACVB),** 233 Peachtree St. NE, Suite 2000, Atlanta 30303 (☎ **404/222-6688**). Call or write in advance to obtain a copy of *Atlanta Now* (the official visitor's guide), a *Metro Atlanta Attractions Guide,* a map, a book of discounts, and a two-month calendar of events. You can call weekdays between 8:30am and 5:30pm. May 1 through December 25 you can also call a toll-free 24-hour number (**800/ATLANTA**) for an informational recording.

In town, you can visit ACVB information centers at:

Lenox Square, 3393 Peachtree Rd. Open Monday to Friday 10am to 5pm. No phone.

Underground Atlanta, 65 Upper Alabama St. (☎ **404/577-2148**). Open Monday to Saturday 10am to 9:30pm, Sunday noon to 6pm.

Hartsfield Atlanta International Airport, near the car rental booths between the north and south baggage claim areas. Open Monday to Saturday 9am to 9pm, Sunday noon to 6pm. No phone.

The **Travelers Aid Society** is a nationwide network of voluntary nonprofit social-service agencies providing help to travelers in difficulty. This might include anything from crisis counseling to straightening out ticket mix-ups, not to mention illness, car breakdowns, reuniting families accidentally separated while traveling, or locating missing relatives (sometimes just at the wrong airport).

In Atlanta, Travelers Aid has offices at the airport (☎ **404/766-4511**) open daily 10am to 6pm; at the Greyhound Bus Terminal, 81 International Blvd. at Williams Street (☎ **404/527-7411**), open Monday to Friday noon to 8pm, Saturday 10am to 6pm; and at 40 Pryor St. SW, at Marietta Street (☎ **404/527-7400,** a 24-hour number), open Monday to Friday 8:30am to 5pm.

WELCOME SOUTH VISITORS CENTER

The Welcome South Visitors Center at the corner of Spring Street and International Boulevard (☎ **404/224-2000**), opened its doors in 1995, leaving itself ample time to gear up for serving the vast influx of visitors arriving for the Olympic Games. After the Games, this 23,000-square-foot facility will continue to welcome visitors and present the culture, history, and attractions of the southeast to tourists and conventioneers from America and abroad. Open Monday through Saturday from 10am to 6pm, Sunday from noon to 6pm, it showcases not only Georgia but six other southeastern states (Alabama, Kentucky, Louisiana, North Carolina, South Carolina, and Tennessee) in an interactive walk-through format. Highlights include:

- A knowledgeable multilingual staff.
- An information counter staffed by the Atlanta Convention & Visitors Bureau and Georgia Department of Industry, Trade, and Tourism.
- Exhibits on major Atlanta attractions and an Atlanta history wall with video components.
- Interactive kiosks where visitors can access information about Atlanta restaurants, shops, and attractions; famous Georgians; regions of Georgia; and more.
- A large store with merchandise related to the Olympic Games.
- Olympic Games and Paralympic Games information and ticket kiosks.
- Olympic-themed exhibits presented by sponsors of the 1996 Games.
- A bookstore stocked with books about Atlanta/Georgia history, the Civil War, the civil rights movement, national parks, and southern cookery.
- An AAA full-service travel agency that can help you with itinerary planning, hotel and airline reservations, ticketing, and more; you can join AAA here as well.
- A ranger-staffed U.S. National Parks Service booth providing information about southeastern parks, historic sites, and outdoor attractions.
- Regional informational kiosks for seven southeastern states.
- A southeastern states exhibit wall adjoining a multipurpose station used for cultural presentations—storytelling, music, etc.
- A Kodak digital-imaging system (you can superimpose your photo against regional images).
- A Thomas Cook foreign exchange office and NationsBank ATM machine.
- A Coca-Cola exhibit where Coke-related merchandise—and Cokes—are sold.
- An art gallery area showcasing the works of Southern artists.

CITY LAYOUT

Atlanta is girded by a beltway called I-285, usually referred to as the Perimeter. As a tourist, you'll be spending most of your time within the confines of the Perimeter. Two interstate highways (I-75 and I-85) converge just above the airport and proceed north, forking off just northwest of Piedmont Park: I-75 goes west, I-85 east. A fourth interstate highway just below the downtown area, I-20, is an east-west artery that cuts all the way through Georgia (and Atlanta), connecting South Carolina with Alabama.

There's a joke that all directions here begin with "Go to Peachtree. . . ." That's because there are a few dozen Peachtrees—Peachtree Street, Lane, Road, Avenue, Circle, Drive, Plaza, and Way, not to mention West Peachtree Street, Peachtree Industrial Boulevard, Peachtree Memorial Drive, Peachtree Battle Avenue, Peachtree Valley Road, etc., etc., etc. So be sure to emphasize which Peachtree you're looking for when you ask for directions. That being said, Peachtree Street (which becomes Peachtree Road above midtown) and Piedmont Avenue are Atlanta's two major north-south arteries. Peachtree is a two-way thoroughfare, while Piedmont has two-way traffic above 14th Street, but south-to-north only below 14th Street. Major east-west streets include Memorial Drive, North Avenue, Ponce de Leon Avenue, 14th Street, and, in Buckhead, East and West Paces Ferry Drives. With map in hand, you'll find getting around Atlanta very easy.

NEIGHBORHOODS IN BRIEF

You can't really get the feel of a city until you understand the characteristics of its neighborhoods. Herewith, a brief rundown of Atlanta's diverse districts.

Downtown   Atlanta's financial and business hub, this beautifully planned area of sleek skyscrapers includes the futuristic Peachtree Center hotel/convention center/trade mart/office-tower complex. Here, too: Underground Atlanta, an exciting mix of shops, restaurants, and nightclubs fronted by a 138-foot light tower; Omni Coliseum, featuring sports action and big-name entertainment; the mammoth Georgia World Congress Center, one of the largest meeting and exhibition halls in the nation; the 71,500-seat Georgia Dome, home of the Atlanta Falcons and site of Super Bowl XXVIII; CNN Center, Ted Turner's media HQ; Georgia-Pacific Center, housing the downtown branch of the High Museum of Art; the golden-domed, century-old State Capitol, a major landmark; the new 21-acre Centennial Olympic Park, which will be a venue for big-name amphitheater concerts during the Games; newly renovated Woodruff Park; and the SciTrek Museum. In the general area are Oakland Cemetery (it's mentioned in *Gone With the Wind,* and Margaret Mitchell is one of the many notables buried here) and Grant Park (the zoo and Cyclorama). This is a downtown with big-city excitement, but its scale is human.

Sweet Auburn   This traditionally black neighborhood, also called the Martin Luther King, Jr., Historic District, is just below downtown's central area. Under the auspices of the National Park Service, it was designated a park in 1980 to honor King, whose boyhood home, crypt, and church are located here. In spite of the yoke of segregation, affluent black businesspeople and professionals flourished here from the early part of the 20th century through the 1950s. Today it's one of Atlanta's major sightseeing draws.

Midtown   Though its boundaries have never been definitively decided, midtown basically encompasses the area north of downtown

Atlanta at a Glance

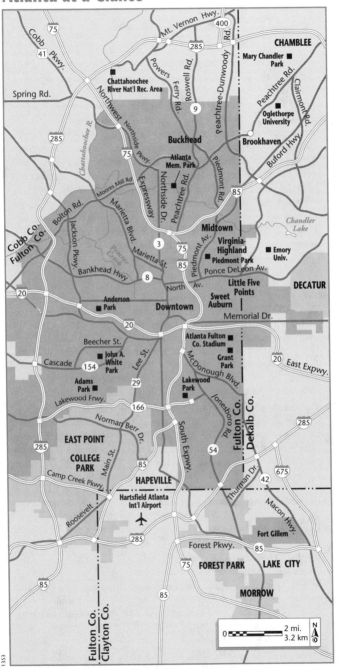

The Olympic Cauldron

Located adjacent to the new Olympic Stadium, the 132-foot-high Olympic Cauldron is the monumental structure designed by American artist and sculptor Siah Armajani to house the famed Olympic flame during the 17 days of the Centennial Olympic Games. Comprised of a tower and a 190-foot-long bridge that connects to the stadium, the structure is constructed of densely interwoven steel painted a warm gray and shaped in the form of the letter "A" for Atlanta. At the top of the tower, the cauldron is rimmed with Georgia red clay. The decking of the bridge is inscribed with the names of all Olympic host cities (beginning with Athens in 1896) and at its center, in gold leaf, are the Olympic Rings and the words "Atlanta 1996." A small park surrounds the gazebo at the cauldron's base, and midway up the tower is a green wooden "house" with windows made of hand-cast colored glass; this house symbolizes the warmth and hospitality of the people of Atlanta and the South.

from about Ponce de Leon Avenue to 26th Street. It includes Piedmont Park, Atlanta's major recreation area; the Woodruff Arts Center, home of the Atlanta Symphony Orchestra, the Alliance Theatre, and the High Museum of Art; the famed Fox Theatre, a 1920s Moorish-motif movie palace; Ansley Park, a 230-acre residential greenbelt area, designed at the turn of the century by Frederick Law Olmsted; and Colony Square, an office/hotel/retail complex. AT&T, IBM, and Southern Bell maintain corporate offices in midtown.

Buckhead　Named for an 1838 tavern called the Buck's Head, this is Atlanta's silk-stocking district—one of America's most beautiful and affluent communities. It begins about six miles north of downtown. Here you'll find tree-shaded residential areas of magnificent mansions surrounded by verdant acreage, elite shops and boutiques (including Lenox Square and Phipps Plaza malls, two exclusive shopping enclaves), superb restaurants, and first-class hotels. Buckhead is also a burgeoning business area. Its major sightseeing attraction is the Atlanta Historical Society, centered on a Palladian villa designed by noted architect Phillip Schutze and surrounded by 32 woodland acres. The Greek Revival Governor's Mansion is also in Buckhead.

Virginia-Highlands　Every major American city has a district that claims kinship (however slight) with New York's Greenwich Village. In Atlanta it's the Virginia-Highlands section, so named for its central avenues, northeast of downtown. Here you'll find ethnic eateries, dozens of antique shops, bookstores, sidewalk cafes, art galleries, lively bars and bistros, and browsable shops selling everything from healing crystals to recycled clothing.

Little Five Points　Just below Virginia-Highlands—and a slightly funkier offshoot of it—Little Five Points offers similar offbeat ambience and emporia. It is also the location of the Jimmy Carter Library/Carter Presidential Center, which opened in 1986 to house the cor-respondence and memorabilia of this Georgia-born president. Many Victorian homes make for an architecturally interesting stroll. The neighborhood is centered at the junction of Euclid and Moreland Avenues.

Decatur   Founded in 1823 by Commodore Stephen Decatur, a dashing naval hero of the War of 1812 who died in a duel, this quaintly charming village centers on an old courthouse square. About a 15-minute drive east from downtown, Decatur is the scene of numerous annual events, festivals, and concerts, and it houses the sprawling Dekalb Farmer's Market, an international food market that must be seen to be believed. Like Virginia-Highland and Little Five Points, Decatur weaves color and texture into Atlanta's tapestry of neighborhoods.

2 Getting Around

If you're here for a few days, you'll get a pretty good feel for the layout of the city. It's not complicated. And getting around the city is easy and affordable.

BY PUBLIC TRANSPORTATION

The Metropolitan Atlanta Rapid Transit Authority (MARTA) operates an extensive and efficient rail (subway) and bus network, making it possible to reach just about any part of town by public transportation.

During the Olympic Games, rail service and some bus routes will operate 24 hours a day. If you have a ticket for any Olympic event you'll be able to ride MARTA buses and trains free the day it takes place. See Section 5, "Transportation," in Chapter 2, "About the Olympic Games," for complete details on transit passes that will be available during the Games.

MARTA RAPID RAIL   MARTA's rapid-rail (subway) service began in 1979. The stations are clean and safe, and it's a pleasure to use. Eventually, this will be a 60-mile, 45-station system. At presstime, the rail system extends 39 miles and includes 33 stations. There are two lines: south-north Orange Line trains travel between the airport and Doraville; east-west Blue Line trains travel between Indian Creek (east of Decatur) and Hightower. They intersect at Five Points Station in downtown Atlanta. By the time you read this, work should be completed on a new line that will begin at the Lindbergh station and travel north paralleling SR 400. Fare is just $1.25 for any ride, payable in exact change, tokens, or TransCards. Tokens, available at the stations, cost $10 for 8. A weekly TransCard, available at Ride Stores—in the Five Points, airport, Lenox, or Lindbergh stations—is good for unlimited bus and rail travel for one week and costs $11.

MARTA trains generally arrive and depart every 8 to 10 minutes during operating hours: Monday to Saturday from 5am to 1am, Sunday and holidays from 6am to 12:30am. Free transfers are available between bus and rail when you board a bus or enter a rail station. Parking is free at all rail stations.

For MARTA schedule and route information, call **404/848-4711** Monday to Friday from 6am to 10pm, Saturday and Sunday from 8am to 4pm. For information regarding services for the elderly and the disabled, call **404/848-5389.**

BUSES   Basically, you can get anywhere in Atlanta by bus. MARTA buses operate on a 1,550-mile network of 150 routes. The fare system is the same as described above for rail service. To find out what bus to take, call **404/848-4711** for route information (same hours as above). Drivers do not carry change; you must have exact change, a token, a transfer, or a TransCard. Special shuttle buses operate from downtown in conjunction with major stadium sports events and conventions; call the above number for details.

BY TAXI

Taxi fares are a bit complicated in Atlanta. In the Downtown Zone (roughly east to west between Piedmont Avenue and Northside Drive, north to south from 14th Street to Ralph Abernathy Boulevard), you pay a flat rate of $4 for one or two passengers, $2 for each additional rider. That's fine if you're going from one end of this extensive zone to the other; unfortunately, though, you pay the same if you only go one block.

There's also a flat rate for rides between downtown and the airport: $15 for one passenger, $8 each for two or more. Between the airport and midtown or Buckhead, the rate is $25 for one passenger, $26 for two, $9 each for three or more.

Outside these specified zones, Atlanta cabs charge a $1.50 drop when you get in and 20¢ for each additional ^{1}/$_6$ mile for the first passenger and a flat rate of $1 for each additional passenger, adult or child.

There are many taxi companies in town. If you need to call for a taxi, try Yellow Cabs (☎ **404/521-0200**) or Checker Cabs (☎ **404/351-1111**).

If you have a complaint about taxi service, call ☎ **404/658-7600.**

BY CAR

Atlanta's transit system (MARTA) is very good. However, a car is certainly a convenience, and, in most places you'll visit, parking isn't a problem. Given my druthers, I prefer to have one. All of the major car-rental companies are, of course, represented here and reachable via toll-free numbers. These include: **Avis** (☎ **800/331-1212**), **Budget** (☎ **800/527-0700**), **Dollar** (☎ **800/800-4000**), **Hertz** (☎ **800/654-3131**), and **Thrifty** (☎ **800/367-2277**).

I always rent from **Atlanta Rent-A-Car** (☎ **404/763-1160**), a local independently owned company that has been serving Atlanta for over 15 years. This company's rates are very low (I've yet to find lower), they stock a full range of compact and midsize cars and vans, and they offer friendly, competent service. They have 18 locations—including one close to the airport—and provide free courtesy pickup anywhere in the city. At presstime, Atlanta Rent-A-Car's compacts begin at just $19.95 a day with 100 free miles, $10 a day and 19¢ a mile with no free miles. The same car costs $99.95 a week with 500 free miles. It's always best to reserve in advance.

FAST FACTS: Atlanta

Airport   See "Getting There" in Chapter 3.

American Express   There's a centrally located office providing travel services in the Colony Square complex at Peachtree and 14th Streets (☎ **404/892-8175**).

Baby-sitters   Most hotels will arrange baby-sitters for you. If yours doesn't, a highly recommended service is A Friend of the Family (☎ **404/643-3000**). All of their sitters are carefully screened, bonded, and at least 21 years of age. On request, they can send someone who is also trained in CPR and first aid and/or who speaks a foreign language. You can interview the sitter in advance on the phone or in person. Rate is $8 to $10 per hour, with a four-hour minimum, plus a $15 agency fee. Advance notice of 24 hours is appreciated but not required. A Friend of the Family also provides pet care and companions for adults. You can call Sunday to Friday 7am to 10pm, Saturday 8am to 10pm.

Buses   See "Getting Around," earlier in this chapter.

Car Rentals   See "Getting Around," earlier in this chapter.

Climate   See "When to Go," in Chapter 3.

Cultural Events   Call the ARTS Hotline at **404/853-3278,** for a 24-hour update on concerts, plays, films, and other cultural events.

Dentists   The Georgia Dental Association of Atlanta (☎ **404/ 636-7553**), offers a free referral service. They'll refer you to a dentist close to your hotel, or if need be, one who can accommodate special needs (for example, a dentist who does cosmetic work, offers home visits or senior-citizen discounts, keeps emergency hours, or otherwise specializes). The service operates weekdays from 8:30am to 5pm. At other times, inquire at your hotel desk.

Doctors   The Medical Association of Atlanta (☎ **404/881-1714**), with over 2,000 member physicians in town, runs a free referral service for every kind of medical specialty and subspecialty. Hours are Monday to Thursday from 9am to 5pm, Friday from 9am to 4pm. At other times, inquire at your hotel desk. (See also "Hospitals," below.)

Drugstores   See "Pharmacies," below.

Emergencies   To report a fire, summon the police, or procure an ambulance, simply dial 911. See also listing for the Travelers Aid Society in "Visitor Information," above.

Eyeglass Repair   Head over to Opti-World, in the Around Lenox Shopping Center (enter the Lenox Square Mall on Peachtree Road, just below Lenox Road, look for Neiman-Marcus, and veer to the right; ☎ **404/262-2020**). This eyeglass department store offers one-hour service on contacts and eyeglasses (including bifocals and trifocals), stocks the largest selection of frames in Atlanta (from designer to economy), provides on-premises eye examinations by independent doctors of optometry, maintains a complete contact-lens center, and gives 15% discounts to senior citizens and college students.

Hairdressers   To some of us, a gifted hairdresser can be the most essential of services. Stan Milton and Rob Davis, 721 Miami Circle NE, off Piedmont Road (☎ **404/233-6241**), are among Atlanta's most talented and celebrated stylists. They've done dozens of makeovers for local TV personalities, and their devoted clientele comes from all over the South. Stan and Rob are wonderful at finding your optimum look. The salon also does superb hair coloring, and an excellent staff proffers a full complement of salon and spa services—facials, manicures/pedicures, waxing, massage, age reversal treatments, extensive skin care (including peelings), paraffin treatments for hands and feet, and full days of beauty services. The salon is elegant but very relaxed and friendly. I appreciate Milton's commitment to the environment; he uses only products that are natural, chemical free, and biodegradable. While you're here, ask for a complimentary Trish McEvoy makeup application. Haircuts are $30 to $60 for women, $20 to $35 for men. Perms are $60 to $80. Reserve as far in advance as possible.

Hospitals/Emergency Rooms   Piedmont Hospital, 1968 Peachtree Rd., just above Collier Road (☎ **404/605-3297**), offers 24-hour full emergency-room service. It also offers a free physician-referral service for all medical problems (☎ **404/605-3556**) weekdays between 9am and 5pm.

Libraries   The Atlanta Fulton Public Library, 1 Margaret Mitchell Sq., at Forsyth Street and Carnegie Way (☎ **404/730-1700**), is the city's central branch. In addition to the usual well-stocked library inventory, it has many books in Spanish and city newspapers from all over the world. Two only-in-Atlanta library features are an extensive collection of first and rare editions of *Gone With the Wind* and a permanent exhibit on Margaret Mitchell. In addition, the library features frequent art exhibits, films, lectures, and storytelling; inquire when you visit. Open Monday to Thursday from 9am to 9pm, Friday and Saturday from 9am to 6pm, and Sunday from 2 to 6pm.

Also of interest is the Auburn Avenue Research Library, 101 Auburn Ave. (☎ **404/370-4001**), which maintains an extensive collection of African-American records, books, photographs, research materials, and multimedia data bases. It also offers related exhibits and programs. Hours are Monday to Thursday noon to 8pm, Saturday and Sunday 2 to 6pm; closed Fridays.

Liquor Laws   No alcohol is served at bars, restaurants, or nightclubs between 2:55am Saturday and 12:30pm Sunday. The drinking age is 21.

Newspapers/Magazines   The major newspaper in town is the *Atlanta Journal-Constitution.* You'll also find it helpful to pick up a current issue of *Atlanta* magazine when you're in town. And keep an eye out for *Creative Loafing,* an offbeat free publication available in shops, restaurants, and on the street; it offers much interesting info.

Pharmacies (Late-Night)   Big B Drugs, 1061 Ponce de Leon Ave. at Highland Avenue (☎ **404/876-0381**), is open 24 hours and offers full pharmaceutical services.

Police   Call **911** in an emergency.

Road Conditions   Call **404/624-7890,** a 24-hour number.

Taxes   Sales tax in Atlanta is 6%. A total of 13% is paid by hotel and motel guests within the city of Atlanta and Fulton County. Of that tax, 6% is sales tax and 7% is room tax.

Taxis   Call Yellow Cabs (☎ **404/521-0200**) or Checker Cabs (☎ **404/351-1111**).

Tickets   For tickets to almost all sports and performing arts events (except Olympic events), call Ticketmaster (☎ **404/249-6400**). For information on getting tickets to Olympic events and the Olympic Arts Festival, see Chapter 2, "About the Olympic Games."

Time   Call **404/603-3333.** Atlanta is on eastern standard time.

Transit Information   (To find out how to get from point A to point B via MARTA (bus and rail), dial **404/848-4711.**

Weather   Call **404/603-3333.**

6

Accommodations

As a major convention city, Atlanta is capable of accommodating vast numbers of visitors. It has 55,337 rooms at 340 properties including budget digs (though not as many as I'd like to see), bed-and-breakfast lodgings, and bastions of luxury. Presented below are my choices in all price brackets, each one offering excellent value in its category.

Note: Although 100% occupancy is a rarity in Atlanta, it is a major convention city; booking well in advance assures you a room in the hotel of your choice.

Many preferential rates are available only when you reserve via toll-free reservation numbers. These numbers are supplied in all applicable listings below. Days Inns offer drastically reduced Super Saver rates if you reserve 30 days or more in advance (subject to availability).

Also inquire about reduced-price packages (they may include extras such as meals, parking, theater tickets, and golf fees) and reduced rates for senior citizens, families, and active-duty military personnel. Reservation agents don't usually volunteer this information, though; you should always take the initiation and ask about special packages yourself.

And finally, keep in mind that a hotel makes zero dollars per night on an empty room. Hence, though they don't exactly advertise it (for obvious reasons), most hotels are willing to bargain on rates rather than leave a room unoccupied. Haggling won't work when hotels are running close to 100% occupancy, but whenever a rate is quoted it's a good idea to ask, "Can I get a better deal?" If the reservations clerk can't help you, ask to speak to the desk captain. I'm not saying you won't risk a snub or two, but those who persevere can nurse wounded feelings all the way to the bank. An especially advantageous time to secure lower rates is late afternoon or early evening on the day of your arrival, when a hotel's likelihood of filling up with full-price bookings is remote.

HOW TO READ THE LISTINGS

The hotels listed below are divided first by location, then alphabetically by price category within a given district. Since most Atlanta attractions are within the downtown/midtown/Buckhead areas, almost all of the hotels here are in, or close to, those sections of town. (See Stone Mountain listings for camping.) When within walking distance, the nearest MARTA subway stop is listed.

Hotels with rates less than $85 are rated **inexpensive** (don't blame me, I didn't create inflation), $85 to $130 rooms make up the

moderate grouping, $130 to $175 I've listed as **expensive,** and anything above that ranks as **very expensive.** Any extras included in the rates (for example, breakfast or other meals) are listed for each property. Add 13% hotel/sales tax to the rates listed, and keep in mind that the prices quoted are subject to change. If you have a car, be sure to consider the price of parking in your hotel garage.

Note: You will spot rates in the above-listed categories higher than those I've quoted. Those are special-events rates (most notably in effect during the Olympics). Most of the year, they will not apply.

BED & BREAKFASTS

Bed & Breakfast Atlanta, 1801 Piedmont Ave. NE, Suite 208 (☎ **404/875-0525** or 800/967-3224), is a professional reservation service that carefully screens facilities in the Atlanta area. Their list comprises more than 100 homes and inns, all accommodations offering private bath. They include—among diverse others—a turreted Queen Anne–style Victorian home with nine fireplaces near the Carter Library, a delightful honeymoon cottage with a Jacuzzi in "Miss Daisy's" Druid Hills, an elegant 1920s Tudor-style home in Buckhead, and a fully furnished garden cottage in Ansley Park. They even have kosher homes on their roster. Many additional B&B accommodations in all price ranges will be available to serve visitors during the 1996 Olympic Summer Games. Owners Madalyne Eplan and Paula Gris have been running B&B Atlanta since 1979. All rates include continental breakfast, in many cases extended considerably beyond the usual roll and coffee. Reserve as far in advance as possible for the greatest number of selections. Call during office hours, which are Monday to Friday from 9am to noon and 2 to 5 pm.

The rates run the gamut from about $52 to $240 (the latter for a luxurious Buckhead guest cottage on a four-acre estate that accommodates four people). Rates during special events may be higher. Weekly and monthly rates are available (in guesthouses and apartments) for long-term visitors. There's no fee. American Express, MasterCard, and Visa are accepted.

ACCOMMODATIONS FOR THE OLYMPIC GAMES

See Chapter 2, "About the Olympics," for details on how to obtain accommodations during the Games.

In addition, several Atlanta bed-and-breakfast operators listed in this chapter have assembled and checked out rosters of homes and apartments to extend their offerings to Olympics visitors. For details call: The Ansley Inn (☎ **404/872-9000** or 800/446-5416), Bed & Breakfast Atlanta (☎ **404/875-0525** or 800/967-3224), and International B&B Reservations (affiliated with the Woodruff Bed & Breakfast Inn; ☎ **404/875-9449** or 800/473-9449).

1 Best Bets

- **Best for Business Travelers.** All the major downtown megahotels—which cater largely to a business and convention clientele—are fully equipped to meet your business needs. Of them all, I'd choose The

Ritz-Carlton Atlanta, 181 Peachtree St. NE (☎ **404/659-0400**), which combines a full business center and a can-do concierge with superb service and peerless elegance.

- **Best for a Romantic Getaway.** The Ansley Inn, 253 15th St. NE (☎ **404/872-9000**), has charming antique-furnished rooms; step outside and you're in one of Atlanta's most beautifully landscaped neighborhoods, perfect for sunset strolls. If you prefer a hotel to a B&B, a stay at The Ritz-Carlton Buckhead, 3434 Peachtree Rd. (☎ **404/237-2700**)—also in a magnificent neighborhood—sets the stage for romance.

- **Best for Families.** The Residence Inn Buckhead, 2960 Piedmont Rd. NE (☎ **404/239-0677**), offers accommodations large enough to insure privacy for all, plus fully equipped kitchens, washers and dryers, indoor and outdoor swimming pools, barbecue grills, and basketball, volleyball, and paddle tennis courts. Many rooms have fireplaces; prepare some popcorn in the microwave and enjoy a fun family evening before the fire.

- **Best Moderately Priced Hotel.** The Quality Inn Habersham, 330 Peachtree St. NE (☎ **404/577-1980**), just a few blocks from downtown, offers solid comfort and congenial surroundings.

- **Best Inexpensive Accommodations.** Biltmore Suites, 30 Fifth St. NE (☎ **404/874-0824**), an elegant property that is on the National Register of Historic Places, delivers a lot of luxury at very low prices. Accommodations are in spacious residentially furnished suites with 10-foot ceilings, hand-carved crown moldings, and French doors.

    The family-run Cheshire Motor Inn, 1865 Cheshire Bridge Rd. (☎ **404/872-9628**), offers unbeatable value for your money; the owners make every effort to please guests. For rock-bottom rates, the Atlanta International Youth Hostel, 223 Ponce de Leon Ave. NE (☎ **404/875-2882**), is the place (and you don't have to be a youth to stay there).

- **Best Location.** For shoppers, the J.W. Marriott, 3300 Lenox Rd. NE (☎ **404/262-3344**), is right in upscale Lenox Square Mall and The Ritz-Carlton Buckhead, 3434 Peachtree Rd. NE (☎ **404/237-2700**), adjoins the even posher Phipps Plaza. To stay in a beautiful area, choose the Ansley Inn, 253 15th St. NE (☎ **404/872-9000**), which is also within walking distance of Piedmont Park and great midtown restaurants.

- **Best Service.** The Ritz-Carlton Atlanta and the Ritz-Carlton Buckhead (see addresses and telephone numbers above) are in a class by themselves.

- **Best Architectural Digest Interior.** The most exquisite interior is found at the Gaslight Inn, 1001 Saint Charles Ave. (☎ **404/875-1001**), a bed-and-breakfast where the rooms might inspire you to redecorate your own home. Its location in charming Virginia-Highland is a plus for vacationers.

- **Best Trendy Hotel.** The Occidental Grand, 75 14th St. (☎ **404/881-9898**), is the glamorous choice of many visiting celebrities and even royalty; sophisticated insiders consider its plushly furnished Segovia Bar the prime setting for afternoon cocktails and rendezvous.

2 Downtown

Downtown hotels primarily cater to the business/convention traveler, but a tourist will also enjoy the services and facilities of these properties.

VERY EXPENSIVE

Atlanta Hilton & Towers

255 Courtland St. (between Baker and Harris sts.), Atlanta, GA 30303. ☎ **404/ 659-2000** or 800/HILTONS. Fax 404/524-0111. 1,224 rms, 41 suites. A/C TV TEL. $119–$225 double, depending on the season. Tower rooms $230 double. Extra person $20. Children of any age free in parents' room. AE, CB, DC, MC, DISC, ER, V. Parking $9 valet, $8 self. MARTA: Peachtree Center.

One of Atlanta's top convention hotels, with 104,000 square feet of meeting and exhibit space, the Hilton is surprisingly upscale for a chain hotel. Cheerfully decorated rooms offer bedside and desk phones, and TVs with On-Command Video pay-movie options, plus video checkout and account-review functions. Many rooms have minibars.

Dining/Entertainment: The Hilton's premier restaurant is the highly acclaimed Nikolai's Roof, a 30th-floor dining room offering spectacular skyline vistas. Only multicourse prix-fixe dinners are offered. Trader Vic's, a South Seas–Polynesian restaurant found at

---

Concierge Levels

If you travel a lot, especially on business, you're probably aware of the concierge-level phenomenon—a hotel-within-a-hotel concept, usually occupying one or more upper floors of a luxury property. Guests on these floors enjoy scenic views as well as upgraded room amenities and private registration and checkout. They're pampered with nightly bed turndown and other special services—including a private concierge—and have access to a plush lounge where complimentary continental breakfast is served. Some hotels also offer a spread of afternoon hors d'oeuvres (in some cases so lavish a meal as to obviate the need for dinner) and late-night petit-fours in these lounges. Though concierge floors (sometimes also called tower floors or club floors) primarily cater to business travelers, vacationers will also enjoy the extra cosseting. In Atlanta you'll find concierge-level accommodations at the Atlanta Hilton & Towers, Hyatt Regency Atlanta, Ritz-Carlton Atlanta, Westin Peachtree Plaza, Marriott Marquis, Best Western American, Sheraton Colony Square, Nikko Atlanta, Ritz-Carlton Buckhead, Swissôtel, JW Marriott at Lenox, and Terrace Garden Inn.

numerous Hiltons, here offers its signature setting and potent rum drinks. The Garden Terrace, a very pretty lobby-level eatery centered around a vast fountain, serves buffet meals at breakfast and lunch and Sunday champagne brunch. Adjoining it are the Cafe Express Deli (a 24-hour facility) and Le Café, the Hilton's casual dining facility. There's live music nightly at the Bogart-and-Bergman–themed Casablanca Bar. Finally, there's Another World, a plush disco adjoining Nikolai's.

Services: Room service, baby-sitting, lobby information desk, airport shuttle.

Facilities: Four outdoor tennis courts, outdoor jogging track, outdoor pool/sundeck, exercise room, sauna, whirlpool, business center, shops, shoeshine stand.

Best Western American Hotel

160 Spring St. NW (at International Blvd.), Atlanta, GA 30303. ☎ **404/688-8600** or 800/621-7885. Fax 404/658-9458. 300 rms, 21 suites. A/C TV TEL. $179–$219 double. Executive Club level $20 additional per night. Parlor suites $245–$385. Extra person $20. Children under 18 stay free in parents' room. Inquire about weekend packages. AE, CB, DC, DISC, MC, V. Parking $8 (valet only). MARTA: Peachtree Center.

When it was first built in 1962 as an American Hotel, this was downtown's most glamorous property, attracting guests like Mary Martin, Carol Channing, Doris Day, and Pearl Bailey. Today, in the shadow of downtown's modern megahotels, the American seems decidedly retro, its public areas, though refurbished, reflecting late-50s/early-60s interior-decorating ideas such as mirrored columns and blond wood paneling. However, everything's in tip-top shape after a recent $2 million renovation. Rooms are equipped with cable TVs offering Spectravision movies and phones with computer jacks and credit card slots.

The pubby, wood-paneled Gatsby's Restaurant, vaguely evoking the 1920s, is open nightly for reasonably priced steak and seafood dinners. In the adjoining lounge, sporting events are aired on a large-screen TV. There's also a poolside coffee shop called the Outside Inn. Other amenities include an airport shuttle, concierge, room service, a medium-size outdoor pool, guest privileges (for a $10 fee) at the very elaborately equipped Peachtree Center Athletic Club, a small on-premises workout room, and a gift shop.

Hyatt Regency Atlanta

265 Peachtree St. NE (between Baker and Harris sts.), Atlanta, GA 30303. ☎ **404/577-1234** or 800/233-1234. Fax 404/588-4137. 1,279 rms, 56 suites. A/C MINIBAR TV TEL. $250 double. Regency Club $250 double. Business Plan $15 over regular rates. Extra person $25. Children under 18 free in parents' room. Packages and promotional rates often available via the toll-free number. AE, CB, DC, DISC, MC, V. Parking $15 (valet only). MARTA: Peachtree Center.

Designed in 1967 by famed Atlanta architect John Portman, this hotel was the prototype not only for future downtown hotels in the city, but for hotel architectural design throughout America. It features a 23-story open-air atrium lobby filled with lush greenery which thrives in the sunlight streaming through a lofty skylight.

Downtown Accommodations

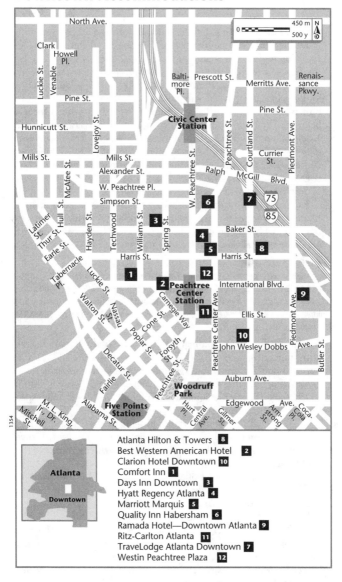

Atlanta Hilton & Towers **8**
Best Western American Hotel **2**
Clarion Hotel Downtown **10**
Comfort Inn **1**
Days Inn Downtown **3**
Hyatt Regency Atlanta **4**
Marriott Marquis **5**
Quality Inn Habersham **6**
Ramada Hotel—Downtown Atlanta **9**
Ritz-Carlton Atlanta **11**
TraveLodge Atlanta Downtown **7**
Westin Peachtree Plaza **12**

The Hyatt accommodates guests not only in this original building, but in two later additions—the 24-story International Tower and the 22-story Ivy Tower. Rooms throughout feature plush modern furnishings and are equipped with safes and TVs offering Spectravision pay movies (video checkout and account review are further options).

The 22nd floor of the main building houses the Regency Club. And on the 21st floor are Business Plan rooms equipped with personal work stations, in-room faxes, desk phones with computer jacks, and coffee-makers. Business Plan guests get free local calls and other perks.

Dining/Entertainment: The blue dome capping Polaris, the Hyatt's revolving rooftop restaurant, is a landmark on the city's skyline. Open for dinner, it features steak, seafood, and prime rib. You can enjoy the same spectacular views over cocktails in the adjoining lounge. Over-looking the lobby is the informal Kafe Köbenhavn, which offers buffets at all meals as well as an à la carte coffee shop menu. One level below the lobby is Avanzare, a charming Italian restaurant with an 1,800-gallon saltwater aquarium along one wall. A coffee cart in the lobby purveys cappuccino, espresso, and pastries for quick breakfasts and desserts. And the Ampersand Lounge airs sporting events on a large-screen TV.

Services: Room service, concierge, airport shuttle.

Facilities: Full health club, barber shop/beauty salon, gift shop, Delta Air Lines desk, large outdoor pool and whirlpool, business center. The Hyatt connects to the vast Peachtree Center shopping mall via a covered walkway.

✪ Marriott Marquis

265 Peachtree Center Ave. (between Baker and Harris sts.), Atlanta, GA 30303. ☎ **404/521-0000** or 800/228-9290. Fax 404/521-6870. 1,674 rms, 80 suites. A/C TV TEL. $220–$250 double. Concierge level $225 double. Extra person $20. Children under 12 free. AE, CB, DC, DISC, MC, V. Parking $15 (self or valet). MARTA: Peachtree Center.

A dramatic downtown landmark, the Marriott Marquis, with its tow-ering tapered-glass exterior, is my personal favorite of Atlanta's Portman-designed megahotels. Fronted by a vast fountain that looks like a flying saucer, it focuses within on a soaring 50-story atrium in which a massive plum-colored fiber sculpture cascades through space from the skylight ceiling to a point just above the lobby. Vines draped over interior balcony railings create a hanging-garden effect. And light classical piano music played in all public areas combines with these natural elements to further humanize a modern environment that might otherwise overwhelm.

Warmly attractive rooms offer TVs (with Video On Command pay movies) and hairdryers in the bath. In your closet, you'll find an iron and full-sized ironing board.

Dining/Entertainment: On the Garden Level, above the lobby, you'll find all the hotel's restaurants and lounges. Allie's American Grille, open for all meals, features light fare. Pompano's, an elegant steak and seafood restaurant, seats diners amid a forest of ficus trees. La Fuente features traditional Southwestern fare in an adobe-walled, south-of-the-border setting. Arbors serves southern buffet lunches weekdays. Pastries, desserts, and coffees are available at Gourmet Bean. And up a brass-railed stairway, seemingly suspended in space, is the Grandstand Lounge. Champions, the Marquis's major nightclub and sports bar, is covered more extensively in Chapter 11.

Services: 24-hour room service, limousine, *USA Today* delivered daily to your room, airport shuttle, concierge.

Facilities: Full health club, large swimming pool with adjoining whirlpool, business center, shops, unisex hairstylist, shoeshine stand. The Marquis connects, via a covered walkway, to dozens of shops at the Peachtree Center Mall.

✪ Ritz-Carlton Atlanta

181 Peachtree St. NE (at Ellis St.; main entrance on Ellis), Atlanta, GA 30303. ☎ **404/ 659-0400** or 800/241-3333. Fax 404/688-0400. 447 rms, 24 suites. A/C MINIBAR TV TEL. Sun–Thurs $169–$295 double, Fri–Sat $122 per room. Club Level $265 double; $450–$985 suite. Extra person $25. AE, CB, DC, DISC, ER, MC, V. Parking $15 (valet only). MARTA: Peachtree Center.

It's hard to believe that this very traditional-looking hostelry—with Persian rugs strewn on marble floors, silk-tapestried and African mahogany-paneled walls hung with a collection of 18th- and 19th-century paintings, and valuable antiques throughout its public areas—was built as late as 1984. The impeccable service also harks back to another, more gracious, era; you'll be cosseted as never before. Elegant rooms, many with bay windows, are furnished with beautiful mahogany pieces (some have four-poster beds). Amenities include terry robes, scales, and extra phones in the bath.

Dining/Entertainment: The hotel's premier dining room is The Restaurant, an equestrian-themed setting with 19th-century, gilt-framed hunt paintings. Open for dinner only, it offers Asian-nuanced French cuisine; a pianist entertains while you dine. Afterward, you might retreat to the adjoining Bar where a jazz trio plays Tuesday to Saturday night till 11:30pm. A reasonably priced lunch buffet is served in The Bar weekdays. The intimate Café, on the lobby level, is the hotel's informal dining room. An afternoon tea, complete with fresh-baked scones and watercress sandwiches, is served in the lobby lounge daily; a pianist entertains here from 4 to 6pm.

Services: 24-hour room service, twice-daily maid service, nightly turndown, complimentary shoeshine, your regional paper delivered to your door on request, evening pressing service, car rental, limousine, multilingual concierge staff.

Facilities: Gift shop, business center, airport shuttle, on-premises fitness center.

✪ The Westin Peachtree Plaza

210 Peachtree St. (at International Blvd.), Atlanta, GA 30303. ☎ **404/659-1400** or 800/228-3000. Fax 404/589-7586. 1,020 rms, 48 suites. A/C TV TEL. Mon–Thurs $190–$210 double. Lower weekend rates are subject to availability. Premier level $235 double. Extra person $25. Children under 18 free. Inquire about packages. AE, CB, DC, DISC, ER, JCB, MC, V. Parking $12.50 self, $13 valet. MARTA: Peachtree Center.

Though the John Portman–designed Westin is a 73-story megahotel with over 1,000 rooms, it is invitingly residential within. The atrium lobby—under a five-story skylight and utilizing acres of pink-hued Portuguese marble—divides into softly lit alcoves where plush sofas, rich mahogany paneling, and Persian rugs combine to create intimate seating areas.

Rooms are decorated in soft hues with walnut furnishings. Handsome armoires house remote-control cable TVs offering Spectravision pay movies and a gratis step-training exercise video (the step is provided). And in-room amenities include TV speakers in the bath, desk and bedside phones, wall safes, irons and full-size ironing boards, and hairdryers. Medium and deluxe rooms are on higher floors; the latter have minibars.

Dining/Entertainment: The revolving Sun Dial Restaurant, on the 71st and 72nd floors, offers a 360-degree city-skyline panorama and sophisticated American cuisine. Its revolving lounge, on the 73rd floor, is a romantic setting for cocktails and light fare. The lobby-level Savannah Fish Company, with seating overlooking a splashing 100-foot horizontal waterfall, specializes in fresh seafood and sushi. A jazz trio entertains nightly in the lobby, near the Café—a delightful restaurant serving both buffet and à la carte American meals plus an award-winning Japanese breakfast. The Oak Bar, a plush venue of warm woods and rich leathers, specializes in liqueurs and coffee drinks. There's also the International Bar and the adjoining Sidewalk Café.

Services: Concierge, 24-hour room service, airport shuttle.

Facilities: Health club, beautiful large pool (under a retractable skylight for year-round indoor/outdoor use), comprehensive business center, car rental, 17,000-square-foot shopping gallery that connects with Macy's Peachtree Center Mall. The Westin Kid's Club offers many free perks for families (call the hotel for details).

MODERATE

The Clarion Hotel Downtown

70 John Wesley Dobbs Ave. (at Courtland St.), Atlanta, GA 30303. ☎ **404/ 659-2660** or 800/241-3828. Fax 404/524-5390. 213 rms, 6 suites. A/C TV TEL. $79–$119 double. Suites $145. Extra person $10. Children under 18 stay free in parents' room. AE, CB, DC, DISC, MC, V. Parking free (self only), subject to availability. MARTA: Peachtree Center.

An eight-story cream stucco building that forms a courtyard around its swimming pool, the Clarion recently completed a $5 million renovation. Rooms, 90% of them with balconies, are charmingly decorated with traditional cherrywood furniture, pretty floral-print bedspreads, and framed botanical prints.

The Courtyard Café, a very pretty garden-motif restaurant, has outdoor balcony seating overlooking the pool. It's open for all meals. A comfortable lounge adjoins. There's also room service during restaurant hours, an airport shuttle, a medium-sized outdoor pool and a gift shop. For a $10 fee, guests can use the state-of-the-art Phoenix Health Club nearby.

Comfort Inn

101 International Blvd. (at Williams St.), Atlanta, GA 30303. ☎ **404/524-5555**, 800/ 535-0707, or 800/228-5150. 257 rms, 3 suites. A/C TV TEL. $99–$149 double. Rates may be higher—up to $250 a night—during major conventions or special events. Extra person $10. Children 18 and under free in parents' room. AE, CB, DC, DISC, ER, JCB, MC, V. Parking $6 (self only), may be higher during special events. MARTA: Peachtree Center or Omni.

Comfort Inns are based on the theory that a low-cost hotel needn't be a no-frills hotel, and this 11-story property is a good example.

Entered via a lobby with a fountain, it offers appealing rooms with oak furnishings, color-coordinated floral-print bedspreads and drapes, and watercolors depicting scenes of France on grasspaper-covered walls. Each room has both a desk and a table with two chairs (or sleeper sofa), and a TV offering Spectravision movies. The Omni Coliseum is two blocks away.

Bistro 101, the on-premises eatery, is rather charming, with tables amid potted ferns and copper cookware on the walls. Many seats overlook the pool. It offers typical American fare. In the adjoining Blind Zebra Bar, sporting events are aired on the TV (proximity to the Omni Coliseum attracts many sports-minded guests).

There's also room service during restaurant hours, an airport shuttle, electric shoeshine machines on each floor, a nice-size outdoor pool/sundeck with adjoining whirlpool, "Discover Atlanta" video machine in the lobby, and a gift shop.

Days Inn Downtown

300 Spring St. (at Baker St.), Atlanta, GA 30308. ☎ **404/523-1144** or 800/ DAYS-INN. Fax 404/577-8495. 262 rms. A/C TV TEL. $99–$225 double (high end reflects major special events). Extra person $10. Children under 18 free in parent's room. Reduced rates may be available if you reserve at least 30 days in advance. AE, DC, DISC, MC, V. Parking $6 (self only). MARTA: Peachtree Center.

This very central Days Inn allows visitors to stay in the heart of the business district at a very moderate cost. In-room amenities include safes and TVs with Spectravision pay movies. Some rooms have refrigerators, and those on floors 3 to 10 have balconies. Although you don't get all the luxury-hotel frills here, accommodations are clean and spiffy-looking, facilities very ample. A Wendy's restaurant adjoins the property. There's also a comfortable lounge in the hotel, open 5pm to midnight, where sporting events are aired. And a large outdoor pool is a plus.

Quality Inn Habersham

330 Peachtree St. NE (between Baker St. and Ralph McGill Blvd.), Atlanta, GA 30308. ☎ **404/577-1980** or 800/241-4288. Fax 404/688-3706. 91 rms. A/C TV TEL. $59–$250 double (high end reflects major special events). Rates include extended continental breakfast. Extra person $10. Children 18 and under free in parents' room. AE, CB, DC, DISC, ER, JCB, MC, V. Parking free (self only). MARTA: Peachtree Center or Civic Center.

Just a few blocks from the center of downtown, this pleasant hotel offers a lot for its price range. Rooms are large and nicely furnished, each equipped with a desk, two armchairs or a sofa, a wet bar/refrigerator, and an in-room coffeemaker.

In a comfortably furnished room off the lobby, complimentary continental breakfast is served each morning. Or, weather permitting, you might breakfast outdoors at patio tables. Room service is available from about a dozen area restaurants (you'll find a comprehensive menu in your room). *USA Today* is free in the lobby. There's also an exercise room and sauna.

Ramada Hotel–Downtown Atlanta

175 Piedmont Ave. NE (at International Blvd.), Atlanta, GA 30303. ☎ **404/659-2727** or 800/228-2828. Fax 404/577-7805. 467 rms, 6 suites. A/C TV TEL. Mon–Thurs

$89–160 double. Fri–Sun $65 per room. Extra person $10. Children 12 and under free in parents' room. Packages available via the toll-free number. AE, CB, DC, DISC, MC, V. Parking free (self only). MARTA: Peachtree Center.

This six-story hotel, opened in the early 1960s, is a particularly nice property entered via a large lobby with intimate, lamplit seating areas. Much of the staff has been here since the hotel's inception, always a sign of a well-run operation. Easy access to all interstates is a plus.

The Pantheon, a pretty plant-filled restaurant-in-the-round, serves typical American fare at all meals. A lounge adjoins. There's also room service 6:30am to 2pm and 5 to 10pm, an airport shuttle, complimentary toiletries on request at the front desk, a lobby gift shop, a large outdoor swimming pool, a whirlpool, and an exercise room.

INEXPENSIVE

TraveLodge Atlanta Downtown

311 Courtland St. NE (between Baker St. and Ralph McGill Blvd.), Atlanta, GA 30303. ☎ **404/659-4545** or 800/578-7878. Fax 404/659-5934. 71 rms. A/C TV TEL. $59–$109 double. Rates include continental breakfast. Extra person $8. Children under 18 free in parents' room. AE, CB, DC, DISC, ER, MC, V. Parking free (self only). MARTA: Peachtree Center.

Operated by the Clark family since 1964, this small TraveLodge offers an inexpensive alternative in the heart of downtown. Its recently renovated rooms look clean and fresh. Each is equipped with a safe, a coffeemaker, and a TV with free HBO; VCRs and rental movies are available at the front desk. Complimentary continental breakfast is served in the lobby each morning, and numerous restaurants are within walking distance. Free daily newspapers are another plus. Facilities include an outdoor pool. And TraveLodge guests can use the extensive facilities of the nearby Peachtree Center Athletic Club for $10 a day.

3 Midtown

Midtown hotels tend to be low-key, catering to tourists and their families rather than conventioneers. Joggers and other outdoor enthusiasts will appreciate proximity to Piedmont Park. The Woodruff Arts Center is also in this section of town.

VERY EXPENSIVE

✪ Occidental Grand Hotel

75 14th St. (between Peachtree and W. Peachtree Sts.), Atlanta, GA 30309. ☎ **404/881-9898** or 800/952-0702. Fax 404/888-8669. 228 rms, 18 suites. A/C MINIBAR TV TEL. Sun–Thurs $153–$275 double; Fri–Sat $112–$132 (range depends on floor and view). Suites $410–$1,500. Extra person $20. Children under 18 stay free in parents' room. Inquire about packages. AE, CB, DC, DISC, ER, JCB, MC, V. Parking $11.50 self, $15 valet. MARTA: Arts Center.

The late 1992 opening of the Occidental Grand brought old-world elegance to Atlanta's midtown hotel scene. It has already hosted the emperor and empress of Japan, the queen of Norway, and the king of

> ### 🅗 Family-Friendly Hotels
>
> **Residence Inn Buckhead** *(see p. 104)* This place has not only a swimming pool but also accommodations with fully equipped kitchens—a potential money-saver when you're traveling with your family. Rates here include breakfast, and there are barbecue grills and picnic tables on the premises. It's like having your own Atlanta apartment, with parking at your door. The property also contains basketball, volleyball, and paddle-tennis courts, and VCRs and movies can be rented at the front desk.
>
> **The Westin Peachtree Plaza** *(see p. 85)* The Westin Kids' Club provides many perks for families: kits filled with children's bath products and activities; kiddie furniture such as high chairs, potty seats, cribs, and bed rails; special children's restaurant and room-service menus, and more—all at no extra charge. And there's a swimming pool on the premises.
>
> **Occidental Grand Hotel** *(see p. 88)* Kids enjoy a special program that includes a toiletries box with baby shampoo and a rubber duck, child-size robes, milk and cookies at nightly turndown, board games, and children's movie videos and video games.

Finland in its Royal Suite and become a haunt of visiting celebrities such as Tony Bennett, Beverly Sills, Isaac Stern, and Jimmy Buffett.

Guests pass from the porte cochère entranceway to a soaring marble-floored three-story atrium lobby with a sweeping curved stairway appropriately reminiscent of *Gone With the Wind*. A massive Baccarat crystal chandelier (which originally graced a turn-of-the-century Paris hotel) sparkles overhead.

Earth-toned accommodations are suitably plush, with large windows, tapestried armchairs at marble desks, handsome armoires, and gilt-framed artworks lit by gallery lights. All rooms are equipped with sofas, TVs offering Spectravision pay movies and tourism-information channels (VCRs and rental movies are available), three phones (bedside, desk, and bath), and safes. Gorgeous marble baths contain scales, terry robes, hairdryers, upscale toiletries, and linen hand towels.

Dining/Entertainment: The magnificent Florencia Restaurant, one of Atlanta's most notable nighttime dining venues, is detailed in Chapter 7. Also beautiful, the Café Opera—with its tapestried banquettes, potted palms, white marble tables set with fresh flowers, and an oil mural evoking 1920s European cafe society—serves all meals. At Overtures, on the mezzanine overlooking the lavishly marbled grand staircase, a pianist entertains from 3:30pm to midnight daily. This facility is also the setting for daily afternoon teas, and, along with the Café Opera, sumptuous Sunday champagne brunches. And the softly lit and very simpatico Segovia Bar is open for business lunches as well as Spanish tapas and sherries until closing at midnight Sunday to Thursday, 1am Friday and Saturday.

Midtown Accommodations

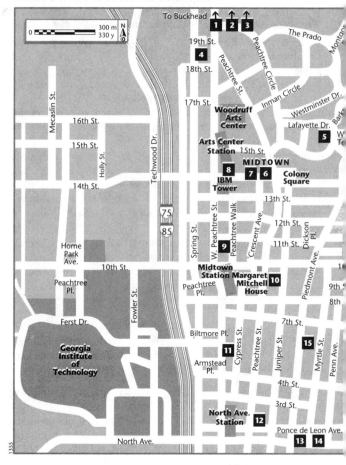

Services: 24-hour room service, 24-hour concierge, nightly bed turndown, newspaper of your choice delivered to your room daily, foreign currency exchange, complimentary shoeshine, limo rental, complimentary round-trip transport via town car from 7am to 7pm to downtown, Buckhead, and points in between.

Facilities: Full-service unisex hair/beauty salon (inquire about "days-of-beauty" packages), extensive business services, gift shop, complete health club, large indoor pool, outdoor sundeck, whirlpool, steam, sauna. Kids enjoy wonderful special gifts and amenities.

EXPENSIVE

✪ Marriott Suites

35 14th St. NE (between Peachtree and W. Peachtree Sts.), Atlanta, GA 30309. ☎ **404/876-8888** or 800/228-9290. Fax 404/876-7727. 254 suites. A/C TV TEL. $179 double. No extra person charge. Discounted rates and packages may be

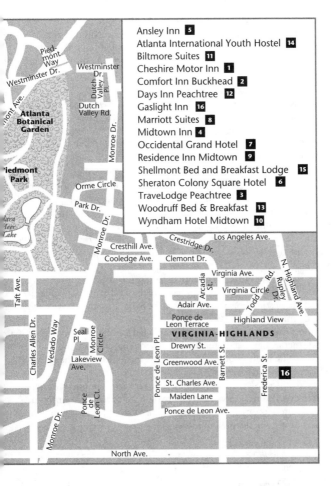

Ansley Inn **5**
Atlanta International Youth Hostel **14**
Biltmore Suites **11**
Cheshire Motor Inn **1**
Comfort Inn Buckhead **2**
Days Inn Peachtree **12**
Gaslight Inn **16**
Marriott Suites **8**
Midtown Inn **4**
Occidental Grand Hotel **7**
Residence Inn Midtown **9**
Shellmont Bed and Breakfast Lodge **15**
Sheraton Colony Square Hotel **6**
TraveLodge Peachtree **3**
Woodruff Bed & Breakfast **13**
Wyndham Hotel Midtown **10**

available through the toll-free number. AE, CB, DC, DISC, ER, MC, V. Parking $9 (self or valet). MARTA: Arts Center.

It would be hard to come by a more agreeable place to stay than this very hospitable, all-suite hotel. Each spacious suite, attractively decorated in a warm, homey style, offers a full living room with a convertible sofa, an extra phone on the desk, a wet bar/refrigerator, and a big console TV. Both this TV and the one in your bedroom offer Video on Command pay movies. Bedrooms are set off from living room areas by lace-curtained French doors. Additional in-suite amenities: coffeemakers, hairdryers, and irons and full-size ironing boards.

Dining/Entertainment: Off the palm court–style lobby, the plant-filled Allies serves lavish buffet breakfasts (everything from blintzes to Belgian waffles) and à la carte lunches and dinners featuring moderately priced American fare. A bar/lounge adjoins.

Services: Room service between 6 and 9:30am and 5:30 and 11pm, airport shuttle, *USA Today* delivered to your door each morning.

Facilities: Gift shop, health club, connecting indoor and outdoor swimming pools (both ample for laps), whirlpool, coin-op washer/dryer.

Sheraton Colony Square Hotel

188 14th St. NE (at Peachtree St.), Atlanta, GA 30361. ☎ **404/892-6000** or 800/422-7895. Fax 404/872-9192. 430 rms, 31 suites. A/C TV TEL. Mon–Thurs $149–$229 double; Fri–Sun lower rates are offered, subject to availability. Colony Club $200 double. Extra person $20. Children 18 and under free in parents' room. AE, CB, DC, DISC, MC, V. Parking $8.50 self, $12 valet. MARTA: Arts Center.

Built in 1974 as an opulent anchor of the Colony Square complex (which includes a mall of 20 shops and restaurants), this theatrically themed property is very popular with entertainers playing at the adjacent Woodruff Arts Center. The Sheraton Colony Square has hosted Frank Sinatra and Linda Ronstadt, not to mention Presidents Reagan, Ford, Carter, Bush, and Clinton. It's also a great choice for tennis and jogging enthusiasts, since Piedmont Park is just a few blocks away.

Rooms are plush and gorgeous. In a handsome armoire, you'll find your cable TV with Spectravision pay movies. Other in-room amenities include electric shoe buffers, and, in the baths, upscale toiletries and cosmetic mirrors.

Dining/Entertainment: The oak-columned 14th Street Bar & Grill serves American fare at all meals. Also here is the cozy lamplit Lobby Bar. There are many good restaurants in the mall, including the Country Place (details in Chapter 7).

Services: Room service 6:30am to 1am, concierge, airport shuttle.

Facilities: Business services, nice-size outdoor pool, workout room. The mall offers a copy shop, shoe repair, photo shop, clothing and shoe stores, a drugstore, florist, and more.

Wyndham Hotel Midtown

125 10th St. NE (just east of Peachtree St.), Atlanta, GA 30309. ☎ **404/873-4800** or 800/822-4200. Fax 404/870-1530. 162 rms, 29 suites. A/C TV TEL. Mon–Thurs $145 double; $155 for an Executive King. Fri–Sun $69 per room. Suites $165–$500. Extra person $10. Children 12 and under free in parents' room. AE, CB, DC, DISC, JCB. Parking $7.50 self, $9.50 valet. MARTA: Midtown.

An 11-story Georgia redbrick building, faced with bronze glass, the Wyndham offers luxuriously appointed rooms, many with bay windows. Each has an armchair and hassock, a handsome armoire concealing a TV (offering pay movie channels), and a coffeemaker. There are hairdryers and cosmetic mirrors in the bath. Executive King rooms feature separate parlors with sofas, extra TVs and phones, and refrigerators.

Dining/Entertainment: An art nouveau entranceway heralds the Juniper Street Café, featuring buffet breakfasts and lunches as well as an à la carte menu at lunch and dinner. A lunchtime pasta bar is a unique feature. The adjoining Butler's bar and lounge specializes in premium wines by the glass.

Services: Comprehensive business services, airport shuttle, room service 5 to 11 pm, complimentary *USA Today* at front desk.

Facilities: 7,000-square-foot fitness center offering Nautilus equipment, steam and sauna, whirlpool, large indoor pool, aerobics classes.

MODERATE

✪ Residence Inn Midtown

1041 W. Peachtree St. (at 11th St.), Atlanta, GA 30309. ☎ **404/872-8885** or 800/331-3131. Fax 404/872-8885, ext. 1805. 66 suites. A/C TV TEL. Suites $119 one bedroom, $149 two bedrooms. Rates include continental breakfast. Rates are reduced off season and for stays of more than 9 nights. AE, DC, DISC, MC, V. Parking free (self only). MARTA: Midtown.

Staying here is like having your own apartment in Atlanta. Accommodations are spacious suites decorated in soft pastel hues with handsome oak and mahogany furnishings—mostly antique reproductions, such as Chippendale-style beds. Both bedrooms and living rooms have their own TVs and telephones, and kitchens are fully equipped. French doors lead to balconies.

Dining/Entertainment: An extended continental breakfast is included in the rates; it's served in a pleasant breakfast room off the lobby, where hot tea and coffee are provided all day. Monday to Thursday night from 5:30 to 7:30pm, there are free beer-and-wine parties in the lobby with a wide array of hot and cold hors d'oeuvres. And every Wednesday night there's a complimentary barbecue dinner. All of these events provide a pleasant opportunity to meet and mingle with fellow guests. A bar, The Vortex, also serves light fare.

Services: Complimentary grocery-shopping service, free newspapers daily.

Facilities: Coin-op washers/dryers, rooftop Jacuzzi, complimentary membership at a nearby health club.

INEXPENSIVE

⑤ Biltmore Suites

30 Fifth St. NE (at W. Peachtree St.), Atlanta, GA 30308. ☎ **404/874-0824** or 800/822-0824. Fax 404/458-5384. 60 suites. A/C TV TEL. Studios and one-bedroom suites (for one or two people) $75–$110; two-bedroom suites (for up to four) $140–$165; penthouses and tri-level honeymoon/anniversary suites $225–$250. Rates include continental breakfast. AE, DISC, MC, V. Parking $5 (self only). MARTA: North Avenue.

A majestic 10-story brick building with a white-columned facade, its courtyard entrance shaded by stately oaks and magnolias, the Biltmore has a rich and glamorous history. Built in 1924 (as a hotel-cum-luxury apartment complex) by Coca-Cola heir William Candler, it played host in its heyday to everyone from *GWTW* stars Vivien Leigh and Olivia de Havilland to Presidents Franklin Roosevelt and Dwight Eisenhower. Closed in 1982, its apartment section was refurbished as an all-suite hotel in 1986.

Lovely, residentially furnished suites offer fully equipped kitchens, dining areas, and (except in some studios) living rooms. They're traditionally furnished (largely in 18th-century style cherrywood and mahogany pieces) with area rugs strewn on glossy oak floors. Lion-head door knockers, 10-foot ceilings, hand-carved crown moldings, multi-paned windows, brass bathroom fixtures, and French doors are additional enhancements. All accommodations but studios feature extra TVs and phones in the living rooms, and the stunning penthouse suites (as well as some two-bedroom suites) contain Jacuzzis.

Dining/Entertainment: Complimentary continental breakfast is served daily in a charming breakfast room off the lobby.

Services: Room service from dozens of area restaurants (there's a menu in your room), airport shuttle, complimentary shuttle from 7 to 11am and 4 to 8pm to anywhere within a five-mile radius of the property.

Facilities: Free health club privileges at the extensively equipped North Side Athletic Club (about a 5-mile drive from here), with an indoor/outdoor Olympic-size pool and tennis courts; coin-op washer/dryer.

☉ Cheshire Motor Inn

1865 Cheshire Bridge Rd. NE (between Wellborne Dr. NE and Manchester St. NE), Atlanta, GA 30324. ☎ **404/872-9628** or 800/827-9628. 58 rms. A/C TV TEL. $35–$42 single. Extra person $6. Children under 12 stay free in parents' room. Rates may be higher during special events. AE, DC, DISC, MC, V. Parking free. MARTA: Lindbergh (about a mile away; you can catch a bus to the station in front of the hotel).

This is my favorite kind of budget hotel, a small property run for decades by caring private owners (the Lacy family) who offer home-like hospitality and many personal touches. On attractively land-scaped, woodsy grounds, the Cheshire offers rooms that are spacious, immaculate, and cozy. Some rooms have sofas. In the bath, you'll find shampoo, a toothbrush, toothpaste, and a razor. A big plus is a famous Atlanta restaurant, the Colonnade, on the premises, serving authentic southern food (see details in Chapter 7). Free newspapers (*USA Today* and the *Atlanta Journal-Constitution*) and coffee are available in the lobby each morning.

Comfort Inn Buckhead

2115 Piedmont Rd. NE (between Lindbergh Dr. and Cheshire Bridge Rd.), Atlanta, GA 30324. ☎ **404/876-4365** or 800/221-2222. Fax 404/873-1007. 177 rms, 5 suites. A/C TV TEL. $63 double. King rooms $6 extra. Suites (for five to eight people) $99. Rates may be higher during special events. Rates include continental breakfast. Children 12 and under stay free in parents' room. AE, CB, DC, DISC, MC, V. Parking free. MARTA: Lindbergh (about three-fourths of a mile north; bus no. 31 stops at the door).

Poised on the border between midtown and Buckhead, this Comfort Inn has large, king-bedded rooms furnished with desks, recliners, and pullout sofas. And suites offer full living rooms, microwave ovens, and refrigerators. In-room amenities include TVs with pay-movie stations, and phones that provide push-button access to dozens of services. Local calls are free, and there's no service charge for credit-card calls. A free copy of *Newsweek* in your room is another plus. Doughnuts, juice, tea, and coffee are served in a pleasant room off the lobby each morning (coffee is available all day). There's also a small outdoor pool and sundeck.

Surprise, surprise! One of Atlanta's finest restaurants, the Chef's Café, leases space on the property. See details in Chapter 7.

Days Inn Peachtree

683 Peachtree St. (between 3rd St. and Ponce de Leon Ave.), Atlanta, GA 30308. ☎ **404/874-9200** or 800/DAYS-INN. Fax 404/873-4245. 141 rms, 1 suite. A/C TV TEL. $79–$119 double. Suites $125–$199. Rates may be higher during conventions and special events. Rates include continental breakfast. Extra person $10. Children under 18 free in parents' room. Weekend rates and packages available via the toll-free number. Super Saver rate of $49 a night may be available if you reserve at least 30 days in advance. AE, DC, DISC, MC, V. Parking $5 (self only). MARTA: North Avenue.

You'll realize this Days Inn is not your average chain motel from the moment you enter its charming lobby with Persian rugs on Saltillo-tile floors and a brass chandelier suspended from a lofty mahogany ceiling.

Nicely decorated rooms feature TVs with free HBO and pay-movie channels; some have comfortable, velvet-upholstered sofas.

Bridgetown Grill, a terrific Caribbean restaurant (see Chapter 7), adjoins the property, and a Wendy's is on the premises. Complimentary wine, cheeses, and hot hors d'oeuvres are served at a cocktail party in the lobby every Thursday night; coffee is served in the lobby throughout the day. There's also an airport shuttle and coin-op washers/dryers.

Midtown Inn

1470 Spring St. NW (at 19th St.), Atlanta, GA 30309. ☎ **404/872-5821**. Fax 404/874-3602. 179 rms. A/C TV TEL. Mon–Thurs $75–$85 double; Fri–Sun $52–$59 per room. Executive Kings $95 double. Extra person $10. Children under 18 free in parents' room. AE, DC, DISC, MC, V. Parking free (self only). MARTA: Arts Center.

The Midtown Inn welcomes guests in a large and inviting plant-filled lobby. Rooms are clean and well maintained—newly renovated for the Olympics. Executive Kings are larger and equipped with sofas.

Services and facilities here include a gift shop, complimentary shuttle to MARTA and local attractions (daily 7am to 11pm), and a swimming pool.

TraveLodge Peachtree

1641 Peachtree St. NE (at I-85), Atlanta, GA 30309. ☎ **404/873-5731** or 800/255-3050. Fax 404/874-5599. 56 rms. A/C TV TEL. $49–$69 double. Rates may be much higher during major conventions or special events. Extra person $4. Children under 18 free in parents' room. AE, CB, DC, DISC, ER, JCB, MC, V. MARTA: Arts Center.

A small property housed in a three-story building, the TraveLodge Peachtree offers a convenient location (the hotel is on the airport shuttle route) and low rates. Rooms are newly renovated. There's no on-premises restaurant, but an International House of Pancakes (among many other eateries) is a block away, and coffee and doughnuts are served in the lobby each morning. There's a small pool out back, and coin-op washers and dryers are available.

BED & BREAKFASTS

✪ Ansley Inn

253 15th St. NE, at Lafayette Dr. (between Piedmont Ave. and Peachtree St.), Atlanta, GA 30309. ☎ **404/872-9000** or 800/446-5416. Fax 404/892-2318. 33 rms,

1 cottage. A/C TV TEL. $99–$495 double; two-bedroom cottage (sleeps six) $200. Extra person $10. Rates include continental breakfast. AE, DC, DISC, ER, MC, V. Parking free. MARTA: Arts Center.

Far and away my favorite accommodation in Atlanta, the Ansley Inn is a delight. Occupying a 1907 yellow-brick Tudor mansion, this former estate of department-store magnate George Muse is located in one of the city's most beautiful and chic residential areas, Ansley Park. Ancient magnolias and white oaks shade the inn's front lawn.

The Persian-carpeted dining room is furnished with a long English Chippendale-style table and Empire sideboards; overhead, two turn-of-the-century Italian crystal chandeliers are suspended from a beautiful arched ceiling carved with fruit motifs. Adjoining is a hand-somely furnished living room, with Chinese rosewood horseshoe-back chairs and a pair of plush Regency-style tufted-leather Chesterfield sofas in front of an eight-foot ceramic-tile fireplace. Deep peach walls in the Italian marble-floored hallways are hung with changing art exhibits, and lavish floral arrangements top a stunning swan table. Classical music or traditional jazz played downstairs during the day further en-hances the inn's ambience, which is refined but never haughty.

Rooms have oak floors, some strewn with Oriental rugs, and are elegantly furnished in antique pieces and reproductions. Your accom-modation might have a brass bed or an 18th-century mahogany four-poster, crystal lamps, or a cushioned window seat overlooking the park. Some rooms have lofty cathedral ceilings and working fireplaces, and all feature wet bars, comfortable armchairs with hassocks, cable TVs, and full baths with whirlpool tubs. The 1,300-square-foot cot-tage has a fully equipped kitchen, two bedrooms, and a living room with a working fireplace.

Most importantly, the Ansley Inn's staff offers warm hospitality and gracious service to guests, creating a friendly, homelike atmosphere that will make your stay a memorable experience.

Dining/Entertainment: Complimentary breakfast includes crois-sants, muffins, dry cereal, pastries, fresh fruit, juices, hot chocolate, and tea or coffee. Complimentary refreshments (coffee, tea, plus cheeses, fresh-baked cookies, and/or crudités with dip) are served in the living room every afternoon.

Services: Newspaper of your choice on request daily, 24-hour con-cierge, room service from area restaurants.

Facilities: Complimentary membership at two local health clubs. The inn itself is building a large outdoor pool/sundeck at this writing.

✪ Shellmont Bed and Breakfast Lodge

821 Piedmont Ave. NE (at 6th St.), Atlanta, GA 30308. ☎ **404/872-9290**. Fax 404/872-5379. 4 rms plus carriage house. A/C TV TEL. $89 double in main house; $109 double in carriage house. Extra person $20. Rates include full breakfast. Children 12 and under allowed in the carriage house only. AE, DC, MC, V. Parking free. MARTA: North Avenue or Midtown.

This charming two-story Victorian mansion looks, from the outside, like a Wedgwood fairy-tale house embellished with ribbons, bows, gar-lands, and shells. Fronted by a small garden, it has both a front porch and a small veranda out back with wicker rocking chairs overlooking a flower garden and fish pond. The building dates to 1891 and is on the National Register of Historic Places. Innkeepers Ed and Debbie McCord have done a superb job of restoration, not only in repairing all functional aspects, but in meticulously researching original paint colors, stencil designs, woodwork, and period furnishings and reproducing them with 100% accuracy.

Breakfast is served in a lovely dining room with a floor-to-ceiling mantel fireplace. Guests might while away an evening reading (the McCords keep a fairly extensive library) before a blazing fire in the oak-furnished living room. There's also a downstairs parlor that was originally a music room, and Ed's favorite room is the Moorish-influenced, kilim-carpeted "Turkish corner."

Up the stairway (its landing graced by an exquisite five-paneled stained-glass window that the McCords believe is an authentic Tiffany) are the four guest rooms. They have gorgeous beds (perhaps you'll have an Eastlake or a bed with a six-foot oak headboard embellished with carved ribbons and bows), leaded-glass or bay windows, Oriental rugs strewn on hand-oiled hard pine floors, and framed botanical prints on the walls. All have private baths, phones (local calls are free), cable TVs, and VCRs. The other accommodation, in an adjoining carriage house, offers a master bedroom, full modern bath with steam bath shower, fully equipped kitchen, living room, and dressing area.

Dining/Entertainment: Daily breakfast, included in rates, consists of fresh-squeezed juice, fresh and dried fruits, an entrée (perhaps Belgian waffles or frittatas), cereal, and tea or coffee.

Services: Ed and Debbie live on the premises and offer all the services of a hotel concierge, plus nightly bed turndown, and fruit and fresh flowers in your room daily.

Woodruff Bed & Breakfast Inn

223 Ponce de Leon Ave. NE (at Myrtle St.), Atlanta, GA 30308. ☎ **404/875-9449** or 800/473-9449. Fax 404/875-2882. 10 rms (8 with bath), 2 suites. A/C TV (on request) TEL. $79–$159 double; $139 for two rooms with a shared bath (for up to four people); $109–$159 for a two-room Jacuzzi suite. Rates include full breakfast. AE, DISC, MC, V. Parking free. MARTA: North Avenue.

This three-story white-brick Victorian house, built in 1906 by an Atlanta physician, went on to a more interesting incarnation in the 1950s when Miss Bessie Woodruff bought the property and turned it into a successful house of ill repute. Officially, it was a licensed massage facility (the "girls" actually wore white nurses' uniforms), and some of Atlanta's most prominent politicians came by frequently to relieve the tensions of public office. Current owners Joan and Doug Jones not only honored Bessie by naming their bed and breakfast for her, they've displayed, in public areas, light boards that were used to keep track of the rooms in use, framed photographs of Bessie (she was a beauty), and her old love letters.

The first floor, entered via a foyer with beautiful beveled-glass doors, has a cozy plant-filled parlor with a bay window; it's furnished with turn-of-the-century antiques, including a plush Empire sofa and an English piano. The dining room, with leaded-glass windows, features an oak table under a crystal chandelier. The rooms, all but three with private baths, contain a mix of 19th- and early 20th-century English antiques, along with pieces one might categorize as "grandma's house" furnishings. Your accommodation might have stained-glass or bay windows or French doors leading to a porch furnished with swings or rocking chairs. The house itself also offers a large front porch overlooking the oak-shaded lawn. Guests in Jacuzzi suites enjoy complimentary flowers and champagne on arrival.

Dining/Entertainment: Rates include a full breakfast—eggs and bacon, fresh fruit, orange juice, jumbo muffins, cereal (on request), and tea or coffee.

Services: Free daily newspaper; magazines and books available.

Facilities: Cable TV with VCR in the parlor.

A YOUTH HOSTEL

☉ The Atlanta International Youth Hostel

223 Ponce de Leon Ave. NE (at Myrtle St.), Atlanta, GA 30308. ☎ **404/875-2882**. 75 beds in 4- to 6-bed dorms, all with shared bath. A/C. $13.25, including tax, for Hostelling International members, $3 additional for nonmembers. Rates include continental breakfast. MC, V (with a $26.50 minimum). Parking free. MARTA: North Avenue.

Operated by Doug and Joan Jones—and adjoining their Woodruff Bed & Breakfast Inn (see above)—this first-rate and fully accredited hostel offers dorm rooms with freshly painted white walls, bunk beds, and fan chandeliers. A unique feature: Doug and Joan have encouraged guests to paint murals in rooms and public areas throughout the building, which adds a homey, if sometimes amateurish, touch. Facilities include a TV room, a game area with a pinball machine and pool table, a fully equipped common kitchen, and a Ping-Pong table. Guests can also use a tree-shaded yard with a barbecue grill on the side of the building; the yard is home to two beagles (named Clinton and Gore) and an aviary of fantail pigeons. About 80% of the hostellers here come from Europe, Japan, and Australia. It's a well-run place where parents can feel safe sending their kids, and the location is wonderfully central. Complimentary coffee and doughnuts are provided each morning. Check-in is from 8am to noon and 5pm to midnight daily; rooms are closed from noon to 5pm, though guests can use public areas. Blankets are provided; lockers and sheets can be rented.

4 Buckhead

Buckhead hotels combine the quiet residential appeal of midtown accommodations with the luxury of downtown properties. Many of Atlanta's best restaurants are close by. In my opinion, it's the optimum hotel location.

VERY EXPENSIVE

☉ Hotel Nikko Atlanta

3300 Peachtree Rd. (just east of Piedmont Rd.), Atlanta, GA 30326. ☎ **404/ 365-8100** or 800-NIKKO-US. Fax 404/233-5686. 418 rms, 22 suites. A/C MINIBAR TV TEL. Mon–Thurs $175–$220 double; Fri–Sun $129–$199 per room. Nikko floor $240 double. Suites $435–$1,500. Extra person $25. Children under 16 stay free in parents' room. AE, CB, DC, DISC, ER, JCB, MC, V. Parking $15. MARTA: Lenox.

The towering Hotel Nikko offers a winning combination of 18th-century American architecture and Japanese attention to aesthetic detail. Its lobby overlooks a 9,000-square-foot garden with traditional plantings, rock formations, and splashing waterfalls created by noted Kyoto landscape architects, and a collection of museum-quality Japanese art, spanning four centuries, is displayed throughout the hotel.

Rooms, decorated in subtle hues, are furnished in 18th-century mahogany reproductions, with crane-motif headboards, fresh orchids, and Japanese prints in black lacquer frames providing Eastern nuance. Every luxury is provided: three phones (bedside, bath, and desk), TVs with Spectravision movie options, terry robes, and baths equipped with hairdryers, TV speakers, cosmetic mirrors, and scales. You'll even find an umbrella in your closet.

Dining/Entertainment: Kamogawa, Atlanta's premier Japanese restaurant, offers an authentic dining experience (see Chapter 7, "Dining"). The delightful Cassis, with soaring arched windows overlooking the Japanese garden, is also much acclaimed for its sophisticated cuisine; all meals are served here, including a Japanese breakfast and lavish Sunday brunch. A pianist entertains daily from 5 to 8pm in the plush Lobby Lounge, also the setting for English-style afternoon teas and a jazz trio, which performs Friday and Saturday nights. Weather permitting, a Japanese tea is also served afternoons in a tranquil garden with pagoda seating on the third floor.

Services: Complimentary overnight shoeshine, 24-hour room service, 24-hour concierge, baby-sitting, toys/activities for children, massage, airport shuttle, complimentary shuttle within a two-mile radius of the hotel.

Facilities: Comprehensive business center, fully equipped health club (with TVs and VCRs on the exercise bikes, Life Trim equipment, stair machines, aerobics videos, steam, and sauna), a lovely outdoor pool and sundeck. Lenox Square and Phipps Plaza shopping malls are two blocks away.

✪ The Ritz-Carlton, Buckhead

3434 Peachtree Rd. NE (at Lenox Rd.), Atlanta, GA 30326. ☎ **404/237-2700** or 800/241-3333. Fax 404/239-0078. 524 rms, 29 suites. A/C MINIBAR TV TEL. Mon–Thurs $165–$225 double, Fri–Sun $125–$185 double. Club Floor $235–$255 double. Extra person $30. Children under 12 stay free in parents' room. Inquire about packages. AE, DC, DISC, JCB, MC, V. Parking $8 self, $12 valet. MARTA: Lenox.

From the lobby, with antique Persian carpets on white marble floors and cut-crystal French chandeliers, to public areas graced with Regency and Georgian antiques and an outstanding collection of 18th- and 19th-century paintings and sculpture, every inch of this hotel bespeaks luxury. And the quality of service matches the sumptuous surroundings.

The rooms, all with large bay windows, are exquisitely decorated, with furnishings including burled-walnut armoires, sofas or armchairs upholstered in raw silk, 18th-century-reproduction beds, beautiful Chinese lamps, and Federalist mirrors. Baths, amply supplied with

Buckhead Accommodations

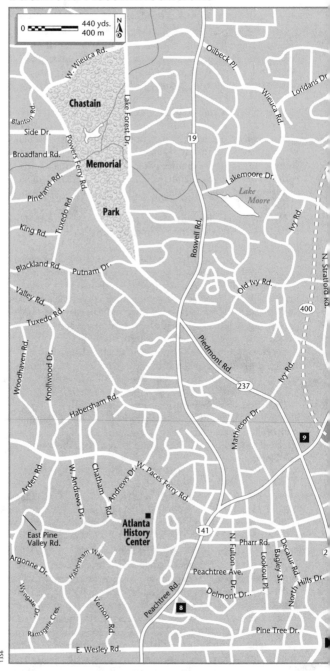

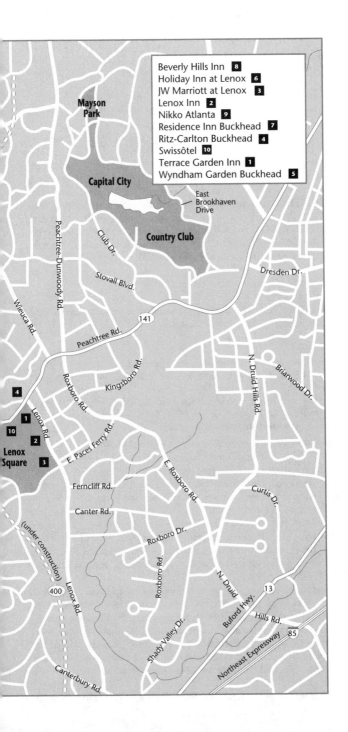

Beverly Hills Inn **8**
Holiday Inn at Lenox **6**
JW Marriott at Lenox **3**
Lenox Inn **2**
Nikko Atlanta **9**
Residence Inn Buckhead **7**
Ritz-Carlton Buckhead **4**
Swissôtel **10**
Terrace Garden Inn **1**
Wyndham Garden Buckhead **5**

Mayson Park

Capital City

Country Club

East Brookhaven Drive

Peachtree-Dunwoody Rd.

Club Dr.

Stovall Blvd.

Dresden Dr.

Wieuca Rd.

141

Peachtree Rd.

Roxboro Rd.

Kingsboro Rd.

N. Druid Hills Rd.

Briarwood Dr.

4

1

10

Lenox Rd.

2

E. Paces Ferry Rd.

Lenox Square

3

Ferncliff Rd.

E. Roxboro Rd.

Curtis Dr.

Canter Rd.

Roxboro Dr.

(under construction)

400

Lenox Rd.

Roxboro Rd.

Shady Valley Dr.

N. Druid

13

Buford Hwy.

Hills Rd.

85

Canterbury Rd.

Northeast Expressway

fine toiletries, contain scales, phones, and makeup mirrors. And you'll find a terry robe in your closet.

Dining/Entertainment: The Dining Room at the Ritz-Carlton Buckhead, one of Atlanta's premier restaurants, is covered extensively in Chapter 7. The Lobby Lounge, with mahogany-paneled walls and a glowing oak-log fire, is the setting for afternoon English-style teas. A classical pianist plays here from 2:30 to 4:30pm daily, jazz artists entertain evenings, and from 5 to 7:30pm 11 different martinis are featured on a special drink menu. The three-tiered Café, an all-day dining room, is a repository of art and antiques. Its classic haute-cuisine menu includes light health-conscious choices. A lavish buffet brunch is served here every Sunday. In the adjoining Café Bar, there's music for dancing Friday and Saturday nights. And Expresso's, with indoor seating as well as outdoor umbrella tables on a poplar-shaded courtyard, serves full breakfasts and deli lunch specials weekdays from 7am to 3pm.

Services: Limousine on request, airport shuttle and shuttle to nearby malls, newspaper delivered to your door each morning, 24-hour room service, nightly bed turndown, currency exchange, concierge, one-hour pressing, on-premises seamstress, personalized shopping, complimentary shoeshine.

Facilities: Full business center, swimming and fitness center, steam and sauna rooms, Jacuzzi, gift shop, hair salon.

✪ Swissôtel

3391 Peachtree Rd. NE (between Lenox and Piedmont Rds.), Atlanta, GA 30326. ☎ **404/365-0065** or 800/63-SWISS. Fax 404/233-8786. 348 rms, 17 suites. A/C MINIBAR TV TEL. Mon–Thurs $175–$245 double. Club level $280 double. Fri–Sun $115 per room, $170 Club Level. Extra person $25. Children under 16 free in parents' room. AE, CB, DC, DISC, ER, JCB, MC, V. Parking $11 valet, $6 self. MARTA: Lenox (complimentary transport to/from station).

Opened in 1991, the Zurich-based Swissôtel (it's owned by Swissair) added a new aesthetic dimension to Atlanta's hotel scene. Its postmodern European architecture and interior spaces utilize Bauhaus elements, notably exemplified in a pristine white tile exterior with a graceful piano curve. An impressive lobby, with floor-to-45-foot-ceiling windows and a grand staircase, is warmed by the extensive use of reddish Australian lacewood paneling. Hallway carpets are designed after a Paul Klee painting, and original works by internationally known contemporary artists—Rauschenberg, Chagall, Schnabel, Stella, and many others—grace public spaces. This is a visually exciting hotel.

Rooms are uniquely furnished in Biedermeier-style bird's-eye maple pieces with black lacquer accents and capacious leather-topped desks. Armoires house cable TVs (with Spectravision/HBO movie options and video checkout), and all rooms are equipped with terry robes, three phones, coffeemakers, irons, and full-size ironing boards. Baths offer cosmetic mirrors, TV speakers, hairdryers, and upscale biodegradable toiletries. Especially nice are corner king rooms (ask for one when you reserve).

Dining/Entertainment: The superb Palm is described in Chapter 7.

Services: Concierge, complimentary shuttle to any destination in a two-mile radius (including MARTA and the plush upscale Lenox Square and Phipps Plaza Malls), multilingual staff, airport shuttle, 24-hour room service, daily newspaper delivery, complimentary shoeshine.

Facilities: Gift shop, unisex hair salon/spa, car rental desk, airline desk (Swissair), 24-hour business/communications center. A small but nicely equipped health club offers massage, exercise equipment, a lap pool, sauna, steam room, and aerobics studio.

EXPENSIVE

✪ JW Marriott at Lenox

3300 Lenox Rd. NE, (a few blocks east of Peachtree Rd. at E. Paces Ferry Rd.), Atlanta, GA 30326. ☎ **404/262-3344** or 800/228-9290. Fax 404/262-8603. 323 rms, 48 suites. A/C MINIBAR TV TEL. Mon–Thurs $139–$220 for up to four people; Fri–Sun $119–$185 per room. Club Level rooms $200. AE, CB, DC, DISC, ER, MC, V. Parking $7 self, $9 valet. MARTA: Lenox.

This luxurious Marriott, with an interior modeled after Atlanta's historic Swan House (see Chapter 8), is striking from the moment you step inside its elegant marble-floored entranceway under a silver-leafed coffered ceiling. The residential-style lobby divides into a series of beautifully appointed, cozy living rooms, its ambience enhanced by classical music and exquisite flower arrangements.

Rooms are charmingly furnished with Chippendale-style mahogany pieces, the walls hung with gilt-framed watercolors of Buckhead mansions. Picture windows offer panoramic vistas. Handsome mahogany armoires house TVs with free HBO and On Command Video pay movie channels. Each room has three phones (bath, beside, and desk), lavish marble baths are equipped with scales and hairdryers, and you'll find an iron and full-sized ironing board in your closet. The Marriott connects from an interior door to the Lenox Square Mall, and the even posher Phipps Plaza Mall is within walking distance.

Dining/Entertainment: At this writing, the Marriott's premier restaurant is undergoing a renovation and concept change—probably to an upscale bistro; call for details. The clubby Ottley's offers piano bar entertainment Wednesday to Saturday evenings. Light fare is available. Yet another plush setting for cocktails/light fare is the cozy Lobby Lounge, with comfortable sofas and armchairs before a working pagoda-style fireplace backed by Brazilian marble.

Services: 24-hour room service, multilingual concierge staff, nightly bed turndown, airport shuttle, one-hour dry cleaning, *USA Today* delivered to your room each morning.

Facilities: Large indoor pool in a setting patterned after a Roman bath, full health club with steam and sauna, car rental desk, full business center, pastry shop.

✪ Terrace Garden Inn

3405 Lenox Rd. NE (between Peachtree and E. Paces Ferry Rds.), Atlanta, GA 30326. ☎ **404/261-9250** or 800/241-8260. Fax 404/848-7391. 360 rms, 6 suites. A/C TV TEL. Mon–Thurs $125–$135 double; Fri–Sun $95–$115 per room. Club level $145 double. Extra person $15. Children under 18 free in parents' room. AE, DC, DISC, MC, V. Parking $5 per night (self only, covered garage). MARTA: Lenox.

This is an especially lovely hotel that offers abundant services and facilities plus a great location (the Lenox Square Mall is just across the street). Rooms are furnished with French country and 18th-century-reproduction mahogany pieces (some have four-poster or brass beds). Most have balconies, and all offer extra phones in the bath and TVs with free HBO and Spectravision pay movies. Phones are equipped with call waiting and computer jacks. Rooms with king-size beds have plush armchairs with ottomans.

Dining/Entertainment: On two levels, the Café, one of Atlanta's prettiest hotel dining rooms, is garden-themed, with gilt-framed botanical prints on the walls and flower-bedecked tables amid lots of leafy greenery. A window wall on the upper level overlooks the pool. The fare is American/continental. The cozy Corner Hearth Lounge offers seating in plush chairs and sofas around a vast stone-walled, copper-hooded fireplace (ablaze in winter).

Services: Room service, free daily newspaper, airport shuttle, concierge.

Facilities: Avis car rental desk, United Airlines desk, gift shop. The extensive Health & Racquet Center offers racquetball, an indoor pool, exercise equipment, steam, sauna, and Jacuzzi. There's also an outdoor swimming pool with waterfalls cascading over bronze dolphins and fish sculptures.

MODERATE

Holiday Inn at Lenox

3777 Peachtree Rd. NE (between Lenox and Piedmont rds.), Atlanta, GA 30326. ☎ **404/264-1111** or 800/HOLIDAY. Fax 404/233-7061. 293 rms, 4 suites. A/C TV TEL. $99–$160 double. Extra person $10. Children under 18 stay free in parents' room. AE, DC, DISC, ER, JCB, MC, V. Parking $6. MARTA: Lenox.

Conveniently located adjacent to the Lenox Square Mall, this 11-story Holiday Inn recently redecorated all of its rooms. They're equipped with coffeemakers, phones with computer jacks, and TVs with free HBO and pay-movie options, plus, uniquely, Game Boy (your kids will be thrilled even if you're not). Most also have small refrigerators.

The Brentwood Café, a pretty dining room with a wall of windows and fresh flowers on every table, serves American fare at all meals. There's also room service 7am to 2pm and 5 to 10pm, an airport shuttle, free *USA Today* in the restaurant, complimentary van transport within three miles of the hotel, an outdoor pool and sundeck, coin-op washers and dryers, and a business center. Guests can use a nearby health club for a fee.

Holiday Inn (an official sponsor of the Olympic Games) has several locations throughout Atlanta in addition to this one. Just call the toll-free number above to book a room at any of their locations.

✪ Residence Inn Buckhead

2960 Piedmont Rd. NE. (between Pharr Rd. and Lindbergh Dr.), Atlanta, GA 30305. ☎ **404/239-0677** or 800/331-3131. Fax 404/262-9638. 136 suites. A/C TV TEL. Studio suites (for up to four people) $120; penthouse suites (for up to six) $160. Reductions are available for stays of seven nights or longer. AE, DC, DISC, MC, V.

Parking free. MARTA: Lindbergh or Lenox (each about a mile away); buses stop half a block away.

This home-away-from-home was designed to meet the needs of travelers making extended visits, but it's marvelous even if you're only spending a single night. It's like having your own luxurious apartment, with a private entrance and a large, fully equipped kitchen.

Accommodations include comfortable living-room areas. About half the suites have working fireplaces (during winter, logs are available from the front desk). The most luxurious accommodations are duplex penthouses with vaulted ceilings, full dining-room/office areas, two baths, and living-room fireplaces. The Residence Inn is located on five attractively landscaped acres backed by woods, and the suites are in two-story cream stucco chalets.

Dining/Entertainment: One of the most salient features here is the cathedral-ceilinged Gatehouse Lounge, among its amenities a TV, a small library, and a blazing fireplace. The Gatehouse provides many opportunities to mingle with fellow guests over breakfast (a buffet of fresh fruits, cereals, yogurt, pastries, juice, tea, and coffee) and at cocktail-hour parties on Monday, Tuesday, and Thursday from 5 to 7pm (featuring gratis beer, wine, and hot and cold hors d'oeuvres); Wednesday a full barbecue or buffet dinner is served during those hours.

Services: Complimentary shuttle service within a three-mile radius of the property at specified hours, complimentary grocery shopping, free daily newspapers in lounge.

Facilities: Outdoor pool and adjoining whirlpool, coin-op washers/dryers, outdoor barbecue grills, on-premises basketball/volleyball/paddle-tennis courts, and complimentary use of an extensively equipped health club nearby (with every kind of workout equipment, a Junior Olympic indoor pool, an outdoor pool, jogging, track, tennis/racquetball/squash courts, and much, much more).

Wyndham Garden Hotel Buckhead

3340 Peachtree Rd. NE (between Lenox and Piedmont rds.), Atlanta, GA 30326. ☎ **404/231-1234** or 800/WYNDHAM. Fax 404/231-5236. 221 rms, 10 suites. A/C TV TEL. Sun–Thurs $129 double; Fri–Sat $89 double. Suites $169–$219. Extra person $10. Children under 14 stay free in parents' room. AE, CB, DC, DISC, JCB, MC, V. Parking $4 (self or valet). MARTA: Lenox.

Designed with the business traveler in mind, this is an equally viable choice for the tourist. Entered via an attractive cherrywood-paneled lobby, it houses comfortable guest rooms fitted out with traditional mahogany furnishings (including large desks) and upholstered recliner chairs. Large king-bedded rooms are especially desirable. In-room amenities include coffeemakers, phones with 25-inch cords and computer jacks, hairdryers, and TVs with free Showtime movies.

Dining/Entertainment: The garden-themed bi-level Savannah Room, with a wall of windows overlooking a brick patio, serves all meals. The menu features steak, seafood, pastas, pizzas, and quesadillas. Beauregard's, a handsome lounge, serves complimentary hors d'oeuvres weekdays from 5 to 7pm.

Services: Room service 5 to 10pm, airport shuttle, complimentary *USA Today* and Atlanta paper at front desk, free courtesy van to/from Lenox Square Mall, Phipps Plaza, and the Lenox MARTA station. The front desk supplies free toothbrushes, toothpaste, razors, shaving cream, deodorant, and other amenities you may have neglected to pack.

Facilities: Pleasantly secluded pool and sundeck bordered by trees, gift shop. Guests enjoy free use of the adjacent state-of-the-art Sports Life Fitness Center, offering a full complement of exercise equipment, massage, steam, sauna, aerobics classes, child care, basketball/racquetball courts, indoor track, and more. Buckhead's posh shopping malls are close by.

INEXPENSIVE

Lenox Inn

3387 Lenox Rd. NE (between Peachtree and E. Paces Ferry rds.), Atlanta, GA 30326. ☎ **404/261-5500** or 800/241-0200. Fax 404/261-1640. 174 rms, 6 suites. A/C TV TEL. Sun–Thurs $79–$125 double; Fri–Sat $69.95 per room. Extra person $15. Children under 18 stay free in parents' room. AE, CB, DC, MC, V. Parking free. MARTA: Lenox.

Considering all you get here, in a great location just across the street from Lenox Square Mall, the Lenox Inn is a great bargain. Under the same ownership as the adjacent Terrace Garden Inn (details above), and sharing many of its facilities, the Lenox offers charming rooms with 18th-century-reproduction mahogany furnishings. Amenities include TVs (with Spectravision pay movies and free HBO) and a full complement of toiletries in the bath. Rooms with king-size beds offer steambaths. Only one building has an elevator, by the way; ask for it, or a first-floor room elsewhere, if stairs are a problem.

Dining/Entertainment: A choice of a complimentary continental breakfast or a large buffet breakfast ($6.25) is offered in a cozy, cherry-paneled restaurant with a working fireplace. Guests also gather here for complimentary cocktails and hors d'oeuvres nightly from 5:30 to 6:30pm. In summer there are occasionally free poolside cookouts/buffets with an open bar.

Services: Airport shuttle, complimentary newspaper (*Atlanta Journal-Constitution*) at front desk, free local calls. Room service is available via a menu compiled from local restaurants.

Facilities: Two outdoor swimming pools, health-club facilities of the Terrace Garden Inn next door at no charge.

A BED & BREAKFAST

✪ Beverly Hills Inn

65 Sheridan Dr. NE (just off Peachtree Rd.), Atlanta, GA 30305. ☎ **404/233-8520** or 800/331-8520. Fax 404/233-8520, ext. 18. 18 suites. A/C TV TEL. $90–$120 double for a one-bedroom suite; $120–$240 for a two-bedroom suite accommodating up to four people. Extra person $7. Children under 12 stay free in parents' room. Rates include continental breakfast. Discounts available for stays of a week or more. AE, CB, DC, DISC, JCB, MC, V. Parking free. MARTA bus: No. 23 at the corner.

Housed in a 1920s California-style building, with forest-green shutters and window awnings, this charming B&B is located on a sedately residential tree-lined street. British owner/host Mit Amin offers warm hospitality to guests. On the first floor is a cozy parlor/library where a decanter of port is available all day. Another library is downstairs in the sunny garden room, which has a skylit conservatory area filled with plants.

Rooms are cheerful and attractive, decorated in an eclectic period mix of antiques (many of them English pieces) and collectibles, with very pretty floral fabric bedspreads and curtains, oak floors strewn with area rugs, and framed botanical prints on the walls. Some have canopied beds. All are equipped with kitchenettes (the housekeeper does your dishes). Private balconies are entered via French doors. Several supermarkets are within easy walking distance, should you want to cook in your room, but the area also abounds with good restaurants. Classical music played in public areas enhances the ambience, as do dozens of flourishing plants.

Dining/Entertainment: An extended continental breakfast is served in the garden room. Or, in good weather, you can enjoy the morning meal at umbrella tables on the front patio.

Services: You'll find a half bottle of burgundy in your room on arrival; four daily newspapers are complimentary; free local calls.

Facilities: Lounge with Xerox machine, fax machine, and computer; complimentary washer/dryer; complimentary membership privileges at the nearby Buckhead Towne Club, a state-of-the-art facility offering two outdoor swimming pools, Lifecycles, Stairmasters, saunas, Jacuzzi, a full complement of Nautilus equipment, racquetball, and squash.

5 Virginia-Highlands

This is a marvelous choice for tourists—very central and within easy walking distance of shops and trendy restaurants. It's one of my favorite areas of town.

✪ The Gaslight Inn

1001 Saint Charles Ave. (between Frederica St. and N. Highland Ave.), Atlanta, GA 30306. ☎ **404/875-1001**. Fax 404/876-1001. 3 rms, 3 suites. A/C TV TEL. $85–$195. Rates include extensive continental breakfast. AE, MC, V. Some parking spaces behind house, otherwise street parking is not usually a problem. MARTA bus: Nos. 2 and 16 stop a block away.

Owner/host Jim Moss, a nationally renowned interior decorator, has turned this charming craftsman-style 1913 house into a delightful B&B, with rooms and public areas of exquisite *Architectural Digest* caliber. As its name implies, much of the inn is lit by flickering gaslight fixtures. A warm ambience—enhanced by classical music—is established as soon as you step into the entrance parlor, where paintings of hunting dogs hang over a working fireplace (one of many here). Another parlor adjoins, there's a lovely screened sunroom, and a comfortably furnished den offers a cable TV, well-stocked bookcases, a baby grand piano, and a large selection of CDs and cassettes. Guests can breakfast in the formal dining room at a long mahogany Sheraton table; pineapples (a traditional symbol of welcome) grace the mantel of its working fireplace. On the other hand, you might opt for an al fresco morning meal in a fountained flower garden or on the front porch furnished with antique wicker chairs and a swing. Guests enjoy many private areas, nooks, and alcoves at the Gaslight. Jim's breakfast includes an array of fresh fruits, fresh-squeezed juices, and oven-fresh muffins, breads, and pastries. Daily papers are provided for your perusal. Sherry is set out in the butler's pantry all day, as is coffee upstairs.

My favorite accommodation here—the perfect venue for a honeymoon or romantic getaway—is the elegant English Suite. It offers a four-poster mahogany bed (among other 18th-century–style furnishings), a vast bathroom equipped with steambath and whirlpool, a working fireplace, and a private deck overlooking the garden. The Ivy Cottage—a detached bungalow with a full kitchen (with washer/dryer) and living-room area—evokes a rustic New England resort; it has a private balcony overlooking a garden. And the Rose Room, with its lace draperies, working fireplace, and mahogany four-poster bed hand-painted with roses, is another charmer. The other accommodations—some of them located in a 1904 house across the street—are equally spectacular. All are equipped with private baths and enhanced by lovingly chosen objets d'art plus fresh flowers and/or live plants; terry robes are provided. On-premises facilities include a kitchen and laundry room.

6 Georgia's Stone Mountain

Georgia's Stone Mountain Park, just 16 miles east of downtown Atlanta, is a recreation area with 3,200 acres of lakes and wooded parkland. It is, in itself, a major travel destination, visited by over six million tourists annually. *Note:* There's a one-time $5 parking fee to enter the park.

EXPENSIVE

✪ Evergreen Conference Center and Resort

One Lakeview Dr., Stone Mountain Park, Stone Mountain, GA 30086. ☎ **404/ 879-9900** or 800/722-1000. Fax 404/469-9013. 220 rms, 29 suites. A/C TV TEL. $125–$160 double; rates depend on view. Extra person $20. Children under 18 free in parents' room. Inquire about packages when you reserve. AE, CB, DC, DISC, ER, MC, V. Parking free (self or valet).

Geared primarily to business travel, the Evergreen is also a good choice for vacationers. A turreted stucco lakefront "castle" nestled in a fragrant forest of pine, it's entered via a lodgelike lobby that centers on a massive stone fireplace. Balconied rooms are large and luxuriously appointed, furnished with floral-tapestried armchairs and 18th-century American reproduction mahogany pieces. Each contains a TV with free HBO and Spectravision pay movies.

Dining/Entertainment: The Waterside Restaurant, part of it under a 35-foot rotunda, offers gorgeous lake, mountain, and treetop views. Buffets are offered at all meals in addition to à la carte regional American fare. Even breakfast can get fancy here, with entrées such as quail eggs and sautéed quail with grits. Both Ivy's, a plush window-walled lounge offering complimentary cocktail-hour hors d'oeuvres, and Vista, a wicker-furnished lobby lounge, overlook the pool. Classical music is played in all public areas and restaurants here.

Services: Complimentary *USA Today* at front desk, 24-hour room service, airport limo, concierge (who sells tickets to all park attractions).

Facilities: Two nightlit tennis courts, two 18-hole championship golf courses, full business/meeting facilities, gift shop, health club, indoor swimming pool, large outdoor pool, whirlpools, kiddie pool, sundeck.

INEXPENSIVE

Ⓢ Stone Mountain Park Inn

Stone Mountain Park, Stone Mountain, GA 30086 ☎ **404/469-3311** or 800/277-0007. Fax 404/498-5691. 92 rms. A/C TV TEL. $59–$125 for one or two people (rates vary seasonally). Extra person $10. Children under 12 stay free in parents' room. Honeymoon package $130, including a bottle of champagne and breakfast. Golf and other packages available. AE, CB, DC, MC, V. Parking free (self only).

This charming inn is housed in a two-story white-colonnaded brick building that wraps around a central courtyard. Rooms are lovely, featuring Chippendale-reproduction furnishings, turn-of-the-century-style ceiling fan/lighting fixtures, and framed Williamsburg sampler embroideries. Most have large vanity/dressing room areas and spacious parlors. Honeymoon suites offer king-size, four-poster beds. Almost all accommodations have courtyard-facing balconies or patios with rocking chairs.

Dining/Entertainment: The inn's attractive dining room has floor-to-ceiling windows overlooking verdant scenery and balcony seating facing the mountain sculptures. All meals here are buffets (very reasonably priced) featuring southern fare.

Services: Limited room service during restaurant hours, airport limo; tickets for all park attractions sold across the street.

Facilities: The park itself offers everything in the way of recreational activities, including two 18-hole championship golf courses. On the premises: coin-op laundry, business services, very large outdoor pool/sundeck in a woodsy setting.

A CAMPGROUND

Family Campground

Stone Mountain Park, P.O. Box 778, Stone Mountain, GA 30086. ☎ **404/498-5710**. $13 for a tent site, $14 for site with water and electricity, $15 for full hookup. Rates cover two people; additional people pay $2 per night. Children 11 and under stay free. AE, DISC, MC, V.

A very large campground, with sections for pop-ups, RVs, and tents, this is a great place to stay. Nestled in the woods, the area has many sites overlooking the lake, especially in the tent section. All have barbecue grills, and picnic tables are scattered throughout. Public facilities include a dining pavilion, playgrounds, laundries, and showers. The park's beach is close by.

7 Druid Hills/Emory University/Brookhaven

Though not a happening section of town in terms of restaurants or attractions, this area, east of midtown and Buckhead, offers good value for your hotel dollar. And if you have a car, the properties listed below are only about a 10-minute drive from the center of things.

MODERATE

Courtyard by Marriott

1236 Executive Park Dr. (off N. Druid Hills Rd.), Atlanta, GA 30329. ☎ **404/ 728-0708** or 800/321-2211. Fax 404/636-4019. 133 rms, 12 suites. A/C TV TEL. Sun–Thurs $99 double; Fri–Sat $89 double. Suites $109 double. Extra person $10. Children under 18 stay free in parents' room. Reduced rates offered for stays of seven days or more. AE, CB, DC, DISC, MC, V. Parking free (self only). MARTA bus: in front of the hotel.

Occupying an attractively landscaped setting of trees, shrubbery, and well-tended flower beds, the Courtyard represents yet another kind of link in the Marriott chain. It's a limited-service (no bellhops, though you can get a luggage cart), moderately priced lodging. But don't picture a spartan, no-frills atmosphere. This property has a pleasant, plant-filled lobby and very nice rooms indeed.

All accommodations here feature large desks, nice-size dressing-room areas, TVs with free HBO and On-Command pay movie channels, and hot-water dispensers so you can make tea or coffee (both available free at the front desk) in your room. Suites—a good bet for families—have full sofa-bedded living rooms with extra phones and TVs plus small refrigerators.

Dining/Entertainment: A lobby restaurant, with seating around a fireplace and overlooking a verdant garden, serves breakfast. A comfortable bar/lounge adjoins.

Services: Airport shuttle, limited room service.

Facilities: Medium-size outdoor pool, indoor whirlpool, poolside gazebo (nice for picnicking), exercise room, coin-op washers/dryers.

Emory Inn

1641 Clifton Rd. NE (between Briarcliff and N. Decatur rds.), Atlanta, GA 30329. ☎ **404/712-6701** or 800/933-6679. Fax 404/712-6701. 107 rms. A/C TV TEL. Sun–Thurs $89–$99 per room, Fri–Sat $69. Conference Center rooms $130–$150. AE, CB, DC, DISC, MC, V. Parking free (self only). MARTA bus: No. 6 Emory stops in front of the hotel.

Owned by Emory University, this delightful hotel is bordered by 14 acres of woodland property. Though it's centrally located—just six miles from downtown—it's peaceful out here; you'll wake to birds singing every morning. This sense of tranquillity is enhanced by classical music played in public areas, which include a charming lobby and a cozy living room/lounge with a working fireplace. Rooms, furnished in Early American–style knotty-pine pieces, are attractively decorated and equipped with TVs (with free HBO and Spectravision pay movies), coffeemakers, irons, and full-size ironing boards. Rooms in the adjoining Emory Conference Center Building are geared to the business traveler.

Dining/Entertainment: The Emory Café, with bamboo and wicker garden furnishings and fresh flowers on every table, serves buffet and à la carte American/continental fare at all meals. There's also outdoor seating for dining or cocktails in a beautiful flower garden.

Services: Airport shuttle, room service during restaurant hours, complimentary *USA Today* in lobby, complimentary morning coffee, complimentary shuttle service to Lenox Square Mall and local MARTA stations.

Facilities: Coin-op washers/dryers, medium-sized L-shaped swimming pool/sundeck bordered by flower beds, Jacuzzi. Guests enjoy free use of a vast fitness complex on campus with an indoor pool, 12 night-lit tennis courts, basketball, indoor track, racquetball, a full complement of Nautilus equipment, and much more.

INEXPENSIVE

Budgetel Inn

2535 Chantilly Dr. NE (just off Cheshire Bridge Rd.), Atlanta, GA 30324. ☎ **404/ 321-0999** or 800/428-3438. Fax 404/634-3384 92 rms, 10 suites. A/C TV TEL. $41–$49 for one or two people. Extra person $7. Children 18 and under stay free in parents' room. AE, CB, DC, DISC, MC, V. Parking free (self only). MARTA bus: No. 47 bus stops at the corner weekdays.

This hotel, part of a Milwaukee-based chain, offers great value to price-conscious travelers. Its small lobby is clean and cozy; its rooms are immaculate and well tended. In-room amenities include dressing areas, coffeemakers, and TVs with Spectravision and Showtime movie stations. Ten larger rooms, called leisure suites, offer refrigerators, microwave ovens, hairdryers, and sofa beds. Coin-op washers and dryers are on the premises. There's no restaurant, but a sweet roll, juice, and coffee are delivered to your room gratis each morning. Local calls are free.

8 Off I-20

Though fairly far out east of town, these two properties are located right off I-20, allowing you to zip into downtown Atlanta in about 10 to 15 minutes by car.

Econo Lodge

2574 Candler Rd. (just off I-20 at Exit 33), Atlanta, GA 30032. ☎ **404/243-4422** or 800/424-4777. 59 rms. A/C TV TEL. $45–$100 double. Rates may be higher during special events. Extra person $4. Children under 12 free. AE, DC, DISC, JCB, MC, V. Parking free. MARTA bus: No. 15 stops in front of hotel.

This Econo Lodge's rooms are spiffy-looking and attractive. They're all equipped with remote-control, 25-inch TVs with HBO, and some rooms with king-size beds have wet bars with sinks and cabinets. The property is just a 10-minute drive from downtown. A Long John Silver's and a Wendy's adjoin the Lodge, numerous other eateries are close by, and free coffee, juice, and doughnuts are served in the lobby each morning.

⑤ Motel 6

2565 Wesley Chapel Rd. (off I-20), Atlanta, GA 30035. ☎ **404/288-6911**. 99 rms. A/C TV TEL. $45.99 double. Rates may be higher during special events. Extra person $3; Children under 18 stay free in parents' room. AE, CB, DC, DISC, MC, V. Parking free.

Located in Decatur, Motel 6 offers all you *really* need in the way of accommodations at a very low cost. It even has a swimming pool. Most of the rooms have two double beds (8 have one double bed), and all offer satellite TVs with free HBO. Dudley's, a western-style restaurant and lounge on the premises (it's like a cowboy version of "Cheers"), serves up steaks, salads, burgers, and sandwiches. Open till 3 or 4am every night, it offers three pool tables, a large-screen TV on which sports events are aired, and friendly conversations with locals. Coin-op washers and dryers are an additional facility.

9 South of Town

Seren-Be Bed and Breakfast Farm

10950 Hutcheson Ferry Rd., Palmetto, GA 30268. ☎ **404/463-2610**. Fax 404/463-4472. 3 rms, 1 cottage. A/C. $95–$140 double. Two-bedroom cottage $130–$175. Rates include full farm breakfast. No credit cards. Parking free. Take I-85 south to Exit 16, follow Spur 14 (S. Fulton Pkwy.) for 13 miles, turn left on GA 154, right onto Carlton Rd., and right again on Hutcheson Ferry Rd.

Thirty-two miles south of Atlanta—amid rolling meadows, horse pasture, verdant woodlands, and fields of sage—Steve and Marie Nygren have created a retreat on 284 acres of farmland. Here they and daughters Quinn (8), Kara (10), and Garnie (12) offer warm southern hospitality to visitors seeking a place to kick back and relax, a romantic getaway, or a family vacation that offers close encounters with farm animals. The latter include horses, cows, goats, geese, a donkey, pigs, and rabbits, not to mention a dog named Scarlett. Visiting kids (and adults) are invited to pet the baby animals, milk cows, feed chickens, and otherwise participate in farm chores. Other activities include occasional hayrides, marshmallow roasts around a bonfire, horseback riding, fishing from a well-stocked lake, hiking trails dotted with streams and waterfalls, moonlit canoe rides, and antiquing in the quaint nearby town of Newman. A rustic recreation room with a working stone fireplace—the setting for evening coffee and fresh-baked desserts—is furnished with comfortable sofas and armchairs and equipped with games, books, puzzles, a TV, and videos. There are also many patios, porches, and gazebos where guests can gather or enjoy peaceful privacy. Other on-premises facilities are a large swimming pool with a water slide and hot tub, an adjoining open-air terrace (where mint tea and southern snacks—such as crackers and cream cheese with red pepper jelly—are served each afternoon), and a communal kitchen and barbecue grill for guest use. A "village" of eight birdhouses draws cardinals, marlins, and bluebirds to the property. The Nygren's window-walled dining room affords gorgeous views of the surrounding countryside and connects, via French doors, to a screened porch with upholstered swings. Here guests enjoy a hearty morning meal—

perhaps cheese grits, baked ham, fresh farm eggs, fried green tomatoes, juices, fresh-baked biscuits, and tea or coffee.

The rooms—all with private bath, one with a Jacuzzi—are country cozy and charming but unpretentious. Yours might have knotty-pine floors strewn with rag rugs, walls hung with patchwork quilts or botanical prints, antique or white painted furnishings, a bed piled high with decorative pillows, or lace-curtained windows. The cottage has its own full kitchen, living room, front porch, and screened dining porch. Georgia folk art, antiques, live plants, and fresh flowers make these accommodations comfortably homelike.

The Nygrens, by the way, are Atlanta restaurant royalty: Steve, now retired, was the founder of the ultrasuccessful Peasant group (including Mick's, City Grill, and others), while Marie is the daughter of Margaret Lupo, who established Mary Mac's Tearoom, a venerated local institution. Marie has additional Georgia pedigree as a distant relation of Margaret Mitchell—Scarlett O'Hara was modeled on her great-great grandmother! The Nygrens are great folks; getting to know them and their kids is one of the joys of staying here.

7

Dining

Although I live in one of the world's top restaurant towns—New York—most of the year, believe it or not I have occasional cravings for various only-in-Atlanta culinary creations—soft-shell crab in lemony red-pepper coulis at Pano's and Paul's plump and juicy fried oysters at French Quarter Food Shop, Rocky's baked rigatoni with chicken balsamico, macaroni and cheese at the OK Café, Oreo cheesecake (the world's best) at Mick's . . . and many delectable others. This is a town that has gastronomically arrived while continuing to nurture its grits-and-greens roots. Atlanta dining options run the gamut from ethnic dishes (Chinese, Thai, and Cajun, to name a few) to the most sophisticated contemporary and traditional haute-cuisine fare. All that and sugar-cured smoked ham with redeye gravy, too!

Atlantans love to dine out. Reservations, where accepted, are always a good idea—in some places, imperative.

HOW TO READ THE LISTINGS

Listings are divided first by location, then alphabetically by price. I've used the following price categories: **very expensive** (dinner is over $45 per person for a full meal, including a glass of wine, tip, and tax), **expensive** ($35 to $45), **moderate** ($25 to $35), **inexpensive** (under $25).

Keep in mind that the above categories refer to dinner prices, and some very expensive restaurants offer more affordable lunches (most notably City Grill) or early-bird dinners. Also, I'm going under the assumption that you're not stinting when you order. Some restaurants, for instance, have main courses ranging from $12 to $20. In most cases, you can dine for less if you order carefully.

Note: MARTA stations are listed where they are within walking distance. If you need bus-routing information, call **404/848-4711.**

1 Best Bets

- **Best Spot for a Romantic Dinner.** When the weather is balmy, there's no better spot than the tree-shaded terrace at Horseradish Grill, 4320 Powers Ferry Rd. (☎ **404/255-7277**) (see "Best View," below). On chillier nights, cozy into a leather booth at the oak-paneled and softly candlelit Florencia at the Occidental Grand, 75 14th St. (☎ **404/881-9898**), its ambience enhanced by lavish floral displays and a blazing fireplace.

- **Best Spot for a Business Lunch.** Few restaurants are as evocative of success and affluence as The Palm, in Swissôtel Atlanta, 3391 Peachtree Rd. (☎ **404/814-1955**), where tables are well-spaced for power-lunch privacy. The food's great, too. Runner-up: Bones, 3130 Piedmont Rd. NE (☎ **404/237-2663**).
- **Best Spot for a Celebration.** The Dining Room at The Ritz-Carlton Buckhead, 3434 Peachtree Rd. NE (☎ **404/237-2700**), under the auspices of nationally celebrated chef Guenter Seeger, is Atlanta's premier dining venue; the cuisine and decor are equally exquisite. A less formal spot is Chow (with branches downtown, at 303 Peachtree Ave. (☎ **404/222-0210**), and in the Virginia-Highland area at 1026^1/$_2$ N. Highland Ave. NE (☎ **404/872-0869**), where a casual-elegant ambience sets a relaxed tone for celebratory conviviality.
- **Best Decor.** The piney Adirondacks-style interior of the Blue Ridge Grill, with a fire blazing in a massive stone hearth, is perhaps the most alluring in town. You'll find it at 1261 W. Paces Ferry Rd., in the Paces Ferry Plaza Shopping Center (☎ **404/233-5030**).
- **Best View.** Even the ride to the Horseradish Grill, along Powers Ferry Road (at W. Wieuca Rd.; ☎ **404/255-7277**), is wonderfully scenic. On the premises, windowed walls and a lushly planted patio overlook the woodlands and meadows of Chastain Park.
- **Best Wine List.** At the opulent City Grill, 50 Hurt Plaza (☎ **404/524-2489**), the culinary creations of chef Roger Kaplan are complemented by a vast wine cellar; follow the steward's superb selections for each course. Other notables: The Dining Room and Bones.
- **Best Cajun Cuisine.** The French Quarter Food Shop at 923 Peachtree St. NE (☎ **404/875-2489**). It looks like a joint, but its jambalaya is divine.
- **Best Italian Cuisine.** Veni Vidi Vici, at 41 14th St. (☎ **404/875-8424**), gets my vote for inspired contemporary Italian cuisine in a glamorous setting.
- **Best Pizza.** Original Rocky's Brick Oven at 1770 Peachtree St. NE (☎ **404/876-1111**) bakes its pies in a hickory- and oak-burning oven from Milan and crowns them with toppings such as homemade mozzarella, sun-dried tomatoes, and rosemary-seasoned roasted new potatoes.
- **Best Seafood.** I often experience serious cravings for oysters rémoulade at the French Quarter Food Shop, 923 Peachtree St. NE (☎ **404/875-2489**), barbecued oysters at City Grill, 50 Hurt Plaza (☎ **404/524-2489**), and hickory-grilled farm-raised trout at the Horseradish Grill, 4320 Powers Ferry Rd. (☎ **404/255-7277**). For

best fresh seafood overall, the Atlanta Fish Market is the ticket, at 265 Pharr Rd. (☎ **404/262-3165**).

- **Best Southern Cuisine.** The competition is stiff; the Horseradish Grill (see address and telephone above) wins by a nose, with the Blue Ridge Grill, 1261 W. Paces Ferry Rd. (☎ **404/233-5030**), and South City Kitchen, at 1144 Crescent Ave. (☎ **404/873-7358**), close contenders.
- **Best Southwestern Cuisine.** Nava, 3060 Peachtree Rd. (☎ **404/240-1984**), a stunning new restaurant with a kitchen under the auspices of a proven southwestern star—Dallas's Kevin Rathbun.
- **Best Tapas.** The ultra-elegant Segovia Bar at the Occidental Grand (see address and telephone above) provides a deluxe setting for sherry and tapas. Sink into a plush velvet sofa and order up crispy fried calamari with aioli, piquant stuffed turnovers, and hot garlic shrimp in olive oil.
- **Best Steak House.** All the major steak houses detailed in this chapter serve up prime succulent steaks, but my favorite for ambience is The Palm, in the Swissôtel Atlanta, 3391 Peachtree Rd. (☎ **404/814-1955**). Great lobsters here, too.
- **Best Desserts.** Lemon buttermilk chess pie at the Horseradish Grill; citrus grits pudding topped with orange crème caramel and vanilla ice cream at the Blue Ridge Grill, 1261 W. Paces Ferry Rd. (☎ **404/233-5030**); Veni Vidi Vici's melt-in-your-mouth crostata layered with almond praline and chocolate ganache found at 41 14th St. (☎ **404/875-8424**); tarte Tatin topped with cinnamon ice cream at the Chef's Cafe, 2115 Piedmont Rd. (☎ **404/872-2284**), and anything at City Grill, at 50 Hurt Plaza (☎ **404/524-2489**), or the Dining Room at The Ritz-Carlton Buckhead, 3434 Peachtree Rd. NE (☎ **404/237-2700**).
- **Best Brunch.** The Occidental Grand offers a sumptuous Sunday brunch complete with carving stations, salads ranging from saffron rice and sausage to Thai shrimp curry, an array of seafood and smoked fish, fresh-baked breads and pastries, egg and waffle dishes, entrées, and desserts—all of it first-rate. Price is $32 per person. Lavish Sunday brunch buffets in luxurious surroundings are also offered at both Ritz-Carltons. For a superior à la carte Sunday brunch, The Palm's the place. See addresses and telephones above.
- **Best Breakfast.** The OK Cafe, 1284 W. Paces Ferry Rd. (☎ **404/233-2888**), serves hearty country breakfasts—such as griddle cakes with Granny Smith apples and pecans or an omelet with grits and homemade biscuits—24 hours a day. Great breakfasts, too, at the Corner Café, 3070 Piedmont Rd. (☎ **404/240-1978**), where choices range from fresh-baked cinnamon buns, croissants, bear claws, and other morning pastries to scrambled eggs with stone-ground grits, applewood-smoked bacon, and slabs of country

toast—all served with fresh-brewed gourmet coffees. Another option: a traditional Japanese breakfast (grilled salmon, rice, miso soup, pickled vegetables, roasted seaweed, rice, and tea) available downtown at the Café in the Westin Peachtree Plaza, 210 Peachtree St. (☎ **404/659-1400**) or at Kamogawa, in Buckhead's Hotel Nikko, 3300 Peachtree Rd. (☎ **404/841-0314**).

- **Best Picnic Fare/Picnic Places.** At Pano's food shop, an adjunct of the Atlanta Fish Market, you might procure smoked fish, herb-roasted chicken, asiago-stuffed roasted red potatoes, and tempting fresh-baked breads and desserts. Good places to picnic include Georgia's Stone Mountain Park, Piedmont Park, Grant Park, and the Yellow River Wild Game Ranch.

- **Best Dim Sum.** Trader Vic's, at the Atlanta Hilton & Towers, 225 Courtland St. (☎ **404/659-2000**), serves a dim sum lunch weekdays from 11:30am to 2pm. Small platters—such as lotus-wrapped sticky rice, pork, and Chinese sausage; delicate pan-fried pot stickers; and doughy buns filled with barbecued pork—average $3.25.

- **Best Late-Night Dining.** At 1812 Peachtree St. NW (☎ **404/881-0246**), R. Thomas never closes, and its plant-filled patio, warmed by heaters in winter, is Atlanta's favorite late-night locale. And you can eat food like mom's around the clock at the OK Cafe (see above); try the baked macaroni made with six cheeses.

- **Best People Watching.** Famous beef-eaters—from Atlanta sports teams to celebs such as Liza Minnelli and Frank Sinatra—flock to Morton's, especially the Buckhead location at 3379 Peachtree Rd. (☎ **404/816-6535**). At The Palm (see address and telephone above), you might run into anyone from Newt Gingrich to Julia Roberts.

- **Best Afternoon Tea.** Fresh-baked scones with Devonshire cream, finger sandwiches, pastries, and tea are served every afternoon in the posh lobby lounge of The Ritz-Carlton Buckhead; in the mahogany-paneled Persian-carpeted lobby lounge of The Ritz-Carlton Atlanta; in the Hotel Nikko Lobby Lounge, which overlooks a Japanese rock garden; and at Overtures in the Occidental Grand Hotel. A pianist entertains during tea at The Ritz-Carlton Atlanta and Overtures.

- **Best for Kids.** Rocky's (see above) has a festive atmosphere kids enjoy, and the food will please the most discriminating adults.

- **Best Pre- and Posttheater Dining.** If you're attending a show at the Woodruff Arts Center—Atlanta's major performance facility—dine at The Country Place, at 1197 Peachtree St. NE (☎ **404/881-0144**), Bistango, at 1100 Peachtree St. (☎ **404/724-0901**), or Veni, Vidi, Vici (see address and telephone above). At any of these, you can valet park, walk to the theater, and return postperformance for late-night desserts and coffee.

2 Restaurants by Cuisine

AMERICAN

The Buckhead Diner (Moderate, Buckhead)

The Country Place (Expensive, Midtown)

Delectables (Inexpensive, Downtown)

Gorin's (Inexpensive, Midtown)

Houston's (Inexpensive, Midtown)

Mick's (Inexpensive, Downtown)

Murphy's (Inexpensive, Virginia-Highlands/ Little Five Points)

The OK Cafe (Inexpensive, Buckhead)

Pano's & Paul's (Expensive, Buckhead)

R. Thomas (Inexpensive, Midtown)

The Swan Coach House (Inexpensive, Buckhead)

The Varsity (Inexpensive, Downtown)

BISTRO

Corner Café/Buckhead Bread Company (Moderate, Buckhead)

CAJUN/CRÉOLE

French Quarter Food Shop (Inexpensive, Midtown)

Taste of New Orleans (Moderate, Midtown)

CANTONESE

Honto (Inexpensive, Chamblee)

CARIBBEAN

Bridgetown Grill (Inexpensive, Virginia-Highlands/ Little Five Points)

CONTEMPORARY AMERICAN

103 West (Very Expensive, Buckhead)

Chef's Café (Moderate, Midtown)

Chow (Expensive, Virginia-Highlands/ Little Five Points)

Chow Downtown (Expensive, Downtown)

Dailey's (Expensive, Downtown)

Florencia, at the Occidental Grand Hotel (Very Expensive, Midtown)

The Peasant Restaurant & Bar (Expensive, Buckhead)

CONTEMPORARY SOUTHERN

Kudzu Café (Moderate, Buckhead)

South City Kitchen (Expensive, Midtown)

CONTINENTAL

The Dining Room, at the Ritz-Carlton Buckhead (Very Expensive, Buckhead)

Florencia at the Occidental Grand Hotel (Very Expensive, Midtown)

Pano's & Paul's (Expensive, Buckhead)

The Pleasant Peasant (Expensive, Downtown)

ICE CREAM

Gorin's (Inexpensive, Midtown)

ITALIAN

Harry & Sons (Expensive, Virginia-Highlands/ Little Five Points)

Original Rocky's Brick Oven Italian Restaurant (Inexpensive, Midtown)

Pricci (Expensive, Buckhead)

Veni Vidi Vici (Expensive, Midtown)

JAPANESE

Kamogawa, in the Hotel Nikko (Very Expensive, Buckhead)

MEDITERRANEAN

Bistango (Expensive, Midtown)

PIZZA

Fellini's Pizza (Inexpensive, Buckhead)

Original Rocky's Brick Oven Italian Restaurant (Inexpensive, Midtown)

SEAFOOD

Atlanta Fish Market (Moderate, Buckhead)

Bone's (Very Expensive, Buckhead)

Chops (Very Expensive, Buckhead)

Morton's of Chicago (Very Expensive, Downtown)

The Palm, in Swissôtel (Very Expensive, Buckhead)

SOUTHERN/REGIONAL

The Beautiful Restaurant (Inexpensive, Sweet Auburn)

Blue Ridge Grill (Expensive, Buckhead)

City Grill (Very Expensive, Downtown)

The Colonnade (Inexpensive, Midtown)

Horseradish Grill (Expensive, Buckhead)

Mary Mac's Tearoom (Inexpensive, Midtown)

SOUTHWESTERN

Nava (Expensive, Buckhead)

SPANISH

La Fonda Latina (Inexpensive, Buckhead)

STEAK

Bone's (Very Expensive, Buckhead)
Chops (Very Expensive, Buckhead)
Morton's of Chicago (Very Expensive, Downtown)
The Palm, in Swissôtel (Very Expensive, Buckhead)

TEXAS BARBECUE

The Rib Ranch (Inexpensive, Buckhead)

THAI

Harry & Sons (Expensive, Virginia-Highlands)
Surin of Thailand (Expensive, Virginia-Highlands)

3 Downtown

Your choices here range from the ultra-elegant City Grill to the world's largest drive-in.

VERY EXPENSIVE

✪ City Grill

50 Hurt Plaza (at Edgewood Ave.). ☎ **404/524-2489.** Reservations recommended. Main courses $9–$14 at lunch, $16–$25 at dinner. AE, CB, DC, MC, V. Mon–Fri 11:30am–2:30pm; Mon–Sat 5:30–10pm. Complimentary valet parking at dinner. MARTA: Peachtree Center. SOUTHERN/REGIONAL.

Atlanta's most opulent restaurant, City Grill opened in 1988 and immediately became a mecca for downtown power-lunchers and a high-society enclave at dinner. Ensconced in the lavishly refurbished Hurt Building, it is entered via a marble-walled rotunda with a rosette-and gold-leaf-adorned dome. Downstairs, murals of misty pastoral scenes adorn the walls, candelabra chandeliers glitter overhead, and floor-to-ceiling windows are framed by gold draperies. An aisle flanked by lofty gilt-topped columns and a staircase with an oak banister leads to balcony seating. It's all rather grand, but service is very relaxed and amiable.

City Grill's setting provides a fitting backdrop for the dazzling creations of executive chef Roger Kaplan. A recent menu (they change daily) included appetizers of southern-fried quail served with black pepper biscuits (spread with raspberry and blackberry preserves) and smothered in sage-sausage cream gravy; plump and piquant barbecued Long Island oysters served atop a salad of fried corn niblets tossed with apple-smoked bacon, spinach, bell peppers, and radicchio; and hickory-fired portabello mushrooms, accompanied by a deep-fried sun-dried tomato risotto, with a nugget of fresh mozzarella buried in its center, and fried leek garnish. A main course of crispy soft-shell crabs was served with crunchy lobster slaw on yellow tomato-champagne vinaigrette. Tender duck, slow-smoked on maple chips, came with a savory vidalia onion pudding studded with toasted pecans and celery

Downtown Dining

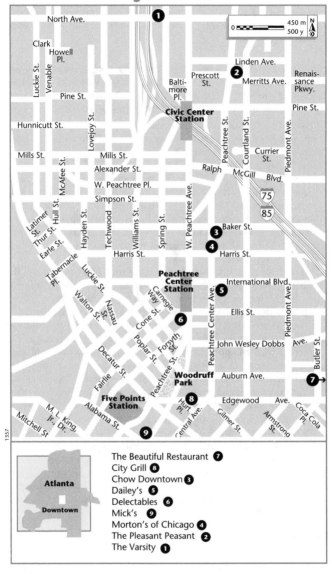

and topped with onion rings and wild mushrooms; it was sauced with ruby grape vinaigrette and garnished with fresh grapes. And yes, it's all as good as it sounds, as are pastry chef Mark Anstey's creations—try a moist chocolate pecan soufflé served warm on vanilla crème anglaise with a topping of chocolate ganache and three scoops of banana ice cream. City Grill's extensive cellar is stocked with over 400 wines (most of them French and Californian) in all price ranges, with about 20 selections available by the glass. Consult friendly wine steward Alan Olegniczak.

Morton's of Chicago

245 Peachtree Center Ave. (at Harris St.). ☎ **404/577-4366.** Reservations required. Main courses $15.95–$29.95. AE, CB, DC, DISC, JCB, MC, V. Mon–Sat 5:30–11pm, Sun 5–10pm. Free valet parking at dinner on Harris St. between Peachtree Center Ave. and Courtland St. MARTA: Peachtree Center. STEAK/SEAFOOD.

The Morton's chain of gourmet steak houses was founded in 1978 by onetime *Playboy* executive vice-president Arnie Morton. His restaurant empire has been as successful as his bunny business, and it's no wonder: These are truly great steak houses. A keynote of every Morton's is a star-studded clientele. Here the cream stucco walls are lined with photos of famous beef eaters ranging from Liza Minnelli to Vice President Al Gore. One night, 15 Atlanta Falcons descended on the restaurant like a swarm of locusts and consumed 56 appetizers in five minutes prior to double and even quadruple steak orders. They worked up a tab of $3,000! As for the Braves, they always order up 24-ounce steaks all around.

Few restaurants offer more in the way of solid comfort. Much of the seating is in roomy horseshoe-shaped cream leather booths at lamp-lit tables adorned with white linen and fresh flowers. An exhibition kitchen is hung with copper pots, and wines are stored in a brick-walled rack.

Servers roll up carts laden with several cuts of meat, a cooked chicken, and a frisky live lobster. What you see is what you get. Do start off with an appetizer—perhaps lump crabmeat cocktail with rémoulade sauce or smoked Pacific salmon. Main course choices include succulent prime midwestern beefsteaks—porterhouse, sirloin, rib eye, or double filet mignon—prepared to your exact specifications—plus lemon oregano chicken, lamb chops, Sicilian veal chop, whole baked Maine lobster, broiled swordfish sauce béarnaise, and prime rib. Side orders such as hash browns or fresh al dente asparagus in hollandaise sauce are highly recommended, and portions are huge, so you can share. Leave room for dessert—perhaps a lemon, Grand Marnier, or chocolate soufflé. There is, of course, an extensive wine list.

Morton's has a second location in the Peachtree Lenox Building in Buckhead, 3379 Peachtree Rd., just south of Lenox Road (☎ **404/816-6535**); hours are the same as above.

EXPENSIVE

Chow Downtown

303 Peachtree Center Ave. (at Baker St., in the Peachtree Center Complex). ☎ **404/222-0210.** Reservations recommended. Main courses $5.95–$8.95 at lunch and brunch, $10.95–$23 (most under $16) at dinner. AE, DC, MC, V. Mon–Thurs 11:30am–10:30pm, Fri 11:30am–11pm, Sat 6–11pm, Sun 11am–10pm. Lunch/brunch menus are in effect through 3pm, cocktails and desserts are served 3 to 6pm, dinner from then on. Free validated parking at the lot on Baker St. between Courtland St. and Peachtree Center Ave. MARTA: Peachtree Center. CONTEMPORARY AMERICAN.

Virginia-Highlands' immensely popular Chow opened this sleek and sophisticated downtown location in 1993. Its casual-elegant ambience (wear a suit or jeans, no one cares) is conducive to convivial candlelit dinners over good food and wine. A stunning interior features a bare oak parquet floor, alabaster hanging lamps, and potted palms. Wraparound windows create a Park Avenue cafe effect (the owners are transplanted New Yorkers). Further adornments include museum-quality paintings, gorgeous flower arrangements, and country baskets overflowing with herbs, breads, fruits, and vegetables. On cool nights, the breezy patio under saillike white canvas awnings is one of my favorite Atlanta venues.

Chow's eclectic menu offers such varied appetizers as smoked Maine trout (served with sliced cucumbers, crusty bread, and sour cream) and piquant southwestern black bean cakes with chunky avocado/tomato salsa and sour cream. For your entrée, consider grilled tuna (marinated in sherry, ginger, soy, and garlic, served with a medley of fresh vegetables) or a hearty Mediterranean-style dish of garlicky chicken chunks sautéed with crushed tomatoes, black olives, and toasted pine nuts, served over linguine and topped with fresh parmesan. At lunch, a blackened salmon salad is highly recommended. And the brunch menu adds eggs, waffles, and other breakfasty fare. Save room for a dessert of rich Oreo-crusted ice cream cake drizzled with chocolate sauce. Chow's wine list features 35 by-the-glass selections as well as single malt scotches and liqueur-laced coffees.

Dailey's

17 International Blvd. (just east of Peachtree St.). ☎ **404/681-3303.** Reservations not accepted; arrive off-peak hours. Main courses $5.95–$11.50 at lunch, $12.95–$24.50 at dinner. AE, CB, DC, MC, V. Mon–Sat 11am–2:30pm; Sun–Thurs 5:30–11pm, Fri–Sat 5:30pm–midnight. Use the garage next door. MARTA: Peachtree Center. CONTEMPORARY AMERICAN.

Entered via a cozy bar, Dailey's is one flight up a majestic staircase. It's a beautiful room, a former warehouse with exposed brick walls, pine-plank floors, and a 20-foot peaked ceiling crisscrossed with dark wooden beams. Two immense train-station lamps are hung on chains from the beams, but they cast little light; Dailey's is romantically dim, with candles aglow on tables covered in white linen. English carousel horses on brass poles are centerpieces, but attention tends to be riveted on a spotlit stage—the marble-topped dessert bar (more about that later).

Waiters, all very efficient and gracious, elucidate the everchanging blackboard menu. On my last visit, there were appetizers of escargots baked in garlic butter; flaky strudel stuffed with cheeses, artichoke hearts, and prosciuttini ham, topped with basil-garlic butter; and a signature dish—steamed broccoli dipped in parmesan-cheese batter and deep-fried. A main dish of swordfish steak was marinated in mustard sauce, rolled in cracked black peppercorns, grilled, and served with mustard-cognac sauce. Another excellent choice: large grilled Gulf shrimp dredged in grated coconut and served in tangy sweet-and-sour sauce. Portions are huge and accompanied by a choice of fresh vegetables or new potatoes roasted in garlic-parsley butter, doughnutlike deep-fried yeast rolls served with whipped herb butter, and a large salad. There's a small but well-chosen wine list.

You can't pass up the above-mentioned dessert bar's array of irresistible oven-fresh temptations. My favorite is the delectable apple caramel pie on a walnut crust, topped with brown-sugary streusel, vanilla ice cream, and ginger-caramel sauce. At lunch, similar fare is supplemented by burgers, omelets, salads, stuffed baked potatoes, and sandwiches.

The Pleasant Peasant

555 Peachtree St. (between Linden and Merritts Aves.). ☎ **404/874-3223.** Reservations accepted. Main courses $7.75–$11.50 at lunch, $10.95–$21.95 at dinner. AE, CB, DC, DISC, MC, V. Mon–Fri 11:30am–2:30pm; nightly 5:30pm–midnight. Free self and valet parking. MARTA: North Avenue. CONTINENTAL.

Housed in a former drugstore, the Pleasant Peasant has all the elements of a typical New York SoHo pub—exposed brick walls, white-tile floors, and a pressed-tin ceiling. At night, the dining room is subtly lit by hurricane lamps on white-linened tables. During the day, you can see that a large ficus and other greenery thrives in the sunshine streaming through a large skylight.

The menu changes daily. At a recent dinner, there were appetizers of shrimp southwestern (five large Gulf shrimp baked in phyllo pastry with cumin/cayenne/chili-flavored cream cheese, served with tomatillo salsa) and piquant sautéed lump crabcakes with seasoned sour cream. Among the entrée choices were honey-sweetened duck in cilantro/jalapeño/lime sauce with macadamia nuts; char-grilled rack of lamb sliced into chops and served with spicy apple-butter barbecue sauce; and grilled filet of fresh grouper served in a rich Calypso stew replete with carrots, potatoes, tomatoes, onions, and green peppers. Sound good? You better believe it. All main dishes include a big salad served with cheese toast and two vegetables.

Lunch offers similar fare, along with soups, omelets, and sandwiches. At either meal, you might order a dessert such as apple-walnut pie with a brown-sugary crust, served warm and topped with cinnamon ice cream.

INEXPENSIVE

Delectables

1 Margaret Mitchell Sq. (at the corner of Carnegie Way and Fairlie St.). ☎ **404/681-2909.** Reservations for large parties only. Small plates $2.95–$4.95, main courses $4.75–$8.50. AE, MC, V. Mon–Fri 11am–2pm. MARTA: Peachtree Center. AMERICAN.

Delectables is the charming domain of society caterers Cary and Nancy Smith. Though service is cafeteria-style, the setting is elegant. Pale peach walls are hung with photographs of Atlanta's original library, built in 1890; menus are propped on music stands; and tables, amid potted ficus trees, are covered in floral chintz and adorned by sprigs of flowers in bud vases. There's also a patio landscaped with terra-cotta planters. Classical music plays in the background.

Everything here is made from fresh, first-quality ingredients. In cold months, order up a hearty bowl of chili served with a Cheddar corn muffin. More filling choices range from pasta pesto tossed with shrimps and scallops to tenderloin of beef with horseradish sauce, served with a salad of ziti tossed with Gouda cheese and broccoli. There are terrific sandwiches, too, like roasted eggplant, peppers, and Montrachet cheese on rosemary six-grain bread. Homemade desserts include fabulous raspberry-almond tarts topped with powdered sugar and white chocolate macadamia nut brownies. Iced tea is served with fresh mint, and coffees are brewed from freshly ground beans. No alcoholic beverages are served.

Note: Delectables may move a few doors down and expand hours to include dinner. Call ahead for details.

Mick's

In Underground Atlanta (at the corner of Pryor and Alabama sts.). ☎ **404/ 525-2825.** Reservations not accepted. Main courses $6.95–$12.95 (burgers, salads, and sandwiches $3.95–$7.95). AE, CB, DC, MC, V. Mon–Thurs 11am–11pm, Fri–Sat 11am–1am, Sun noon–10:30pm. MARTA: Five Points. AMERICAN.

My favorite of the Underground eateries is Mick's, an imposing turn-of-the-century-themed two-story restaurant in Humbug Square. It's fronted by a gaslit wraparound porch enclosed by black wrought-iron fencing, great for viewing indoor "street" action while sipping vodka-spiked pink lemonade. The main dining room, done up in Victorian-saloon red and black, has whitewashed brick walls hung with Early American patchwork quilts. It's a casual but very simpatico setting with candlelit tables and large candelabra chandeliers overhead. Upstairs is a cozy bar. There's also cafe seating on both levels, the upper actually outdoors on a patio overlooking the fountain plaza.

Mick's is great for anything from a snack to a full meal. Nachos here are as good as nachos get—piled high with melted Monterey Jack, cheddar, and jalapeños. Also fabulous: a po'boy sandwich on fresh-baked French bread stuffed with Cajun shrimp, andouille sausage, shredded romaine lettuce, jalapeño slaw, and Tabasco mayonnaise. Yet another option is southern fried chicken fingers served with savory peach and honey-mustard dipping sauces and fries or pasta salad. Whatever you order, leave room for dessert—perhaps the rich, silky-smooth chocolate-cream pie topped with whipped cream.

Mick's has additional locations at 557 Peachtree St. (☎ **404/ 875-6425**), 229 Peachtree St. (☎ **404/688-6425**), the Lenox Square Mall, (☎ **404/262-6425**), and 2110 Peachtree Rd. (☎ **404/ 351-6425**).

The Varsity

61 North Ave. (at Spring St.). ☎ **404/881-1706.** Reservations not accepted. Everything under $5. No credit cards. Sun–Thurs 9am–11:30pm, Fri–Sat 9am–1:30pm. Free parking. AMERICAN.

Atlanta grew up around the Varsity, the world's largest drive-in restaurant, opened in 1928 by Frank Gordy and today run by his daughter Nancy Simms. This fast-food mecca's greasy feasts are an essential element of the Atlanta experience. A 150-foot stainless-steel counter is the hub of the operation, behind which red-shirted cooks and counterpeople rush out thousands of orders. It's a constant chorus of

"What'll ya have?" with customer responses translated into such esoteric orders as "walk a dog sideways, bag of rags" (a hot dog with onions on the side and potato chips). It takes 200 employees to process the ton of onions, 2,500 pounds of potatoes, 2 miles of hot dogs, and 300 gallons of chili consumed here by some 16,000 hungry customers each day. The Varsity's interior is spartan, with tiered seating consisting in the main of large, windowed rooms with Formica tables. Five big TVs are always on.

Order up a chili dog or a couple of chili burgers (they're only two ounces each), with fries, onion rings, and a frosted orange (it's a creamy frozen orange drink). Barbecued pork, homemade chicken salad, and deviled-egg sandwiches are other options. And since none of this is health food (though it's all fresh and made from scratch), don't resist the fried apple or peach pie à la mode for dessert.

4 Midtown

Many Midtown restaurants are a little less flashy than those in downtown or Buckhead, perhaps because they're primarily patronized by locals rather than tourists. But to this rule, the first two listings are glamorous exceptions.

VERY EXPENSIVE

✪ Florencia

At the Occidental Grand Hotel, 75 14th St. (between Peachtree and W. Peachtree sts.). ☎ **404/881-9898.** Reservations recommended. Main courses $18–$23. AE, CB, DC, DISC, ER, JCB, MC, V. Mon–Sat 6–11pm. Complimentary valet parking. MARTA: Arts Center. CONTEMPORARY AMERICAN/CONTINENTAL.

The signature restaurant of the deluxe Occidental Grand Hotel is a warmly intimate dining room offering solid comfort, culinary excellence, and deft, professional service. Pale oak walls, with panels of burled carpathian elm and pleated fabric, are hung with gilt-framed oil paintings and antique mirrors. Seating is in high-backed tapestried chairs and roomy forest-green leather booths. And the romantic glow of candle lamps on elegantly appointed white-linened tables is augmented by flickering sconces, gorgeous crystal chandeliers, and a fire ablaze in the massive hand-carved limestone hearth.

Talented chef Scott Dangerfield changes his menus seasonally. When last I dined, there were appetizers of savory escargots (sautéed with shallots, garlic, shiitake mushrooms, and herbs, finished with a touch of cream, and served over black squid-ink pasta) and quick-seared foie gras and smoked duck wrapped in a speckled wild rice crêpe topped with a sprinkling of duck cracklings. A main course of roasted rack and loin of lamb came poised on a goat cheese and spinach pie with a rosemary-garlic-brushed buttery phyllo crust; the plate was further embellished with baby carrots and crunchy shoestring potatoes. And pan-seared North Atlantic salmon was ringed with steamed green-lip New Zealand mussels drizzled with pesto, "leaves" of quick steamed roma tomatoes, and spinach capellini tossed with pesto. Desserts ranged from a classic chocolate soufflé to a scrumptious warm strudel filled with cheese and amaretto-splashed bing cherries, served on zabaglione dotted with dried cherries. There were complimentary petit fours as well. Ask the wine steward to recommend wines that complement your main course selections; Florencia's impressive list includes Spanish wines, sherries, and ports.

EXPENSIVE

Bistango

1100 Peachtree St. (at 12th St.). ☎ **404/724-0901.** Reservations recommended. Main courses $6.95–$13.95 at lunch, $11.95–$21.95 at dinner. AE, CB, DC, MC, V. Mon–Fri 11:30am–2:30pm; Mon–Thurs 5:30–10:30pm, Fri–Sat 5:30–11pm. Complimentary valet parking. MARTA: Midtown. CREATIVE MEDITERRANEAN.

Entered via an elegant bar/lounge, Bistango features the Mediterranean culinary creations of noted Atlanta chef Tom Coohill. Toting an impressive resume ranging from a Michelin three-star restaurant in France to Los Angeles' chic Ma Maison, he came to local prominence as the original executive chef of the City Grill (described above). His upscale midtown bistro is dramatic in design. Sun-drenched by day via floor-to-ceiling windows, softly lit by night, its earth-toned interior centers on a massive alabaster chandelier suspended from a 35-foot skylit dome. An elaborate dried-flower arrangement in subtle wildflower hues graces a central cherrywood pedestal, and art deco elements include a bold geometrically patterned carpet and colorful Matisse-like cut-out motifs embellishing chandeliers and upholstery. Large

---

🄰 Family-Friendly Restaurants

McDonald's   Every parent knows that burgers from McDonald's are a surefire way to keep kids happy. An official sponsor of the 1996 Olympic Games, McDonald's has locations throughout the city, including one on Peachtree Street that's within the center of the Olympic Ring.

The Varsity   *(see p. 125)* The greasy feasts of the world's largest drive-in restaurant are of course big kid-pleasers.

Gorin's   *(see p. 134)* This place offers the best kind of fast food— everything is homemade and fresh, prices are low, you can have quiche while the kids eat grilled cheese, and there are yummy ice-cream sundaes for dessert.

Fellini's Pizza   *(see p. 150)* The New York–style pizza Fellini's serves is a treat that will please everyone. There's an outdoor patio upstairs.

Mick's   *(see p. 125)* If you're looking for real sit-down meals in pleasant surroundings, the four locations of this excellent chain all serve the simple foods kids love at moderate to budget prices.

The OK Cafe   *(see p. 151)* This casual, low-priced restaurant serves excellent home cooking–style food, and has a special brunch menu Saturday and Sunday.

Midtown/Virginia-Highlands Dining

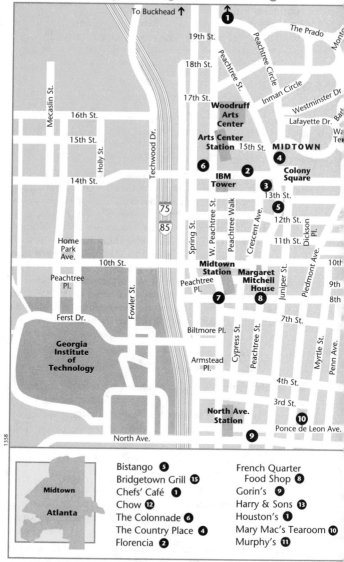

Bistango ❺	French Quarter
Bridgetown Grill ⓯	Food Shop ❽
Chefs' Café ❶	Gorin's ❾
Chow ⓬	Harry & Sons ⓭
The Colonnade ❻	Houston's ❶
The Country Place ❹	Mary Mac's Tearoom ❿
Florencia ❷	Murphy's ⓫

white-linened tables are luxuriously spaced. In good weather, you can also dine al fresco on a lovely outdoor patio.

Coohill's seasonally changing menus range from the French and Italian Rivieras to the Costa Brava. I most recently experienced Tom's refreshing summer fare, which included appetizers of ravioli filled with Gorgonzola and oven-dried tomato served with a compote of tomato chunks and sautéed arugula in light virgin olive oil; thin slices of Parma

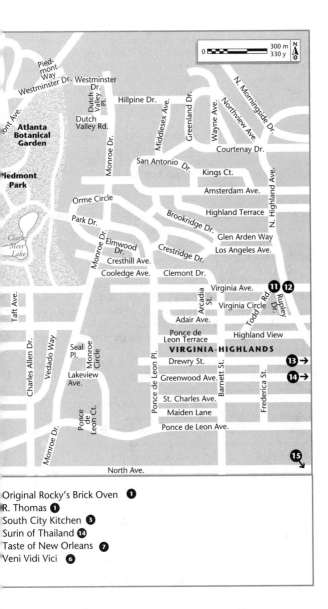

ham served with canteloupe and a crostini spread with dried figs; and alderwood-smoked salmon, grilled, chilled, and served over a gazpacholike summer salad tossed with goat cheese in balsamic vinaigrette. A main course of grilled scampi—made with plumply sweet New Zealand prawns—was served atop a chewy saffroned risotto spiced with Moroccan chilies and studded with morsels of stewed tomato, asparagus, and rock shrimp. And a thick, grilled pork chop stuffed with oven-dried tomatoes, crisp sautéed spinach, and romano cheese was served with chunky mashed red bliss garlicky potatoes and sautéed shiitake mushrooms in a pork jus. Bistango's wine list is first-rate, and the pastry chef offers ethereal endings, such as a buttery bread pudding afloat on rich caramel sauce studded with golden raisins, topped with fresh whipped cream, and garnished with berries.

❂ The Country Place

1197 Peachtree St. NE (at 14th St., in the Colony Square complex). ☎ **404/ 881-0144.** Reservations accepted. Main courses $6.95–$10.95 at lunch and brunch, $10.95–$22.95 at dinner (burgers, salads, and sandwiches $7.95–$8.95). AE, CB, DC, MC, V. Mon–Fri 11:30am–2:30pm, Sun 11am–3pm; Sun–Thurs 5:30–11pm, Fri–Sat 5:30pm–midnight. Free validated parking in the Colony Sq. lot. MARTA: Arts Center. CREATIVE AMERICAN.

This charming low-key restaurant just across from the Woodruff Arts Center is a local favorite for pretheater dining and posttheater desserts and cocktails. Its attractions include a pianist and singer Tuesday through Saturday nights, great food, friendly service, and a mellow ambience. At night soft lighting emanates from shaded table lamps poised atop booth dividers, while a wall of French windows makes for sun-drenched daytime lunches. Floors are terra-cotta, walls and columns embellished with beautiful, hand-painted blue-and-white Portuguese tiles. Diners are seated in comfortable upholstered bamboo chairs, banquettes, and booths amid planters of greenery, potted palms, and big ceramic urns.

The kitchen is innovative and exciting. A Country Place dinner might begin with a trio of crisp sautéed crabcakes seasoned with cumin and chili powder, served with rémoulade sauce; baked elephant garlic with marinated goat cheese, roasted plum tomatoes, and rounds of hickory-grilled French bread; or a hearty red bean/bacon/Cheddar soup topped with sour cream. A recent menu offered entrées of maple-basted peppercorn salmon (on pesto mashed potatoes with julienned carrots, scallions, bacon, and whole-grain mustard sauce) and apple-walnut-stuffed pork loin served with whipped sweet potatoes, green beans, and natural gravy. Desserts are of the not-to-be-missed variety, such as a brown-sugary six-nut pie, served warm with vanilla ice cream. At lunch there are salads, sandwiches, and burgers in addition to regular main courses. And the brunch menu adds options such as crabcakes Benedict and apple-walnut French toast. The wine list features many premium selections by the glass.

South City Kitchen

1144 Crescent Ave. (between 13th and 14th sts.). ☎ **404/873-7358.** Reservations recommended after 6pm. Main courses $5.95–$11.25 at lunch (most are under $10), $13.75–$18.50 at dinner ($6.95–$8.95 for sandwiches and light fare). AE, CB, DC, DISC, MC, V. Sun–Thurs 11am–11pm, Fri–Sat 11am–midnight. Free parking in lot behind restaurant. MARTA: Arts Center. CONTEMPORARY SOUTHERN.

Fronted by a brick patio lined with pear trees, South City Kitchen is ensconced in a converted two-story house with charming dining areas upstairs and down. On the lower level, light filters in through large windows and a bustling marble-countered exhibition kitchen serves as a visual focus. My favorite spot, however, is a pristine pine-floored alcove painted pale yellow with glossy white trim. Working fireplaces on both floors, large floral arrangements, bay windows, and candlelit white-linened tables further enhance this friendly restaurant's appeal. Weather permitting, patio seating is also very pleasant.

The seasonally changing menu reflects widely varied southern influences, and the food is enhanced by its presentation on creamy white Royal Doulton platters or in big china bowls. A basket of fresh-baked buttermilk biscuits and corn muffins accompanies all main courses. Start off with a steaming bowl of creamy she-crab soup with jumbo lump crabmeat and enlivened by a shot of sherry. Also tempting: a Tex-Mex–style quesadilla layered with grilled chicken, jack cheese, and roasted poblano peppers. Entrées are likely to range from jambalaya to pastas—such as fettuccine tossed with fresh seafood, chopped tomatoes, and andouille sausage in white wine cream sauce garnished with fresh-shaved parmesan. Or there might be tangy barbecued swordfish served atop creamy cheese grits. A rather extensive wine list includes small signature acquisitions and other unusual finds, plus 20 or more premium wines available by the glass. And daily-changing desserts always feature a fruit cobbler topped with vanilla bean ice cream.

✪ Veni Vidi Vici

41 14th St. (between W. Peachtree and Spring sts.). ☎ **404/875-8424.** Reservations recommended. Pasta dishes $8.75–$10.50 at lunch, $9.50–$12.50 at dinner; other main courses $6.95–$15.75 at lunch, $13.75–$21 at dinner (most under $17). AE, CB, DC, DISC, ER, MC, V. Mon–Fri 11:30am–4pm; Mon–Thurs 4–11pm, Fri 4pm–midnight, Sat 5pm–midnight, Sun 5–10pm. Complimentary valet parking. MARTA: Arts Center. SOUTHERN-INFLUENCED CONTEMPORARY ITALIAN.

This elegant theater-district restaurant manages to create an intimate ambience in a 5,000-square-foot space. Its cutting-edge design (handsome cherrywood wine cabinets, stenciled oak flooring, and sophisticated track lighting that replaces the glow of candles with a pinpoint splash of light on each white-linened table) is effectively complemented by more traditional elements, such as a bustling exhibition rôtisserie kitchen flanked by big baskets of dried flowers. There's additional seating on an awninged, candlelit terrace bordered by planters of geraniums and overlooking the midtown skyline beyond an expanse of lawn and garden.

Inspired chef Jamie Adams apprenticed for $4^1/_2$ years in some of northern Italy's most acclaimed restaurants. His menus change seasonally. A recent one offered an appetizer of chilled octopus salad in lemon olive oil nuanced with tomato sauce and perked up by a spicy crushed-red-pepper punch; it was served with chunks of poached new potato. Another was goat cheese mixed with pine nuts, raisins, and herbs, rolled into grilled eggplant and served with panzanella (a tomato/cucumber salad in a light vinaigrette). Jamie's pasta entrées—which ranged from linguine with clams in white wine sauce (the house specialty) to gnocchi (oven-baked with a cheesy parmesan-Gorgonzola crust)—were superb, his risottos equally exquisite. But the pièce de résistance was a crisp and juicy herb-marinated rôtisseried duck topped with baked artichokes gratinée; it was served with spicy lentils and cipollini onions in orange grappa sauce. Desserts—such as a crostata of crunchy almond praline and silky Italian chocolate ganache served with fresh cream and blackberries—are not to be resisted. An extensive and well-chosen wine list is almost 100% Italian; knowledgeable waiters can make good recommendations. Lunch options additionally include sandwiches on fresh-baked focaccia.

MODERATE

✪ Chef's Café

2115 Piedmont Rd. NE (between Lindbergh Dr. and Cheshire Bridge Rd.). ☎ **404/ 872-2284.** Reservations recommended. Main courses $5.95–$9.95 at lunch, $10.95–$16.95 at dinner, $4.95–$10.95 at brunch. AE, CB, DC, DISC, MC, V. Tues–Fri 11:30am–2pm; Sun–Thurs 6–10pm, Fri–Sat 6–11pm; Sun brunch 11am–2:30pm. MARTA: Lindbergh. CONTEMPORARY AMERICAN.

Though unpretentiously located adjacent to a Comfort Inn, this charming cafe is surprisingly sophisticated. Chef Georges Màrtin creates main courses that are both innovative and tantalizing, using only the finest and freshest of ingredients. The setting is lovely—textured peach walls are hung with whimsical oil paintings of rotund chefs pursuing crabs and other would-be food sources, soft lighting emanates from candles and sconces, and flower-bedecked tables are covered in crisp white linen.

Appetizers here might include grilled prosciutto-wrapped shrimp with balsamic vinaigrette and exquisitely light Gulf Coast crabcakes served with jalapeño tartar sauce. As for main dishes the Chef's Café makes a superb spicy paella replete with scallops, shrimp, littleneck clams, saffron rice, chorizo sausage, peas, peppers, tomatoes, and mushrooms. Grilled lamb loin is served with rosemary aioli chilled white bean salad, and ratatouille. Beautiful plate presentations further enhance your meal, as does a carefully constructed (mostly Californian) wine list, with 35 premium wines available by the glass.

Don't pass up the delectable desserts, such as a rich Frangelico-flavored Belgian chocolate pâté studded with pistachios and served afloat an espresso crème anglaise. The lunch menu lists salads, gourmet burgers, and sandwiches, along with a few entrées. Brunch fare ranges from crabcakes Benedict to smoked Irish salmon on a toasted bagel with herbed cream cheese and capers.

Taste of New Orleans

889 W. Peachtree St. (at 8th St.). ☎ **404/874-5535.** Reservations recommended at dinner. Main courses $5.99–$7.99 at lunch, $8.95–$16.95 at dinner. AE, CB, DC, DISC, MC, V. Mon–Fri 11:30am–2pm; Mon–Thurs 6–10pm, Fri–Sat 5:30–11pm. Free parking in adjoining lot. MARTA: Midtown. NEW AMERICAN CREOLE.

Taste of New Orleans offers a comfortable setting for owner/chef John Beck's light version of Créole cookery. A slightly austere gray and burgundy interior is warmed by soft sconce lighting and candlelight. Whimsical New Orleans–themed paintings and posters adorn pale gray walls, and an actual street lamp fronting a mural of a French Quarter brick-walled garden creates a trompe l'oeil effect.

Begin with an appetizer of delicious Long Island oysters en bro-
chette; lightly battered, they're wrapped in bacon, deep-fried, and
served on a piquant rémoulade. Seafood gumbo and oyster/andouille
sausage soup are also first-rate here. Delicate, fluffy crawfish cakes
(available as an appetizer or main course) are seasoned with garlic, hot
sauce, fresh basil, and romano cheese and served with jalapeño tartar
sauce on tomato buerre blanc. Blackened grouper (crispy here, not
charred) is dusted with Créole spices and lightly brushed with Dijon
mustard, topped with hollandaise and toasted almonds, and served with
a boiled red potato and a medley of fresh vegetables. You can also opt
for tender Long Island duck, deboned, roasted, and glazed with a
semisweet Grand Marnier orange sauce on a bed of pecan rice. The
restaurant's peanut butter velvet pie and classic bread pudding are renowned, and its wine list is reasonably priced, with many by-the-glass
offerings. Luncheon fare includes chicken andouille po'boys, jambalaya,
and salads.

INEXPENSIVE

The Colonnade

1879 Cheshire Bridge Rd. NE (between Wellborne Dr. and Manchester St.). ☎ **404/
874-5642.** Reservations not accepted. Main courses $6–$9 at lunch, $8–$14 at dinner. No credit cards. Mon–Sat 11am–2:30pm; Mon–Thurs 5–9pm, Fri–Sat 5–10pm,
Sun 11am–9pm. Free parking. SOUTHERN.

This Atlanta institution, established in 1927, offers authentic and
savory southern specialties. It has an enormous local clientele of
devoted regulars—many of whom look like they might enjoy a birthday greeting from Willard Scott any day—and some of the waitstaff
have worked here for decades. The Colonnade is totally unpretentious
and comfortable, a vast room with seating at butcher-block tables. A
cozy bar with a working fireplace adjoins, a nice place to sit if you have
to wait for a table.

At lunch or dinner, you can order fresh-from-the-oven turkey with
dressing (they roast about a dozen a day), sugar-cured ham in redeye
gravy, or roast leg of lamb, all of which are served with a choice of two
vegetables (choose from among homemade whipped potatoes,
black-eyed peas, macaroni and cheese, sweet-potato soufflé, lima beans,
greens, fried okra, and others). Homemade cornbread and yeast rolls
accompany all meals. In addition to menu listings, there are fancy specials ranging from Cornish game hens to frogs' legs and low-priced
blue-plate specials. Everything is fresh and made from scratch, including desserts like the yellow cake topped with ice cream and drenched
in semisweet hot fudge. Portions are very large.

✪ French Quarter Food Shop

923 Peachtree St. NE (just north of 8th St.). ☎ **404/875-2489.** Reservations not
accepted. Po'boy sandwiches $5.95–$7.50, main courses $6.95–$13.95 (most under
$10). AE, DC, DISC, MC, V. Mon–Thurs 11am–10pm, Fri–Sat 11am–11pm. Free
parking in lot behind restaurant off 8th St. MARTA: Midtown. CAJUN.

This little eatery is 100% authentic; Cajun owners Tony and Missy
Privat (they met in a Louisiana cooking school) grew up on this

cuisine and know its every nuance. Their restaurant is unpretentious—almost a joint—decorated in black and gold (colors of the New Orleans Saints), with burgundy plastic cloths on the tables. Cajun/zydeco music adds ambience. I like to sit on the patio out front, which is heated and enclosed by plastic flaps in cool weather.

Everything here is just scrumptious. Daily-changing soups range from dark, rich, spicy gumbos, thickened with roux, to velvety oyster-andouille bisque. Cajun signature dishes—red beans and rice, po'boy and muffaletta sandwiches, crawfish étouffée, and jambalaya—reach their culinary apogee here, and plumply juicy lightly battered fried oysters, served with rémoulade sauce, rice, beans, and Cajun fries, are memorable.

One of the best things I ever tasted was a special here of fried soft-shell crab stuffed with béchamel-sauced crawfish in a roasted garlic cream sauce. For dessert, the pièce de résistance is nutmeg/cinnamon-flavored bread pudding. Studded with crushed pineapple, pecans, and raisins, it's smothered in fresh whipped cream and buttery bourbon sauce. The French Quarter serves beer and wine. A small on-premises shop sells Louisiana food products.

Gorin's

620 Peachtree St. (between Ponce de Leon and North aves.). ☎ **404/874-0550.** Reservations not accepted. Everything under $5. No credit cards. Mon–Fri 9:30am–5pm, Sat–Sun 10am–6pm; open till show time for many Fox Theatre events. Parking difficult on street. MARTA: North Avenue. AMERICAN/ICE CREAM.

Gorin's homemade ice cream is Atlanta's answer to Häagen-Dazs. And Gorin's locations, which also serve food in an ice-cream-parlor setting, are a great choice for casual meals with the kids. Not only is the ice cream homemade, sandwich meats and salads are also freshly prepared on the premises. Menu selections include a classic Reuben sandwich with Thousand Island dressing, ham and cheese with honey mustard on grilled egg bread, an almond chicken/pasta salad platter, and homemade soups. For dessert there are oven-fresh cakes and, of course, ice cream, over 200 flavors—everything from amaretto almond to peach cobbler. Light ice creams, frozen yogurts, sherbets, and sorbets are also served, as, of course, are milk shakes, malts, ice-cream sodas, and sundaes. In nice weather you can indulge at tables on the front patio.

A few blocks from this location is **Gorin's Diner,** at 1170 Peachtree St., at 14th Street (☎ **404/892-2500**). Similar fare—but with a broader menu including items such as grilled Cajun chicken with rémoulade sauce—is served here in a re-creation of a classic American diner, complete with stainless-steel facade, gleaming neon, and checkerboard-tile floors. Open Sunday to Thursday from 7am to midnight, Friday and Saturday from 7am to 2am. Check your phone book for other locations.

Houston's

2166 Peachtree Rd. (at Colonial Homes Dr. in the Brookwood Square Shopping Center). ☎ **404/351-2442.** Reservations not accepted; arrive off-peak hours. Burgers and salads $5.95–$8.95; main courses $8.25–$16.95. AE, MC, V. Sun–Thurs 11am–11pm, Fri–Sat 11am–midnight. Free parking. AMERICAN.

Part of an Atlanta-based chain with restaurants throughout the country, Houston's serves up lavish portions of fresh, first-quality fare. The spacious dining room has a rustic ambience, with exposed brick walls and a crisscross of rough-hewn rafters under a skylight ceiling. Seating is in roomy burgundy leather booths at bare oak tables, with cozy lighting emanating from shaded table lamps. If you're in a rush, there's counter seating; and weather permitting, you can dine on the patio at tables with red umbrellas.

Thick, hickory-grilled burgers are served with skillet beans, fries, or coleslaw. The same fixings come with barbecued chicken or tender, meaty ribs. But my favorite main course is the salad of sliced grilled chicken (big chunks), tossed with chopped greens and julienned tortilla strips in a honey-lime vinaigrette, garnished with a light peanut sauce. Marvelous, too, are appetizers such as creamed spinach and artichoke hearts in parmesan cream sauce. For dessert you can indulge in a huge, chewy brownie topped with vanilla ice cream and Kahlúa. A second location is in Buckhead at 3321 Lenox Rd., at East Paces Ferry Road (☎ **404/237-7534**). Menu and hours are the same.

Mary Mac's Tearoom

224 Ponce de Leon Ave. NE (at Myrtle St.). ☎ **404/876-1800.** Reservations not accepted. Main courses $5–$8 at lunch, $6–$10 at dinner; junior plates (you can order them if you're 9 or 90) $3. No credit cards. Sun–Fri 11am–3pm, Mon–Sat 5–9pm. Free parking. MARTA: North Avenue. SOUTHERN.

In business since 1945, Mary Mac's is a quaint and colorful Atlanta institution, a bastion of classic southern cuisine that is patronized by everyone from truck drivers to bank presidents. Jimmy Carter often came by for lunch when he was governor, as does Zell Miller, and the state legislature can almost be said to meet here. Walls in the four dining rooms are covered with photos of famous clients and Atlanta sites (including the original house used for Tara in *Gone With the Wind*), along with murals of the Carter Center and the city skyline. Service is friendly and very southern. You'll find a glass of pencils on your table; check off menu items you desire (they change daily) and hand your selections to your server.

Among the famous entrées are fried chicken dredged in buttermilk and flour, fried or baked catfish, and chicken pan pie topped with thick giblet gravy. All come with a choice of side dishes. You might select corn bread with pot likker (a scrumptious broth made with chicken drippings and turnip greens), black-eyed peas, whipped potatoes, steamed okra, macaroni and cheese, or sweet-potato soufflé. Fresh-from-the-oven corn and bran muffins and yeast rolls are served with lunches; at night there are hot cinnamon rolls as well. Desserts include Georgia peach cobbler and pound cake topped with strawberries and whipped cream. There's a full bar.

✪ Original Rocky's Brick Oven Italian Restaurant

1770 Peachtree St. NE (at 26th St.). ☎ **404/876-1111.** Reservations not accepted. $7.95 for an individual pizza; $14.95 for a pie serving two to three people; $17.95 for a pie serving four; $9.95–$11.95 for pasta dishes. AE, DC, DISC, MC, V. Mon–Fri 11:30am–2:30pm; Fri 5pm–midnight, Sat 4pm–midnight, Sun 4–11pm. Free parking. ITALIAN/PIZZA.

When I want pizza I want to be in Atlanta—at Rocky's—where irrepressible ex-Brooklynite Bob Russo (his father was Rocky) makes his own mozzarella fresh every day, grows his own herbs and tomatoes, uses garlic lavishly, and bakes the pies in a hickory- and oakwood-burning oven from Milan.

Rocky's is comfortable and candlelit (at night), with seating in leather booths at tables covered with red-and-white-checkered cloths. Walls are brightly painted with Sicilian donkey-cart motifs, an enticing garlicky aroma emanates from the display kitchen, and opera and Italian classical music enhance a convivial atmosphere; it's not unusual for local opera singers to stand up and belt out arias here. In fact, as photos lining the entrance wall attest, Rocky's attracts a lot of media people and celebrities. In addition to its cozy interior, the restaurant has a rustic screened patio with umbrella tables (it's heated in winter by a fireplace), and additional totally al fresco seating framed by trellising.

My favorite pizzas are the chicken bianca oreganato (topped with sautéed chicken breast, virgin olive oil, fresh oregano and rosemary, white wine, garlic, lemon juice, red onions, and Gorgonzola and mozzarella cheeses) and the Rudolph Valentino, with sweet-onion sauce and rosemary-seasoned roasted new potatoes. Consider ordering a salad of homemade mozzarella layered with ripe tomatoes, finely chopped onion, and fresh basil in extra-virgin olive oil drizzled with balsamic vinegar. Rocky's baked pasta balsamico is another unforgettable dish— a baked rigatoni quattro formaggio arrayed with chicken tenderloins and smothered in a chicken-broth/white-wine sauce enhanced by aged black balsamico wine vinegar, extra virgin olive oil, and fresh rosemary and garlic. Finally, cioppino here is a hearty amalgam of fresh clams, New Zealand mussels, Gulf shrimp, bay scallops, fresh grouper, and marinated calamari served over homemade linguine with zesty marinara sauce in a round nest of wood-fired Italian bread. For dessert, the tiramisu here is first rate. Kids get free gelato.

Note: For hotel pizza delivery, dial **404/262-ROCK.**

R. Thomas

1812 Peachtree St. NW (between Collier Rd. and 26th St.). ☎ **404/881-0246.** Reservations not accepted. $5.95–$8.95 for main courses, sandwiches, salads, omelets, and burgers. AE, MC, V. Daily 24 hours. Free parking in lot behind restaurant. AMERICAN.

Richard Thomas is king of late-night Atlanta, his 24-hour eatery a mecca for postdisco/posttheater crowds and actors unwinding after performances. Tom Cruise, Madonna, Emilio Estevez, Halle Berry, and Val Kilmer have all dined here after hours. They come, like everyone else, to relax on the beautiful plant-filled tented patio, which is festively lit by multicolored globe lights strung overhead. Don't get the idea this is a fancy place, however. It's supercasual. Comfort is the keynote, enhanced by good music—light jazz or rock—and a friendly waitstaff. Thomas is an avid gardener. His premises are so lushly planted with pansies, petunias, rose bushes, geraniums, irises, sunflowers, and more—that passersby have stopped in thinking it was a nursery. He also maintains an aviary here of doves, canaries, parakeets, cockatiels, and parrots. Open year-round, the patio is cooled by fans in summer and warmed in winter by 12 heaters.

Nature-loving Thomas is health and ecology conscious. He serves free-range chickens and steroid-free lean beef, grows his own fresh herbs, and squeezes fresh fruit and vegetable juices (organic if possible). Come by for breakfast any time—perhaps a California omelet stuffed with shrimp, crabmeat, and Cheddar, served with freshly made home fries. There are pasta dishes (for example, penne tossed with rosé tomato marinara, fresh-grated cheeses, and fresh herbs), terrific salads, sandwiches served on organic nine-seed bread with home fries, homemade soups, tacos, and quesadillas. For dessert, you can indulge in anything from raspberry white-chocolate cheesecake to bananas Foster. Beer and wine are available.

5 Buckhead

Buckhead contains the majority of Atlanta's posh dining venues.

Note: There's another **Morton's of Chicago** (see description above in "Downtown" listings) at 3379 Peachtree Rd., between Stratford Road and Wooddale Drive (☎ **404/816-6535**). It's open for lunch Monday to Friday from 11:30am to 2:30pm; for dinner Monday to Saturday from 5:30 to 11pm, Sunday from 5 to 10pm.

VERY EXPENSIVE

✪ Bone's

3130 Piedmont Rd. NE (a half-block below Peachtree Rd.). ☎ **404/237-2663.** Reservations essential. Main courses $8.95–$24.95 at lunch, mostly $19.95–$26.95 at dinner. AE, CB, DC, DISC, MC, V. Mon–Fri 11:30am–2:30pm; nightly 6–11pm. Closed most major holidays. Complimentary valet parking. STEAK/SEAFOOD.

Atlanta's most famous steak house, Bone's is a top power-lunch venue for the expense-account crowd (as many deals as steaks are cut here), which is provided with notepads and phones at the midday meal. And celebrity stories abound. When Bob Hope dined here, everyone respected his privacy until he rose to leave; then the entire dining room stood up and gave him a standing ovation. And during his presidency, George Bush came in for dinner one night, booking six surrounding tables for Secret Service men (they ate, too).

The setting is traditional masculine-clubby, with deep-red leather chairs at tables covered in crisp white-linen, wide-plank oak floors, and globe-light fans overhead. The walls are covered with vintage museum-quality photographs depicting the history of Atlanta and caricatures of local personalities.

As noted for its seafood as for its steaks and chops, Bone's flies Maine lobster in daily and serves fresh Gulf Coast crabmeat and shrimp. As for the steak, it's prime aged, corn-fed Iowa beef, butchered on the premises. A good beginning here is a salad of crabmeat, romaine and iceberg lettuce, chunks of avocado, mushrooms, and hearts of palm in a classic vinaigrette. Thick, juicy lamb chops (two nine-ounce chops, served with mint jelly) and tender char-grilled steak are prepared to your exact specification and served in more than ample portions. Of

Buckhead Dining

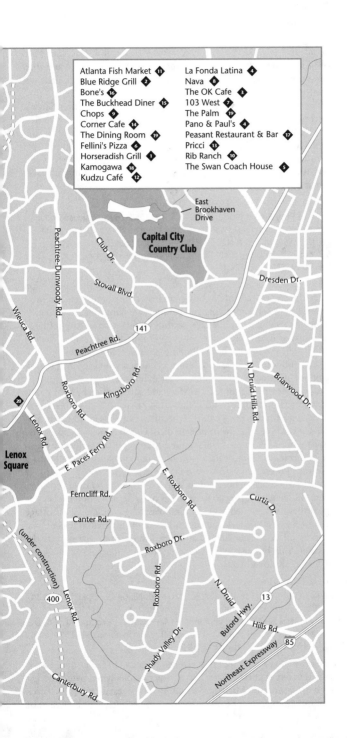

Atlanta Fish Market ◆11
Blue Ridge Grill ◆2
Bone's ◆16
The Buckhead Diner ◆15
Chops ◆9
Corner Cafe ◆14
The Dining Room ◆19
Fellini's Pizza ◆6
Horseradish Grill ◆1
Kamogawa ◆18
Kudzu Café ◆12

La Fonda Latina ◆4
Nava ◆8
The OK Cafe ◆3
103 West ◆7
The Palm ◆19
Pano & Paul's ◆4
Peasant Restaurant & Bar ◆17
Pricci ◆13
Rib Ranch ◆10
The Swan Coach House ◆5

East Brookhaven Drive

Capital City Country Club

Peachtree-Dunwoody Rd.
Club Dr.
Stovall Blvd.
Dresden Dr.
Wieuca Rd.
141
Peachtree Rd.
Roxboro Rd.
Kingsboro Rd.
N. Druid Hills Rd.
Brianwood Dr.
20
Lenox Rd.
Lenox Square
E. Paces Ferry Rd.
Ferncliff Rd.
E. Roxboro Rd.
Curtis Dr.
Canter Rd.
Roxboro Dr.
Roxboro Rd.
(under construction)
400
Lenox Rd.
N. Druid
13
Shady Valley Dr.
Buford Hwy.
Hills Rd.
85
Canterbury Rd.
Northeast Expressway

the side dishes, I like the sea-breeze baked potato (brushed with egg and rolled in kosher salt to seal in moistness), sautéed snow peas, and fried onion rings. Similar entrées are available at lunch, along with salads and sandwiches.

The wine gallery at Bone's houses over 500 selections; international in scope, it highlights French and California wines. There are rich desserts like mountain-high pie—layers of chocolate chip, rum raisin, and vanilla ice cream on a crème-de-menthe-soaked brownie, topped with chocolate sauce, whipped cream, and meringue. And finally, at this unabashedly macho enclave, a cigar humidor is brought to your table on request after dinner.

✪ Chops

70 W. Paces Ferry Rd. (at Peachtree Rd.). ☎ **404/262-2675.** Reservations highly recommended. Main courses $8.50–$13.95 at lunch, $14.75–$29.50 at dinner. AE, CB, DC, DISC, MC, V. Mon–Fri 11:30am–2:30pm; Mon–Thurs 5:30–11pm, Fri–Sat 5:30pm–midnight, Sun 5:30–10pm. Complimentary valet parking at W. Paces Ferry entrance. STEAK/SEAFOOD.

This very popular Atlanta steak house is an extremely elegant version of its clubby genre. Soft lighting emanates from art deco alabaster chandeliers, a coffered ceiling and columns are handsomely paneled in California redwood, and tri-level seating is in comfortable upholstered armchairs or roomy banquettes at crisply white-linened tables. White-hatted chefs can be seen busily broiling, steaming, and sautéeing clams, oysters, and lobsters in an exhibition kitchen; seafood is a real option here, not an afterthought as in most steak houses.

A good beginning, in fact, is Maryland soft-shell crab, lightly battered in seasoned flour and quick-fried crisp, served with lemon-mustard and red-pepper coulis. A recommended seafood main dish is boneless whole rainbow trout with diced lemon croutons, capers, and mushrooms. Meat entrées will require a hearty appetite (or doggy bags), for example, a 22-ounce portion of triple cut lamb loin chops, a 24-ounce porterhouse steak, or a hearty serving of roast prime rib of beef au jus in creamy horseradish sauce. All the meats are fork tender, juicy, and delicious, prepared exactly as ordered. Traditional à la carte side dishes like creamed spinach, jumbo asparagus hollandaise, cottage fries, or a skillet of steak mushrooms are a must. A large selection of wines is, of course, available, and if you have room for dessert the chocolate chip butterscotch pie is noteworthy. At lunch, delicious sandwiches are options.

✪ The Dining Room

At the Ritz-Carlton Buckhead, 3434 Peachtree Rd. NE (at Lenox Rd.). ☎ **404/237-2700.** Reservations essential, and as far in advance as possible. Four-course prix-fixe dinner $56, $80 with appropriate wines with each course. AE, CB, DC, MC, V. Mon–Sat 6:30–11pm. Complimentary valet parking. MARTA: Lenox. CONTINENTAL/EUROPEAN HAUTE CUISINE.

One of Atlanta's most highly acclaimed restaurants, the Dining Room is the domain of chef Guenter Seeger. Internationally renowned, Seeger received the coveted Michelin Star rating for his restaurant in the Black Forest of Germany—one of the few restaurants outside of France to be so honored. His traditional European haute-cuisine creations (with American regional overtones) are magical, drawing the maximum of flavor from the very freshest of ingredients.

Seeger's refined cuisine is a gem in a worthy setting. The Dining Room's mahogany-paneled walls are hung with a museum-quality collection of gilt-framed British hunt paintings. Diners sink into comfortable silk-upholstered armchairs and banquettes at elegantly appointed tables adorned with stunning arrangements of Hawaiian flowers—tropically hued orchids, birds of paradise, and anthurium. Shaded table lamps provide soft lighting, and background music is classical. Service is impeccable ("The waiters, the wine steward, all move in a well-orchestrated dance," raved one reviewer).

Menus change daily. On a recent visit, I began with delicately cubed tuna ceviche with cilantro and osetra caviar garnish in extra-virgin olive oil. It was followed by grapefruit-garnished Gulf red snapper in a croustade of thinly sliced potatoes with citrus vinaigrette. Next came a crispy fan of rosemary-garnished duck breast with date purée in caramelized sherry-vinaigrette sauce. And dessert was a heavenly fig tart topped with vanilla ice cream and garnished with fresh mint and raspberries. Everything is sensational, and presentations, on white German Hutschenreuther china platters, are works of art. A very comprehensive list of over 300 wines is dominated by French and California selections, but also offers many German and Italian vintages. Master Sommelier Michael McNeill, one of only 24 master sommeliers in the United States, oversees wine selections and confers daily with Seeger to match wines for his prix-fixe menus.

Kamogawa

In the Hotel Nikko, 3300 Peachtree Rd. (just east of Piedmont Rd.). ☎ **404/ 841-0314.** Reservations highly recommended, especially for tatami rooms. Main courses $7.75–$19.75 at lunch, $16.75–$28.50 at dinner; prix-fixe complete lunch $6.75; kaiseki dinner $50, $70, or $100. AE, CB, DC, JCB, MC, V. Daily 11:30am–2pm and 6–10:30pm. Complimentary valet parking. MARTA: Lenox. JAPANESE.

Built by temple craftsmen from Kyoto, Kamogawa has an understated decor authentically reflective of traditional Japanese interior design. Its clean lines derive from simple materials—rice paper, bamboo, pale cedar paneling, and granite pathways. And in lush contrast, large windows overlook a classic Japanese garden—a serene backdrop of waterfalls, carefully placed rocks and plants, and a "teahouse" structure meant for meditation.

Dining at Kamogawa, you'll experience subtle nuances of food preparation and presentation. Every aesthetic element is considered. An appetizer of grilled salmon with shiitake mushrooms, for instance, comes wrapped in an artistically knotted leaf secured by a bamboo skewer; it's served on a lovely ceramic fan with a cherry blossom. And dobinmushi—an exotically herbed consommé infused with shrimp, chicken, oyster mushrooms, and gingko nuts—is served in a delicate ceramic spouted pot from which the soup is poured into a beautiful little dish and sipped. One of my favorite entrées here is filets of yellowtail tuna basted with teriyaki sauce and grilled to a crisp, aromatic flavor enhanced by ginger and shredded burdock root. And a unique delicacy is nasu dengaku—a deep-fried eggplant dish; the cooked pulp is scooped out, mashed with sweet rice wine and a soupçon of miso sauce, stuffed into the shell, and served caramelized with ginger and shrimp garnishes. Plum wines and sake are essential accompaniments, though your server can also recommend appropriate French and California wines. A specialty here is the prix-fixe kaiseki dinner, an esoteric ceremonial meal with multiple courses selected by the chef.

103 West

103 W. Paces Ferry Rd. (off Peachtree Rd.). ☎ **404/233-5993.** Reservations recommended. Main courses $15.50–$26.75 (most under $20). AE, CB, DC, DISC, MC, V. Mon–Sat 6–11pm. Complimentary valet parking. FRENCH-INFLUENCED CONTEMPORARY AMERICAN.

Unrestrained Victorian opulence is the keynote of 103 West, from its porte-cochère entranceway lit by 19th-century coach lights to its posh interior with rose silk moiré wall coverings, Venetian sky-painted domes, and Aubusson tapestries. Walls are hung with gilt-framed mirrors and oil paintings, plants in ornately carved urns grace faux-marble columns, and arched windows are framed by heavy silk draperies. A pianist entertains during dinner.

Begin your meal with an appetizer of thick, scallion-studded crabcakes topped with a nest of sautéed shredded leeks, the cakes afloat on a basil-flavored beurre blanc sauce ringed with red-pepper rouille. Also superb are shrimp- and lobster-filled ravioli in lobster bisque garnished with cilantro and sour cream. Main dishes—all accompanied by a beautiful bouquetière of vegetables—include roasted duck breast with peppered red wine sauce and a gratin of turnips and plums; Dover sole rolled with lemony garlic butter, dredged in brioche crumbs, and quickly deep-fried; and pinkly juicy roast rack of lamb seasoned with rosemary. The dessert menu offers many temptations—a luscious crème brûlée and hot soufflé Grand Marnier served with cold vanilla sauce, among others—but most tempting is the sampler of six. An extensive wine list offers over 600 wines, 54 of them available by the glass.

✪ The Palm

In Swissôtel, 3391 Peachtree Rd. (between Lenox and Piedmont rds.). ☎ **404/814-1955.** Reservations recommended. Main courses $8.50–$14 at lunch, $7.50–$15 (many under $10) at brunch, $14–$27.50 at dinner. AE, CB, DC, MC, V. Daily 11:30am–11pm. Complimentary valet parking. STEAK/CHOPS/SEAFOOD/ PASTA.

New York's legendary purveyor of juicy prime steaks and succulent outsized lobsters—established in 1926 and still run by its founding family—now has a branch in Atlanta, and it's a beauty. Glossy oak floors, soft sconce lighting, a lofty pressed-tin ceiling, potted palms, and white-linened tables well spaced for power-lunch privacy, create the classic Palm setting—a setting that would not be complete without the restaurant's signature oak-wainscoted "Wall of Fame," plastered with celebrity caricatures—everyone from Frank Sinatra to famous locals Jane Fonda and Ted Turner. Additional dining areas include a convivial bar and a flower-bordered awninged patio, candlelit at night.

Food preparation is simple here (nothing is drizzled, infused, or nuanced); the emphasis is on the freshest fish and seafood, the highest-quality cuts of meat—all served up in satisfying hungry-man portions. Great starters include shrimp Bruno (sautéed and served in a buttery/Dijon mustard/white wine sauce) and baked clams oreganata redolent of garlic and browned to perfection. Salads are perfected by superlative blue cheese dressing (ask for it). The Palm is famous for its steak and lobster entrées; other excellent choices are fluffy jumbo lump crabcakes and al dente linguine with garlicky white clam sauce. And at lunch, I adore the lobster salad in rémoulade dressing. The wine list nicely complements the menu, while desserts include a superbly light and creamy New York cheesecake. Do consider the reasonably priced Sunday brunch; it features entrées ranging from waffles topped with fresh berries and whipped cream to leg of lamb slow-roasted with garlic and rosemary, served with garlic mashed potatoes. A cocktail is included.

EXPENSIVE

Blue Ridge Grill

1261 W. Paces Ferry Rd. (just east of Northside Pkwy. in the Paces Ferry Plaza Shopping Center). ☎ **404/233-5030.** Reservations not accepted. Main courses $6.95–$13.95 at lunch and brunch, $12.95–$24.95 (most under $18) at dinner. AE, DISC, MC, V. Daily 11:30am–3pm and 5:30–11pm. Complimentary valet parking. SOPHISTICATED SOUTHERN.

The Blue Ridge Grill's inviting Adirondacks-style interior has the woodsy warmth of a national park lodge. Antique canoes and turn-of-the-century Central Asian rugs adorn the rafters of a soaring knotty-pine ceiling that is supported by stone and rough-hewn wood pillars from a Georgia cotton mill, and walls are comprised of weathered logs. Stunning flower arrangements add upscale elegance to the rusticity, as does the soft light that emanates from a wood fire ablaze in the massive stone hearth, a gleaming copper-hooded rôtisserie kitchen, and the glow of shaded brass lamps on white-linened tables. Consider adjourning for dessert or after-dinner drinks to the cozy screened porch.

Chef Bob Carter puts a sophisticated spin on traditional southern fare. An appetizer of hickory-grilled quail stuffed with pecan-apple spoon bread is served atop a sweet corn/spinach compote and topped with julienned fried leeks; its sauce is flavored with Red Brick ale and molasses. A must here is a salad course of mixed greens tossed with roasted walnuts and pears in zingy blue cheese dressing. As for entrées, crabcakes—made with a mix of crabmeat and smoked trout, served over creamed leeks, and topped, once again, with julienned fried leeks—are divine. Also very good are iron-skillet trout sprinkled with crunchy roasted pecans and barbecued pork chops with spicy tomato jam. A loaf of hot sourdough bread, spicy peach chutney, and two vegetables accompany each main dish. A uniquely southern dessert of citrus grits pudding topped with orange crème caramel and vanilla ice cream yields an ambrosial mix of tastes and textures. The Grill's wine list is extensive. Lunch fare includes sandwiches, and brunch offers the likes of shrimp-andouille sausage hash with poached eggs and tomato hollandaise.

Note: Driving here along beautiful Paces Ferry Road, remember you're looking for Northside Parkway—not Northside Drive—which you'll pass first.

✪ Horseradish Grill

4320 Powers Ferry Rd. (at W. Wieuca Rd.). ☎ **404/255-7277.** Reservations not accepted. Main courses $5.95–$14.95 at lunch (most items under $10), $11.50–$19.95 at dinner. AE, CB, DC, DISC, ER, MC, V. Mon–Thurs 11:30am–10pm, Fri 11:30am–11pm, Sat 11:30am–3pm and 5–11pm, Sun 11am–3pm and 5–9pm. Complimentary valet parking. Bus 38. SOUTHERN REGIONAL REVIVAL.

This restaurant had a previous incarnation as the Red Barn Inn, and it still retains some of the rustic components that name evokes—barnwood walls hung with horse tack and equestrian photographs, a raftered pine ceiling, a massive stone fireplace, and rows of upholstered pine booths vaguely suggestive of horse stalls. Big windows overlook a vegetable garden on one side, Chastain Park on the other. What was previously a porch now comprises an intimate dining area adjoining an elegant bar. And perhaps the Grill's most alluring attribute is its flower-bordered garden patio overlooking the park, with seating amid lush foliage under ancient oaks.

The kitchen here is in the capable hands of Scott Peacock, former chef of two Georgia governors. His appetizers are hearty—foccacialike Georgia flat bread topped with crunchy caramelized onions, toasted pecans, goat cheese, and fresh rosemary; pecan-crusted baked goat cheese served on arugula salad with candied figs; and hot Georgia browns—smoked turkey in creamy Mornay sauce topped with crumbled bacon and poised atop buttermilk biscuits. The entrée of choice is hickory-grilled farm-raised trout wrapped in bacon and drizzled with an aiolilike onion-mayonnaise sauce; it's served with yummy mashed potatoes and garlicky string beans. Skillet-fried chicken is also tender and flavorful here. At lunch there are sandwiches (try the oyster po'boy), and the brunch menu adds items such as eggs and country ham steak with redeye gravy. In keeping with the restaurant's regional theme, the wine list—which includes numerous by-the-glass selections—is predominantly, but not completely, American. Lemon buttermilk chess pie with bourbon whipped cream (*see recipe on p. 146*) is the not-to-be-missed dessert.

Nava

3060 Peachtree Rd. (at W. Paces Ferry Rd.). ☎ **404/240-1984.** Reservations recommended. Totopos $2.50–$5; main courses $10–$14 at lunch (sandwiches $7–$10), $15–$24.50 at dinner. AE, DC, DISC, MC, V. Sun–Thurs 5:30–11pm, Fri–Sat 5pm–midnight; Sat–Sun 10:30am–3pm. Complimentary valet parking. CONTEMPORARY SOUTHWESTERN.

Nava's tri-level earth-toned interior is gorgeous, with a bundled spruce ceiling beamed with tree trunks; a kiva-style fireplace on the upper tier; a copper-hooded exhibition kitchen; and a rustic-elegant decorative scheme that utilizes southwestern art as well as Native American blankets, pottery, and petroglyph motifs. Large windows are framed by shutterlike willow twig *sombrajes* and diffused lighting issues from jewel-toned copper and steel chandeliers fitted with hand-blown glass. A beautiful brick terrace offers seating amid holly, pear, and river birch trees; candlelit tables out here overlook a flower-bordered reflecting pool and waterfall.

Chef Kevin Rathbun, formerly of Dallas' famed Baby Routh, is a rising star on the national culinary scene who has consistently garnered rave reviews. A typical dinner here might begin with mussels dry roasted in a very hot iron skillet and served in spicy chipotle broth with cayenne-nuanced sunflower seed Indian bread. Rathbun creates an entrée of chile-cured lamb by rubbing the meat with ancho chilies, cilantro, and garlic and grilling it to crusty perfection outside, pink juiciness within; it's served with red pepper chilliquiles composed of tortilla, Monterey Jack cheese, chilies, pepper, sweated onion, and garlic. Another entrée, sautéed filet of red snapper, is crusted with sun-dried corn ground up with chilies and cilantro; it's served with whipped potatoes spread with chili oil and corn garnish. At lunch there are sandwiches stuffed with goodies like grilled shrimp and cilantro aioli. And at either meal you can enjoy totopos (a southwestern answer to tapas). For dessert, try warm Mexican chocolate crispy cake served atop mango coulis with cinnamon whipped cream. Nava's extensive list of Californian and French wines was composed to complement southwestern dishes. There's also a large selection of tequilas and beers, and—a bow to Atlanta—peach margaritas.

✪ Pano's & Paul's

1232 W. Paces Ferry Rd. (at Northside Pkwy., in the West Paces Ferry Shopping Center). ☎ **404/261**-3662. Reservations recommended. Main courses $15.95–$27.95. AE, CB, DC, DISC, MC, V. Mon–Thurs 6–10:30pm, Fri–Sat 6–11pm. Free parking. AMERICAN/CONTINENTAL.

When Pano and Paul opened their deluxe dining emporium in 1979, they brought big-city sophistication to Atlanta's restaurant scene. For over a decade, they've continued to dazzle the dining public with culinary creations that have garnered countless awards. Well-heeled Atlanta business and society people consider the place a kind of posh private club. And very posh it is, with intimate canopied booths framed by forest-green velvet curtains; delicate vases of fresh-cut flowers on rose damask-clothed tables; ornate gilt-framed mirrors; and antique chandeliers and wall sconces. A pianist entertains nightly in the opulent adjoining piano bar.

Dinner here might begin with an appetizer of spinach- and ricotta-filled tortellini tossed in browned butter with fresh sage leaves and walnuts. Or you might opt for house-smoked salmon on a potato pancake. In season, be sure to order an entrée of soft-shell crabs, lightly battered and sautéed crisp, a succulent treat served with white lemon butter and red-pepper coulis. Also highly recommendable is the grilled filet of lightly smoked salmon with Pommery honey cream, served on a bed of vegetable "noodles" with fried mashed potatoes. Yet another suggestion: crisp Chinese-style roast duck in orange-ginger sauce, served with wild rice and asparagus. Desserts are lush—from a classic crème brûlée to Kahlúa-flavored ice-cream pie with Oreo crust, topped with bourbon-flavored whipped cream, roasted pecans, and chocolate sauce.

The Peasant Restaurant & Bar

3402 Piedmont Rd. NE (a block north of Peachtree Rd.). ☎ **404/231-8740.**
Reservations accepted. Main courses $8.95–$10.95 at lunch/brunch, $10.95–$20.95 at dinner. AE, DC, DISC, MC, V. Sun–Fri 11:30am–2:30pm; Sun–Thurs 5:30–10pm, Fri–Sat 5:30–11pm. Complimentary valet parking. CONTEMPORARY AMERICAN.

The Peasant group owns 18 restaurants in Atlanta, many of which are described above (Mick's, The Country Place, the Pleasant Peasant, Dailey's, even the posh City Grill). The setting here is romantic, with candlelit tables amid potted palms. Shaded table lamps, English landscape paintings, French antiques, and lovely dried-flower arrangements add charm. There's an elegant bar area, and a glass-walled conservatory section is full of lush plantings.

A Recipe for Lemon Buttermilk Chess Pie

Recipe from Scott Peacock, chef at the Horseradish Grill.

1¹/₂	cups sugar
1	tablespoon yellow cornmeal
1	tablespoon flour
¹/₄	teaspoon salt
4	large eggs, room temperature
¹/₃	cup unsalted butter, melted, cooled
1	tablespoon finely grated lemon zest
¹/₃	cup lemon juice
¹/₂	cup buttermilk, room temperature
1	teaspoon vanilla
1	unbaked 9-inch pie shell
1	tablespoon confectioners' sugar
	Whipped cream for garnish

- Preheat oven to 350 degrees.
- In a bowl, combine sugar, cornmeal, flour, and salt.
- In another bowl, beat eggs thoroughly. Add sugar mixture; mix well.
- Add melted butter, lemon zest and juice, buttermilk, and vanilla to egg mixture, mixing to blend thoroughly after each addition to prevent lumping.
- Pour the mixture into the unbaked pie shell; bake for 30 to 45 minutes or until the top is golden brown and custard is set.
- Remove pie to rack; cool completely.
- Sprinkle top with confectioners' sugar and garnish each serving with whipped cream.

You might begin your meal here with a grilled quesadilla stuffed with shrimp, black beans, melted Cheddar and Monterey Jack cheeses, and jalapeños, served with guacamole and sour cream. Another notable appetizer is sea scallops in a hot and spicy soy-chili sauce, with black beans on a bed of crisp-fried spinach leaves. Main dishes come with delicious cheese toast and a huge salad. A good choice is grilled grouper (seafood is always fresh here) served with avocado slices, roasted tomatoes, and butter-browned couscous tossed with mushrooms, macadamia nuts, and ginger. The brunch menu adds options such as challah French toast stuffed with strawberry cream cheese. Portions are huge. Desserts are no exception, with lavish offerings like caramel-butter pecan pie on pecan cookie crust, slathered with whipped cream, and topped with warm caramel and pecans. The wine list features California wines; about a dozen premium selections are offered by the glass.

Pricci

500 Pharr Rd. (at Maple Dr.). ☎ **404/237-2941.** Reservations recommended. Pizzas and calzones $6.50–$8.50 at lunch or dinner; main courses $8.25–$11.50 at lunch, $14.75–$21.50 at dinner (pastas $10.50–$12.95). AE, CB, DC, DISC, MC, V. Sun–Thurs 11am–11pm, Fri 11am–midnight, Sat 5pm–midnight. Complimentary valet parking. ITALIAN REGIONAL.

One of Atlanta's hottest restaurants, Pricci is strikingly glamorous. Part of the drama ensues from an exhibition kitchen where a team of white-hatted chefs are engaged in culinary frenzy around an oak-fired pizza oven. A theatrical interior utilizes gorgeous terrazzo marble floors, art deco chrome and brass dividers, rich decorative woods such as African turtle shell sapelle and East India rosewood, and stunning, whimsical hand-blown lighting fixtures. White-linened tables, potted palms, and lavish floral arrangements add traditional panache.

Pricci's fare is the hearty cuisine of Italy's Tuscan, Ligurian, and Milanese regions. Your meal might begin with a crisp Gorgonzola- and walnut-filled risotto on fresh tomatoes. I prefer, though, to begin with one of the thin-crusted oak-fired pizzas. Among the pasta dishes (available as appetizers or main courses) I love the arrechiette (small ear-shaped pasta) tossed with roast chicken, braised baby greens, crushed red pepper, and pecorino-romano cheese. More substantial entrées range from spicy Tuscan seafood stew served with garlicky bruschetta to juicy baby lamb shank in Barolo wine sauce, served with pastina, sliced artichokes, and roasted garlic. For dessert, a caramelized upside-down apple tart with homemade vanilla ice cream was memorable. The lunch menu lists focaccia sandwiches, pastas, salads, pizzas, and calzones. The award-winning wine list highlights every wine-producing region of Italy and features a good selection of grappas.

MODERATE

Atlanta Fish Market

265 Pharr Rd. (between Peachtree Rd. and N. Fulton Dr.). ☎ **404/262-3165.** Reservations accepted. Main courses mostly $12.50–$15.95 (luncheon sandwiches $7.95–$9.95). AE, CB, DC, DISC, ER, MC, V. Mon–Fri 11:30am–2:30pm; Mon–Thurs 5:30–11pm, Fri–Sat 5:30pm–midnight, Sun 4–10pm. The Geechee Crab Lounge and

Porch are open daily 2:30–5:30pm for light fare and desserts. Complimentary valet parking. SEAFOOD.

Like the Buckhead Diner (under the same ownership, details below), the Atlanta Fish Market offers a winning combination of glamour and laid-back casual ambience. Housed in a brick building inspired by a 1920s Savannah train station, it is fronted by a covered veranda furnished with rocking chairs. Diners enter a dramatic interior space, where vast globe lights ringed by brightly colored stars are suspended from a lofty 24-foot beamed ceiling, creating an airy dining-in-outer-space sensation. Plush leather booths lit by art deco sconces contrast with distressed-look pine tables and wide-plank pine floors. Potted palms add a traditional note. To the rear, a bustling exhibition kitchen is fronted by display cases of fresh seafood on ice and backed by a mural of famous Georgia people and places. Another venue is the 1990s room—an elegant glass-walled cafe with exterior cedar shutters filtering the sunlight. The Geechee Crab Lounge is low lit and pubby, and there's also a cozy enclosed porch area.

A vast daily-changing menu offers appetizers such as barbecued oysters topped with applewood-smoked bacon and big fluffy broiled Dungeness crabcakes served with tartar and red mustard sauces. A list of over a dozen fresh catch items can be ordered charbroiled or steamed; they're served with vegetables, creamy mashed potatoes, and tartar sauce. Or you can opt for daily specials: I recently enjoyed a sautéed swordfish that had been dredged in ground cashews and black peppercorns to form a flavorful crust; it was served on white corn cheese grits with haricots verts and mushrooms poached in white wine. There are pasta dishes and salads as well. Desserts include rich chocolate toffee crunch pie drenched in caramel sauce, garnished with fresh fruit, and topped with whipped cream and morsels of toffee.

The Buckhead Diner

3073 Piedmont Rd. (at E. Paces Ferry Rd.). ☎ **404/262-3336.** Reservations not accepted; arrive off-peak hours. Snacks, sandwiches, and salads mostly $4.50–$9; main courses $7.95–$12.50 at lunch, mostly $10.95–$14.50 at dinner. AE, CB, DC, DISC, MC, V. Mon–Sat 11am–midnight, Sun (including brunch) 11am–10pm. Complimentary valet parking. AMERICAN.

Year after year, this nouvelle-diner-chic reconstructed roadhouse remains *the* place to see and be seen in Atlanta. Princess Stephanie of Monaco once stood patiently in line waiting for a table, then returned for another meal a few days later. And local boy Elton John comes in regularly. As sleek as a Thunderbird convertible, the Buckhead's exterior glitters with stainless-steel and neon tubing. Inside there's a trompe-l'oeil Italian marble floor, a "bar car" inspired by the opulence of the Orient Express, and a gorgeous counter of Honduran mahogany with ebony, cherrywood, and bird's-eye maple marquetry detail. Bustling white-hatted chefs behind the counter work in an exhibition-kitchen area. Most diners opt for the intimate transom-windowed, upholstered mahogany booths. Classic recorded jazz (Louis Armstrong, Ella Fitzgerald) creates the ambience.

A contemporary American menu highlights southern and south-western cookery. That means main courses are a mix of Mom and modern: for example, thick-cut grilled smoked pork chops with spinach, cheese grits, and blackeyed pea salsa; crispy fried oysters and scallops with shoestring potatoes and jalapeño coleslaw; and a grilled cheese sandwich of Jarlsberg and Cheddar with plum tomato, scallions, and grainy mustard on three-cheese bread. Many low-priced little snack items—such as tamarind-glazed baby back ribs with fried plaintains and black bean mango salsa—make grazing fun here. Both the menu and the wine list change seasonally. Desserts are great, ranging from peach bread pudding with Southern Comfort–flavored cream to upside-down apple pie topped with homemade cinnamon ice cream.

✪ Corner Café/Buckhead Bread Company

3070 Piedmont Rd. (at E. Paces Ferry Rd.). ☎ **404/240-1978.** Reservations not accepted. Main courses $6.50–$13.95 at lunch (sandwiches and salads all under $10), $5.95–$9.75 at brunch, $8.50–$14.50 (sandwiches and salads all under $12) at dinner. AE, DC, DISC, MC, V. Mon–Thurs 6:30am–11pm, Fri 6:30am–midnight, Sat 6:30am–3pm and 5pm–midnight, Sun 6:30am–3pm and 5–11pm. Complimentary self and valet parking. SOPHISTICATED BISTRO FARE.

The decor of this friendly and casual Atlanta bistro—like its kitchen—combines southern hominess (cafe-curtained windows with wooden venetian blinds, big planters of philodrendrons and sansevieria, flagstone flooring) with whimsical sophistication (pinspot lighting, red and pink neon tubing, black lacquer tables, and murals of workers in the style of Soviet Realism). Nostalgia music (Cole Porter, big band) creates an appropriate audio backdrop. About half the space is given over to a vast marble-floored bakery (the Buckhead Bread Company) that displays about 30 varieties of fresh-baked breads each day—everything from focaccia flavored with fresh rosemary and basil to honeyed eight-grain loaves studded with roasted sunflower seeds. Self-service breakfasts here feature oven-fresh cinnamon buns, bear claws, bagels, muffins, and croissants along with fresh-squeezed orange juice and gourmet coffees. Those with heartier morning appetites might opt for scrambled eggs with stone-ground grits, applewood-smoked bacon, and slabs of country toast. As for the decadent—let them eat cake.

Chef Tomas Lee's seasonally changing menus proffer internationally diverse items. On a recent visit, appetizers ranged from crispy Long Island oysters (drizzled with wasabi mayonnaise and accompanied by daikon cucumber "noodles" in sesame oil/rice wine vinaigrette) to braised duck quesadillas (stuffed with smoked Cheddar and served with salad and guacamole). An entrée of tender grilled rosemary- and garlic-marinated roast rack of lamb was presented in a pyramid over onion-thyme confit and ratatouille with shaved sweet potato chips. A lighter choice was a sandwich of grilled portabello mushroom, roasted red peppers, baby spinach, and soft goat cheese on a focaccialike olive-oil infused boule; it came with potato-leek salad in Pommery mustard dressing. You can peruse dessert offerings—such as warm apple tart Tatin topped by a scoop of fresh vanilla gelato—in bakery display cases. At brunch try a Scotch egg; it's hard-cooked, encased in sausage, crusted with Japanese bread crumbs, deep-fried, and served on roast garlic-cheese grits with country toast.

Kudzu Café

3215 Peachtree Rd. (at E. Shadowlawn Ave.). ☎ **404/262-0661.** Reservations not accepted. Main courses $8.95–$15.95 at lunch and brunch (burgers, sandwiches, and salads $6.50–$7.95), $8.95–$19.95 at dinner. AE, DISC, MC, V. Mon–Thurs 11am–11pm, Fri 11am–midnight, Sat 2:30pm–midnight, Sun 2:30–11pm. Complimentary valet parking. CONTEMPORARY SOUTHERN.

Themed around a vine that flourishes in the South, the Kudzu Café brings new vigor to traditional southern cookery. And in similar vein, its thoroughly contemporary sage, green, and burgundy interior has southern roots (wooden venetian blinds, a plant-filled oak-floored porch area cooled by overhead fans and lit by gaslight sconces, and a display of museum-quality historic photographs of the Old South on exposed brick columns). Dining room floors are covered with specially designed kudzu-motif carpeting, sprigs of sculpted metal kudzu vine embellish the walls, and you'll also spot the curly kudzu leaf on menu covers, lampshades, and server's vests. Most seating is in comfortable leather booths lit by shaded lamps, though some diners prefer to perch on stools at an oval bar overlooking a busy display kitchen. Background music is mellow rock and oldies.

If you've been hankering after fried green tomatoes since the movie came out, you'll find them here battered with cornmeal and served with chunky Créole tomato sauce. Entrées, such as roast chicken with red pepper jelly or hickory-grilled smoked pork chops with spicy applesauce, though delicious, are, for me, merely pretexts to garner accompanying vegetables—perhaps hickory-grilled corn on the cob, apple cider slaw studded with golden raisins, sautéed spinach, and chunky red skin mashed potatoes nuanced with horseradish. You get two with your main course but I always order extras or simply opt for a vegetable plate. At lunch or brunch, a hickory-grilled turkey burger served with cranberry mayonnaise and fries is noteworthy. The dessert of choice is hot peach bread pudding with rum sauce. A small list of California wines—all offered by the glass or bottle—is supplemented by a good choice of American beers.

INEXPENSIVE

Fellini's Pizza

2809 Peachtree Rd. (at Rumson Rd.). ☎ **404/266-0082.** Reservations not accepted. $1.10–$2.50 for a slice; $7.50–$12.50 for a medium pie, with additional toppings $1–$1.50; $4.50–$5 for calzones. No credit cards. Mon–Sat 11:30am–2am, Sun noon–midnight. Free parking. PIZZA.

You won't get chèvre or cilantro on your pies here, but you will get traditional toppings like anchovies, Italian sausage, meatballs, pepperoni, fresh mushrooms, and onions piled on cheesy New York–style pies with thin, doughy crusts that exude the heavenly aroma of fresh-baked bread. Fellini's is a classic pizza joint, and a damn good one. It's a wacky place, very atypical for Buckhead. Most of the seating is at white-canvas umbrella tables on a large outdoor patio centered on a tiered fountain, with statues of angels, the god Pan, gargoyles, and King Tut here and there. A yellow awning overhead provides shade. At night, citronella candles and strings of colored lights overhead make for a festive ambience. The patio is lit by gas heaters in winter, but when the heat is wilting, you can retreat to a cheerful air-conditioned interior space with red plastic booths, brick walls painted bright jade and coral, and exposed overhead pipes painted yellow, lavender, rose, and orange.

The pizzas, regular and thick-crusted Sicilian, are made with only the freshest ingredients. Other options are immense calzones stuffed with fillings like sausage and cheese and tasty Italian salads.

There are additional locations at 422 Seminole Ave. in Little Five Points (☎ **404/525-2530**) and in midtown at 923 Ponce de Leon Ave. (☎ **404/873-3088**).

ⓢ La Fonda Latina

2813 Peachtree Rd. NE (between Rumson Rd. and Sheridan Dr.). ☎ **404/816-8311.** Reservations not accepted. Main courses $3.50–$7.95. No credit cards. Sun–Thurs 11:30am–11pm, Fri–Sat 11:30am–1am. Free parking in lot behind restaurant. SPANISH.

Funky and festive, La Fonda is brightly painted in tropical resort hues, with hibiscus, palm trees, parrots, and other colorful island motifs adorning every inch of wall space. It comprises a small interior dining area with an open kitchen, an outdoor patio under a striped awning, and an awninged, open-air rooftop patio with seating in wooden booths amid lots of plants. Outdoor areas are heated in winter and cooled by large fans in summer. Well-chosen Spanish and Brazilian music enhances the mood.

The food is both fresh and refreshingly authentic. You might simply order up a bottle of vino blanco and a delicious ensalada mixta (tuna, black olives, lettuce, onions, and peppers in a classic vinaigrette you can soak up with Cuban bread). Grilled quesadillas layered with Cheddar, Monterey Jack, sautéed shrimp, and tomato salsa come with yellow rice and black beans. The paella—yellow rice cooked with herbed baked chicken, calamari, shrimp, chorizo sausage, peppers, onions, and pimientos—is heartily satisfying here. Ditto La Fonda's mesquite-grilled chicken served with rice and black beans and sandwiches on crusty Cuban bread (try one stuffed with roast pork, ham, Swiss cheese, mayo, mustard, and mojo sauce, served with rice and beans). There are flans for dessert.

Note: There's another location in Little Five Points at 1150B Euclid Ave., off Colquitt Avenue (☎ **404/577-8317**).

The OK Cafe

1284 W. Paces Ferry Rd. (at Northside Pkwy., in the West Paces Ferry Shopping Center). ☎ **404/233-2888.** Reservations not accepted. Lunch and dinner burgers, salads, and sandwiches $4.95–$6.95; blue-plate specials $7.95–$8.95 at lunch, $8.95–$9.50 at dinner. AE, MC, V. Daily 24 hours. Free parking. AMERICAN.

Though it was actually built in 1987, it's hard to believe this isn't an authentic 1950s rural Georgia roadhouse. A low yellow cement-block building, with striped aluminum awnings and a green shingled roof, it's heralded by the requisite neon roadhouse sign. Within, seating is in roomy leather booths at old-style Formica tables, windows are shaded with venetian blinds and framed by retro-look curtains, the jukebox is stocked with oldies, and waitresses are attired in white diner uniforms. Shaded table lamps further enhance the cozy ambience.

As for the food, it evokes memories of Mom, with blue-plate specials such as meat loaf, pot roast, and roast turkey with corn bread dressing (they change seasonally), all served with scrumptious home-made corn muffins and two side dishes—your choices including, among many others, creamy macaroni and cheese made with six cheeses (the best I've ever had), collard greens, squash soufflé, green beans, and sweet potatoes seasoned with nutmeg and cinnamon, studded with honeyed pecans, and topped with a cornflake crust. Sandwiches, burgers, and salads are additional options, not to mention old-fashioned thick shakes and malteds served in the tumbler. And leave room for a dessert of homemade hot apple pie topped with brown sugar, pecans, and a scoop of vanilla ice cream. The OK is also a great place for country-style breakfasts and brunches. Stop in for a three-egg omelet (with a filling of smoked turkey, leeks, and Monterey Jack) served with grits and homemade biscuits.

The Rib Ranch

25 Irby Ave. NW (just west of Roswell Rd. between W. Paces Ferry Rd. and E. Andrews Dr.). ☎ **404/233-7644.** Reservations not accepted. Barbecue sandwiches $3.45–$7.25; platters $6.50–$15.95; ribs $6.95–$19.50; children's plates $2.95. MC, V. Mon–Sat 11am–11pm, Sun noon–10pm. Free parking in a few spaces here; validated parking 10am–5pm Mon–Fri in a lot. TEXAS BARBECUE.

Fronted by a Texas flag awning shading a few picnic tables, the Rib Ranch is your archetypical Lone Star rib joint. The cozy interior, with dark-stained pine floors and café-curtained windows, is cluttered with long horn skulls, neon beer signs, license plates, and university football banners suspended from a low-beamed ceiling. Tables are covered with homey red and white checker cloths, and of course, the jukebox is stocked with country tunes.

Come here for fork-tender Texas-style ribs that have been slow-cooked over hickory wood and basted with tangy sauce. The beef ribs are the most truly Texan, but the pork ribs are equally delicious. Don't bother with the chicken; it's undistinguished. There are all kinds of side dishes, the best being spicy Brunswick stew—a mix of tomato, shredded pork and beef, okra, onions, and lima beans. Also noteworthy: authentic all-beef chili, crisp fresh-made onion rings, and homemade sweet and creamy coleslaw. Beer is the beverage of choice, and you can have a brownie or blackberry cobbler for dessert.

The Swan Coach House

3130 Slaton Dr. NW (at the Atlanta History Center). ☎ **404/261-0636.** Reservations not accepted. Main courses $6–$8. MC, V. Mon–Sat 11:30am–2:30pm. Closed Jan 1, Memorial Day, July 4, Thanksgiving, and Dec 25. AMERICAN.

If you visit the Atlanta History Center in Buckhead (see Chapter 8, "What to See & Do in Atlanta," below), this delightful restaurant is a great lunch option. Tables are adorned with lovely flower arrangements, crystal chandeliers glitter overhead, and multipaned windows overlook wooded grounds. A vast gift shop and art gallery adjoin the dining room.

The menu mirrors the ambience, featuring fare such as salmon croquettes topped with white caper sauce and served with a spiced peach, vegetables, and congealed salad (chopped apples, pecans, and walnuts in a lime-jello mold). Or you might opt for chicken salad in pastry timbales served with cheese straws and creamy frozen fruit salad. There's even chicken à la king. For dessert, order a French silk swan—a meringue base filled with chocolate mousse and whipped cream, topped with slivered almonds, and garnished with a swan-shaped cracker. There's a full bar. *Note:* You don't have to be visiting the AHC to dine here; it has a separate entrance.

6   Virginia-Highlands/Little Five Points

Make a meal in this charming district the occasion to see a nontouristy part of Atlanta. Come a little early, so you can browse in the area's great little shops and boutiques.

EXPENSIVE

Chow

1026 ¹/₂ N. Highland Ave. NE (at Virginia Ave.). ☎ **404/872-0869.** Reservations not accepted. Main courses $5.95–$8.50 at lunch/brunch, $9.95–$17.95 (most under $15) at dinner. AE, DC, MC, V. Mon–Fri 11:30am–3pm; Sat–Sun 11am–3pm; Sun–Mon 6–10pm, Tues–Thurs 6–10:30pm, Fri–Sat 6–11:30pm. Free parking behind restaurant on Highland, north of Virginia. CONTEMPORARY AMERICAN.

At the very hub of Atlanta's arty Virginia-Highlands area, Chow evokes the casual chic of New York's trendy SoHo district. Glossy cream walls function as gallery space for quality artworks, large halaphane lamps are suspended from a high pressed-tin ceiling (very Big Apple), and bare oak floors further an uncluttered, less-is-more ambience. However, the setting is warmly inviting rather than stark. Highly polished black granite tables are candlelit and adorned by exquisite flower arrangements, the soft lighting is flattering, and a rough-hewn stone wall adds rustic charm. In good weather, outdoor balcony seating under a striped awning is very popular.

Everything on the menu is fresh and prepared from scratch. Dinner might begin with rosemary- and thyme-marinated baked garlic cloves served with feta cheese spread and toasted French bread croutons. A platter of hummus dip with pita bread, plump black olives, and cucumber slices is another option. Main courses include many pasta dishes such as Gulf shrimp and sea scallops tossed with linguine in olive oil, garlic, fresh-grated parmesan, and parsley. Also featured is fresh seafood. Try the sautéed Cyprus grouper in lemon-butter sauce served with yellow rice and a bed of spinach topped with plum tomatoes and a generous crumble of feta cheese. The lunch menu features delicious salads, half-pound burgers, overstuffed sandwiches, pasta dishes, and quesadillas. And Chow is one of the most popular Sunday brunch venues in town (one local critic described its regulars as a cult). Selected lunch menu items are augmented by breakfasty omelets, strawberry French toast, and Belgian waffles.

Harry & Sons

820 N. Highland Ave. (between Greenwood Ave. and Drewry St.). ☎ **404/ 873-2009.** Reservations not accepted. Main courses $4.95–$7.95 at lunch, $7.95–$14.95 at dinner. AE, DISC, MC, V. Mon–Sat 11:30am–2:30pm; Mon–Thurs 5:30–10:30pm, Fri–Sat 5:30–11:30pm; bar and sushi bar open till 2am. Free parking in lot behind restaurant. THAI/ITALIAN.

Under the same ownership as Surin of Thailand (see below), this comfortable neighborhood restaurant offers great food in a friendly, casual setting. Owner Harry House considers his employees extended family (hence the name), and that warm relationship is clearly reflected in the happy mien of everyone who works here. The room is bistrolike, with bare wood floors, exposed brick walls hung with works by local artists, a row of black leather booths lining an upper tier, and tables (candlelit at night) covered with paisley cloths. It's one of my favorite places for relaxed schmoozy meals.

The Thai and Italian menu provides diverse dining choices. For instance, you might start off with wings of angels (battered, deep-fried Thai-style deboned chicken wings stuffed with pork, shrimp, straw mushrooms, and onions) or with fried calamari in a tangy red sauce. Thai dishes include chicken panang in red curry paste—a savory (but mild) mix of chili peppers, peanuts, lemongrass, galanga (a gingerlike root), lime peel, fresh Thai basil, and other spices—served over saffroned rice. In the Italian mode, there's delicious grilled shrimp scampi served over angelhair pasta tossed with garlic butter, oregano leaf, and chunks of fresh tomato. Also an option here: 25 varieties of sushi. And at night there's a satay (kebab) grill at the bar. Entrées are served with big soft yeasty buns—the perfect foil for spicy fare. And speaking of spicy, if you want hot dishes toned down, be sure to tell your server; the kitchen will accommodate. There's a full bar, and first-rate desserts include a rich amaretto Chambord cheesecake on a buttery almond-graham cracker crust.

✪ Surin of Thailand

810 N. Highland Ave. (at Greenwood Ave.). ☎ **404/892-7789.** Reservations not accepted. Main courses $5.95–$6.50 at lunch, $6.95–$14.95 at dinner. AE, DISC, MC, V. Mon–Fri 11:30am–11:30pm, Sat noon–11:30pm, Sun noon–10:30pm. Free parking in lot behind restaurant. If that's full there's paid parking close by. THAI.

This pristinely charming Thai restaurant opened in 1991 to rave reviews, and it has continued to enjoy hearty acclaim for its scrumptious and authentic fare. It's a very comfortable setting, with bare oak floors and candlelit tables covered in royal blue linen cloths. Colorful Thai banners are suspended from a lofty pressed-tin ceiling, and cheerful yellow walls are hung with striking color photographs of Thailand. During the day, light streams in through a wall of windows overlooking the street.

The same menu is offered throughout the day, with specials at both meals. There are many tempting appetizers, my favorites of which are chef Surin Techarukpong's perfectly crispy mee-krob—a pungent rice noodle dish sauced with tamarind and garnished with plump shrimp, egg, and bean sprouts—and his exquisite deep-fried edible "baskets" filled with shrimp, chicken, and corn, served with a piquant vinegar-chili-peanut sauce. Entrées include a hearty chicken curry with potatoes, carrots, and other vegetables in an unsweetened coconut milk sauce. And if it's on the specials menu, opt for neur nam tok—strips of grilled beef tenderloin seasoned with lime, hot Serrano chili peppers, fresh basil, fish sauce, and green onion; it's eaten rolled in cabbage leaves. This is a complex cuisine in which each dish yields a kaleidoscopic spectrum of spicy flavors. Beverage choices include exotic drinks like mango daiquiris, sake, a small wine list, and creamy-sweet Thai herbal iced tea. For dessert there's homemade coconut ice cream as well as mango, green tea, and ginger versions—all fittingly light and cooling finales. On weekends, arrive early or late to avoid a wait for seating.

INEXPENSIVE

Bridgetown Grill

1156 Euclid Ave. NE (between Moreland and Colquitt aves.). ☎ **404/653-0110.** Reservations not accepted. Main courses $4.95–$8.95 at lunch, $5.50–$12.95 at dinner. AE, MC, V. Sun–Thurs 11:30am–10:30pm, Fri–Sat 11:30am–midnight. (Dinner menu begins at 5pm.) Bus nos. 3, 6, and 48 stop here. Free parking in a lot on Seminole Ave. behind restaurant. CARIBBEAN.

I adore long, leisurely weekend lunches, comfortably ensconced in a roomy white wooden booth of Bridgetown's airy skylit patio. Lush tropical plantings, reggae music, and a Caribbean-style beach bar nestling in the corner further enhance the island ambience. And since it's heated in winter, this sun-dappled setting can be enjoyed year-round. The interior is also simpatico, with Saltillo-tile floors and exposed brick walls hung with Haitian folk art painted on oil drums. At night, candlelight sets the mood.

To get things going, order up delicious flaky-crusted Jamaican patties stuffed with spicy chicken or shredded vegetables. Bay scallops ceviche, another good beginning, comes garnished with mandarin oranges, tomato wedges, and pineapple chunks. Jerk chicken is a specialty here, seasoned in a mix of spices that yield an explosion of subtle flavors with every bite. You can order it grilled in a sandwich; as a main dish served with raspberry-tamarind sauce (like all entrées here, it comes with salad, black beans, and rice); or in a terrific salad tossed with greens, grated Monterey Jack cheese, fresh mushrooms, tomatoes, pineapple chunks, and orange sections in mango vinaigrette dressing. Also available jerk-seasoned are grilled pork chops with honey apricot glaze, sautéed plump Gulf shrimp served with chipotle pepper sauce, and grilled filet of salmon in Jamaican rémoulade. After such hearty fare, I think a light piña colada flan is the best dessert choice. Beverages include beer and wine, as well as nonalcoholic ginger beer, an excellent foil for spicy fare. Tropical coolers are also available.

There's another Bridgetown Grill at 689 Peachtree St., at 3rd Street (☎ **404/873-5361**). It's open Sunday to Thursday 11am to 11pm, Friday to Saturday 11am to midnight.

Murphy's

997 Virginia Ave. NE (at N. Highland Ave.). ☎ **404/872-0904.** Reservations not accepted. Main courses $4.25–$6.25 at lunch and for breakfast/brunch fare, $4.75–$11.95 at dinner. AE, MC, V. Mon–Thurs 7am–10pm, Fri 7am–midnight, Sat

8am–midnight, Sun 8am–10pm (Sat–Sun brunch served 8am–4pm). A few on-site parking spots, otherwise street only. Evenings you can park at the Texaco station across the street. AMERICAN.

Murphy's, originally a wine-and-cheese shop that evolved into a restaurant and bakery, today comprises a cozy warren of rooms separated by French doors. Charming and innlike, its softly lit interior has low-beamed ceilings, exposed wine racks, and beautiful dried-flower arrangements here and there. A large open-air patio, cooled by fans suspended from an aqua ceiling, nestles in a lush garden. And up front is the now-expanded bakery-cum-shop, a rustic cracker-barrel setting with baskets suspended from rough-hewn pine rafters overhead and maple cabinets and glass display cases overflowing with pastries, gourmet foods, crusty fresh-baked breads, charcuterie and salad items, and luscious-looking cakes. You can sit at the counter here and bask in the heavenly aroma of fresh coffee being ground. Classical music and light jazz enhance the ambience.

Everything here is fresh. At lunch and dinner there are haute-deli sandwiches such as grilled eggplant and creamy goat cheese on focaccia with balsamic vinaigrette; hearty homemade soups; and entrées running the gamut from a shrimp Créole frittata to thick-cut smoked pork chops served with macaroni and cheese and sautéed spinach. Breakfast/brunch items include omelets, Mexican breakfasts rolled in tortillas, Belgian waffles, French toast, and much, much more. And luscious fresh-baked desserts range from peanut butter pie topped with white chocolate mousse to a perfect creamy custard flan.

7 Sweet Auburn

The Beautiful Restaurant

397 Auburn Ave. (at Jackson St.). ☎ **404/223-0080.** Reservations not accepted. Everything, except steaks, under $5. No credit cards. Daily 7am–8:30pm. Free parking. MARTA: King Memorial. SOUTHERN/SOUL FOOD.

It's not really all that beautiful, but this tiny eatery—one of a chain of soul-food cafeterias run by the Perfect Church—is a very good place for a lunch break when you're touring the Sweet Auburn district of Atlanta (see Chapter 9). There's seating in a few orange plastic booths and at long Formica tables; counterpersons are also attired in orange, and orange curtains frame the windows. A few plants and shell hangings constitute the sole attempt at decoration. You don't come here for ambience but for hearty homemade southern fare. There's always a choice of meat dishes—baked pork chops, baked chicken in thick gravy, barbecued beef tips, meat loaf—plus a half dozen or so side dishes. These might include collard greens, candied yams, black-eyed peas, baked macaroni, lima beans, and spiced rice, all of them delicious. Fresh-baked corn bread is served with all entrées. And there are homemade desserts such as peach cobbler, sweet-potato pie, and banana pudding topped with vanilla wafers, along with an intriguing southern specialty called red velvet cake—a rich chocolate cake that is dyed red with food coloring! No alcoholic beverages are served. Good southern-style breakfasts here, too.

8 Chamblee

✪ Honto

3295 Chamblee-Dunwoody Rd. (between Buford Hwy. and Peachtree Industrial Blvd.). ☎ **404/458-8088.** Reservations for large parties only. Main courses mostly $6.25–$11.95, $3.50–$4.75 for lunch specials served with soup, fried rice, and egg rolls; dim sum items $1.75–$5.50 per plate. AE, MC, V. Sun–Thurs 11:30am–9:45pm, Fri–Sat 11:30am–10:45pm; special dim sum meals Sat–Mon 11am–2pm, Tues–Fri 11:30am–2pm. Free parking. CANTONESE.

Almost all the restaurants listed in this book are very centrally located, but this one's well worth an extra 10 minutes on the road. *Atlanta* magazine calls it the city's best Chinese restaurant. Honto isn't a fancy place. Large and well lit, it has peach walls hung with Chinese art and dining areas separated by carved golden arches. The most important aspect of its decor, however, is a row of pink strips of paper marked with Chinese characters that inform diners (those who can read Chinese) of fresh seafood and other market specialties available on any given day. Ignore the printed menu; instead, put yourself in the expert hands of chef Johnny To, indicating the amount you wish to spend and any food preferences (for shrimp, beef, lobster, or pork dishes), and let him create a feast for you.

On a recent visit, seasonally fresh main courses included delectably tender sautéed beef with snow peas, thinly sliced carrots, and oyster mushrooms in a brown sauce; crispy fresh pan-fried pompano, garnished with cilantro, in a delicately seasoned soy sauce; a superb dish of clams steamed in garlic butter and served in a piquant cilantro-flavored broth (it comes in a big cast-iron pot); and sautéed Dungeness crab with ginger or black-bean sauce. Though these dishes may sound prosaic, you'll find they are exquisitely flavored and very unique. Every morsel is a delight, and many morsels there are—portions are vast. This is also a great place for dim sum (Chinese tea lunch) meals consisting of numerous appetizer-size dishes.

8

What to See & Do in Atlanta

People used to say Atlanta was a great place to live, but you wouldn't want to visit. I'm happy to report that this is no longer the case. You can picnic in one of the nation's most scenic parks, discover important black history landmarks, visit a presidential center or enchant your kids with a puppetry museum. The area is rich in Civil War sites, and, in a related area, in *Gone With the Wind* memorabilia.

MARTA stops close to attractions are listed where applicable. If you need bus-routing information, call **404/848-4711.**

SUGGESTED ITINERARIES

If You Have 1 Day

Head up to Buckhead and visit the Atlanta History Center—pretty much a full day's activity, with house tours, museum exhibits, and woodland trails to explore. Have lunch at the Swan Coach House on the premises. If you have extra time (and energy) in the afternoon, take a stroll around this beautiful neighborhood where almost every home is a mansion. From the History Center go south on Andrews Drive and/or west on West Paces Ferry Road. If the weather is not right for a leisurely stroll, head downtown to Underground Atlanta, see the shops and sights, and have dinner at Mick's.

If You Have 2 Days

Follow the suggestions above on the first day. On the second day, get up early, go over to Auburn Avenue (see the walking tour later in this chapter) and visit the Martin Luther King, Jr., National Historic Site and surrounding attractions. In the afternoon, time and energy permitting, head over to Grant Park and see Cyclorama and/or Zoo Atlanta.

If You Have 3 Days

On your first two days, see as many of the sights described above as a comfortable pace allows. If the weather is fine on the morning of your last day, nothing could be more pleasurable than a day at Georgia's Stone Mountain Park. In summer, be sure to stay late and see Lasershow.

On the other hand, if it's cold or rainy, plan a morning tour of the Carter Presidential Center or CNN Center, possibly doing the other in the afternoon. If you're traveling with kids, spend the day at the Fernbank Museum of Natural History instead.

What's Special About Atlanta

Architectural Highlights

- Peachtree Center, a downtown "urban village" comprising 14 city blocks.
- Swan House, designed in the manner of a 16th-century Palladian villa.
- The fabulous Fox Theatre, a lavish 1920s movie palace featuring replicas of art and furnishings from King Tut's tomb.

Parks and Gardens

- Piedmont Park and the adjacent Atlanta Botanical Garden.
- Grant Park, a Civil War battle site that now houses the zoo and Cyclorama, a 360-degree cylindrical painting of the Battle of Atlanta.
- Georgia's Stone Mountain Park, with 3,200 acres of lakes and wooded parkland.

For Kids

- Zoo Atlanta, with animals housed in large open enclosures that simulate natural habitats.
- The Birth Home of Martin Luther King, Jr.—along with the nearby Martin Luther King, Jr., Center for Nonviolent Social Change, an opportunity for kids to learn about the history of the civil rights movement.
- The Center for Puppetry Arts, with first-rate productions.
- The Yellow River Wildlife Game Ranch, where kids can feed, pet, and mingle with friendly animals along a tree-shaded forest trail.
- Six Flags Over Georgia, a major theme park with more than 100 rides, shows, and attractions.
- The Fernbank Museum of Natural History, with an IMAX Theater, children's discovery rooms, and many fascinating exhibits.

After Dark

- The Coca-Cola Lakewood Amphitheatre, used for headliner entertainment, with most seating on a sloping lawn.
- The Alliance Theatre, the largest resident professional theater in the southeast.
- The well-regarded Atlanta Symphony Orchestra.
- Kenny's Alley in Underground Atlanta—a nightlife complex perfect for an evening of clubhopping.

If You Have 5 Days or More

Take it easy. Over the first four days, juggle the above suggestions as you see fit. On the fifth day, go to Six Flags Over Georgia, White Water, or the marvelous Yellow River Wildlife Game Ranch. Civil War buffs should take in the Big Shanty Museum and Kennesaw Mountain/National Battlefield Park (both can be done in one day). Or do the Day 3 activity you didn't choose.

1 The Top Attractions

During the Olympic Games, the Atlanta History Center, the High Museum of Art, and the Michael C. Carlos Museum of Emory University will have special exhibits. See Chapter 2, "About the Olympic Games," for details on all Olympic Arts Festival events.

✪ Atlanta History Center

130 W. Paces Ferry Rd. (at Slaton Dr.). ☎ **404/814-4000.** Admission $7 for adults, $5 for seniors and students 18 or older, $4 for children 6–17, under 6 free. General admission includes the museum and gardens. House tour tickets $1 additional per house, free for children under 6. Mon–Sat 10am–5:30pm, Sun and some holidays noon–5:30pm. Ticket sales stop at 4:30pm. Closed Thanksgiving, Christmas Eve, Christmas, and New Year's Day. Take MARTA rail to Lenox station; from there bus no. 23 to Peachtree Street and West Paces Ferry Road, then walk three blocks west on the latter.

The Atlanta History Center has, in recent years, expanded its concept to encompass Georgian and southern history as well. The Center maintains a vast collection of photographs, maps, books, newspaper accounts, furnishings, Civil War artifacts, decorative arts, and Margaret Mitchell memorabilia. It occupies 32 woodland acres, with self-guided walking trails and five gardens. Plan to spend the better part of a day here. And call ahead, or inquire on the premises, about lectures, films, festivals, and other events that take place here on a regular basis; activities range from sheepshearing demonstrations to decorative arts forums. When you call, also check on house-tour times for the day of your visit. Plan to have lunch at the delightful **Swan Coach House** restaurant on the premises (details in Chapter 7).

Note: House-tour tickets are limited and can only be purchased on the day of your visit. Arrive early to avoid disappointment.

Begin your visit at the **Atlanta History Museum.** Neoclassic in design (to harmonize with the Swan House), it was built with native materials such as locally quarried granite and Georgia heart-pine flooring; its interior is painted to evoke Georgia clay. This is where you can purchase tickets and get information about historic-house tours (see below) and other on-premises activities. The museum's major permanent exhibit, "Metropolitan Frontiers: Atlanta, 1835–2000," traces Atlanta's history from the days of Native American and rural pioneer settlements to the 1996 Olympic Games. Displays, enhanced by hands-on discovery areas and informative videos, include hundreds of photographs, documents, and artifacts; an entire 1890s shotgun house; a fire engine that was used in Atlanta's great fire of 1917 (when 50 city blocks were ravaged by flames); a rare 1920 Hanson Six touring car; and a model of Atlanta's most complex interstate intersection, known locally as "Spaghetti Junction." Additional exhibits focus on southern folklife and crafts and the Civil War.

Also on the center's grounds is the **Swan House,** the 1928 estate of Edward Hamilton Inman, scion of an old Atlanta family and owner of one of the world's largest cotton brokerages. The house and gardens were designed by renowned architect Philip Trammell Shutze and are considered his finest residential work. The house is interesting not only architecturally but for its eclectic contents and furnishings, which comprise a veritable museum of decorative arts. Mr. Inman died three years after the house was completed at the age of 49, but his wife, Emily, lived here until her death in 1965.

Swan House is fronted by a classical colonnaded porte cochère, leading to a circular entrance hall with Ionic columns and a dramatic floating stairway. The formal gardens include terraced lawns and waterfalls, retaining walls with recessed ivied arches, and fountain statuary. In the entrance hall, you'll notice that the fanlight over the door centers on a swan, announcing the theme of the house.

Family china (including a lavender Royal Doulton set custom-made for Tiffany) is displayed in the dining room. (Note the rococo marble-topped swan tables.) The Inmans took their morning meal in a charming octagonal breakfast room, with windows overlooking woodland scenery and a beautifully detailed vaulted ceiling.

Upstairs, Mrs. Inman's bedroom is furnished with a high-post bed and a silk-upholstered Sheraton settee. Her adjoining faux-marble bathroom has a toilet hidden in a rattan chair (a Victorian holdover) and a huge-headed shower that must have provided heavenly cascades of water.

As you tour the house, you'll also see many museum-quality 17th- and 18th-century English paintings. And on the upstairs level is the Philip Shutze Collection of Decorative Arts—a marvelous array of china, silver, furnishings, textiles, rugs, and objets d'art. A must for aficionados, it can be seen only on tours weekdays at 11:15am and 3:15pm or by appointment. Half-hour tours of the house itself take place throughout the day on a continual basis.

Tullie Smith Farm depicts the life of Georgia's mid-19th-century farmers. A two-story "plantation-plain" house built in the early 1840s, it was brought here along with period outbuildings in 1972. The farm was originally located outside 1864 city limits, so it survived Atlanta's destruction during the Civil War. This was no Tara-like colonnaded mansion—just an everyday farmhouse whose occupants lived in rustic simplicity. The "plantation-plain" style derives from English architecture. It features a gabled roof with twin chimneys and a full front porch with a room at one end to lodge travelers and itinerant parsons. (In premedia days, travelers were an important source of news.)

A bedroom has a rope bed with a feather mattress and a crib that was always occupied by the youngest baby. Here, demonstrations are given on a spinning wheel, and you'll learn that the term *spinster* derives from the fact that unmarried women had so much time to spin. A basket of pomander balls was typical—the 19th-century answer to today's air fresheners.

In a back room, there are weaving demonstrations, and a display shows natural materials used to dye yarns. During cooler months, demonstrations of 19th-century hearth cookery (Brunswick stew, corn bread) take place in the whitewashed kitchen, where game and herbs hang from the rafters. Additional outbuildings are a barn, corncrib, root cellar, blacksmith shop, and smokehouse. The gardens and grounds are authentic to the period. Costumed docents give tours throughout the day, and there are frequent demonstrations of 19th-century farm activities.

Leave some time to stroll the gardens, most notably the forested mile-long **Swan Woods Trail.** It includes plants native to Georgia and the Garden for Peace where you will see a sculpture by noted Soviet artist Georgi Dzhaparidze and Atlanta artist Hans Godo Frabel.

✪ Birth Home of Martin Luther King, Jr.

501 Auburn Ave. (at Hogue St.). ☎ **404/331-3920.** Admission free. Daily 10am–5pm. Closed Christmas and New Year's Day. Take bus no. 3 from the Five Points MARTA station.

Note: At this writing, tickets are available from the National Park Service Visitor Contact Station at 522 Auburn Ave., open daily from 9am to 5pm. However, when the new visitor center opens at 450 Auburn Ave., across from the King Center, tickets will be sold there. Best to call ahead (☎ **404/331-3920**) for up-to-the-minute information. Tours depart from the ticket-purchase point about every 30 minutes, taking in sights en route to the house. In summer months, especially, tickets often run out early; arrive at 9:30am to optimize your chances of getting in. If summer crowds prevent you from getting on a tour, you can view a slide presentation about the Birth Home at the Martin Luther King Center.

Martin Luther King, Jr. was born in this two-story Queen Anne–style house on January 15, 1929, the oldest son of a Baptist minister and an elementary school music teacher. His childhood was a normal one. He preferred playing baseball to piano lessons, liked to play Monopoly, and got a kick out of tearing the heads off his older sister's dolls. (Nonviolence came later.) To quote his sister, Christine King Farris, ". . . my brother was no saint ordained at birth, instead he was an average and ordinary man, called by . . . God . . . to perform extraordinary deeds."

King lived here through the age of 12, then moved with his family to a house a few blocks away. A visit provides many insights into the formative influences on one of the greatest leaders of our time. The Rev. A. D. Williams, King's maternal grandfather and pastor of Ebenezer Baptist Church, bought the house in 1909. Reverend Williams was active not only in the church, but in the community and early manifestations of the civil rights movement. He was a charter member of Atlanta's NAACP and led a series of black registration and voting drives as far back as 1917. He was instrumental in getting black officers on the Atlanta police force. Martin Luther King, Sr. moved in on Thanksgiving Day, 1926, when he married Williams's daughter Alberta. When Reverend Williams died in 1931, Martin's father became head of the household and also took over Williams's pulpit at Ebenezer Church.

The King family retained ownership of the house at 501 Auburn even after they moved away. Martin's younger brother, Alfred Daniel, lived here with his family from 1954 to 1963. In 1971, King's mother deeded the home to the Martin Luther King, Jr., Center. It has since been restored to its appearance during the years of Martin's boyhood. The furnishings are all originals or similar period reproductions, and

Martin Luther King, Jr., National Historic Site

Under the auspices of the National Park Service is an area of about 10 blocks around Auburn Avenue, established in 1980 to "preserve the birthplace and boyhood surroundings of the nation's foremost civil rights leader." It includes King's boyhood home and the Ebenezer Baptist Church, of which King, his father, and his grandfather were ministers. Other Auburn Avenue attractions, not under NPS auspices, include the Martin Luther King, Jr., Center for Nonviolent Social Change (where King is buried) and the APEX Museum.

The area is known as Sweet Auburn. John Wesley Dobbs, maternal grandfather of former Atlanta mayor Maynard Jackson, is the person who first called it such, after Oliver Goldsmith's *The Deserted Village,* the first line of which reads, "Sweet Auburn! loveliest village of the plains." Mayor Jackson says his grandfather called the area "sweet" because the keys to black liberation existed here in the form of "the three b's—bucks, ballots, and books."

See Chapter 9, "A Walking Tour of Sweet Auburn," for a walking tour of the area.

Information: As I go to press, a new visitor center is under construction at 450 Auburn Ave., across from the King Center. It will provide a complete orientation to area attractions and include a theater for audiovisual and interpretive programs, exhibits, and a bookstore. Guided tours of the area (including those of the Birth Home) will originate here. The visitor center will be fronted by a beautifully landscaped plaza with a reflecting pool and outdoor amphitheater for Park Service programs. Call **404/331-3920** to find out if this new facility is open when you visit.

many personal items belonging to the family are on display. Christine was actively involved in the restoration, providing a wealth of detail about its former appearance, as well as anecdotal material about life in the King family.

Tours of the house, conducted by National Park rangers, begin in the downstairs parlor, where you'll see family photographs showing Martin Luther King as a child. The parlor was also used for choir practice, for the dreaded piano lessons, and as a rec room where the family gathered around the radio to listen to shows like "The Shadow." In the dining room, world events were regularly discussed over meals, and every Sunday, before dinner, each child was required to recite a newly learned Bible verse from memory. You'll also see the coal cellar (stoking coal was one of Martin's childhood chores); the children's play area; the upstairs bedroom of Martin's parents in which Christine, Martin, and Alfred Daniel were born; Reverend Williams's den, where the family gathered for nightly Bible study; the bedroom Martin shared with his brother ("always in disarray," says Christine); and Christine's bedroom.

✪ Martin Luther King, Jr., Center for Nonviolent Social Change

449 Auburn Ave. (between Boulevard and Jackson St.). ☎ **404/524-1956.** Admission free. To see the videos, adults pay $1, children 6–12 pay 50¢, under 6 free. Daily 9:30am–5:30pm. Closed Thanksgiving, Christmas, New Year's Day. Take bus no. 3, from the Five Points MARTA station.

Martin Luther King, Jr.'s commitment to nonviolent social change lives on at this memorial and educational center under the direction of his son, Dexter Scott King. On the premises is an information counter where you can find out about all Auburn Avenue attractions and obtain tickets to tour the King birth home (details above). A nongovernmental member of the United Nations, the center works with government agencies and the private sector to reduce violence within the community and among nations. It provides day care for low-income families, assists students in developing leadership skills in nonviolence, and holds workshops on topics like hunger and illiteracy. Its library and archives house the world's largest collection of books and other materials documenting the civil rights movement, including Dr. King's personal papers and a rare 87-volume edition of *The Collected Works of Mahatma Gandhi,* a gift from the government of India. Equally important, it is Martin Luther King's final resting place, a living memorial to an inspiring leader which is visited by tens of thousands each year, including heads of foreign governments.

Visitors are given a self-guided tour brochure. The tour begins in the Exhibition Hall, where memorabilia of King and the civil rights movement are displayed. Here you can see his Bible and clerical robe, a hand-written sermon, a photographic essay on his life and work, and, on a grim note, the suit he was wearing when a deranged woman stabbed him in New York City and the key to his room at the Lorraine Motel in Memphis, Tennessee, where he was assassinated. In an alcove off the main exhibit area is a video display on Martin Luther King's life and works. Additional exhibits—including a room honoring Rosa Parks (whose refusal to give up her seat on a city bus led to the Montgomery bus boycott) and another honoring Gandhi—are in Freedom Hall.

Outside is Freedom Plaza, where Dr. King's white marble crypt rests on a beautiful five-tiered Reflecting Pool, a symbol of the life-giving nature of water. The tomb is inscribed with his words: "Free at Last. Free at Last. Thank God Almighty I'm Free at Last." An eternal flame burns in a small circular pavilion directly fronting the crypt. The Freedom Walkway, a vaulted colonnade paralleling the pool, will eventually be painted with murals depicting the civil rights struggle. Located at the end of Freedom Walkway is the Chapel of All Faiths, symbolizing the ecumenical nature of Dr. King's work and the universality of the basic tenets of all the world's great religions.

A very important part of your visit is the Screening Room, where four excellent half-hour videos about Martin Luther King play continuously throughout the day. Enhanced by music that ranges from spirituals to rap, they show many of his most stirring sermons and speeches, including "I've Been to the Mountaintop" and "I Have a Dream"—speeches that are as much a part of America's heritage as the Gettysburg Address.

A store on the premises offers King memorabilia and a wide selection of books and cassettes. Inquire about events (including puppet shows for kids) and workshops taking place during your stay. Ranger talks focusing on the community and the civil rights movement take place frequently on Freedom Plaza. The annual Kingfest, held mid-May and mid-June, features music, theatrical performances, a kids' day, and many other events. And every October 2, Gandhi's birthday is celebrated with Indian food, music, and entertainment. A very nice cafeteria is on the premises.

APEX Museum

125–135 Auburn Ave. (at Courtland St.). ☎ **404/521-APEX.** Admission $3 adults, $2 seniors and students, children under 4 free. Tues–Sat 10am–5pm, till 6pm Wed nights; also Sun 1–5pm Feb and June–Aug. Closed Thanksgiving, Christmas, and New Year's Day. Take bus no. 3 from the Five Points MARTA station.

The APEX (African-American Panoramic Experience) Museum both chronicles the history of Sweet Auburn, Atlanta's foremost black residential and business district, and serves as a national African-American museum and cultural center. In the museum's Trolley Car Theater, a replica of a turn-of-the-century tram that ran on Auburn Avenue, a 12-minute multimedia presentation, *Sweet Auburn: Street of Pride,* acquaints visitors with the area's history. Sweet Auburn history is also represented in tableaux such as a replica of the barbershop run by Alonzo Herndon and a re-creation of the Gate City Drugstore (Atlanta's first black pharmacy) in the 1920s, including some original furnishings. There are interactive displays for children as well.

A new three-story wing scheduled to open shortly after we go to press will include: art and history galleries; a rotunda with a 360-degree screen used for live performances and multimedia presentations; a walk-through exhibit that traces Afro-American history from its African roots to contemporary times; galleries portraying the contributions of Africans and African-Americans in science, music, and other fields; a vast library of films, slides, videotapes, and audiovisual materials that is open to visitors; and a vast gift shop. Inquire about special events and workshops taking place during your visit to Atlanta.

Across the street from the APEX Museum, at 100 Auburn Ave., is Herndon Plaza, where you can see a permanent exhibit on the Herndon family and changing shows of the works of African-American artists.

Ebenezer Baptist Church

407–413 Auburn Ave. ☎ **404/688-7263.** Admission free (donations appreciated). Mon–Fri 9:30am–4:30pm, Sun for services only at 7:45 and 10:45am. MARTA: King Memorial Station is about eight blocks away. You can also take a no. 3 bus from anywhere on Peachtree St.

Founded in 1886, Ebenezer was a spiritual center of the civil rights movement during the years 1960 to 1968, when Martin Luther King, Jr., served as copastor. His grandfather, the Rev. A. D. Williams, dedicated the church to "the advancement of black people and every righteous and social movement." Williams's activist example was followed by his son-in-law and successor, Martin Luther King, Sr., who worked for voting rights and other aspects of black civil and social advancement. Later, Martin Luther King, Jr., would join his forebears in pursuing justice for black Americans. You can listen to a taped message on the history of the church and/or take a 10-minute guided tour. An ecumenical service takes place here every year during King week.

Note: At this writing, the congregation has begun work on a new church across the street. When it is completed, the original church will remain as a historic site under Parks Department auspices.

✪ Fernbank Museum of Natural History

767 Clifton Rd. (off Ponce de Leon Ave.). ☎ **404/378-0127.** Admission $9.50 adults ($13.50 inclusive of an IMAX Theater ticket), $7.50 students and seniors ($10.50 inclusive of an IMAX Theater ticket), free children 2 and under. IMAX Theater admission alone $5.50 adults, $4.50 students and seniors, $4 children 3–12, under 3 free. Mon–Thurs and Sat 10am–5pm, Fri 10am–9pm, Sun noon–5pm. Closed Thanksgiving and Christmas.

The largest museum of natural sciences in the southeast, this architecturally stunning facility adjoins 65 acres of pristine forest. The building centers on a soaring three-story, skylit Great Hall—a gorgeous Italianate brick atrium with spiral staircases, lofty columns, and windows embracing the verdant woodlands beyond. Architect Graham Gund has achieved one of the best integrations of interior/exterior space I've ever seen. Museum floors are imbedded with ancient fossil remains from the late Jurassic period.

The major permanent exhibit, "A Walk Through Time in Georgia," uses the state as a microcosm to tell the story of the earth's development through time and the chronology of life upon it. Seventeen galleries here re-create landform regions from the rolling pine-forested foothills of the Piedmont Plateau to the mossy Okefenokee Swamp, from the Cumberland Plateau (where you can walk through a typical "limestone cavern") to the marshy Coast and Barrier Islands. Exhibits are enhanced by creative state-of-the-art films and videos, informational audiophones, interactive computers, sound effects, and old-fashioned field guides—not to mention more than 1,500 fabricated plants and mounted specimens of birds and animals. Visitors travel back 15 billion years—to experience the origins of the universe (the Big Bang) and the formation of galaxies and solar systems—and into the future to consider the fate of our planet. It's a fascinating journey.

Another major permanent installation, "Spectrum of the Senses," comprises 65 participatory displays shown on a rotating basis—all of them designed by physicists to illustrate scientific principles. Here you can step into a life-size kaleidoscope, play with perspective, gaze into infinity, see physical evidence of sound waves, mix colors on a computer, blow giant bubbles, and see a steam fog tornado in formation. In Fantasy Forest, a colorful play area designed for preschoolers (ages 3 to 5), kids become bees and pollinate flowers, climb a treehouse, walk through a swamp, and play at being farmers. The state-shaped Georgia Adventure is a similar discovery room for ages 6 to 10. While you're here, be sure to catch a thrilling IMAX film (buy tickets as soon as you enter the museum; they sometimes sell out). And if it's a weekend, see if there are any programs going on at the Harris Naturalist Center, a

Central Atlanta Sights

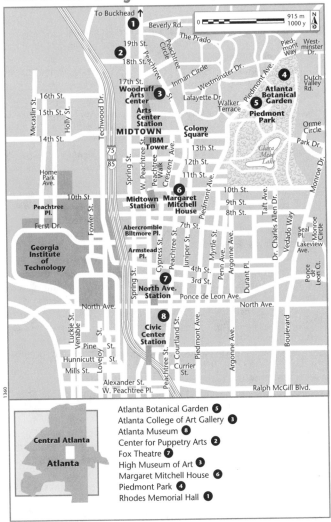

To Buckhead ↑

0   915 m
0   1000 y

N

① Beverly Rd.

The Prado

Peachtree Circle

Piedmont Way

Westminster Dr.

② 19th St.
18th St.

Peachtree St.

Inman Circle

Westminster Dr.

Piedmont Ave.

④ Atlanta Botanical Garden

Dutch Valley Rd.

17th St.
③ Woodruff Arts Center

16th St.

Mecaslin St.

15th St.
Holly St.

14th St.

Techwood Dr.

Lafayette Dr.

Walker Terrace

⑤ Piedmont Park

Arts Center Station

MIDTOWN

Colony Square

Orme Circle

Park Dr.

IBM Tower

13th St.

12th St.

11th St.

Spring St.

W. Peachtree St.

Peachtree Walk

Crescent Ave.

Piedmont Ave.

Clara Meer Lake

Home Park Ave.

10th St.

⑥ Margaret Mitchell House

9th St.

8th St.

Taft Ave.

Dr. Charles Allen Dr.

Vedado Way

Monroe Dr.

Peachtree Pl.

Ferst Dr.

Fowler St.

Midtown Station

Abercrombie Biltmore Pl.

7th St.

Cypress St.

Peachtree St.

Juniper St.

Myrtle St.

Penn Ave.

Argonne Ave.

Durant Pl.

Seal Pl.

Monroe Circle

Lakeview Ave.

Georgia Institute of Technology

Armstead Pl.

4th St.

3rd St.

Ponce de Leon Ct.

⑦ North Ave. Station

Ponce de Leon Ave.

Spring St.

North Ave.

Luckie St.
Venable St.

Pine St.

Lovejoy St.

Hunnicutt St.

Mills St.

⑧ Civic Center Station

W. Peachtree St.

Courtland St.

Piedmont Ave.

Argonne Ave.

Boulevard

North Ave.

Currier St.

Alexander St.
W. Peachtree Pl.

Peachtree St.

Ralph McGill Blvd.

1360

Central Atlanta

Atlanta

cluster of science laboratories where visitors often get to examine items under an electron microscope.

Other museum attractions include a Caribbean coral reef aquarium, the Star Gallery (where 542 fiber-optic stars create a twinkling evening sky), The World of Shells (a vast and beautiful collection), and the McClatchey Collection of jewelry and textiles from the old silk road countries. A museum store is stocked with entertaining and educational gifts and books, and there's a delightful on-premises restaurant with arched windows overlooking Fernbank Forest as well as outdoor patio seating.

✪ Cyclorama

800 Cherokee Ave. (in Grant Park). ☎ **404/624-1071** or 404/658-7625. Admission $5 adults, $4 seniors, $3 children 6–12, under 6 free (not recommended for very young children). Daily June–Labor Day 9:20am–5:30pm, the day after Labor Day–May 31 9:20am–4:30pm. Shows begin every half hour on the half hour starting at 9:30am. Closed Thanksgiving, Christmas, New Year's Day, and Martin Luther King Day. Take Georgia Ave. bus no. 97 from Five Points Station.

Though it sounds like something out of Disney World, this Cyclorama was created in the 1880s, and its concept—a huge, 360-degree cylindrical painting displayed on a rotating platform—dates back to a century earlier. Cycloramas were the rage of 18th- and 19th-century Europe, Russia, Japan, and later, the United States, depicting subject matter ranging from the splendors of Pompeii to Napoleonic battles. Enhanced by multimedia effects and faux-terrain dioramas extending 30 feet from the painting into the foreground, they were the forerunners of newsreels, travelogues, and TV war coverage.

The one you'll see here—a 42-foot-high cylindrical oil painting, 358 feet in circumference (on about 16,000 square feet of canvas)—depicts in meticulous detail the events of the Battle of Atlanta, July 22, 1864. It took 11 eastern European artists, working in America in the studio of William Wehner, 22 months to complete. For 20th-century tourists, the concept itself is as interesting as the action depicted, and the restoration is incredibly impressive. Though painted on fine Belgian linen in the painstaking methodology of the 19th-century academies, the work suffered in moves from city to city, and later (when motion-picture epics made cycloramas passé) from neglect. Well-intentioned but incompetent attempts at restoration caused further damage. In the 1970s, a severe storm waterlogged the painting, causing seemingly irreversible damage. But Mayor Maynard Jackson recognized the historic and artistic importance of Cyclorama; under his auspices $11 million was raised for its restoration. It took $2^1/_2$ years for renowned conservator Gustav Berger and his crew to repair the damaged work, a process that included mending over 700 rips and tears in the canvas. In the auditorium itself the Cyclorama viewing is preceded by a 14-minute film about the Battle of Atlanta narrated by James Earl Jones.

The fascinating story of Cyclorama's development and restoration is related in a video format near the auditorium entrance. Cyclorama's central theme is General John B. Hood's desperate attempt to halt Sherman's inexorable advance into the city. Comprehensively narrated, and complete with music and sound effects including galloping horses and cannon fire, it vividly depicts the troop movements and battles of the day in which the Confederates lost 8,000 men, the Federals 3,722. A figure highlighted far beyond his historic importance is Gen. John A. Logan of the Federal Army of Tennessee. He commissioned the painting at a cost of $42,000 as a campaign move in his bid for the vice presidency. He's shown gloriously galloping into the fray, bravely exposing himself and his men to enemy fire. The work was originally called *Logan's Great Battle.*

The building housing Cyclorama also comprises a museum of related artifacts, most importantly the steam locomotive Texas from the

Downtown Sights

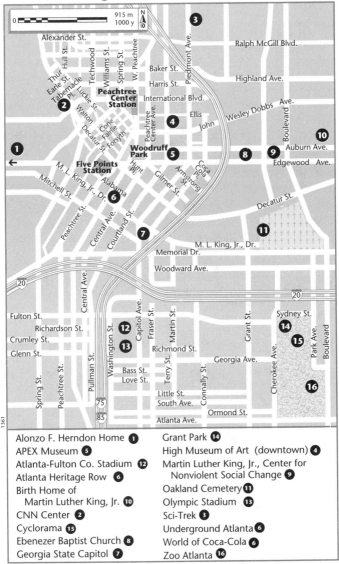

Alonzo F. Herndon Home ❶
APEX Museum ❺
Atlanta-Fulton Co. Stadium ⓬
Atlanta Heritage Row ❻
Birth Home of
    Martin Luther King, Jr. ❿
CNN Center ❷
Cyclorama ⓯
Ebenezer Baptist Church ❽
Georgia State Capitol ❼

Grant Park ⓮
High Museum of Art (downtown) ❹
Martin Luther King, Jr., Center for
    Nonviolent Social Change ❾
Oakland Cemetery ⓫
Olympic Stadium ⓭
Sci-Trek ❸
Underground Atlanta ❻
World of Coca-Cola ❻
Zoo Atlanta ⓰

1862 Great Locomotive Chase. Other exhibits include displays of Civil War arms and artillery, Civil War–themed paintings, portraits of Confederate and Union leaders, "life in camp" artifacts and photographs, and uniforms. A bookstore on the premises is a repository of Civil War literature, including a sizable black history section.

✪ Oakland Cemetery

248 Oakland Ave. SE (main entrance at Oakland Ave. and Martin Luther King Dr.).
☎ **404/688-2107.** Admission free. Daily sunrise to 7pm (6pm in winter); Visitor
Center Mon–Fri 9am–5pm. Purchase an informative self-guide walking tour map
brochure at the Visitor Center for $1.25. Parking inside the cemetery, near the Visi-
tor Center. MARTA: King Memorial.

On the National Register of Historic Places, this outstanding 88-acre
Victorian cemetery was founded in 1850. It survived the Civil War and
remained the only cemetery in Atlanta for 34 years. Among the over
48,000 people buried here are Confederate and Union soldiers (including five Southern generals), prominent families and paupers, governors
and mayors, golfing great Bobby Jones, and Atlanta's most famous
personage, *Gone With the Wind* author Margaret Mitchell. There's a
Jewish section (consecrated by a temple), a black section (dating from
segregation days), and a potter's field. Two monuments honor the
Confederate war dead. And standing at the marker that commemorates
the Great Locomotive Chase, you can see the trees from which the
Yankee raiders were hanged (Confederate conductor Captain William
Fuller is buried here).

Almost every grave has a story. Real-estate tycoon Jasper Newton
Smith had a life-size statue of himself erected on his grave so he could
watch the city's goings-on into eternity. The sculptor originally gave
Smith a tie, but Smith, who never wore one, refused to pay for the
piece until the tie was chiseled off. Dr. James Nissen, Oakland's first
burial, feared being buried alive; his will stated that his jugular vein be
severed prior to interment. And John Morgan Dye was a baby who
died during the siege of Atlanta; his mother walked through the
raging battle to the cemetery carrying the small corpse. The smallest
grave, however, is that of "Tweet," a pet mockingbird buried in his
family's lot. You'll also learn about graveyard symbolism on the tour: a
lopped-tree-trunk marker indicates a life cut short or goals unachieved,
rocks on a grave denote a life built on a solid foundation, a shell means
resurrection, and so on.

The cemetery is renowned not only for historical reasons, but as an
outdoor "museum" of Gothic and classical-revival mausolea, bronze
urns, stained glass, and Victorian statuary. Atlanta residents also view
Oakland's rolling terrain as parkland; dozens of people actually jog here
every day, and picnickers are a common sight. Every October, there's
a celebration to commemorate the cemetery's founding, with
turn-of-the-century music, food, and storytelling. Though you can visit
whenever the cemetery is open, try to come when you can take a
guided tour. It's fascinating.

✪ Georgia's Stone Mountain Park

16 miles east of downtown on U.S. 78. ☎ **404/498-5600.** Major attractions
$3 each adults, $2 children 3–11, children under 3 free. A ticket for all six major
attractions is $13.50 adults, $9 children. Year-round, gates open 6am–midnight.
Major attractions open fall and winter 10am–5pm, spring and summer 10am–9pm.
Parking charge $5 a day, $20 annually (one-time-only charge if you stay on the
grounds). Attractions only are closed Christmas Day; park is open. Take a MARTA train
to Indian Trail Station where you can transfer to a bus to Memorial Hall in the park.

A monolithic gray granite outcropping (the world's largest), carved with a massive monument to the Confederacy, Stone Mountain is a distinctive landmark on Atlanta's horizon and the focal point of its major recreation area—3,200 acres of lakes and beautiful wooded parkland. It's Georgia's number-one tourist mecca and the third most visited paid attraction in the United States.

Over half a century in the making, Stone Mountain's neoclassic carving—90 feet high and 190 feet wide—is the world's largest piece of sculpture. Originally conceived by Gutzon Borglum, it depicts Confederate leaders Jefferson Davis, Robert E. Lee, and Stonewall Jackson galloping on horseback throughout eternity. Borglum started work on the mountain sculpture in 1923; after 10 years he abandoned it, due to insurmountable technical problems and rifts with its sponsors. He went on to South Dakota, where he gained fame carving Mount Rushmore. No sign of his work remains at Stone Mountain, but it was his vision that inspired the project. Augustus Lukeman took over in 1925, but three years later, the work still far from complete, the family that owned the mountain lost patience and reclaimed the property. It wasn't until 1963, the state having purchased the mountain and surrounding property for a park, that work resumed under Walter Kirtland Hancock and Roy Faulkner. It was completed in 1970.

The best view of the mountain is from below, but you can ascend a walking trail up and down its moss-covered slopes, especially lovely in spring when they're blanketed in wildflowers, or take the narrated tram ride to the top. Trams run about every 20 minutes in both directions.

A highlight at Stone Mountain is **Lasershow,** a spectacular display of laser lights and fireworks with animation and music. It begins in April (Friday, Saturday, and Sunday night at 9pm); from early May through Labor Day it can be seen nightly at 9:30pm; then it resumes its Friday-through-Sunday schedule during September; Friday and Saturday night only in October. Don't miss it.

Other major park attractions include: the **Stone Mountain Scenic Railroad** that chugs around the five-mile base of Stone Mountain. The ride takes 25 minutes. Trains depart from Railroad Depot, an old-fashioned train station with a very attractive restaurant on the premises serving ice cream, lemonade, and chicken dinners with all the fixings.

The *Scarlett O'Hara,* a paddlewheel riverboat, cruises the 363-acre Stone Mountain Lake.

The **Antique Auto & Music Museum** is a jumble of old radios, jukeboxes, working nickelodeons, pianos, Lionel trains, carousel horses, and clocks along with classic cars such as a 1925 Ford Model T truck and a 1928 Martin built for World War I ace Gen. Billy Mitchell out of airplane parts.

The 19-building **Antebellum Plantation** offers self-guided tours assisted by hosts in period dress at each structure. Highlights include an authentic 1830s country store; the 1845 Kingston House (it represents a typical overseer's house); the clapboard slave cabins; the 1790s Thornton House, elegant home of a large landowner; the smokehouse and well; a doctor's office; a barn, a coach house, and crop-storage cribs; a necessary; a cook house; and the 1850 neoclassical Tara-like Dickey House. The grounds also contain formal gardens and a kitchen garden. It takes at least an hour to tour the entire complex (a map is provided at the entrance), really a major Atlanta sightseeing attraction in itself. Often (especially in summer), there are crafts and cooking demonstrations, medicine shows, storytellers, and balladeers on the premises. You can even take a 20-minute horse-drawn carriage ride around the area ($5 for adults, $3 for children 3 to 11; free for children under 3).

Confederate Hall, an information center, houses a large narrated exhibit called "The War in Georgia," a chronological picture story of the Civil War.

At **Memorial Hall,** another information center, a nine-minute tape on Stone Mountain history and geology is played throughout the day. A Civil War museum is upstairs.

Additional activities: golf (on a top-rated 36-hole course designed by Robert Trent Jones and John LaFoy), miniature golf, eight night-lighted Laykold tennis courts, a sizable stretch of sandy lakefront beach with wonderful water slides, 20 acres of wildlife trails with natural animal habitats and a petting zoo, carillon concerts, boating (rowboats, canoes, sailboats, and paddleboats), bicycle rental, fishing, hiking, picnicking, and more.

Stone Mountain is one of the most beautiful parks in the nation. Consider spending a few days of your trip here; it's a great place for a romantic getaway or a family vacation. On-site accommodations are detailed in Chapter 6, "Accommodations." If you can only spare a day, it's an easy drive (about 30 minutes) from downtown.

Note: Stone Mountain Park will host three Olympic events—tennis, archery, and cycling.

The Jimmy Carter Library

Freedom Pkwy. (Exit 96 off I-75/85). ☎ **404/331-0296.** Admission $4 adults, $3 seniors, free children under 16. Mon–Sat 9am–4:45pm, Sun noon–4:45pm. Closed New Year's Day, Thanksgiving, Christmas.

Opened in October 1986 on 30 acres of gardens, lakes, and waterfalls, this impressive presidential library houses some 27 million pages of documents, memoranda, and correspondence from Jimmy Carter's White House years. There are also $1^1/_2$ million photographs and hundreds of hours of audio- and videotapes, the latter documenting everything from meetings with world leaders to a footrace between the president and his daughter, Amy. The library's hilltop site is a historic one; it was from this spot that Sherman watched the Battle of Atlanta.

In the facility's extensive museum, you'll see an exact replica of the Oval Office during Carter's presidency, an exhibit enhanced by a recording of Carter speaking about his experiences in that office. A large display of "gifts of state" runs the gamut from a Dresden figurine of George and Martha Washington (a gift from Ireland) to a carpet from the Shah of Iran. You'll see the table setting used when the Carters entertained Chinese vice premier Deng Xiaoping and his wife in the State Dining Room; a video of artists such as the late pianist Vladimir Horowitz performing in the East Room; campaign memorabilia;

Georgia's Stone Mountain Park

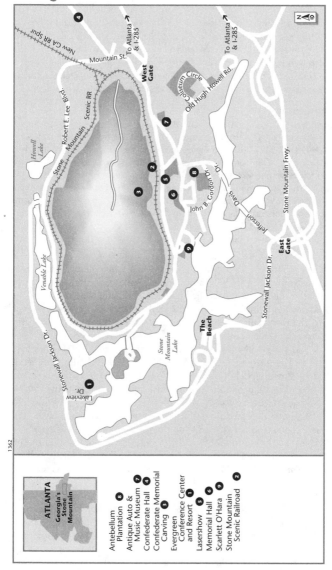

ATLANTA
Georgia's Stone Mountain

Antebellum Plantation **8**
Antique Auto & Music Museum **7**
Confederate Hall **4**
Confederate Memorial Carving **3**
Evergreen Conference Center and Resort **1**
Lasershow **5**
Memorial Hall **6**
Scarlett O'Hara **9**
Stone Mountain Scenic Railroad **2**

and a large display devoted to the activities of Rosalynn Carter. A changing exhibit area houses art and historically themed shows.

Other exhibits focus on Carter's support of human rights (there's a letter from Soviet dissident Andrei Sakharov and Carter's reply); his boyhood days (his sixth-grade report card and a photo of the Plains High baseball team are two of the items on display); and his pre-presidential life as a peanut farmer, governor, and state senator.

There are informative videos throughout, including an interactive "town meeting" format in which visitors can ask Carter questions on subjects ranging from world affairs to his personal life. And a most interesting participatory video lets you choose your response to a terrorist crisis and learn the probable consequences of your choice.

Consider having lunch here. There's an attractive cafeteria on the premises with patio seating overlooking a Japanese garden and pond.

CNN Center

Marietta St. (at Techwood Dr.). ☎ **404/827-2300.** Admission $7 adults, $5 seniors, $4.50 children 6–12; under 5 free (though the tour is not recommended for young children; they'll be bored). A more in-depth hour-long tour costs $24.50. *Note:* Tickets are available on a first-come, first-served basis on the day of the tour. Arrive early for the tour you wish to take, since only 35 tickets are sold per tour, and they often sell out. Best bet is to reserve in advance via MasterCard or VISA. 35-minute tours given daily every 15 minutes between 9am and 6pm; tickets go on sale at 8:30am. Hour-long tours take place at 3:30pm daily. Closed New Year's Day, Easter, Memorial Day, July 4, Labor Day, Thanksgiving, and Dec 24–25. MARTA: Omni. Many parking lots around the building.

The CNN Center is headquarters for media magnate Ted Turner's 24-hour cable news networks, CNN, CNN International, and Headline News. During 35-minute guided walking tours, visitors get a behind-the-scenes look at the high-tech world of TV network news in action. You'll find the Tour Desk in the main lobby near the base of an eight-story escalator. While you're waiting for the tour to begin, have your photograph taken behind a CNN anchor desk replica.

Tours begin in an exhibit area where displays include MGM movie stills (Turner owns a portion of the MGM/RKO film library); a scaled-down model of the Galaxy 5 satellite that carries the signal for the company's networks; exhibits on Jacques Cousteau and *National Geographic* (both subjects of numerous specials on Turner-owned TBS); an exhibit on TBS sports (Turner owns the Atlanta Hawks and the Atlanta Braves); an exhibit on the Goodwill Games; a 12-monitor video wall that continuously airs all Turner networks; a display on the 24-hour cartoon network; a duplicate of MGM's Oscar for *Gone With the Wind;* and items involved in CNN's much-lauded coverage of the Gulf War.

On another level, visitors observe the CNN newsroom from a glass-walled viewing station. You'll see the domestic and international desks, and writers composing news scripts. On a monitor, you can observe what newscasters are up to during their breaks (often chomping sandwiches), and if a live broadcast is in progress, you can see CNN newscasters at work. Tour guides are knowledgeable and can answer virtually any question.

There are over a dozen restaurants and fast-food outlets on the premises, a variety of shops, and a movie theater. The Turner Store on the premises carries network-logo clothing and gift items, along with MGM movie memorabilia (this is your chance to buy a Rhett Butler jack-in-the-box or a *Gone With the Wind* beach towel). There are frequent exhibits, concerts, crafts shows, and other special events in the atrium lobby; ask your tour guide what's on.

The Winecoff Hotel Fire

The deadliest hotel fire in U.S. history—which killed 119 people—broke out shortly before 4am on December 7, 1946, at the Winecoff Hotel at Peachtree and Ellis Streets. Many who died were killed jumping out of windows. Though on its stationery, the hotel billed itself as fireproof, it had, in fact, no sprinkler system, fire escapes, or fire doors. For $2^1/2$ hours, firefighters from Atlanta and nearby towns battled the blaze in the cold predawn hours, but their ladders reached only to the eighth floor, and their nets were not strong enough to withstand jumps of more than 70 feet. For a long time, the 15-story building has stood empty, but it is going to reopen as a hotel this year. In December 1994, 500 survivors and their relatives (there were 161 actual survivors) gathered at the site for the dedication of a plaque commemorating the dead and the heroes who fought to save those trapped in the inferno. The tragedy led to the enactment of more stringent fire codes throughout America.

✪ High Museum of Art

1280 Peachtree St. NE, (at 16th St.). ☎ **404/733-HIGH.** Admission $6 adults, $4 seniors and students with ID, $2 children 6–17, children under 6 free. Free to all on Thurs 1–5pm. Tues–Sat 10am–5pm, Sun noon–5pm. Closed July 4, Thanksgiving, Christmas, and New Year's Day. MARTA: Arts Center. A parking garage is located behind the museum on Lombardy Way between 15th and 16th Sts.

Designed by architect Richard Meier, this facility—part of the Woodruff Arts Center complex—is itself a work of art. A dazzling white porcelain-tiled edifice with an equally pristine white interior (the *New York Times* jokingly cautioned that visitors risk snow blindness on a sunny day), it houses four floors of galleries connected by semicircular pedestrian ramps girding a spacious, sun-filled, four-story atrium. The north wall of this atrium is enhanced by a 62-foot-high jewel-toned ink drawing by Sol Le Witt. It's a very favorable setting in which to view art. It's not the Met, but this New Yorker enjoys the intimacy of the experience. I also find it fascinating to see lesser-known works by major artists.

The permanent collection includes over 10,000 pieces, among them a significant group of 19th- and 20th-century American paintings. It features Hudson River School artists such as Thomas Cole and Frederic Church, as well as works by Thomas Sully, John Singer Sargent, and William Harnett. The Virginia Carroll Crawford Collection of American Decorative Arts comprehensively documents styles from 1825 to 1917. The Samuel H. Kress Foundation collection comprises Italian paintings and sculpture from the 14th through the 18th century. The Uhry Print Collection contains important works by French impressionists and postimpressionists, German expressionists, and American 20th-century artists. Also notable are collections of sub-Saharan African art, a folk art collection, and works by noted 19th- and 20th-century American and European photographers.

In addition to its permanent collection—which is shown on a rotating basis—the museum hosts a number of traveling exhibitions each year, complemented by films, lectures, workshops, gallery talks, concerts, and other cultural events. Inquire at the desk about happenings during your stay, and call in advance to find out when you can take a free gallery tour.

✪ Fox Theatre

660 Peachtree St. NE (at Ponce de Leon Ave.). ☎ **404/817-8700** for box office, **404/876-2041** for tours. Tours $5 adults, $4 seniors, $3 students. The Atlanta Preservation Center conducts walking tours of the Fox Theatre and its surrounding area Mon and Thurs at 10am and Sat at 10 and 11:30am. Call to verify tour times before you go. MARTA: North Avenue.

Originally conceived as a Shriners' temple in 1916, this lavish, blocklong Moorish-Egyptian fantasyland ended up as a movie theater when the Shriners realized their grandiose conception had far exceeded their budget. In 1927, they sold the "temple" to movie magnate William Fox, who amended their plans and created a peerless pleasure palace. The building was designed by French architect Oliver J. Vinour, who utilized design motifs of the Middle East in his creation, including replicas of art and furnishings from King Tut's tomb.

Atlanta's new theater opened in 1929 as a masterpiece of Oriental splendor, its Moorish facade, onion domes, and minarets an exotic contrast to the surrounding Victorian boardinghouses. A brass-trimmed marble kiosk imported from Italy served as a ticket booth. The 140-foot entrance arcade led to a lushly carpeted lobby with blue-tiled goldfish pools. And the auditorium was an Arabian courtyard under a twinkling starlit sky that could, with state-of-the-art technology, be transformed to a sky at sunrise or sunset. A striped bedouin canopy sheltered the balcony, and sequin- and rhinestone-studded stage curtains depicted mosques and Moorish horsemen. As the show began, a gigantic gilded 3,610-pipe Möller organ rose majestically from its vault, its rich chords accompanied by a full orchestra. A medley of popular songs, cartoons, a follow-the-bouncing-ball sing-along, a stage-show extravaganza by a bevy of Rockette-like chorines called the Fanchon and Marco Sunkist Beauties, and a newsreel preceded every main feature. At night there were dances in the Egyptian Ballroom, designed to replicate Ramses' temple. And even the men's lounge was exotically appointed with hieroglyphic adornments, winged scarab-motif friezes, bas-reliefs of royal figures, and throne chairs.

Unfortunately, the Fox's opening coincided with the Great Depression, and it proved impossible to maintain its unstinting opulence. In 1932 the company declared bankruptcy and closed its doors. The theater reopened three years later for occasional concerts featuring cultural superstars such as Leopold Stokowski and Yehudi Menuhin. By the '40s, it was a viable concern once more, and in 1947 the Metropolitan Opera began a 20-year stint of week-long performances here. An oversize panoramic screen was installed in the 1950s, along with a 26-speaker stereophonic system. But like monumental movie palaces nationwide, the Fox inevitably declined in the age of television. In 1975 its doors were padlocked once again.

An organization of concerned citizens calling themselves Atlanta Landmarks raised $1.8 million and saved the Fox from the wrecking ball in 1978, foiling Southern Bell's plans to purchase and demolish it to make way for a regional headquarters building. Ever since, it's been a thriving entity, featuring Broadway shows, headliners (Ray Charles, Liza Minnelli), dance companies such as Alvin Ailey, and comedy stars such as Jay Leno and Whoopi Goldberg. A big event every summer is the Summer Film Festival, which features organ concerts, sing-alongs, and cartoons with classic and current blockbuster movies (see the "Calendar of Events" in Chapter 3 for details). Best of all, the theater has been restored to its former glory, its fabulous furnishings and fixtures, terrazzo-tile floors and elaborately stenciled ceilings, gilded columns and velvet draperies all refurbished or replaced with replicas.

To tour the Fox is to enter the fantasy world of Hollywood's heyday. I guarantee you'll be caught up in its glamorous mystique.

○ Atlanta Botanical Garden

In Piedmont Park (at Piedmont Ave. and The Prado). ☎ **404/876-5859.** Admission $6 adults, $4.75 seniors, $3 students with ID, free children 6 and under. Free every Thurs 3pm–closing. A $2 taped audio tour is available in five languages. Tues–Sun 9am–6pm, till 7pm during daylight saving time. Free parking.

This delightful botanical garden, occupying 30 acres in Piedmont Park, consists of three main sections. **The Gardens** highlight plants that flourish in North Georgia's extended growing season. Displays in this section include a carnivorous plant bog, a rock garden, a dwarf conifer garden, an English knot-designed herb garden, a tranquil moongated Japanese garden, a rose garden, and a fragrance garden built for the blind. These lovely gardens are enhanced by fountains, stone statuary, benches, and pagodas. Lunch is served Tuesday to Sunday from April through October on Lanier Terrace, overlooking the Rose Garden.

Two natural arboretum settings comprise 15 acres of hardwood forest. The **Upper Woodlands,** with a paved path, contains a fern glade, a camellia garden, gurgling streams, beautiful statuary, and a habitat designed to show visitors how to attract wildlife to their own backyards. Still more rustic is **Storza Woods,** with an unpaved path. Both make for easy and very pleasant walks.

Most exciting is the 16,000-square-foot, glass-walled **Dorothy Chapman Fuqua Conservatory,** housing rare and endangered plants from exotic climes. With 54 acres of irreplaceable rain forest being bulldozed every minute, facilities such as this provide a much-needed haven for technology-threatened plant species. Approached via an arbored promenade and fronted by a water lily pond, the conservatory has a revolving globe outside its entrance showing the many regions worldwide where plant life is endangered. An interactive video display enhances visitor understanding of exhibits.

The focal point of the conservatory is the misty Tropical Rotunda, housing fern collections, cycads (the most primitive seed-bearing plants known), epiphytes (plants that don't require soil to grow), gorgeous orchids, carnivorous plants (always intriguing), a wide variety of begonias, and towering tropical palms. It's a lush and humid jungle, with brightly hued tropical birds warbling overhead, a splashing waterfall, and winding pathways lined with fragrant hibiscus, African violets, and flowering jasmine vines. Of special interest is a double coconut palm seed from the Seychelles, the largest and heaviest seed in the plant kingdom. Its first 12-foot leaves have already begun to grow, but it will be 100 years before the tree reaches its full height.

The arid Desert House displays Madagascan succulents such as a unique family of spiky plants called Didieriaceae. Here, too, are "living stones" (desert succulents that nature designed to look like pebbles to protect them from being eaten by animals), tree aloes, caudici-forms (with swollen stems and roots for storing water), and conifers from Africa and the Canary Islands. Adjoining is an area for special exhibits.

The building also houses an orangery of rare tropical mango, papaya, star fruit, lychee, coffee, and citrus trees. And a new addition is an "Olympic" olive tree presented by Greece in honor of the 1996 event.

There are flower shows throughout the year, along with lectures and other activities. Call to find out what's on during your stay. A marvelous gift shop is on the premises; your purchases help support the garden.

Georgia State Capitol

Capitol Hill (at Washington St.). ☎ **404/656-2844.** Admission free. Mon–Fri 8am–5pm, Sat 10am–4pm, Sun noon–4pm. Tours given weekdays only at 10 and 11am and 1 and 2pm. Closed major holidays, including state holidays. Parking lot behind the capitol building on Capitol Ave. is closed to the public during legislative sessions; other lots are on M. L. King Dr. at Central Ave. and on Courtland St. between M. L. King Dr. and Central Ave. MARTA: Georgia State.

It wasn't until after the Civil War (1868) that Atlanta became, once and for all, the state capital; its present capitol building, completed July 4, 1889, was hailed as a testament to the city's recovery. Assuming office in the new building, Governor (and former Confederate general) John Brown Gordon eloquently expressed the sentiments of his constituency: "Built upon the crowning hill of her capital city, whose transformation from desolation and ashes to life . . . and beauty so aptly symbolizes the State's resurrection, this proud structure will stand through the coming centuries as a fit memorial to the indomitable will of this people." And so it does.

Modeled after the nation's Capitol, another neoclassical edifice atop a "crowning hill," its 75-foot dome, covered in gold leaf and topped by a statue of Freedom, is a major Atlanta landmark. The building is fronted by a massive four-story portico with a pediment supported by six Corinthian columns set on large stone piers. In the rotunda, with its soaring 237-foot ceiling, are busts of famous Georgians, including signers of the Declaration of Independence and the Constitution.

Tours begin in the entrance hallway of the main floor, this level also serving as an information center for city and state attractions. The governor's office is off the main hall. The tours take 45 minutes; allow at least another 30 minutes to browse around on your own after the tour. Highlights of the grounds are detailed in a brochure available at the tour desk. *Note:* For security reasons, your bag will be searched when you enter.

Grand staircases in both wings rise to the third floor, where you'll enter the House of Representatives, and, across the hall, the Senate chambers. The legislature meets for 40 days, beginning the second Monday in January (it can also be called into special sessions); all of its sessions are open to the public. The fourth floor houses legislative galleries and the State Museum of Science & Industry, with exhibits on cotton, peach, and peanut growing; cases of mounted birds, fish, deer, insects, and other species native to Georgia; weaponry; rocks and minerals; Indian artifacts; and more. During the Olympics, these will be augmented by additional Georgia-themed exhibits. Note, too, museum displays on the first floor.

Some events of note: The week before Thanksgiving is Indian Heritage Week at the capitol. A wattle-and-daub Indian dwelling is constructed in the rotunda, and there are Native American lecturers, music, and arts-and-crafts demonstrations. At Christmas, a beautifully decorated 40-foot tree adorns the rotunda. And on January 15, Dr. Martin Luther King, Jr's., birthday, there's an annual memorial program; local dignitaries, including the governor, give speeches, and King's family attends.

Underground Atlanta

Bounded by Wall St., Central Ave., Martin Luther King, Jr., Dr., and Peachtree St. ☎ **404/523-2311.** Admission free. There is a charge for parking in the garage on Central Ave. off Martin Luther King Dr., but it's reduced if you get your ticket validated at a store or restaurant. Mon–Sat 10am–9:30pm, Sun noon–6pm. Most restaurants and clubs stay open until midnight (or later) nightly. MARTA: Five Points Station has a short pedestrian tunnel that connects directly with Underground Atlanta.

The site of Underground Atlanta is the historic hub of the city, centered on the Zero Milepost that marked the terminus of the Western & Atlantic Railroad in the 1800s. For many years a flourishing locale, the area became so congested in the early 1900s that permanent concrete viaducts were constructed over it, elevating the street system and routing traffic over a maze of railroad tracks. Merchants moved their operations up to the new level, using the lower level for storage space. For most of the 20th century, it remained a deserted catacomb. Then, in 1969, a group of Atlanta businesspeople decided to create an underground entertainment complex of restaurants, shops, and bars in a setting that retained the historic feel of the area. The idea was great, but perhaps the time wasn't right; the complex declined and closed after a little over a decade. Since 1989, however, it has become one of Atlanta's most ballyhooed sightseeing extravaganzas.

Occupying 12 acres in the center of downtown, this $142 million entertainment mecca and urban marketplace is heralded by a beacon of oscillating searchlights emanating from a 138-foot light tower, an outdoor staging area used for performances and concerts, and the cascading waters of Peachtree Fountain Plaza. It offers over 150 retail operations, restaurants, and nightclubs. Humbug Square—where street vendors and con artists flourished in the early 1900s—is again a colorful street market with turn-of-the-century pushcarts and wagons displaying offbeat wares. Clustered around a section called Kenny's Alley, restaurants and nightclubs (see Chapter 11, "Atlanta After Dark") offer a wide spectrum of food and entertainment. And like

Rouse projects everywhere, Underground has a food court purveying everything from egg rolls to stuffed baked potatoes.

Markers throughout the complex indicate historic sites. The Atlanta Convention and Visitors Bureau (☎ **404/577-2148**) maintains an information center at Underground on the corner of Pryor and Alabama Streets. And the Olympic Experience, at the corner of Alabama and Peachtree Streets (☎ **404/658-1996**), offers information about the Olympic games, exhibits, and a gift shop retailing official Olympic merchandise.

✪ Atlanta Heritage Row: The Museum at Underground

55 Upper Alabama St. (at Underground Atlanta). ☎ **404/584-7879.** Ages 6 and up pay $2, under 6 free. Tues–Sat 10am–5pm, Sun 1–5pm. Parking in garage on Central Ave. off Martin Luther King Dr. MARTA: Five Points.

This informative and highly entertaining attraction tells the story of Atlanta from its humble beginnings as a wilderness village through its eventful 200-year history to its present-day status as an international city. It's divided into five themed sections.

In the Civil War section, amid bombed rubble, with shells bursting in the background, you'll hear readings of the poignant diaries of people who experienced the siege of Atlanta.

In "New South City" (1866 through 1895), skyscrapers go up as Atlantans begin recovering from the ravages of war. In a reconstruction of *Atlanta Constitution* editor Henry Grady's office you can hear excerpts from his famous speech advancing the ideals of the "New South."

"Forward Atlanta" (1896 through 1945) deals with the surge in the business community and prominent roles played by major companies. It also examines the Jim Crow Laws and the prosperous black-owned businesses and thriving music scene that developed in Sweet Auburn.

"A City too Busy to Hate" (1946 through 1973) documents Atlanta's continued emergence as a business center and as the cradle of the civil rights movement.

Transportation and communications are the themes of "The World's Next Great City," focusing on the role of Turner Broadcasting and Delta Air Lines. You can step inside a 1970 Convair 880 Delta jet cockpit (photos inside contrast the infinitely more complex controls of a present-day jet) and listen to pilots conversing with the tower at Hartsfield International Airport. Baseball buffs will enjoy a video of Hank Aaron's record-breaking home run.

Exhibits are interactive, enhanced by audio and video presentations, and you can ask to view additional videos about various aspects of Atlanta history. Be sure to check out the gift shop here.

The World of Coca-Cola

55 Martin Luther King, Jr., Dr. SW, at Central Ave. (adjacent to Underground Atlanta). ☎ **404/676-5151.** Admission $3.50 adults, $3 seniors 55 and over, $2.50 children 6–12, under 6 free. Mon–Sat 10am–8:30pm, Sun noon–5pm. Closed New Year's Day, the second Mon in Jan, Easter, Thanksgiving, Christmas Eve, and Christmas Day. Parking garage on Central Ave. off Martin Luther King Dr. MARTA: Five Points.

This expositionlike attraction showcases "the world's most popular product." Its vast three-story pavilion houses a massive collection of

Coca-Cola memorabilia, along with numerous interactive displays, high-tech exhibits, and video presentations. A self-guided tour begins on the third level where visitors are greeted by a Rube Goldberg–like kinetic sculpture called a "Bottling Fantasy." Exhibits throughout trace the history of Coca-Cola from its 1886 debut at Jacob's Pharmacy in downtown Atlanta to its current worldwide fame. Highlights include: a re-creation of Barnes Soda Fountain in Baxley, Georgia (ca. 1930) (a jukebox on the premises plays Coke-themed pop songs of yesteryear like "Sweet Coca-Cola Bush" sung by Shirley Temple); diverse advertising campaigns over the years (did you know that Maxwell House's "good to the last drop" was originally a Coke slogan?); a video on the making of the "Hilltop Reunion" Coke commercial (it kicked off the "I'd Like to Teach the World to Sing" campaign); print ads featuring screen stars such as Jean Harlow, Claudette Colbert, Clark Gable, and Cary Grant; and an interactive audio exhibit that lets you listen to Coke commercials sung by pop stars like Al Jarreau, Loretta Lynn, Jerry Lee Lewis, and the Supremes. And, in case you've worked up a thirst by this time, you can sample unlimited amounts of 38 Coca-Cola Company beverages at Club Coca-Cola, including 18 international drinks that are not sold in the United States (for example, a pineapple/orange/banana beverage marketed only in Kenya). The tour ends in the first-floor gift shop, which vends a mind-boggling array of Coca-Cola logo items—everything from T-shirts to Coke polar bears. There's much, much more; this experience is a total immersion in Coca-Cola.

✪ Michael C. Carlos Museum of Emory University

571 S. Kilgo St. (near the intersection of Oxford and N. Decatur rds. on the Main Quadrangle of the Emory Campus). ☎ **404/727-4282.** $3 donation suggested. Mon–Thurs 10am–5pm, Fri 10am–9pm, Sat 10am–5pm, Sun noon–5pm. Closed New Year's Day, Thanksgiving, and Christmas.

Emory University's antiquities collection dates to 1875 and this intriguing museum to 1919, when it was founded to display the art and artifacts collected by Emory faculty in Egypt, Cyprus, Greece, Sicily, the Sea of Galilee, and the sites of ancient Babylon and Palestine. Today the museum also maintains collections of ancient art and archaeology of Rome, Central and South America, the Near East, and Mesoamerica; works of the native cultures of North America; art of Asia and Oceania; and some 1,000 objects from sub-Saharan Africa. Additionally, a sizable collection of works on paper encompasses illuminated manuscript pages, drawings, and prints from the Middle Ages and the Renaissance to the 20th century. It's all housed partly in a 1916 beaux-arts building that is on the National Register of Historic Places, its interior redesigned in 1985 by postmodernist architect Michael Graves. The remainder is in a 35,000-square-foot exhibition space (also designed by Graves) that opened in 1993.

The first-floor galleries feature exhibits from the extensive permanent collection—objects that were part of the daily life of people from five continents as early as the seventh millenium B.C. They include Bronze and Iron Age clay pots, jugs, loom weights, and oil lamps from Palestine; Egyptian mummies, pottery, cosmetic containers, and headrests; Greek and Cypriot pottery, flasks, and statuary; and Mesopotamian pottery, coins, tools, sculpture, and cuneiform tablets inscribed with ancient writing. Also on this level: the Thibadeau Pre-Columbian collection, comprising over 1,300 objects spanning 2,000 years of creativity—gold jewelry, pottery, and statues, including many ceramic, volcanic stone, greenstone, and gold sculptures from ancient Costa Rica.

The upper floor is used for changing exhibits ranging in subject matter from Pueblo Indian pottery to impressionist art. This level also houses a café serving light fare. Throughout the museum, 210 plaster casts of ancient architectural elements—reliefs, friezes, column capitals, and decorative elements from temples and monuments—adorn hallway and lobby walls. There are many interesting workshops, lectures, films, and gallery tours here; call to find out what's on during your stay. Allow about an hour to see the collection.

2 More Attractions

Château Elan Winery & Resort

30 miles north of Atlanta at Exit 48 off I-85 in Braselton. ☎ **404/932-0900** or in Georgia 800/233-WINE. Admission free. Daily 11am–7pm. Closed Christmas.

Château Elan is a hilltop winery that replicates a 16th-century French estate surrounded by verdant countryside. Its first wines were produced in 1985, and already they have garnered 205 awards. Guided tours are given daily between 11am and 4pm (call ahead for hours; you can also take self-guided tours from 5pm to closing).

On view are the crushing and pressing machines, oak barrels used to age and flavor wines, the cask room, and the bottling area. Tours conclude with a wine tasting. Vines ripen in July/August, so if you're here during harvesting in August and September, you'll actually see the winemaking procedure. More than 500 tons of grapes are harvested and processed each year. The interior of the château, a stage-set version of a Paris street, has a quarry-stone floor, wrought-iron fences, and streetlamps. Walls are adorned with large murals depicting the history of winemaking and two Parisian sites—La Gare du Nord and the place des Vosges. The building houses an art gallery offering changing exhibits by regional and national artists, displays of antique European winemaking equipment, and a wine market.

There are also two on-premises restaurants, so plan to dine here. Café Elan, open daily from 11am (closing hours vary; call before you go), features sandwiches, salads, and continental entrées such as trout amandine and beef bourguignonne for $7.25 to $12.95 at lunch, $12.95 to $17.95 at dinner. It's a charming setting, with seating under a green awning. The fancier Le Clos—with pale pink walls, lace-curtained French doors, and tables covered with crisp white linen—is open for dinner only Wednesday through Saturday evenings, with seatings from 6:30 to 10pm. A six-course prix-fixe meal for $65 features haute-cuisine entrées such as Barbarie duck breast with cerise sauce and Dover sole aux champignons meunière; appropriate Château Elan wines with each course are included. Reservations are imperative. Men are requested to wear a coat and tie. There are also several restaurants at the adjoining

Château Elan resort. And there are picnic areas on the lovely grounds; custom picnic baskets can be purchased here.

In addition to its interior attractions, Château Elan has nature trails along St. Emilion Creek and by Romanée-Conti pond. On select Saturday evenings between Memorial Day and Labor Day there's dancing to live beach music in an adjoining outdoor facility called Le Pavillon. Admission is $20; you can order a picnic box in advance or enjoy a themed buffet (call ahead for prices). Shag (jitterbugging) lessons begin at 7:30pm, but you should arrive at least an hour earlier for dinner. In addition, there are numerous events at Château Elan, ranging from harvest celebrations to equestrian shows; call to find out what's on during your visit.

You might also consider an overnight or longer stay at the 144-room **Inn at Château Elan,** a luxurious on-premises resort where facilities include three golf courses (two 18-hole and one par-3, 9-hole), and seven tennis courts (both offering pro shops and instruction), a full European-style spa and salon (days of beauty are an option), an outdoor Olympic-size pool and an indoor heated pool, a fitness center, and lawn games; boating and fishing can be arranged nearby. Room rates are quite reasonable; call the above numbers for details and inquire about golf, tennis, spa, and other packages.

Big Shanty Museum

2829 Cherokee St., Kennesaw. ☎ **404/427-2117** or 800/742-6897. Admission $3 adults; $2.50 seniors, service people, and AAA members; $1.50 children 7–15; children 6 and under free. Families pay a maximum of $12. Mon–Sat 9:30am–5:30pm, Sun noon–5:30pm. Take exit 118 off I-75N and follow the signs.

On this site began the wild adventure known as "the Great Locomotive Chase." The Civil War had been underway for a year on April 12, 1862, when Union spy James J. Andrews and a group of 21 Northern soldiers disguised as civilians boarded a locomotive called the *General* in Marietta, buying tickets for diverse destinations to avert suspicion. When the train made a breakfast stop at the Lacy Hotel in Big Shanty, they seized the locomotive and several boxcars and fled northward to Chattanooga. The goal of these daring raiders was to destroy tracks, telegraph wires, and bridges behind them, thus cutting off the Confederate supply route between Virginia and Mississippi.

Conductor William A. Fuller, his breakfast interrupted by the sound of the *General* chugging out of the station, gave chase on foot, then grabbed a platform car and poled along the tracks. With him were a railroad superintendent and the *General*'s engineer. At the Etowah River, Fuller and crew commandeered a small locomotive called the *Yonah* and made better progress. Meanwhile, the raiders tore up track behind them, and when the pursuers got close, the raiders slowed them down by throwing ties and firewood onto the tracks. Andrews, a very smooth talker, managed to convince station attendants en route that he was on an emergency mission running ammunition to Confederate general Beauregard in Mississippi. Fuller's chances of catching the *General* improved when he seized the southbound *Texas* and began running it backward toward the raiders, picking up reinforcements along the way and eventually managing to get a telegraph message through to Gen. Danville Leadbetter, commander at Chattanooga. The

Regional Atlanta Sights

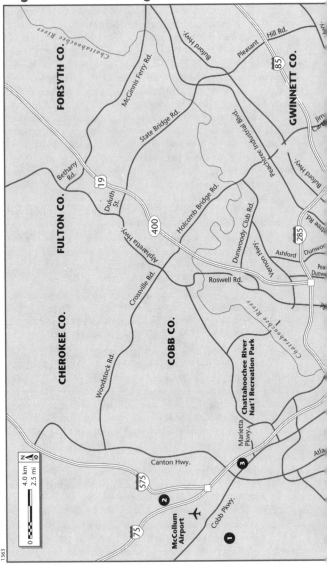

chase went on, with Andrews sending uncoupled boxcars careening back toward Fuller as obstructions. Fuller, however, who was running in reverse, merely attached the rolling boxcars to his engine and kept on. At the wooden-covered Oostanaula Bridge, the raiders detached a boxcar and set it on fire in hopes of finally creating an impassable obstacle—a burning bridge behind them. But the *Texas* was able to

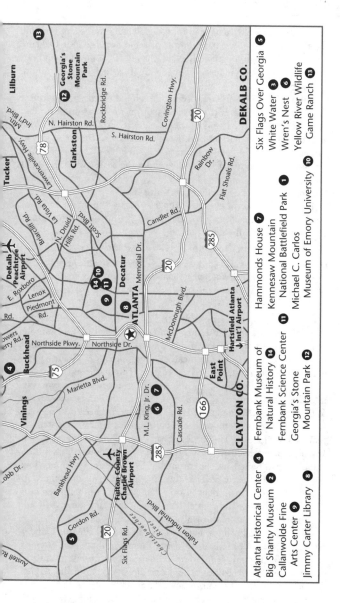

Atlanta Historical Center	4
Big Shanty Museum	2
Callanwolde Fine Arts Center	9
Jimmy Carter Library	8

Fernbank Museum of Natural History	14
Fernbank Science Center	11
Georgia's Stone Mountain Park	12

Hammonds House	7
Kennesaw Mountain National Battlefield Park	1
Michael C. Carlos Museum of Emory University	10

Six Flags Over Georgia	5
White Water	3
Wren's Nest	6
Yellow River Wildlife Game Ranch	13

push the flaming car off the bridge; it soon burned out, and Fuller tossed it off the track and continued.

By this time the *General* was running low on fuel and water, the *Texas* was hot on its heels, and the raiders realized that all was lost. Andrews gave his final command: "Jump off and scatter! Every man for himself!" All were captured and imprisoned within a few days. Some escaped, others were exchanged for Confederate prisoners of war, and the rest were hung in Atlanta, most of them at a site near Oakland Cemetery. Though the mission failed, the raiders, some of them post-humously, received the newly created Congressional Medal of Honor for their valor.

The Big Shanty Museum, occupying a building that was once the Frey cotton gin, houses the *General* (still in running condition, but don't get any ideas), a walk-through caboose, exhibits of Civil War artifacts, memorabilia and photographs relating to the chase and its participants, and, for good measure, a *Gone With the Wind* exhibit. You can view a 20-minute narrated video about the chase, but if you really want the full story, rent the Disney movie, *The Great Locomotive Chase,* starring Fess Parker as the dashing Andrews.

The museum is three miles from Kennesaw Mountain/National Battlefield Park (details below), so consider visiting both of these Civil War–related sights the same day.

Kennesaw Mountain/National Battlefield Park

Old Highway 41 and Stilesboro Rd., Kennesaw. ☎ **404/427-4686.** Admission free. Visitor Center open daily 8:30am–5pm, till 6pm weekends June–Aug; front gate closes at 8pm Jun–Aug, 6pm the rest of the year. Closed Christmas. Take 1–75 north to Barrett Pkwy. (Exit 116), then follow the signs.

This 2,882-acre park was established in 1917 on the site of a crucial Civil War battle in the Atlanta campaign of 1864. A very popular attraction, it draws some two million visitors annually. The action began in June 1864. A month earlier, Gen. Ulysses S. Grant had or-dered Sherman to attack the Confederate army in Georgia, "break it up, and go into the interior of the enemy's country as far as you can, inflicting all the damage you can upon their war resources." In response to this order, Sherman's army, 100,000 strong, had been pushing back Confederate forces composed of 65,000 men under Gen. Joseph E. Johnston. By June 19, Union troops had driven Johnston's men back to a well-prepared defensive position on Kennesaw Mountain. Southern engineers had built a line of entrenchments in its rocky slopes allow-ing the Confederates to cover every approach with rifle or cannon. An Ohio officer later commented that if the mountain had been con-structed for the sole purpose of repelling an invading army, "it could not have been better made or placed."

On June 27, following a few weeks of skirmishing, Sherman, under-estimating the strength and still-feisty morale of the rebels, attempt-ed to break through Confederate lines and annihilate them in a grand no-holds-barred assault from two directions. Confederate Gen. Samuel French described the onset of the attack thusly: "As if by magic, there sprang from the earth a host of men, and in one long, waving line of blue the infantry advanced and the battle of Kennesaw Mountain began."

Sherman's men were repelled by massive bursts of firepower and huge rocks rolling down the mountain at them. Federal casualties far outnumbered Confederate losses. Meanwhile, 8,000 Union infantry-men in five brigades attacked from another angle; in this battle the Union lost 3,000 men, the Confederates 500. Weeks of torrential rain, which had turned these battlegrounds into a muddy mire, added significantly to the misery quotient on both sides. There was no rain the day of the battle, but the day was swelteringly hot and muggy.

Allow at least two hours for exploring. Start your tour at the **Visitor Center,** where you can pick up a map, watch a 10-minute slide show about the battle, and view exhibits of Civil War artifacts and memorabilia. You can drive weekdays (on weekends take a shuttle bus) or hike up the mountain to see the actual Confederate entrenchments and earthworks, some of them equipped with Civil War artillery. The trail is about one steep mile long, so wear comfortable shoes. Interpretive signs at key spots enhance the experience, and, weekends spring through fall, interpretive programs further elucidate the battle. You'll also want to drive to **Cheatham Hill,** site of some of the fiercest fighting. There are 16 miles of hiking trails for those who want a more extensive tour (trail maps are available at the Visitor Center), and picnicking is permitted in designated areas, some with barbecue grills. The scenery, by the way, is gorgeous, so even if Civil War battles are not your thing (that is, if you're reluctantly accompanying an enthusiastic spouse), it makes for beautiful hiking or driving.

Note: Special interactive displays and living-history programs will be offered during the Olympic Games when Visitor Center hours will also be extended to 7am to 9pm daily.

High Museum of Art, Folk Art and Photography Galleries

30 John Wesley Dobbs Ave. (at Peachtree St. NE). ☎ **404/577-6940.** Admission free. Mon–Sat 10am–5pm. MARTA: Peachtree Center.

This downtown branch of the High Museum of Art displays folk art and photography. Allow about an hour for your visit. Visitors can enter via an elegantly landscaped courtyard on John Wesley Dobbs Avenue or via the imposing lobby of the Georgia-Pacific Building off Peachtree Street, itself the setting for Louise Nevelson's vast indoor environmental sculpture in white wood, *Dawn's Forest.* Spanning three levels, the museum has beautiful walls paneled in an African wood called angré, and pedestrian ramps affording visitors a view of the downtown skyline as they descend to the galleries.

The two levels of galleries provide approximately 5,000 square feet of exhibition space. The upper gallery has a barrel-vaulted ceiling with Plexiglas inserts allowing daylight to flood the space. In addition to exhibitions, the museum offers free films, lectures, concerts, and gallery talks (call for details). The Georgia-Pacific Building, by the way, occupies the hallowed site of the Loew's Grand Theatre, where *Gone With the Wind* premiered in 1939.

The Alonzo F. Herndon Home

587 University Place (between Vine and Walnut Sts.). ☎ **404/581-9813.** Admission free (donations appreciated). Tues–Sat 10am–4pm, with tours on the hour. Closed New Year's Day, July 4, Thanksgiving, and Christmas. MARTA: Vine City.

Alonzo Herndon was born into the last decade of slavery in 1858. After emancipation, he worked as a field hand and sharecropper, supplementing his meager income by selling peanuts, homemade molasses, and axle grease. He arrived in Atlanta in the early 1880s, where he worked as a barber and eventually owned several barbershops of his own. He acquired real estate with earnings from these shops. By 1900, with only a year of formal education and less than 40 years out of slavery, Herndon was the richest black man in Atlanta. In 1905, he purchased a church burial association, which, with other small companies, became the nucleus of the Atlanta Life Insurance Company, today the nation's second-largest black-owned insurance company.

In 1910, Herndon built this elegant 15-room house in the beaux-arts neoclassical style with a stately colonnaded entrance. Today, visitors enter from the back. The tour begins in a receiving room with a 10-minute introductory video called *The Herndon Legacy.* Herndon and his wife, Adrienne McNeil, a drama teacher at Atlanta University, were the primary architects of the house, and construction was accomplished almost completely by black artisans. Since the home was occupied until 1977 by their son Norris, much of the original furniture remains, and there are family photographs throughout. Adrienne died about a week after the house was completed. Two years later, Herndon married Jessie Gillespie, who later became a vice president of Atlanta Life.

The tour takes you through the reception hall; the music room with rococo gilt-trim walls and Louis XV–style furnishings; the living room, with a frieze on its walls depicting the accomplishments of Herndon's life; the dining room, furnished in late Renaissance style with family china and Venetian glass displayed in a mahogany cabinet; the butler's pantry; and the sunny breakfast room. Upstairs, you'll see Jessie Herndon's bedroom, with its Jacobean suite and Louis XV–style furnishings; Herndon's Empire-furnished bedroom, where a book from a Republican National Convention displayed on a table lets you know his political bent; the collection room (Norris collected ancient Greek and Roman vases and funerary objects); Norris's bedroom; a sitting room; and a guest bedroom.

Atlanta College of Art Gallery

In the Memorial Arts Building of the Woodruff Arts Center, 1280 Peachtree St. NE. ☎ **404/733-5050.** Admission free. Mon–Sat 10am–5pm; fall–spring Sun 1–6pm as well. MARTA: Arts Center.

The Atlanta College of Art, housed in the Woodruff Arts Center complex, features an ongoing series of gallery shows. Some recent examples: "Subject Male Violence" (an installation of 80 study tables by Richard Bolton), "Make Yourself At Home: Race and Ethnicity in the American Family"; and "A Family Affair: Gay and Lesbian Issues of Domestic Life." There are also faculty exhibitions, juried student shows, lectures, and concerts here. Call for details.

Atlanta Museum

537 Peachtree St. (between Renaissance Pkwy. and Linden Ave.). ☎ **404/872-8233.** Admission $3 adults, $2 children under 12 and seniors. Mon–Fri 10am–5pm (hours may vary; call ahead). Parking on the side and rear of the building. MARTA: North Avenue or Civic Center.

If, like me, you love to come upon musty collections of curiosities, this will be a thrill. Antique dealer James Elliott, Sr., started his mini-Smithsonian in 1936; today, his son, James Elliott, Jr., is in charge of its 2,500 or so diverse exhibits. They're displayed in a 1900 Historic Register Victorian home. Mr. Elliott runs a cluttery antique shop on the first floor. The museum is upstairs.

Exhibits include: the throne of Haile Selassie, paw signatures of movie dogs, Franklin D. Roosevelt's fishing hat, personal articles that belonged to Adolf Hitler, a carved stone from King Tut's tomb, a lock of Napoléon's hair and a pair of chairs from his throne room (the latter were given to Admiral Dewey while on a goodwill tour of France), a World War II Japanese field telephone, a vase with an Egyptian curse, the desk on which the Georgia secession was written, General Custer's hairbrush, Davy Crockett's gun, furnishings and books that belonged to Margaret Mitchell, an original model of the cotton gin from Eli Whitney's shop, spoons made by Paul Revere, and a piece of root from the apple tree under which Robert E. Lee stood when he surrendered at Appomattox. Another collector of curiosities, Michael Jackson, once came in and tried to buy a thing or two, but Elliott wouldn't part with his treasures.

Hammonds House Galleries & Resource Center of African-American Art

503 Peeples St. (at Lucile St. two blocks north of R. D. Abernathy Blvd.). ☎ **404/ 752-8730**. Admission $2 adults, $1 seniors and students. Tues–Fri 10am–6pm, Sat–Sun 1–5pm. MARTA: West End (4^1/$_2$ blocks away).

Occupying the 1857 Eastlake Victorian-style former home of Dr. Otis T. Hammonds, a black anesthesiologist and art patron, Hammonds House is a national center for the exhibition, preservation, research, and documentation of African-American art and artists. The house was purchased with these aims in mind by the Fulton County Commission after Hammonds's death in 1985. Hammonds's extensive collection included works by African-American and Haitian artists, as well as African masks and carvings. Along with later acquisitions—including works by Romare Bearden, William H. Johnson, Robert S. Duncanson, and Elizabeth Catlett—the permanent collection is shown on a rotating basis and supplemented by exhibitions of renowned black artists from all over the world. The Resource Center on the premises, housing documents on African-American art and artists, is open to the public by appointment.

Callanwolde Fine Arts Center

980 Briarcliff Rd. NE (north of Ponce de Leon Ave). ☎ **404/872-5338**. Admission free. Guided tours, by special appointment only, $1.50 adults, 50¢ children under 12. If you're interested in a tour, call to arrange it as far in advance as possible. Mon–Fri 9am–9pm, Sat 10am–4pm.

A magnificent Gothic/Tudor–style mansion, built for Coca-Cola heir Charles Howard Candler in 1920, Callanwolde today serves as a fine-arts center for DeKalb County. Classes are given in pottery, painting, photography, drawing, and more, and there are numerous workshops for adults and children. Though it's a lovely setting for art students, I can't help wishing that some preservation committee had instead restored the house to its former grandeur and re-created its

---

❓ Did You Know?

- Atlanta has 32 streets named Peachtree.
- Georgia's major agricultural crop is peanuts, not peaches.
- Atlanta's earliest street lights burned whale oil.
- The world's largest bas-relief sculpture (Stone Mountain—90 feet by 190 feet) and the world's largest painting (Cyclorama, utilizing 20,000 square feet of canvas) are in Atlanta.
- Georgia Tech's Yellow Jackets set a world record football score in 1916—222 to 0 (they were the zero).
- Because it has received over $250 million from Coca-Cola, Emory University is known as "Coca-Cola U."
- *Fortune Magazine* rates Atlanta the nation's "best place to do business."
- Not a single scene from the movie *Gone With the Wind* was filmed in Georgia, though a few bushels of Georgia red clay were transported to the Hollywood set to add verisimilitude.
- Hartsfield is the world's third-busiest airport and is consistently ranked among the best airports in the world. Eighty percent of the United States population is within a three-hour flight of Atlanta.

---

furnishings and appointments. As it is, most of the rooms are bare, and only Callanwolde's exquisite walnut paneling, beautifully carved ceilings and moldings, grand staircase, magnificent marble and stone fireplaces, and leaded-glass windows evoke its luxurious past.

The estate occupies 12 acres (originally 27) in the Druid Hills section of Atlanta, an area planned by Frederick Law Olmsted, designer of New York's Central Park. Visitors are welcome to peruse shows of local artists in the Petite Hall gallery upstairs; enjoy the lawns, formal gardens, and nature trails, which are maintained by the county; and participate in the many events here—concerts, storytelling evenings, dance performances (see the "Calendar of Events" in Chapter 3). Attending a function here is the best way to experience the estate.

Rhodes Memorial Hall

1516 Peachtree St. NW (at Peachtree Circle). ☎ **404/881-9980.** Admission $2 adults, $1 seniors, students, and children under 12. Mon–Fri 11am–4pm. MARTA: Arts Center.

Rhodes Hall is one of a few remaining pre–World War I Peachtree Street mansions. It was designed shortly after the turn of the century by Willis Franklin Denny (at the time Atlanta's leading residential architect) as a residence for affluent Atlanta businessman Amos Giles Rhodes and his family. Its medieval baronial-cum-high Victorian Romanesque style was inspired by Rhineland castles. The granite exterior is replete with arched Romanesque windows, battlements and buttresses, parapets, towers, and turrets. A large Syrian-arched veranda wraps the east and north facades. And the interior is grandiose, with maple- and mahogany-bordered oak parquet floors, mosaics surrounding the fireplaces, and a gracefully winding hand-carved Honduran mahogany staircase with nine stained-glass stairwell panels depicting "The Rise and Fall of the Confederacy." The house and stables originally occupied 150 acres of land and included servants' quarters, a carriage house, and other outbuildings. When it was built, this site was in suburbia, an afternoon's drive from downtown.

Upon Rhodes's death in 1929, his residence was deeded to the state of Georgia in keeping with his desire to preserve it. The house was entered on the National Register of Historic Places in 1974. Today it is headquarters for the Georgia Trust for Historic Preservation and is in an ongoing process of restoration. To date, the original dining-room suite and some other furnishings are in place, and all the mahogany woodwork and decorated ceilings on the first floor have been restored. Original landscaping—with white and red cedars, dogwoods, banana trees, and a circular flower bed—is being re-created in the front yard.

The Margaret Mitchell House (Birthplace of *Gone With the Wind*)
Peachtree and 10th sts. ☎ 404/249-7012.

In Atlanta, *Gone With the Wind* comes up daily, and Margaret Mitchell is an almost-hallowed name. So it's rather surprising that only at this late date is restoration underway on the dilapidated turn-of-the-century Tudor-revival Peachtree Street apartment house where Mitchell lived with her husband, John Marsh, from 1925 to 1932 (they called it "The Dump") and wrote most of her epic novel. They even held their wedding reception there. Since everyone comes to Atlanta seeking *GWTW*-related attractions, and few exist (the white-colonnaded mansion at 1401 Peachtree St., where Mitchell grew up, was razed in 1952), it is estimated that the restored home will draw millions of visitors annually. Plans call for a re-creation of Mitchell's apartment and utilization of the rest of the building for a museum. Despite an arson fire in September 1994, it is the goal of the organization behind the restoration to have the exterior of the building and Mitchell's apartment reconstructed by June 1996, the 60th anniversary of the publication of the book. Call for details.

PARKS

Refer to Section 1, "The Top Attractions," earlier in this chapter, for full details on Georgia's Stone Mountain Park.

Piedmont Park, the city's most popular and centrally located recreation area (with its main entrance on Piedmont Avenue at 14th Street), was created around the turn of the century. Its first public usage was by the elite Gentlemen's Driving Club, which bought the property as a site for horseback riding and racing. It soon became a venue for state fairs, culminating with the spectacular Cotton States and International Exposition of 1895. In 1904, the property's 180-plus acres of woodsy meadow and farm acreage were transformed into a city park with a varied terrain of rolling hillsides, verdant lawns, and lush forest around beautiful Lake Clara Meer.

Today, Piedmont Park is the setting for many popular regional attractions: jazz and symphony concerts, art and music festivals, marathons, etc. It contains a large baseball field, tennis courts, a public swimming pool, and paths for jogging, skating, and cycling. The magnificent Atlanta Botanical Garden (see "The Top Attractions," above) is adjacent. At this writing, the Piedmont Park Conservancy and the City of Atlanta have been upgrading the park's landscaping, including the planting of 150 new trees, and a Visitors' Center is underway in the Boathouse Building at the Piedmont Avenue and 12th Street entrance.

A very pleasant way to see the park is on an Atlanta Preservation Center **walking tour.** Departures are from the 12th Street gate Saturdays at 2pm and Sundays at 3pm March through November. Tour charges are $5 for adults, $4 for seniors, $3 for students. For further details call **404/876-2041.**

The park is open daily from 6am to 11pm. The nearest MARTA stop is Midtown or Arts Center.

Named for Confederate captain Lemuel P. Grant, who helped build Atlanta's defense line, **Grant Park** (bordered by Sydney Street and Atlanta Avenue, Boulevard and Cherokee Avenues) still contains vestiges of his fortifications. Grant also donated its 100 acres to the city for a park on this site. Near the intersection of Boulevard and Atlanta Avenue, you can see the remaining earthwork slopes of Fort Walker, a commanding artillery bastion with its original gun emplacements. Its cannons and caissons can be seen in the museum area of Cyclorama (see "The Top Attractions," above), one of Grant Park's two major attractions. The other is Zoo Atlanta (see "Especially for Kids," below). The park is open daily from 6am to 11pm.

3 Especially for Kids

Though the following attractions are great choices if you're traveling with kids, don't pass them up if you're not. I especially love Wren's Nest, the Center for Puppetry Arts, the Yellow River Wildlife Game Ranch (visit in conjunction with Stone Mountain), and Zoo Atlanta (visit in conjunction with Cyclorama and Oakland Cemetery). In addition, be sure to take the kids to the Fernbank Museum of Natural History and the Martin Luther King, Jr. birth home and Center for Nonviolent Social Change (all described above).

✪ Zoo Atlanta

800 Cherokee Ave. (in Grant Park). ☎ **404/624-5600.** Admission $7.50 adults, $6.50 seniors, $5.50 children 3–11, children 2 and under free. Strollers can be rented. Daily 10am–5:30pm, till 6:30pm during daylight saving time. The admission booth closes an hour before zoo closing. Closed New Year's Day, Thanksgiving, Christmas. Take I-75 south to I-20 east. Get off at the Boulevard exit and follow the signs to Grant Park. Or take a no. 31, 32, or 97 bus from the Five Points rail station.

This absolutely delightful 40-acre zoo dates from 1889, when George W. Hall (aka "Popcorn George") brought his traveling circus to town. Employee claims against Hall for back wages forced him to relinquish his menagerie, and the animal entourage was purchased by a prominent Atlanta businessman who donated the collection to the city as the basis for a zoological garden in Grant Park. It's grown considerably since then, but the real turnaround came in 1985, when the zoo began a still-ongoing multimillion-dollar renovation.

Today, Zoo Atlanta is a very exciting and creatively run facility, with animals housed in large open enclosures that simulate their natural geographical habitats. The zoo participates in breeding programs, many of them focusing on endangered species. Signs, some translated into Swahili, use a cartoon format to inform visitors about environmental and conservational issues pertinent to wildlife. All areas are beautifully landscaped and adorned with animal sculptures. There are video displays in the Elephant Barn, Tiger Forest, and Gorilla museum, and safari carts throughout the zoo serve as educational stations. Plan to catch entertaining and informative free animal shows in the Kroger Wildlife Theater, presented daily at 11:30am and 1:30 and 3:30pm May through September. Ditto the African Elephant Demonstration given daily year-round at 11am, 1, and 3pm.

Flamingo Plaza is the first habitat you'll see upon entering the zoo. Farther on, **Masai Mara** houses elephants, rhinos, lions, zebras, giraffes, gazelles, and other African animals and birds. Its landscape resembles the plains of East Africa, with honey locust trees and yuccas; and the lion enclosure replicates an East African kopje (rocky outcropping). A café called the **Swahili Market** overlooks the zebras. Frequent animal demonstrations, African storytelling, and educational programs take place under the Elder's Tree in Masai Mara.

The lushly landscaped **Ford African Rain Forest** centers on four vast gorilla habitats separated by moats. Studies on gorilla behavior take place here, and there are often quite a few adorable babies. A gorilla named Willie B. and his daughter Kudzoo are the zoo's mascots. Also in the section: a walk-through aviary of West African birds, small African primates, and the Gorillas of Cameroon museum. Landscaping includes burned-out areas of forest and deadfall trees—gorillas do not live in manicured gardens.

Sumatran tigers (a very endangered species) and orangutans live in the **Ketambe** section, an Indonesian tropical rain forest with clusters of bamboo and a waterfall. Ketambe also includes a Reptile House and a special exhibit area, often used to house visiting animals.

A zoo train travels through the **Children's Zoo** area, a peaceful enclave with a playground and children's zoo where kids can pet baby llamas, sheep, pigs, and goats. There are aviaries here, too. In the works are **Okefenokee Swamp** and a hands-on educational facility with animal exhibits and **Coastal Georgia** exhibits. There are shops and snack bars throughout the zoo and tree-shaded picnic areas in Grant Park.

✪ Wren's Nest

1050 Ralph Abernathy Blvd. (two blocks from Ashby St.). ☎ **404/753-7735.** Admission $4 adults, $3 seniors and students 13–19, $2 children 4–12, under 4 free; storytelling $2 per person additional. Tues–Sat 10am–4pm, Sun 1–4pm, with tours departing every 30 minutes on the hour and half hour. Closed Jan 1, July 4, Thanksgiving, Dec 24–25. Take I-20 to Ashby St., turn left on Ashby, right on Ralph Abernathy Blvd.; Wren's Nest is two blocks down on the left. MARTA: West End (three long blocks away).

Named for a family of wrens that once nested in the mailbox (and at this writing wrens are nesting there again), Wren's Nest is the former home of Joel Chandler Harris, who chronicled the wily deeds of Br'er Rabbit and Br'er Fox. It's been open to the public since 1913, when his widow sold it to the Uncle Remus Memorial Association. Harris's literary career began at the age of 13, when he apprenticed on *The Countryman,* a quarterly plantation newspaper. In four years spent learning journalism there, young Harris spent many an evening hanging about the slave quarters, drinking in African folk tales and fables spun by George Terrell, a plantation patriarch who became the prototype for Uncle Remus. Sherman's army put *The Countryman* out of business, and Harris went on to other newspapers, working his way up to editorial writer at the *Atlanta Constitution* by age 28. There, plagued by writer's block one gloomy winter afternoon, he remembered the plantation stories of his youth and evoked Uncle Remus to fill his column. Enthralled readers clamored for more, and the rest is history.

The house itself is an 1870s farmhouse with a Queen Anne Victorian facade added in 1884. Harris lived here from 1881 until his death in 1908, doing most of his writing in a rocking chair on the wraparound front porch. On a 30-minute tour, including a slide presentation about Harris's life, you'll see much Uncle Remus memorabilia. The stuffed great horned owl over the study door was a gift from Theodore Roosevelt, whose White House Harris visited; the original wren's nest mailbox reposes on the study mantel; and all of Harris's books, along with signed first editions of major authors of his day (Mark Twain and others) are displayed in a bookcase.

The house is restored to its 1900 appearance, and an interpretation center is in the works. Call ahead to find out when storyteller-in-residence Akbar Imhotep will be telling stories culled from African and African-American folklore; it's a real treat. Mid-June through mid-August, Akbar and storytellers perform daily at 11:30am and 12:30 and 1:30pm. There are other storytelling programs year-round; call for details.

Joel Chandler Harris died at the age of 62 on July 3, 1908. He penned these words, which later appeared on his gravestone:

> I seem to see before me the smiling faces of thousands of children—some young and fresh—and some wearing the friendly marks of age, but all children at heart, and not an unfriendly face among them. And while I am trying hard to speak the right word, I seem to hear a voice lifted above the rest saying, "You have made some of us happy." And so I feel my heart fluttering and my lips trembling and I have to bow silently and turn away and hurry into the obscurity that fits me best.

✪ Center for Puppetry Arts

1404 Spring St. NW (at 18th St.). ☎ **404/873-3089,** box office 404/873-3391. Admission $3 adults, $2 children 14 and under; free if you see a show or take a workshop. Show prices vary; call ahead for details. Mon–Sat 9am–5pm. Closed New Year's Day, Memorial Day, July 4, Labor Day, Thanksgiving, and Christmas. MARTA: Arts Center.

If you're traveling with the kids, this is in the not-to-be-missed category. In fact, I wouldn't miss it even without kids in tow. The center is dedicated to expanding public awareness of puppetry as a fine art and to presenting all its international and historic forms. Opened in 1978, with Kermit the Frog cutting the official ribbon (he had a little help from the late Jim Henson), it contains a 300-seat theater, two smaller theaters, gallery space, and a permanent museum. The puppet shows are marvelous—sophisticated, riveting, full-stage productions with elaborate scenery. Some are family oriented; others, with nighttime showings, are geared to adults. Call ahead to find out what's on; reservations are essential. You can also call a week or so in advance to enroll yourself or your kids in a puppet-making workshop here.

The museum area displays puppets ranging from ritualistic African figures to Punch and Judy. It's an excellent collection, one of the largest in North America, including turn-of-the-century Thai shadow puppets, Indonesian wayang golek puppets used to tell classic stories (a centuries-old tradition), Chinese hand puppets, rod-operated marionettes from all over Europe, original Muppets, pre-Columbian clay puppets that were used in religious ceremonies circa A.D. 1200, Turkish shadow figures made of dried animal skins, and a Nigerian Yoruba puppet, among many, many others. The permanent collection is augmented by short-term exhibits such as a Bill Baird retrospective (he created the puppets used in *The Sound of Music*).

As part of the Cultural Olympiad, the museum will feature a special exhibit focusing on the global aspects of puppetry called "Uniting Nations Through Puppetry."

✪ Yellow River Wildlife Game Ranch

4525 Hwy. 78, Lilburn. ☎ **404/972-6643.** Admission $5 adults, $4 children 3–11, one child under 3 admitted free. Memorial Day–Labor Day daily 9:30am–dusk; till 6pm the rest of the year. Closed Thanksgiving and Christmas. Take I-85N to I-285E. Exit to State Hwy. 78 (30B), and follow it east for 10 miles.

This 24-acre animal preserve bordering the Yellow River is one of the most special places I've ever visited. Owner Art Rilling has created an environment that offers close encounters of the four-legged kind—a chance to view, pet, feed, and generally mingle with some 600 animals (always including quite a few babies) living in open enclosures, or right out in the open, along a one-mile oak- and hickory-shaded forest trail. Art knows every animal on the ranch by name and can give you chapter and verse on the personality, preferences, and in some cases, even romantic history of them. You'll feel like you're in a Disney movie when the deer (there are over 100 whitetail deer) sidle up and nuzzle you. The animals know they're among friends here and are highly socialized, so you have a unique chance to study them up close. Inhabitants include donkeys named Rhett and Scarlett, Georgia black bears that stand up and beg for marshmallows, the goats at Billy Goat Gruff Memorial Bridge (they climb it to get food at the top), dozens of rabbits in Bunny Burrows (kids can walk right into this enclosure and pet the bunnies), a wide assortment of interesting-looking chickens, a herd of buffalo, sheep, burros, ponies, a skunk named General Sherman (we are in Atlanta, after all), and a groundhog named

General Beauregard Lee who lives in a white colonnaded southern mansion complete with miniature satellite dish. You can get animal food in the gift shop at the entrance or buy it along the trail.

Bring your camera (or sketchbook) and consider packing a picnic lunch; there are tables throughout the property, and one especially nice picnic area overlooks the river. An exciting time to visit is Sheep Shearing Saturday in mid-May; in the fall there are after-hours "wilderness hayrides."

SciTrek (The Science and Technology Museum of Atlanta)

395 Piedmont Ave. (between Ralph McGill Blvd. and Pine St.). ☎ **404/522-5500.** Admission $7.50 adults, $5 seniors, students, and children 3–17; free for children under 3. Parking $4. Mon–Sat 10am–5pm, Sun noon–5pm. Closed Thanksgiving, Christmas, Easter, New Year's Day. MARTA: Civic Center.

This museum offers hands-on adventures for adults and kids in science and technology. It houses over 150 interactive exhibits.

Here you can create a magnetic field to hurl a disc upward, change light into electricity, produce electric current using your own hand as a "battery," see how much electricity you can generate pedaling a bicycle (how many bulbs can you light up?), and test various metals for electrical conductivity.

A kinetic light sculpture lets you vary frequency, intensity, and revolutions to create an infinite variety of designs. You can also examine the range of your peripheral vision, step inside a kaleidoscope, watch yourself on video while walking through a distorted room (demonstrating how the brain visually perceives things based on past experience), mix over 16 million colors (time permitting) on a computer, bend light beams, and look into infinity. My own favorite exhibit is the frozen shadow room, in which you can "freeze" your shadow on a wall of light-sensitive phosphorous vinyl film; a bright flash causes the panel to glow except in the area your body shields from the light. It's lots of fun dancing and jumping to create shadow art on the wall.

KIDSPACE has simple exhibits geared to the 2- to 7-year-old set. Here the kids can paint their faces in a mirror, explore a crystal cave, squirt water to float toys downstream, play electronic instruments, make images on heat-sensitive liquid crystal with their hands, and use furnished play environments including an office, puppet theater, and a TV news/weather station. There are also very easy computer games.

Pulleys, levers, wheels, axles, and suchlike are explored in another area. You can lift billiard balls with a screw auger, become a human gyroscope, and suspend a ball in the air using a Bernouilli blower (don't ask me to explain what that is; I'm low-tech).

In Mathematica, a history wall portrays the achievements of major mathematicians from the 12th century to the present. Other hands-on displays here demonstrate various aspects of mathematics from the laws of planetary motion to probability theory. And Power Your Future provides a glimpse at technical innovations that will shape future electrical energy use.

Exhibits are supplemented by an ongoing series of lectures, demonstrations, workshops, and temporary shows. An on-premises McDonald's restaurant is in the works at this writing.

Fernbank Science Center

156 Heaton Park Dr. NE (at Artwood Rd. off Ponce de Leon Ave.). ☎ **404/ 378-4311.** Admission free. Planetarium shows $2 adults, $1 students, free for senior citizens. Note: Children under 5 not admitted to the planetarium. Mon 8:30am–5pm, Tues–Fri 8:30am–10pm, Sat 10am–5pm, Sun 1–5pm. Planetarium shows at 8pm Tues–Fri and 3pm Wed and Fri–Sun. The Observatory open Thurs–Fri 8 (or whenever it gets dark)–10:30pm, weather permitting. Forest trails open Sun–Fri 2–5pm, Sat 10am–5pm. The Greenhouse open Sun only 1–5pm. Closed all school holidays.

Owned and funded by the DeKalb County School System, this museum/planetarium/observatory, located adjacent to the verdant 65-acre Fernbank Forest, is an educational partner of the Fernbank Museum of Natural History (details above in "The Top Attractions"). Plan to visit the entire complex the same day. There's a 1¹/₂-mile forest trail here, with trees, shrubs, ferns, wildflowers, mosses, and other plants marked for identification.

The indoor facility houses museum exhibits such as: a video display on geological phenomena (volcanoes, earthquakes, mountain formation); a gem collection; development of life in Georgia from 500 million years ago to a million years ago; a complete weather station; fossil trees; the original *Apollo 6* space capsule and space suit (on loan from the Smithsonian); computer games; a replica of the Okefenokee Swamp, complete with sound effects; and replicas of dinosaurs that roamed Atlanta in prehistoric times. There are planetarium shows, and, at the Observatory, which contains the largest telescope in the world dedicated to public education, an astronomer gives a talk and lets visitors use the telescope.

If you're here on a Sunday, allow time to visit the nearby greenhouse, about 2¹/₂ miles from the Center. A horticulturist gives a talk to visitors, and children can pot a plant and take it home. There are many workshops, lectures, tours, and films for adults and children on subjects ranging from nature photography to weather forecasting.

Six Flags Over Georgia

Six Flags exit off I-20W. ☎ **404/948-9290.** Admission $28 adults, $20 for children ages 3–9, $14 for seniors (55 and over), under 3 free. A nominal fee ($3–$6) is charged for amphitheater concerts. Weekends only Mar to mid-May, Sept, and Oct; daily Memorial Day–Labor Day. Gates open 10am daily; closing hours vary. Parking $5.

One of the state's major family attractions, Six Flags offers a great day's entertainment. Arrive early (at least 30 minutes before opening), note where you've parked in the vast lot, and take 10 minutes or so to plan out your show and ride schedule.

The park's eight themed areas reflect the historical heritage of the region, both southern (Cotton States, Confederate, Georgia, and Lickskillet) and European (France, Britain, Spain, and U.S.A.). The Spanish section contains Bugs Bunny World, which is especially geared to young children. The "wascally wabbit" is just one of many costumed Looney Tune characters (Sylvester, Daffy Duck, and others) that roam the park greeting kids. Bugs even has a signature restaurant, The Carrot Club, where Warner Brothers cartoons are aired on a video wall and Looney Tunes characters make appearances.

Thrill rides include several wet ones such as Ragin' Rivers (two-person inflatable boats that careen down contoured water channels), a log flume, and Thunder River (a simulated whitewater rafting adventure). White-knuckler coasters include The Viper (which goes from 0 to 60 m.p.h. in less than six seconds and has a 360-degree loop), Ninja (the "black belt" of roller coasters that turns riders upside down five times and offers thrilling loops, dives, and corkscrew turns), the Georgia Cyclone (a classic wooden roller coaster with 11 dramatic drops, patterned after Coney Island's), the Great American Scream Machine (another classic wooden coaster), and Mind Bender, a triple-looper. Other highlights are the Great Gasp (a 20-story parachute jump), Splashwater Falls (plummet down a soaring 50-foot waterfall), and Free Fall (ever wonder what it would be like to fall off a 10-story building?). A less dizzying adventure is Monster Plantation, a Disneyesque boat ride through an antebellum mansion haunted by over 100 animated monsters. There's much, much more.

Shows vary from year to year, but they usually include a major musical revue, a country music show, a golden-oldies show, thrill cinema adventures on a 180-degree screen, a Don Rickles–style comic (much modified, of course) in the form of a sharp-tongued bird named Buford Buzzard, a Batman stunt spectacular show, and an animated character show. In addition, headliners such as Ray Charles, Faith Hill, Doug Stone, Smokey Robinson, Tanya Tucker, and the Steve Miller Band play the 8,072-seat (with lawn seating for 4,000) Southern Star Amphitheatre.

There are restaurants and snack bars throughout the park, though you might consider bringing a picnic. Gift shops also abound.

White Water

Exit 113 off I-75 on North Cobb Pkwy., Marietta. ☎ **404/424-WAVE.** Admission $17.99 adults, $10.99 children from age 3 and up to 48 inches tall; children under 3 and senior citizens free. Weekends only in May, daily Memorial Day–late summer and Labor Day weekend 10am–late evening (closing hours vary). Closed Sept–Apr.

Forty acres of wet, splashy fun await you at White Water, the largest water-theme park in the south. Its star attraction is the $1 million Tree House Island, a four-story fantasy treehouse with over 100 different activities—curvy slides, net bridges, water cannons, chutes, etc. A giant 1,000-gallon bucket of water empties over the whole attraction every few minutes! Other park highlights include: Black River Falls, with two enclosed 400-foot flumes creating a twisting "river of darkness" enhanced by strobe lights; the "Atlanta Ocean," a 750,000-gallon wave pool; the Bahama Bob-Slide, a group tube ride down a chute the length of two football fields; Caribbean Plunge, a 100-foot free-fall water flume drop; and Dragon's Tail Falls, which sends riders plummeting down a 250-foot triple drop at speeds up to 30 miles per hour. There's much more, including water jet and high-dive stunt shows and a special section for children 48 inches and under called Little Squirt's Island, offering 25 tot-size water attractions. Captain Kid's Cove, adjacent to it, has dozens of additional activities for kids 12 and under. Restaurants and snack bars are on the premises, as are rental lockers and shower facilities. Swimsuits are essential.

Adjacent to White Water is **American Adventures** (☎ 404/424-9283), an indoor/outdoor family amusement park featuring 15 children's rides in Fun Forest (bumper cars, a small roller coaster, a tilt-a-whirl, and others); a classic carousel; a penny arcade with over 130 games; Professor Plinker's Laboratory—a large children's play area with ball crawls and nets to climb; 18-hole miniature golf; and Imagination Station—a creative play area with arts and crafts, costumes, children's shows, and games. It's all geared to children 12 and under. A 180-seat family-style restaurant is on the grounds. Admission to American Adventures is free (you pay per ride; a pass for unlimited rides is $12.99 for children 18 and under, $4.99 for adults and children under 3; adults ride free with toddlers). The park is open daily year-round (hours vary seasonally).

4 Organized Tours

BUS TOURS

Gray Line of Atlanta   This company (☎ **404/767-0594**) offers several comprehensive tours aboard comfortable sightseeing buses. Departures are from the Hyatt Regency Downtown. Since departure times and prices are subject to change, call before you go.

All Around Atlanta is a 3$^{1}/_{2}$-hour excursion that takes in Peachtree Street, Peachtree Center (you'll see the city's notable downtown architecture), the capitol, Georgia Tech, Coca-Cola headquarters, the Governor's Mansion, the Woodruff Arts Center, Swan House, and Cyclorama. It's a great introduction to the city. Adults pay $20, children 6 to 11 pay $15, under 6 free. Departures are daily at 1pm.

The **Atlanta Grand Circle,** an 8-hour tour, includes all of the above plus the city's grand homes, history-rich Five Points, the CNN complex, Underground Atlanta, and Georgia's Stone Mountain. Adults pay $30, children $22.50. Departures are daily at 8:30am.

The **Black Heritage Tour,** a 3$^{1}/_{2}$-hour trip, concentrates on the Sweet Auburn district, where Dr. Martin Luther King, Jr., spent his boyhood years. In addition, you'll visit the Herndon mansion and the world's largest predominantly black center for higher education—the Atlanta University complex. Adults pay $20, children $15. Departures are on Saturdays only, June to Labor Day, at 1pm.

SPECIAL-INTEREST TOURS

The Atlanta Preservation Center   This private, nonprofit organization (156 7th St. NE, Suite 3, ☎ **404/876-2040**) is dedicated to "the preservation of Atlanta's architecturally, historically, and culturally significant buildings and neighborhoods," and offers 10 1$^{1}/_{2}$- to 2-hour guided walking tours in the city. In addition, a self-guided Civil Rights Tour will be offered by the time you read this, and several special tours will be offered during the Olympics. Cost of each tour is $5 for adults, $4 for seniors, $3 for students, free for children under 5. Tours of the Fox Theatre District are given year-round; the remaining tours are offered March through November only. Call for days and hours.

The **Fox Theatre District Tour** is outstanding. You'll explore in depth this restored 1920s Moorish movie palace, a theater whose auditorium resembles the courtyard of a Cairo mosque and whose architecture and interior were influenced by the discoveries at King Tut's tomb. The tour also includes turn-of-the-century buildings in the area.

The **Historic Downtown Tour** is an architectural survey of Atlanta's downtown edifices from Victorian buildings to modern high-rises. You'll learn about the architects, the businessmen, and the prominent families who created the city's early commercial center.

The **Inman Park Tour** visits Atlanta's first garden suburb, where you'll see preserved and restored Victorian mansions (exterior views only). Highlights include the homes of Coca-Cola magnates Asa Candler and Ernest Woodruff and the interior of the Inman Park Methodist Church.

The **Underground Atlanta Tour** explores the city's historic hub—today a flourishing complex of shops, restaurants, and nightclubs.

The **Sweet Auburn Tour** focuses on the area 20th-century African-American entrepreneurs developed into a prosperous commercial hub. You'll also visit Martin Luther King's boyhood home and the church where he preached.

Walking Miss Daisy's Druid Hills explores the neighborhood that was the setting for the play and film *Driving Miss Daisy*. The gracious parklike area was laid out by noted landscapist Frederick Law Olmsted and contains many architecturally important homes.

West End, Hammonds House, and Wren's Nest Tour focuses on the home of Joel Chandler Harris (author of the Uncle Remus stories) and Hammonds House (a museum; details above), while also noting Victorian homes and churches in the West End area, Atlanta's oldest neighborhood.

The **Ansley Park Tour** explores one of Atlanta's first garden suburbs (today a charming midtown neighborhood), partly designed by Frederick Law Olmsted. Its broad lawns, majestic trees, parks, and beautiful houses make for a lovely tour.

The **Piedmont Park Tour** focuses on the history of this central Atlanta park. In previous incarnations, it was a farm, a Civil War encampment, a driving club, and the grounds for the 1895 Cotton States and International Exposition.

Finally, the **Atlanta University Center Tour** focuses on the Vine City area, home to the largest concentration of African-American colleges in the U.S., including Spelman, Morehouse, Morris Brown, and Clark Atlanta University. This area was the birthplace of many civil rights leaders (Julian Bond and Hosea Williams, among others).

5 Outdoor Activities

See also Section 1, "The Top Attractions," earlier in this chapter, for a full description of **Georgia's Stone Mountain Park,** one of the best places in the region for all kinds of outdoor activities: picnicking, boating (rowboats, canoes, and sailboats), biking (rentals are available), fishing, hiking, golf, tennis, and swimming.

FISHING

There's good trout fishing on the **Chattahoochee River,** in the North Georgia Mountains, about 1¹/₂ hours from downtown. Many lakes in the area are good for bass and striper, including **Lake Lanier,** a 38,000-acre reservoir about 45 minutes away. Fishing licenses are $7 for seven days, $13 for a trout-fishing license valid for one year.

The **Fish Hawk,** 279 Buckhead Ave. NE, between Peachtree and Piedmont Roads (☎ **404/237-3473**), is the largest supplier in Atlanta for quality tackle. It carries all manner of fishing gear and outdoor clothing and can also supply the requisite license. The staff is extremely knowledgeable and can tell you where to find the fish you seek and anything you need to know about applicable state regulations. They're open Monday through Friday from 9am to 6pm, Saturday from 9am to 5pm.

For additional information, serious anglers can write or call the Georgia Department of Natural Resources, Wildlife Resources Division, 2070 U.S. Hwy. 278 SE, Social Circle, GA 30279 (☎ **404/918-6406**).

GOLF

✪ **Georgia's Stone Mountain Park Golf Course** (☎ **404/498-5717**) is nationally ranked. A 36-hole Robert Trent Jones course, it's a beautiful facility, some parts of it adjacent to the park's lake. To quote *Gene's Guide to Atlanta's Public Courses,* "Its narrow rolling fairways lead to well trapped, tiered bent grass greens. When the tees are back the course demands both strength and accuracy." I don't know what that means, but if you're a golfer, I guess it communicates something. A pro shop is on the premises, and lessons are available. For weekends and holidays, reserve the Tuesday prior to the day you want to play; other times reserve a week in advance. A restaurant/clubhouse has a large deck overlooking the lake. Greens fees are $40, including cart. There is a fee of $5 per car to enter the park. The course is open Monday to Friday from 8am to dark, from 7am until dark weekends and holidays.

IN-LINE SKATING

Piedmont Park is the place. **Skate Escape,** 1086 Piedmont Ave. NE, at 12th Street (☎ **404/892-1292**), is located conveniently close by. It offers all kinds of bicycles and skates for rent or sale, as well as helmets, bicycle locks, and accessories. (You can also buy skateboards here.) Conventional or in-line skates can be rented for $4 per hour, $12 per day (it's $5 per hour if you'd like to rent a single-speed or children's bike). A driver's license or major credit card is required for ID, or you can leave a deposit of $100 for skates, $200 for bikes. Skate Escape is open Monday through Saturday from 10am to 7pm, Sunday from noon to 7pm. MARTA: Midtown.

NATURE WALKS & SCENIC STROLLS

In addition to city strolls, Atlanta offers many wonderful places for quiet nature walks and easy day hikes.

The **Atlanta History Center,** 130 W. Paces Ferry Rd. (☎ **404/ 814-4000**), described fully in Section 1 of this chapter, stands on 32 woodland acres and offers self-guided walking trails and five gardens. You'll discover many plants native to the region along the forested mile-long Swan Woods Trail.

Georgia's Stone Mountain Park, 16 miles east of downtown on U.S. 78, is also covered in Section 1 of this chapter. It offers thousands of acres of beautiful wooded parkland and lakes. There's a walking trail that goes up and down the moss-covered slopes of the mountain; you'll be delighted by the wildflowers that bloom here each spring. There are also 20 acres of wildlife trails in the park with natural animal habitats and a petting zoo, as well as more challenging hiking trails.

Château Elan, 30 miles north of Atlanta at Exit 48 off I-85 in Braselton (☎ **404/932-0900**), has nature trails along St. Emilion Creek (forested with tulip poplar, oak, hickory, and beech trees) and by Romanée-Conti Pond. And there are picnic areas on the lovely grounds; custom picnics can be purchased here. See Section 2 of this chapter for a complete description of its other attractions.

There are 16 miles of extensive hiking trails at **Kennesaw Mountain/National Battlefield Park,** Old Highway 41 and Stilesboro Road, Kennesaw (☎ **404/427-4686**). The scenery is beautiful, and trail maps are available at the Visitor Center. See Section 2.

Piedmont Park, centrally located with its main entrance on Piedmont Avenue at 14th Street, offers a glorious setting for strolls, jogging, and biking. The wonderful Atlanta Botanical Garden is adjacent. See Section 2 of this chapter for a full description of the park, Section 1 for coverage of the botanical garden.

Yellow River Wildlife Game Ranch, 4525 Hwy. 78, Lilburn (☎ **404/ 972-6643**), offers a mile-long shady forest trail along which you can meet the many animal residents that live here, from deer to buffalo. See Section 3 of this chapter for complete details.

Also described in Section 3 is the **Fernbank Science Center,** 156 Heaton Park Dr. NE (☎ **404/378-4311**), which has a 1 1/2-mile nature trail with trees, wildflowers, and plants labeled for identification. This unspoiled natural environment is home to many animals and birds, and a small pond teems with aquatic life.

RIVER RAFTING/CANOEING/KAYAKING

Southeastern Expeditions (☎ **404/329-0433** or **800/868-RAFT**) offers white-water adventures on the scenic Chattooga River in North Georgia (it's the one you saw in the movie *Deliverance*) and the Ocoee in Tennessee (which will be an Olympic venue). Put-in points for both rivers are about a two-hour drive from Atlanta. Trips vary in length (from a few hours to a few days) and difficulty.

A favorite of mine is a sunrise trip on the Chattooga; you'll find the exquisite morning peacefulness of river and forest soon contrasted by the thrill of running some of the toughest rapids around. After lunch you can hike to the magnificent Opossum Creek Falls. Days like that are magical.

The Chattooga offers Class II and III rapids in Section III and Class III, IV, and V in Section IV. The roller-coaster Ocoee has Class III and IV rapids only. Kids must be at least 10 for easy trips, 12 or 13 for more difficult rapids. The company also offers canoeing and kayaking. All of these expeditions are immensely popular, so make your reservations as far in advance as possible.

Prices vary depending on length and difficulty of the trip. Weekends are more expensive than weekdays. Half-day trips begin at about $28, full-day trips at about $50, both rates including lunch, equipment, a guide, and transportation from the outpost to the river. Rafting season is April 1 to October 31, with occasional trips in March and November.

SWIMMING

Almost every Atlanta hotel features a swimming pool. In addition, there is a large public swimming pool in Piedmont Park, plus a sandy lakefront beach (complete with water slides) in Stone Mountain Park.

If you're *really* serious about getting wet, there's also **White Water,** Exit 113 off I-75 on North Cobb Parkway, in Marietta (☎ **404/ 424-WAVE**), a water-theme park described in detail in Section 3 of this chapter.

TENNIS

The City of Atlanta Parks and Recreation Department operates 12 outdoor hard courts at **Piedmont Park,** all of them lit for night play. No reservations are taken; it's first-come, first-served. There's free parking at the courts, and showers, lockers, and a pro shop are on the premises. Hours are weekdays from 10am to 9pm (noon to 9pm in winter), Saturdays and Sundays from 9am to 6pm (till 7pm in summer). Fees are $1.50 per person per hour during the day, $1.75 per person per hour when courts are lit for night play.

Leased from the Atlanta Parks and Recreation Department are 13 outdoor clay courts (six of them lit for night play) and 10 outdoor hard courts (four lit) at the **Bitsy Grant Tennis Center,** 2125 Northside Dr., between I-75N and Peachtree Battle Avenue (☎ **404/351-2774**). Courts are available on a first-come, first-served basis. No reservations. There are showers, lockers, and a pro shop on the premises. The courts are open Monday to Friday from 9am to 9pm, Saturday and Sunday from 8am to 5pm (sometimes the courts close at 6pm on Friday). It's $2.50 per person per hour for clay courts, $1.50 per person per hour for hard courts.

6 Spectator Sports

Atlanta is the only U.S. city with professional baseball, basketball, and football teams, none of which has ever won a national championship. "Go, Braves—and take the Falcons with you!" used to be a popular saying. But with the Braves perennially challenging for the pennant, and the Falcons playing in the still-new Georgia Dome, tickets to Atlanta sporting events are harder to come by than you might imagine.

You can charge tickets by phone for all the sports listed below by calling **Ticketmaster** (☎ **404/249-6400**).

BASEBALL

Once the laughingstock of the National League, the **Atlanta Braves** now boast one of the best pitching staffs in baseball and are often favored to win the National League pennant. Their home games are currently played in Atlanta–Fulton County Stadium, where in 1974, Hammerin' Hank Aaron hit home run no. 715 to break Babe Ruth's all-time record. Call **404/522-7630** for information. Seats run from $5 (bleachers) to about $20, and ticket availability is inversely proportional to the team's success. (See "Stadiums," below, for additional details.) Nobody in Atlanta will call you politically incorrect if you join the crowd in the Tomahawk Chop; you may spot owner Ted Turner and his wife, Jane Fonda, participating with the rest of the fans. After the 1996 Olympic Games, the Braves will move into the 85,000-seat Olympic Stadium, which will be modified for major league baseball after the Games, currently being built across the street. Tickets should be easier to come by then.

BASKETBALL

The **Atlanta Hawks** are the local NBA franchise, though not a particularly outstanding team. The season runs from November to April, with 41 regular home games played in the Omni Coliseum (see "Stadiums," below, for details). Tickets range from $10 for a nosebleed seat in the rafters to about $55 for center court. Call **404/827-3800** for information.

On the college basketball front, the **Georgia Tech Yellow Jackets** play in the highly competitive ACC. The season runs from November through March; the 1995–96 season should prove interesting, since coach Bobby Cremins has recruited Stephon Marbury, the most highly sought-after high school player in the country. Their home games are played in Alexander Memorial Coliseum, on campus at 10th and Fowler Streets (see "Stadiums," below, for details). Tickets are usually $14, but are difficult to come by. Call **404/894-5400** for information.

FOOTBALL

The **Atlanta Falcons** are the city's NFL franchise, playing eight games (plus exhibition games) each season in the Georgia Dome (see "Stadiums," below, for details).

As for college football, the "Ramblin' Wrecks from Georgia Tech" have played their home games at 43,000-seat Bobby Dodd Stadium/Grant Field, on campus at North Avenue and Techwood Drive (MARTA: North Avenue) since 1913. The season runs from September through November. Call **404/894-5447** for information. Tickets are usually $21 if you can manage to get them.

The **Peach Bowl** is played each January in Atlanta in the Georgia Dome, with tickets priced at around $35.

HOCKEY

Fall through spring, the **Atlanta Knights** (IHL) play around 40 home games in the Omni Coliseum, which also occasionally hosts NHL exhibition games. Call **404/681-2100** for information. Tickets run from $8 to $16.

MOTOR SPORTS

Situated on 750 scenic wooded acres about 50 miles north of downtown Atlanta, **Road Atlanta** is one of the southeast's premier road-racing motor-sports facilities. Its 2.5-mile Grand Prix racecourse offers a challenging combination of turns, elevation changes, and high-speed straights.

A year-round season of events include sports car, motorcycle, vintage/historic, motocross, and go-kart racing, including the annual International Motor Sports Association (IMSA) Exxon WSC for prototype sports cars, AMA-sanctioned motocross events, and Sports Car Club of America (SCCA) America Road Race of Champions and SCCA Trans-AM. Call **404/967-6143** for information. Tickets usually run $10 to $45.

Road Atlanta is located on Georgia Highway 53 between I-85 and I-985 (take I-85N to Exit 49, make a left, and follow the signs). You can camp free on the property if you're attending an event.

STADIUMS

Georgia Dome

1 Georgia Dome Dr. (at International Blvd. and Northside Dr.). ☎ **404/223-9200** for information or 404/223-8427 (the Dome box office) to charge tickets. MARTA: Omni/GWCC/Georgia Dome.

Atlanta's $214 million, 71,500-seat domed megastadium, which hosted Super Bowl XXVIII in 1994, is also the home of the Atlanta Falcons (NFL). It will be the site of Olympic basketball and gymnastics competitions. The facility combines with the adjacent 2-million-square-foot Georgia World Congress Center to form the world's largest entertainment complex. Its oval shape provides a close view of stadium action from every seat. It is also the site for the annual Peach Bowl, while other targeted events include the NCAA Final Four in 2002. The dome additionally hosts tennis matches, tractor pulls, college basketball, track and field events, Supercross events, and the SEC Championship Football game every December. Check the papers or call the above number to find out what's on during your stay.

Forty-five minute **tours of the Georgia Dome** (including the visitors locker and dressing rooms, press box, executive suites, sports lounge, and other areas of interest) are offered on the hour Tuesday to Saturday between 10am and 4pm, Sunday between noon and 4pm. Call **404/223-TOUR** for reservations and details. Adults pay $4, seniors and children 5 to 12 pay $2.50, under 5 free.

Omni Coliseum

100 Techwood Dr. NW. (at Marietta St.). ☎ **404/681-2100**. MARTA: Omni.

The 17,000-seat oval-shaped Omni Coliseum is home to the Atlanta Hawks (NBA). Also fall through spring, the Atlanta Knights hockey team (IHL) plays 41 games here. In September, the Omni hosts NHL exhibition games. At other times, the Omni is used for varied sporting and entertainment events, including Harlem Globetrotter games, college basketball, and tennis exhibitions. Call or check the papers to find out what's on during your stay. During the Olympic Games the Omni will be the host venue for the men's and women's volleyball.

Atlanta–Fulton County Stadium

521 Capitol Ave. SW (between Fulton St. and Ralph David Abernathy Blvd.). ☎ **404/522-7630** for information. Parking $7. MARTA: Shuttle bus service (fare is $1.25) operates between the stadium and West End Station (at Lee and Oglethorpe Sts.) starting 2¹/₂ hours before game time. Call 404/848-7711 for shuttle–bus information.

The circular open-air Atlanta–Fulton County Stadium, built in 1965, has 52,710 seats and is home to the Atlanta Braves (NL). The 85,000-seat Olympic Stadium is being constructed across the street at this writing. After the 1996 Olympic Games, it will be modified to become the new home of the Braves, and the old Atlanta–Fulton County Stadium will be torn down.

Alexander Memorial Coliseum

Georgia Institute of Technology, 10th and Fowler sts. ☎ **404/894-5400** for information. MARTA: North Avenue.

This 10,000-seat stadium—undergoing a $12 million renovation at this writing—is home to Georgia Tech's Yellow Jackets college basketball team. It will also be the host venue for Olympic boxing.

9

A Walking Tour of Sweet Auburn

I t's my feeling that you never really understand a city unless you walk around it a bit. Atlanta's lovely climate makes walking tours a marvelous option just about year round. In addition to the tour below, consider the excellent guided walking tours listed in Chapter 8, "What to See and Do in Atlanta." Also, note that the following attractions detailed in that chapter comprise walking tours in and of themselves: Georgia's Stone Mountain Park, Kennesaw Mountain/National Battlefield Park, Oakland Cemetery, and the Atlanta Historical Society in Buckhead. Auburn Avenue is specially set up for a walking tour.

Start: The corner of Howell and Irwin streets. To get to this intersection take bus no. 3. If you're driving, you can park in a lot on the north side of Irwin Street between Boulevard and Jackson Street.

Finish: Auburn Avenue and Courtland Street

Time: Allow at least half a day to explore this area thoroughly. If you want to include a tour of Martin Luther King, Jr.'s Birth Home (stop no. 3)—and I urge you to do so—start out early in the day and obtain your tickets at the Center for Nonviolent Social Change (stop no. 2).

Sweet Auburn includes the Martin Luther King, Jr., National Historic District, which comprises about 12 blocks along Auburn Avenue. A neighborhood that nurtured scores of 20th-century black businesspeople and professionals, it contains the birthplace, church, and gravesite of Martin Luther King, Jr. Under the auspices of the National Park Service, portions of Auburn Avenue are in an ongoing process of restoration as an important historic district. The street has been beautified by much new landscaping, and about 80 percent of the homes and businesses on the "Birth Home" block have been restored to their 1920s appearance. This tour provides insight into black history, the civil rights movement, and black urban culture in the South. If you're traveling with children, it's a wonderful opportunity to teach them about a great American. The major attractions are covered in detail in Chapter 8.

Begin your stroll at:

1. **Howell and Irwin Streets.** Walk south along Howell Street where renovated historic homes and recently built housing (designed to

Walking Tour—Sweet Auburn

finish here

☆ **16** Herndon Plaza

17 **15**

❶ Howell & Irwin Streets
❷ Martin Luther King, Jr., Center for Nonviolent Social Change
❸ Birth Home of Martin Luther King, Jr.
❹ Double "Shotgun" Row Houses
❺ Fire Station No. 6
❻ Ebenezer Baptist Church
❼ Wheat Street Baptist Chu[rch]
❽ Prince Hall Masonic Buil[ding]

Atlanta

Sweet Auburn

harmonize with the architecture of the neighborhood) provide heartwarming testimony to the area's renaissance. Note no. 102 Howell, built between 1890 and 1895, which was the home of Alexander Hamilton, Jr., Atlanta's leading turn-of-the-century black contractor. Its architectural details include Corinthian columns and a Palladian window.

Turn right on Auburn Avenue, and as you proceed be sure to look for interpretive markers indicating historic homes (mostly Victorian and Queen Anne) and other points of interest en route to:

2. **The Martin Luther King, Jr., Center for Nonviolent Social Change,** 449 Auburn Ave. This organization continues the work to which King was dedicated—reducing violence within the community and among nations. Freedom Plaza, on the premises, is his final resting place. The center functions as an information station for area attractions. This is where you obtain tickets to view the Birth Home of Martin Luther King, Jr. (on weekends, especially, arrive early, since demand for tickets often exceeds supply). Here,

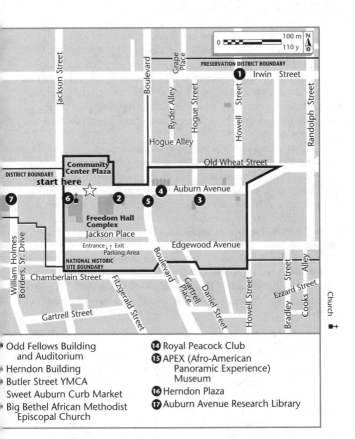

too, you can take a self-guided tour of exhibits on King's life and the civil rights movement and see videos which include some of his most stirring speeches. Including the videos (which shouldn't be missed), plan to spend about two hours at the center.

Now double back a few blocks east to:

3. **The Birth Home of Martin Luther King, Jr.,** 501 Auburn Ave., at Hogue Street, where free half-hour guided tours are given on a continual basis September through May 10am to 5pm, the rest of the year 10am to 7pm. Get tickets at the MLK, Jr., Center, listed above.

After you leave, note some turn-of-the-century homes in the area such as:

4. **The Double "Shotgun" Row Houses,** 472–488 Auburn Ave., two-family dwellings with separate hip roofs that were built in 1905 to house workers for the Empire Textile Company. They were so named because rooms were lined up in a row; if you so desired, you could fire a shotgun right through them.

At the corner of Auburn and Boulevard is:

5. **Fire Station No. 6,** one of Atlanta's eight original firehouses, completed in 1894. The two-story Romanesque-revival building was situated to protect the eastern section of the city. The station houses a museum, open daily from 9am to 5pm, where exhibits include restored fire engines and vintage fire-fighting paraphernalia. Admission is free. Note the Italianate arched windows on the second story.

Continuing west, a notable stop on your tour is:

6. **Ebenezer Baptist Church,** 407 Auburn Ave., founded in 1886, where Martin Luther King, Jr., served as co-pastor from 1960–68. Ten-minute guided tours are given throughout the day. At this writing, a new sanctuary is going up across the street; when it is completed, the original building will remain as an historic site under Parks Department auspices.

🔖 **TAKE A BREAK**   At the corner of Auburn Avenue and Jackson Street is a very good, and very inexpensive, southern/soul food cafeteria, the **Beautiful Restaurant** (☎ **404/223-0080**). It's open daily from 7:30am to 8pm. No credit cards. See Chapter 7 for details.

One block west is the:

7. **Wheat Street Baptist Church,** 365 Auburn Ave., built in the 1920s, but serving a congregation since the late 1800s. Auburn Avenue was originally called Wheat Street in honor of Augustus W. Wheat, one of Atlanta's early merchants. The name was changed in 1893.

Further west, on Auburn between Hilliard and Fort Streets, is:

8. **The Prince Hall Masonic Building,** an influential black lodge led for several decades by John Wesley Dobbs. Today it houses the national headquarters of the Southern Christian Leadership Conference.

On the other side of the expressway, note:

9. **The Odd Fellows Building and Auditorium,** 228–250 Auburn Ave., another black fraternal lodge, which originated in Atlanta in 1870. Completed in 1914, the building later became headquarters for an insurance company.

Across the street is:

10. **The Herndon Building,** 231–45 Auburn Ave., named for Alonzo Herndon, an ex-slave who went on to found the Atlanta Life Insurance Company. It was erected in 1924. By 1930, the Auburn business district supported 121 black-owned businesses and 39 black professionals.

Make a left and you'll see:

11. **The Butler Street YMCA,** built in the early 1900s, today augmented by a new YMCA, across the street.

Continue south along Butler Street to the:

12. Sweet Auburn Curb Market, just below Edgewood Avenue. This historic market dates to 1924 when Atlanta was still a segregated city. Whites shopped within, but blacks were only permitted to patronize stalls lining the curb. The market's current name reflects that era. Today, following a $7^1/$_2$ million renovation, this is a vibrant and colorful food emporium. Light and airy, it's filled with tempting displays of gorgeous groceries and fresh produce—including many regional and ethnic items such as hamhocks and chitlins ("We sell every part of the pig here but the oink," quips the owner); collard, mustard, and turnip greens; red velvet cake (one of many fresh-baked items); and home remedies such as yellowroot tea (for arthritis) and Georgia white dirt (ingested by pregnant women in the rural South to settle their stomachs). Sometimes there are farmer's market and flea market stalls out front, and there's a food court on the premises with covered outdoor seating. Another open-air market is in the works nearby on Auburn Avenue between Fort and Bell Streets under the expressway; it will feature a changing array of merchandise (food, crafts, and more) sold by vendor carts and a stage for entertainment. If it's open by the time you read this, you'll have passed it on your way here.

Walk back to Auburn Avenue on Butler Street and turn left.

☕ **TAKE A BREAK** **The Caribbean Restaurant,** 180 Auburn Ave., between Piedmont Avenue and Butler Street (☎ **404/ 658-9829**), has a plain but pleasant interior. Walls are hung with posters of Caribbean destinations and musicians, diners are seated on glossy white wooden benches at big picnic-style tables, and reggae and calypso music provide appropriate ambience. The low-priced menu lists authentic—and very tasty—Caribbean foods such as oxtail soup, curried goat, spicy jerk chicken, red snapper stew, fried plantains (served with blue cheese dressing), and rôti skin (a pancakelike bread). All entrées come with rice and two vegetables (perhaps lima beans and steamed cabbage). The homemade carrot cake is a good dessert choice. Drink options range from beer and stout to fresh-squeezed lemonade, Ting (a Jamaican grapefruit drink), and Ashanti roots drink (which has health benefits). Major credit cards are accepted. Open daily.

13. The Big Bethel African Methodist Episcopal Church, at no. 220, was originally built in the 1890s and then rebuilt in 1924 after a fire. In the 1920s, John Wesley Dobbs called the Bethel "a towering edifice to black freedom."

Farther along is:

14. The Royal Peacock Club, 184–186 Auburn Ave. Its walls painted floor to ceiling with peacocks, it presented top black entertainers such as Ray Charles, Aretha Franklin, and Dizzy Gillespie in its heyday. There is talk of restoring the club to its former glamour.

At Auburn Avenue and Courtland Street is:

15. The APEX (African-American Panoramic Experience) Museum, 135 Auburn Ave.—with a recently completed 90,000-square-foot adjacent addition at 125 Auburn Ave. (☎ **404/521-APEX**). It features exhibits on the history of Sweet Auburn and the African-American experience, including a children's gallery with interactive displays. See Chapter 8 for further details.

   Cross the street to:

16. Herndon Plaza, where exhibits on the Herndon family can be seen. If you'd like to do further research on the history of Auburn Avenue—or on any aspect of African-American history and culture—continue on to:

17. The Auburn Avenue Research Library on African-American Culture and History, 101 Auburn Ave. (☎ **404/730-4001**). A Heritage Center on the premises features special exhibits, workshops, seminars, lectures, and events. Open Monday to Thursday noon to 8pm, Saturday and Sunday 2 to 6pm; closed Friday.

10

Atlanta Shopping

Atlanta is the shopping mecca of the southeast. Its vast—and very chic—malls serve not only locals but a large number of consumers who come from neighboring states just to shop. Buckhead boutiques such as Sasha Frisson can hold their own with the most fashionable emporiums of New York and Los Angeles. There are also browsable areas of quaint shops in Little Five Points and Virginia-Highland. This is a great town for antiquing, and I love the big old-fashioned downtown Macy's.

1 Great Shopping Areas

CHAMBLEE'S ANTIQUE ROW

✪ Antique Row, on Peachtree Road at Broad Street and North Peachtree Road (☎ 404/458-6316), is a quaint complex of more than 30 shops located in historic homes, churches, and other buildings. Some of them date as far back as the 1800s. There are dealers of antique American and European furniture, glassware, pottery, Victoriana, Orientalia, wicker, collector toys, quilts, sports equipment, coke memorabilia, jewelry, architectural antiques, Olympic collectibles, and crafts items. It's a great afternoon ramble. Hours vary with each store. Almost all are open Monday through Saturday from 10:30am to 5pm; most are open Sunday from 1 to 5pm as well. You can take a MARTA train to Chamblee Station; it's about three-fourths of a mile from the shops. On weekdays you can get the no. 132 Tilly Mill bus from there; on weekends walk or take a taxi.

VIRGINIA-HIGHLANDS

This charming area of town, centered on North Highland Avenue between Virginia and Ponce de Leon Avenue, teems with antique shops, junk stores, trendy boutiques, and art galleries. Since you'll want to browse through all its shops in one excursion, they're grouped together here in the order in which you will find them while walking north through the neighborhood. Take a lunch break at Murphy's (see Chapter 7, "Dining").

ANTIQUES & GIFTS

20th Century
1044 N. Highland Ave. (between Los Angeles and Virginia aves.). ☎ **404/892-2065.**

As its name implies, this shop specializes in international antiques and reproductions made during this century. The inventory is wide-ranging, including some terrific jewelry, Limoges porcelain boxes, whimsical clocks, art deco items, Belgian tapestries, and furnishings running the gamut from 19th-century reproductions to '50s Heywood-Wakefield blond-wood pieces. Also in the mix: campy nostalgia items such as back issues of *Life* magazine, Elvis trading cards, and antique radios and telephones. Great browsing. Open Monday to Wednesday 11am to 7pm, Thursday to Saturday 11am to 9pm, Sunday noon to 6pm. In summer the store stays open till 9pm Monday to Wednesday.

Affairs

1401 N. Highland Ave. (just below University Dr.). ☎ **404/876-3342.**

This charming shop—its ambience enhanced by well-chosen classical, jazz, and show music tapes—offers many exquisite giftware items. Some examples: a mother-of-pearl toothbrush, a rabbit- or cow-shaped clock, one-of-a-kind picture frames, stuffed dolls and animals, beautiful dinnerware, and gourmet foods. Affairs also carries French and Italian kitchenware and a full line of Crabtree & Evelyn products. Delightful browsing. Open Monday to Saturday 10am to 9:30pm, Sunday 11am to 6pm.

BODY & BATH

Natural Body

1403 N. Highland Ave. (just below University Dr.). ☎ **404/876-9642.**

This very appealing shop invites you to pamper yourself with all manner of skin treatments, bubble baths, massage and body oils, potpourris, soaps, lotions, and cosmetics. All of their products are 100% natural, chemical free, and biodegradable, and none is tested on animals. They carry, among other lines, Kiehl (from New York), Aveda, Ahava (made in Israel with minerals from the Dead Sea), and Bindi (products made in India from ayurvedic herbs, roots, and flowers). Natural Body also runs a spa across the street (☎ **404/872-1039**), offering massages, facials, aromatherapy, manicures, pedicures, and other beauty spa treatments. Open Monday 10:30am to 6pm, Tuesday to Saturday 10:30am to 9pm, Sunday noon to 6pm.

This emporium and spa has another location at 3209 Paces Ferry Pl. in Buckhead (☎ **404/237-7712**).

CLOTHING BOUTIQUES

Mitzi & Romano

1038 N. Highland Ave. (between Virginia and Los Angeles aves.). ☎ **404/876-7228.**

Mitzi Ugolini buys designer clothes in New York and California. Her clothing is fashion-forward—the kind that makes a statement instead of blending in with the crowd. Great jewelry and accessories, too. Prices are affordable. Open Monday 11am to 8pm, Tuesday to Thursday 11am to 9pm, Friday and Saturday 11am to 10pm, Sunday noon to 7pm.

Porter's

994 Virginia Ave. (just off N. Highland Ave.). ☎ **404/874-7834.**

Stop by for carefully chosen men's clothing and men's and women's accessories, unique imported and designer ties for men, beautiful T-shirts, jewelry, and other lovely items. Open Tuesday to Thursday 11am to 9pm, Friday and Saturday 11am to 10pm, Sunday and Monday noon to 6pm.

Mooncake

1019 Virginia Ave. NE (just off N. Highland Ave.). ☎ **404/892-8043.**

The ever-changing inventory of whimsical wearables for women here might include cloche and straw hats, black-printed cotton dresses, and oddments that range from ethnic and handcrafted jewelry to nomadic shoes from Turkey. The retro-style clothing looks vintage, but it's all new. You'll also find body and bath items, hair accessories, diaries, greeting cards, and carved wooden angels here. Open April to December Monday to Thursday 11:30am to 9pm, Friday and Saturday 11am to 10pm; January to March Monday to Saturday 11am to 7pm.

Rapture/Bang!

1039 N. Highland Ave. (between Los Angeles and Virginia aves.). ☎ **404/873-0444.**

This emporium houses two stores at one address. Rapture sells elegant, cutting-edge women's clothing, featuring contemporary designers such as Leon Max and BCBG, as well as great shoes. Especially fun are Audley shoes, made in England; you can design your own, changing such variables as heel style, color, and type of leather. Some men's shoes here, too. Bang! features *GQ*-look clothing for men—French Connection shirts, snazzy-looking suits (linen in summer), hats, and accessories among them. Open Monday and Tuesday noon to 8pm, Wednesday and Thursday noon to 9pm, Friday and Saturday 11am to 10pm, Sunday noon to 6pm.

Earth Angel

1196 N. Highland Ave. (at Amsterdam Ave.). ☎ **404/607-7755.**

This very feminine and frou-frou shop is stocked with lacy wedding gowns, romantic and dressy frocks, beautiful lingerie, rosette-embellished ballet slippers, handmade antique-lace veils, hats decorated with antique flowers, ribbons, gift items such as potpourri and sachets, jewelry, and hair accessories, as well as upscale linens and towels. Open Monday to Saturday 11am to 7pm.

NEW AGE

Reader's Loft

1402 N. Highland Ave. (between University and Morningside drs.). ☎ **404/ 881-6511.**

Billing itself as a "metaphysical resource center," Reader's Loft sells books (there's a comfortable reading balcony), audiotapes, and CDs relating to meditation, channeling, self-help and recovery, Eastern philosophy, women's and men's spirituality, astrology, and angels. It also carries related items, such as crystals, incense, Chilean rain sticks, and

Zuni fetishes, as well as New Age greeting cards and Native American and contemporary jewelry. Psychics are often on hand to do readings. Open Monday 11am to 6pm, Tuesday to Thursday 11am to 9pm, Friday and Saturday 11am to 10pm, Sunday noon to 5pm.

CRAFTS SUPPLIES

Intown Crafter

1062 St. Charles Ave. (between N. Highland Ave. and Frederica St.). ☎ **404/ 874-9276.**

If you like crafts, it's great fun browsing in this shop filled with stencils, jewelry-making supplies, ribbons, beads, feathers, dried flowers, needlework patterns, decoupage materials, candlemaking equipment, modeling clay, and much, much more, including a good supply of how-to books. Open Monday to Saturday 11am to 7pm, Sunday 1 to 6pm.

AN ART GALLERY

Aliya Gallery

1402 N. Highland Ave. NE (in the Highland Walk Center between University and Morningside drs.). ☎ **404/892-2835.**

Steve Fleenor and Gary Alembik (Gary lived a year in Jerusalem, hence the name Aliya), are the owners of this very lovely gallery. They represent 45 artists, both American and international, whose works range from contemporary paintings (abstracts, landscapes, and figurative), to pottery, sculpture, and jewelry. Open Monday to Thursday 2 to 10pm, Friday 2 to 11pm, Saturday noon to 11pm, Sunday 11:30am to 10pm.

LITTLE FIVE POINTS

An area similar to Virginia-Highlands (see above)—though a little funkier—Little Five Points reminds me of Berkeley in the 1960s. There are still authentic hippies here. It is also close to Virginia-Highlands, so if you crave additional boutique browsing, both areas are easily covered in a few hours. While you're shopping here, plan a leisurely lunch at the delightful Bridgetown Grill (details in Chapter 7). Begin your shopping stroll at Euclid and Moreland Avenues and proceed southwest along Euclid. Because shopping here is more of a browsing experience than a search for specific merchandise, stores in this area are listed in geographic order rather than by type of store.

Crystal Blue

1168 Euclid Ave. (between Moreland and Colquitt aves.). ☎ **404/522-4605.**

Wayne and Debbie Vaillancourt's esoteric emporium specializes in crystals and minerals touted for healing and other purposes. For example: black tourmaline promotes balance to the endocrine system, rose quartz perks up the kidneys and circulatory system, and meteorite helps reveal past lives from other planets and galaxies. Other items here include New Age books and cassettes, incense, chimes, chakra oils, and Acusphere exercise balls to stimulate acupuncture points. Open Monday to Saturday 11am to 7pm, Sunday noon to 6pm.

Stefan's

1160 Euclid Ave. (between Moreland and Colquitt aves.). ☎ **404/688-4929.**

Most of Stefan's merchandise is vintage clothing for men and women from the 1890s through the early 1960s, the rest accessories like belts, suspenders, cummerbunds, and glitzy period costume jewelry. There are 1950s net-skirt prom dresses, Mamie Eisenhower gowns, tuxedos, wedding gowns, Hawaiian shirts, and many many hats. Prices are low. Open Monday to Saturday 11am to 7pm, Sunday noon to 6pm.

Boomerang

1145 Euclid Ave. (between Moreland and Colquitt aves.). ☎ **404/577-8158.**

This eclectic shop carries funky furniture (it ranges from 1950s Formica to handmade and painted contemporary pieces), and a wide array of gift items—pink French poodle salt and pepper shakers, Mona Lisa magnets, a wide array of picture frames, Indian cut-tin wall ornaments, hand-blown glass perfume bottles, Botticelli and Da Vinci shower curtains, tapestries, Chilean wood animals, and more. Open daily except Tuesday noon to 6pm.

Rene Rene

1142 Euclid Ave. (between Moreland and Colquitt aves.). ☎ **404/522-RENE.**

Atlanta magazine, in a "best and worst" awards issue, once named Rene Rene the city's "best women's clothing" shop in the "funky club scene" category. It's true, but some of owner Rene Sanning's designs are more sophisticated—even possibly wearable for business. She even has high-fashion menswear in her line ("not for the IBM man," says Rene). Interesting accessories here, too, such as black gloves adorned with silk roses. Open Monday to Friday 11:30am to 6:30pm, Saturday 11am to 7pm, Sunday noon to 6pm.

Throb

1140 Euclid Ave. (between Moreland and Colquitt aves.). ☎ **404/522-0355.**

Throb specializes in unconventional (to put it mildly) club wear for men and women. You can shop here for see-through vinyl minis, hot pants, bondage-look clothing, black fishnet and silver vinyl dresses, intergalactic plastic jewelry, the latex look, leather lingerie, lingerie meant to be worn as outerwear, chartreuse wigs, and, to complete the look, wild hair dye and makeup colors. Open Monday to Thursday 11am to 8pm, Friday and Saturday 11am to 9pm, Sunday noon to 7pm.

The Junkman's Daughter

464 Moreland Ave. (between Euclid and North aves.). ☎ **404/577-3188.**

This funky 10,000-square-foot store looks like a transplant from New York's East Village. Owner Pamela Mills, whose parents and grandparents were in the salvage/junk-store business, inherited a bizarre assortment of family treasures, including cartons of Mickey Mouse toys, the remains of a perfume factory, and cases of stockings from World War II. This legacy formed the nucleus of her collection, which today includes a large array of costumes (everything from Elvis to Mardi Gras garb), Japanese military capes, '50s saddle shoes and crinolines, feather boas, leather jackets, posters, cards, Elvis key chains, puppets from Sri Lanka, and toys, not to mention a large selection of international masks and folk art, sequin-covered Haitian voodoo flags and bottles, and new and used tapes and CDs. Today, however, Pamela's vintage wares are secondary to more modern merchandise—forward-look club clothing for men and women, thousands of T-shirts, shoes (from fetish footwear to Dr. Marten's), and more. The staircase leading to the mezzanine is in the shape of a 20-foot red high-heeled shoe. And a tattoo parlor, smoking-accessories room, and body-piercing operation are on the premises. Open Monday to Saturday 11am to 7pm, Sunday noon to 6pm.

A Cappella Books

1133 Euclid Ave. (at Colquitt Ave.). ☎ **404/681-5128.**

This is the kind of offbeat bookstore that makes for great browsing. They carry new, used, and out-of-print books, many of them relating to counterculture, literature, history, and the arts. Signed editions here, too. Open Monday to Saturday 11am to 7pm, Sunday noon to 6pm, with extended hours spring and summer.

African Connections

1107 Euclid Ave. (between Colquitt and Washita aves.). ☎ **404/589-1834.**

This fascinating shop carries soapstone carvings from Kenya; textiles, such as *asooke* cloth from Nigeria and *kente* cloth from Ghana; hand-crafted jewelry from Africa, India, and Indonesia, as well as pieces made by African-American jewelers using African materials; traditional and contemporary clothing from the Ivory Coast, Ghana, and Nigeria; traditional West African masks; Nigerian Fulani wedding bead necklaces; Indonesian and African baskets; and African ceremonial combs and medicine bowls. There's much more. Open Tuesday to Saturday 11am to 6pm, Sunday 2 to 6pm.

STONE MOUNTAIN

✪ **Stone Mountain Village,** just outside the West Gate of Georgia's Stone Mountain Park (bounded by Second and Main streets north and south, Lucille Street and Memorial Drive east and west; ☎ **404/879-4971**), is well worth a visit. It's been developing since the 1800s, and many of the 60-plus shops are housed in historic buildings (for example, a winery in a 160-year-old log cabin). Merchants here keep to a very high standard, and their wares are tasteful and of good quality. A lot of the stores specialize in antiques, crafts, and collectibles. Some examples: country furniture, canning jars, dried-flower wreaths, imported toys, handmade candles, jewelers, dolls, baskets, homemade jams, potpourri, patchwork quilts and quilting fabrics, handcrafted dulcimers, Civil War memorabilia, and out-of-print books.

It's great fun to wander about this quaint village, and there's usually some festive event going on—perhaps an arts-and-crafts fair or live entertainment. During Christmas season, the streets are candle-lit and the village becomes a magical place populated by St. Nick, elves, carolers, and harpists. Hours for most shops are Monday

A Day of Rejuvenation

Why not set aside just one day to forget about your boss, your mother, your kids, and your mortgage and spend it being pampered, relaxed, refreshed, and rubbed the right way? No place does these things better than Atlanta's luxurious **Spa Sydell,** which has 6,200 square feet of facilities running the gamut from oversized hot tubs to herbal-wrap rooms and an impressively professional and charming staff to coddle its clients. Among the services offered here are massage (Swedish, deep-tissue, acupressure), herbal wraps, body scrubs, body polishes, facials and masks, hydromassage, hair removal, makeup lessons, manicures and nail treatments, pedicures, and foot reflexology. Highly recommended is a five-hour package that includes a facial with aromatherapy, manicure, pedicure, and massage, with complimentary champagne served between services and a lovely spa lunch prior to a cosmetic make-over. Price is $175, plus tax and tips. For couples, a romantic option is a same-room massage (with champagne). Owner Sydell Harris carries a very extensive line of her own products should you want to continue moisturizing, toning, and exfoliating yourself at home. And if you need to get somewhere directly from your spa day, you'll find showers, hair products, cosmetics, and whatever else you might require.

Spa Sydell is at 3060 Peachtree Rd., at West Paces Ferry Road, in the Buckhead Plaza office complex (☎ **404/237-2505**). Hours are Monday to Saturday from 9am to 9pm, Sunday 11am to 7pm.

Note: Spa Sydell doesn't do hair. If after you've been buffed and polished, you'd like to continue soothing your spirit at a superb salon nearby, make an appointment with **Stan Milton/Rob Davis,** 721 Miami Circle NE (☎ **404/233-6241**).

through Saturday from 10am to 6pm; many are also open Sunday from 1 to 5pm.

Be sure to stop by the Village Visitor Center housed in a restored 1915 caboose at the corner of Main and Poole Streets to find out about special sales and events. It's open Monday to Saturday from 10am to 4pm, Sunday 1 to 4pm. Parking is free at several lots in town.

Stop for a meal at the nearby **Basket Bakery and Garden Café,** 6655 Memorial Dr., at Main Street (☎ **404/498-0329**). For breakfast there are croissants, German apple pancakes, or ham-and-egg platters with homemade biscuits. Later, you can opt for sandwiches on fresh-baked breads, homemade salads, quiche, soups, and home-baked desserts. And the dinner menu highlights European specialties. Open Tuesday to Thursday 7am to 9pm, Friday and Saturday 7am to 10pm, Sunday for brunch only 11am to 4pm. Major credit cards (AE, MC, V) accepted.

2 Department Stores & Malls

So many malls, so little time. I've covered the most central shopping clusters only; there are many more in suburbia.

Lenox Square Mall

3393 Peachtree Rd. NE (at Lenox Rd.). ☎ **404/233-6767** or 800/344-5222. MARTA: Lenox.

The vast upscale Lenox Square was built in 1959 and has since undergone three major expansions. And a fourth (170,000 square feet of merchandise space to house 50 or 60 new shops) is nearing completion at this writing. Anchors include Neiman-Marcus, Macy's, and Rich's department stores, and the J. W. Marriott hotel. There are six movie theaters in the complex, 25 restaurants (including Mick's, detailed in Chapter 7, "Dining"), and over 200 specialty shops. Among the best-known emporia are Ann Taylor, Britches of Georgetowne, Burberrys, J. Crew, Warner Bros. Studio Store, a Metropolitan Museum of Art store, Forgotten Woman, Cartier, Disney Store, The Sharper Image, Laura Ashley, The Nature Company, Brooks Brothers, Polo/Ralph Lauren, B. Dalton, Waldenbooks, Bally of Switzerland, F.A.O. Schwarz, and Louis Vuitton. Basically, you can purchase just about anything here, from hiking boots to an engagement ring (there are 10 jewelry stores). A full complement of service shops are here as well—shoe repair, optician, locksmith, post office, airline offices, you name it. Open Monday to Saturday 10am to 9pm, Sunday noon to 6pm, with extended hours during the Christmas season. Valet parking is complimentary.

Macy's Peachtree

180 Peachtree St. (between International Blvd. and Ellis St.). ☎ **404/221-7221.** MARTA: Peachtree Center.

Opened in 1927, this downtown branch of Macy's is a department store in the grand tradition, its main floor featuring 30 lofty Corinthian columns, marble floors, and glittering crystal chandeliers. However, it's perfectly up to date when it comes to merchandise. Like most branches of Macy's nowadays, it has a Cellar—a street market with tiled brick floors and shops specializing in housewares. The mezzanine houses an Olympics shop, a shop selling Atlanta sports team merchandise, other Atlanta-themed merchandise, and shops based on current fads. There's also a conveniently located visitor's center on the Cellar level; stop in for information on Atlanta attractions and a complimentary cup of coffee. Five floors of merchandise comprise everything you'd expect—clothing and shoes for the whole family, china, silver, bedding, the works. And dining options range from grilled seafood to a buttery hot cinnamon bun. Open Monday to Saturday 10am to 6pm, Sunday noon to 6pm.

Mall at Peachtree Center

Peachtree St. at International Blvd. ☎ **404/614-5000.** MARTA: Peachtree Center.

Part of the vast 14-block Portman-designed Peachtree Center complex, this downtown mall offers 80 shops, restaurants, and services on three levels. Its location couldn't be more convenient—three adjoining hotels even offer direct access to it via indoor passageways. It's a very complete shopping center, all in a smart setting of Italian marble, fountains, and greenery. There are branches of Muse's Department Store and Brooks Brothers. Services include florists, hairstylists, a travel agency, Federal Express, UPS, a dry cleaner, and an optician. As for dining, a food court dishes up everything from gyros to Mrs. Field's cookies, and full-service restaurants include some great choices: Chow Downtown, Micks, and Morton's of Chicago (see Chapter 7, "Dining"). Most stores are open Monday to Saturday 10am to 6pm, with some stores open Sunday noon to 5pm.

✪ Phipp's Plaza

3500 Peachtree Rd. NE (at the Buckhead Loop). ☎ **404/262-0992** or 800/810-7700. MARTA: Lenox.

Atlanta's most exclusive shopping venue, Phipp's Plaza serves the affluent Buckhead community. In 1992, it underwent a vast multimillion-dollar renovation/expansion, adding shops, spacious promenades, and grand interior courts. And another 550,000 square feet of merchandising space (which will include a Bloomingdale's and 130 specialty stores) is due to open soon after presstime. Phipp's 100-plus shops and restaurants are anchored by Lord & Taylor, Muse's, Parisian (a Birmingham, Alabama–based department store), and Saks Fifth Avenue, and the exclusive Ritz-Carlton Buckhead hotel is adjacent. Its posh emporia (many of them area exclusives) include Gucci, Tiffany & Co., Jaeger International, Gianni Versace, Timberland, Niketown, Paul & Shark (upscale men's clothing), Designs by Levi's (with computerized fitting), A/X Armani Exchange, Ross-Simons (upscale jewelry, china, and silver), and Cole Haan for shoes. You'll also find chic boutiques selling ladies and men's apparel, luggage, jewelry, home furnishings, shoes, and specialty gifts. The ambience is sedately elegant, and there's usually something special going on—perhaps an art or fashion show. Services include personal shoppers, gift locators, and a concierge, and among the mall's first-class restaurants is the highly recommended Peasant Uptown. Also on the premises: a restaurant complex called The Veranda Food Court and a 14-screen movie theater. Stores are open Monday to Saturday 10am to 9pm, Sunday noon to 5:30pm. Valet parking is complimentary.

Underground Atlanta

Alabama St. (between Peachtree St. and Central Ave.). ☎ **404/523-2311.** MARTA: Five Points.

This 12-acre mix of colorful shops, nightclubs, and restaurants makes for a fun-filled day or evening. There are dozens of shops here, plus vendors in Humbug Square selling merchandise off antique pushcarts. Shopping options include numerous clothing shops for men, women, and children, running the gamut from upscale T-shirts at Dallas Alice, to unisex active wear at Gadzooks, to Victoria's Secret's sexy lingerie. Other interesting emporia include Art by God (fossils and rare mineral specimens), First World Book (African-American literature), Kandlestix (where candle-makers display their craft), Starlog (for futuristic and sci-fi stuff), Papier D'Couleur (papier-mâché birds, fruit, and animals), and Georgia Grande General (Georgia-related gifts and crafts). There are also novelty stores such as the bargain mecca, Everything's A $1. And don't miss Olympic Experience, headquarters and retail outlet for the 1996 Games. Of course, eateries—from pizza and taco stands to elegant restaurants—abound. If you're driving, there's parking in a garage on Central Avenue off Martin Luther King Drive. Be sure to get your ticket validated inside for discounted parking. Open Monday to Saturday 10am to 9:30pm, Sunday noon to 6pm.

3 Shopping Around Town

In addition to the independent bookstores in Atlanta, the nationwide chain stores of **B. Dalton** and **Waldenbooks** are represented locally (see "Department Stores & Malls," earlier in this chapter).

BOOKS

Chapter 11—The Discount Bookstore

1544 Piedmont Rd. (in the Ansley Mall at the corner of Monroe Dr.). ☎ **404/ 872-7986.**

These large, first-class bookstores, in distinctive yellow and black, make up the largest bookstore chain in Atlanta. They are also the least expensive. They take 30% off the cover price for the top 15 hardcover *New York Times* bestsellers, and all other books in the store are at an everyday discount of 11%. Their service also sets them apart. The staff, all serious readers themselves, excel at answering questions and finding particular titles. Chapter 11 will also special order books at no additional cost. Open Monday to Saturday 10am to 9pm, Sunday 12pm to 6pm.

Besides the Ansley Mall store, there are Chapter 11 branches at **Sandy Springs Plaza** (6237 Roswell Rd. ☎ 404/256-5518. Open Monday to Saturday 10am to 9pm, Sunday 11am to 6pm.), **Briarcliff Village** (2100 Henderson Mill Rd. ☎ 404/414-9288. Open Monday to Saturday 9am to 9pm, Sunday 12pm to 6pm.), and **Emory Commons** in Decatur (2091 N. Decatur Rd. ☎ 404/325-1505. Open Monday to Saturday 10am to 10pm, Sunday 12pm to 6pm.). There should also be a new store opening soon at Paces Ferry Plaza, 3509 Northside Pkwy.

Engineer's Bookstore

748 Marietta St. NW (at the corner of Means Street, just off Tech Parkway and approximately one mile from Georgia World Congress Center). ☎ **404/221-1669** or 800/635-5919.

The largest technical bookstore in Atlanta, Engineer's has an incredible selection of computer and engineering titles as well as the graduate and undergraduate texts for Georgia Tech. Relocated in 1993 to make way for the Olympic Village Dormitories, Engineer's Bookstore has been in business since 1954. The 10,000-square-foot store, a rehabbed 1930s brick building, is located in a historic district of Marietta

Street, near art galleries, restaurants, and the Georgia Institute of Technology (Olympic Village). Open Monday to Friday 9am to 5:30pm, Saturday 10am to 2 pm.

Latitudes

Lenox Square Mall, 3393 Peachtree Rd. NE. ☎ **404/237-6144.**

A great store for map lovers, Latitudes offers a wide variety of atlases, globes, wall maps, road maps, and travel guidebooks, as well as travel accessories such as money belts, backpacks, toiletry kits, and kids' car games. Open Monday to Saturday 10am to 9pm, Sunday noon to 6pm.

There's another Latitudes in the Perimeter Mall, 4400 Ashford-Dunwoody Rd. (☎ 404/394-2772).

Oxford Books

360 Pharr Rd. (between Peachtree and Piedmont rds.). ☎ **404/262-3333** or 800/476-3311.

Few cities can boast of bookstores like Oxford Books. Founded in 1970, this independent Atlanta bookseller has four stores that collectively contain 250,000 titles, making it the largest bookstore south of New York City.

Oxford at Buckhead, at 33,000 square feet, is the flagship store (its address and phone number are given above). Formerly a Mercedes dealership, the store consists of three linked rotundas that house, in addition to books, a coffee shop, a complete video store, vast audio tape/CD selections, a comic shop, rare and collectible books, and a giant magazine/newspaper selection. Browsers are invited to relax in the store's informal seating throughout and peruse the *Oxford Review,* a 200,000-circulation newspaper that offers book reviews and an Oxford events calendar. A knowledgeable staff is available at all stores to help locate or order books. Hours are Sunday to Thursday 9am to midnight, Friday and Saturday 9am to 1am.

The Buckhead store, in the heart of the city's entertainment and restaurant district, is also the site of frequent appearances by celebrated authors. These have included Anne Rice, Pat Conroy, Amy Tan, Isabel Allende, Dick Francis, Deepak Chopra, Alan Shepard, Walter Mosely, Lauren Bacall, Maya Angelou, and Barbara Taylor Bradford, as well as local celebrities such as Newt Gingrich and Jimmy Carter.

Other branches include **Oxford at Peachtree Battle,** 2345 Peachtree Rd. NE (☎ 404/364-3040), a 13,000-square-foot store that features a coffee shop and a large magazine and newspaper department. It is located in the Peachtree Battle Shopping Center, site of several fine restaurants. Hours are Sunday to Thursday from 9am to 11pm, Friday and Saturday from 9am to midnight.

Adjacent to the Peachtree Battle store is **Oxford Too,** 2395 Peachtree Rd. NE (☎ 404/262-3411), one of the largest used, collectible, and bargain bookstores in the South. Oxford Too specializes in hard-to-find books on Southern and Civil War history as well as books by Southern writers. The Oxford Comic Shop is located here. Hours are Sunday to Thursday 10am to 10pm, Friday and Saturday 10am to 11pm.

Slightly north of the Buckhead stores is the 12,000-square-foot **Oxford at Sandy Springs,** 6320 Roswell Rd. (☎ 404/364-3040). A smaller neighborhood version of the main store, Oxford at Sandy Springs brings a wide array of books and services to a convenient location for suburban readers. Hours are Sunday to Thursday 9am to 10pm, Friday and Saturday 9am to 1pm.

Books can be shipped from any store to anywhere in the world. Orders can be placed and charged during store hours from anywhere in the U.S. by calling 800/476-3311, or 404/262-3333 from anywhere in the world. You can also fax orders to 404/364-2729 or place an order on the Internet at http://www.oxfordbooks.com.

Tall Tales Book Shop, Inc.
2999 N. Druid Hills Rd. ☎**404/636-2498.**

This general bookstore in the Emory University area offers a large selection of mainstream titles with an emphasis on literary selections. All large publishers are represented as well as university and small presses. There's a coffeehouse in the store, and a friendly atmosphere prevails. The staff is knowledgeable and will be happy to process special orders. Open Monday to Thursday 9:30am to 9:30pm, Friday and Saturday 9:30am to 10pm, Sunday 12:30pm to 6pm.

WOMEN'S CLOTHING

See also "Department Stores & Malls," above, for more stores.

A Pea in the Pod
In the Phipp's Plaza Mall, 3500 Peachtree Rd. (at Lenox Rd.). ☎ **404/261-0808.** MARTA: Lenox.

This cleverly named shop features maternity clothes, but we're not talking T-shirts with an arrow pointing to your stomach and the word *baby*. These are gorgeous clothes—the kind you wore when you weren't pregnant—including designer lines by Adrienne Vittadini, Carol Little, Laundry, David Dart, and Joan Vass. They run the gamut from really elegant business garb (perfect for board meetings) to evening wear and chic sports clothing. In fact, the clothes are so beautiful that women who are not pregnant shop here as well. Open Monday to Saturday 10am to 9pm, Sunday noon to 5:30pm.

✪ Sasha Frisson
3094 E. Shadowlawn Ave. NE (between Peachtree and E. Paces Ferry rds.). ☎ **404/231-0393.**

Without a doubt, the most high-fashion boutique in town. This is the stuff best-dressed lists are made of. Owners Emma Nassar and Laura Seydel carry only the smartest European and American designers—Fendi, Anna Lisa Ferro, John Galiano, Vestimenta, Chantal Thomas, Karl Lagerfeld, and others. Wonderful accessories and jewelry here, too. This delightful and impeccably elegant boutique is located in a peach-brick 1930s house. There are other chic emporia occupying residential buildings on the same street if you feel like doing some upscale browsing. Open Monday to Saturday 10am to 6pm.

FACTORY OUTLETS

Tanger Factory Outlet

198 Tanger Dr. (at Exit 53 off I-85N), Commerce. ☎ **706/335-4537.**

Tanger is a bargain-hunter's paradise, with 45 factory-outlet stores on a 22-acre property. Included are Oneida, Liz Claiborne, Corning, American Tourister, Farberware, Gitano, Levi's, Reebok, Mikasa, L'Eggs, Hanes, Bali, Maidenform, and Van Heusen, among others. It's about a 50-minute drive from downtown. Open Monday to Saturday 9am to 9pm, Sunday noon to 6pm.

FARMER'S MARKETS

Atlanta State Farmer's Market

16 Forest Pkwy., Forest Park. ☎ **404/366-6910.**

The State Farmer's Market is a vast 146-acre outdoor facility where stall after stall is piled high with produce. There are also vendors of home-canned pickles, jams, and relishes; plants and flowers; and seasonal items such as pumpkins in October, holly and Christmas trees in December. It's a colorful spectacle. You can have a good meal at a restaurant on the premises. If you're driving, take I-75 south to Exit 78; the market is on your left. Open 24 hours daily except Christmas.

DeKalb Farmer's Market

3000 E. Ponce de Leon Ave., Decatur. ☎ **404/377-6400.**

Even if you have no intention of purchasing comestibles, this incredible market, started in 1977 by Robert Blazer, merits a visit. A mind-boggling array of international food items is temptingly displayed in a 140,000-square-foot cedar-paneled building that harmonizes nicely with its wooded surroundings. It's about a 20-minute drive from downtown. International flags from Australia to Zaire are hung from the rafters. Tables are laden with mountains of produce from broccoli to bok choy, not to mention winter melons and water chestnuts, lily root, curry leaves, breadfruit, Jamaican jerk marinade, Korean daikon, a multiplicity of mushrooms, chick-pea miso, cheese fudge, a vast beer and wine section, dried fruits, plants and flowers, seafood, meat, poultry, every imaginable variety of fresh herbs and hot peppers, fresh-baked breads and pastries, stalks of sugarcane, 450 varieties of cheese, frogs' legs, conch meat, quail, and so on. As you shop, you can nibble grilled red snapper, knishes, sections of grapefruit, Ecuadorian octopus, or whatever else is offered at sample tables throughout the facility. Open daily 9am to 9pm.

11

Atlanta After Dark

The Allman Brothers dubbed it "Hot'lanta!" This is a city that sizzles after dark, with numerous music clubs featuring jazz, rock, country, and blues. It also offers a comprehensive cultural scene, including symphony, ballet, opera, and theater productions. And major artists headline regularly at Atlanta's many large-scale performance facilities.

To find out what's on during your stay, consult the "Weekend" section of Saturday's *Atlanta Journal-Constitution* or *Creative Loafing,* a free publication you'll see in stores, restaurants, and other places around town (to obtain a free copy prior to your visit call **800/950-5623**). Another source is the **ARTS Hotline** (☎ **404/853-3278**), a 24-hour recording that provides up-to-the-minute listings of concerts, plays, films, and other cultural events.

Tickets to many performances are handled by Ticketmaster. Call **404/249-6400** to charge tickets. *Note:* Oxford Bookstores (see Chapter 10) function as Ticketmaster outlets.

1 The Performing Arts

See the listing for the Fox Theatre below for details on the Atlanta Ballet.

CLASSICAL MUSIC

In addition to the city's symphony, listed below, the **Atlanta Chamber Players** perform a wide spectrum of classical and contemporary masterpieces, and each year they commission works by leading composers. Their season runs from fall through spring, and most concerts are $12 (free for students with ID). Call **404/651-1228** to find out where they'll be playing during your stay.

Atlanta Symphony Orchestra

Performing in the Woodruff Arts Center, 1280 Peachtree St. NE (at 15th St.). ☎ **404/733-5000** (box office) for information and tickets. Most tickets $16–$45. Parking available in the Arts Center Garage on Lombardy Way between 15th and 16th sts. MARTA: Arts Center.

Having celebrated its 50th anniversary during its 1994–95 season, the Atlanta Symphony Orchestra (ASO) performs under musical director Yoel Levi. Complementing it is the 200-voice Atlanta Symphony Orchestra Chorus, enabling performances of large-scale symphonic-choral works. The season runs from September through May in the

Woodruff Arts Center, plus summer concerts in Chastain Park Amphitheatre and in various Atlanta parks.

The ASO's annual schedule is extensive. The main offerings are the **Master Season Series** and the **Champagne and Coffee Series.** Master Season concerts, held on selected Thursday, Friday, and Saturday evenings in the plush 1,762-seat Symphony Hall, feature renowned guest artists such as violinists Pinchas Zukerman and Joshua Bell, cellist Lynn Harrell, pianists Alicia de Larrocha and Tzimon Barto, and sopranos Barbara Hendricks and Sylvia McNair. There are 24 different programs. The Champagne and Coffee Series offers thematic programs of light classics and popular favorites on selected Friday and Saturday evenings as well as Saturday mornings. Also held during this season is a series of three **Family Concerts** geared to children. In addition, there are **Holiday Concerts** at Halloween and Christmas and **Saturday Sampler Matinees** (classical concerts) on selected dates at 2pm.

The ASO's **Classic Chastain Series** concerts, held in the 7,000-seat Chastain Park Amphitheatre, begin at 8:30pm on Wednesday, Friday, and Saturday evenings between June and August. All except lawn seating is reserved. It's customary to bring elaborate picnics and wine to these events. The series features headliner performers such as Natalie Cole, Tony Bennett, Diana Ross, Tom Jones, Mel Tormé, Mary Chapin Carpenter, and Trisha Yearwood performing with the ASO. Another warm-weather event is the **Summer Classical Series,** which takes place for three weeks in July. There are also free concerts in parks throughout the Atlanta area on selected summer evenings. These run the gamut from full symphony performances to light classical repertoires.

The ASO will present six concerts—two of them featuring soprano Jessye Norman—during the summer of 1996 as part of the Olympic Arts Festival.

OPERA

Atlanta Opera

Fox Theatre, 660 Peachtree St. NE (at Ponce de Leon Ave.). ☎ **404/355-3311** or 800/35-OPERA for information and tickets; tickets also available via Ticketmaster (☎ 404/249-6400). Tickets $15–$100. MARTA: North Avenue.

Under the artistic direction of William Fred Scott, the Atlanta Opera offers three fully staged productions each summer at the Fox Theatre and performs additional operas and concerts at varied locations throughout the year. Principal performers are drawn from top opera companies from across the United States and Europe. Three to five performances are given of each opera. A recent season's productions included Puccini's *Turandot,* Bellini's *Norma,* and Bizet's *The Pearl Fishers.* Future plans call for a more extensive season. Tickets can be difficult to obtain; charge them in advance if possible.

THEATER

Alliance Theatre Company

Performing in the Woodruff Arts Center, 1280 Peachtree St. NE (at 15th St.). ☎ **404/733-5000** for information or to charge tickets. Tickets $14–$34. Discounts for students and seniors; "rush tickets" often available on the night of a performance. Parking in the Arts Center Garage on Lombardy Way between 15th and 16th sts. MARTA: Arts Center.

The Alliance Theatre Company, under the artistic direction of Kenny Leon, is the largest regional theater in the southeast. On two stages, it produces about 10 plays a year (the season runs from September through May, with occasional productions during the summer). Many well-known actors have played these stages, among them Jane Alexander, Richard Dreyfuss, Esther Rolle, Phylicia Rashad, and Morgan Freeman. A recent season's productions included Dickens's *A Christmas Carol* (performed annually), the complete *Angels in America*, Nobel Prize–winner Jacinto Benavente's *The Art of Swindling*, James Baldwin's *Amen Corner*, and more.

The Alliance Lunchtime Theatre series offers one-act plays ranging from vaudeville to Shakespeare, presented on designated Tuesdays and Thursdays between September and May (admission is $3). And the Alliance Children's Theatre presents plays geared to youngsters from September through April (tickets are $8).

Seven Stages Performing Arts Center

1105 Euclid Ave. (two blocks west of Moreland Ave.). ☎ **404/523-7647** for information and tickets. Tickets $8–$14 for most shows; discounts for students and seniors. Parking $3. MARTA: Inman Park.

Under the direction of Del Hamilton, this company has been producing new, experimental, and issues-oriented works of international scope since 1979. Many worthy new works and new playwrights find a stage here, and both local and international acting groups supplement the resident company. But not everything done here is avant-garde or controversial, however; the company has also performed Shakespeare, Molière, and Jacques Brel, and there are frequent children's theater productions. The center has two stages, the 100-seat Backdoor Theatre and the 300-seat Main Stage.

MAJOR VENUES

To find out who'll be playing during your stay, call the ARTS Hotline (☎ **404/853-3278**) for an up-to-date 24-hour recording.

In addition to the special places I've listed below, many of the stadiums listed in Section 6, "Spectator Sports," in Chapter 8, host major concerts from time to time. These include the Alexander Memorial Coliseum and Bobby Dodd Stadium/Grant Field at Georgia Tech, Road Atlanta, the Georgia Dome, and the Omni Coliseum.

Atlanta Civic Center

395 Piedmont Ave. NE (between Ralph McGill Blvd. and Pine St.). ☎ **404/523-6275** for general information or to charge tickets. MARTA: Civic Center (about five blocks away); buses go to the door.

The Civic Center offers a wealth of entertainment options in its 4,600-seat auditorium. It hosts headliners, touring Broadway shows, traveling symphonies and opera companies, fashion shows, and body-builder contests—quite a mixed bag.

Call the Civic Center or check local newspapers and magazines to find out what's on during your stay. Many Cultural Olympiad performances will take place here.

Chastain Park Amphitheatre

In Chastain Park at Powers Ferry Rd. and Stella Dr. ☎ **404/231-5888** for information.

This delightful 7,000-seat outdoor facility offers concerts under the stars from May to October. Everyone brings food; a picnic on the grass or at your amphitheater seat is a tradition (people bring gourmet feasts and even candelabra). Big-name performers are featured. It's hard to get tickets, so order as far in advance as possible (months ahead if you can). See also the listing for the Atlanta Symphony Orchestra, which offers a summer series here.

Coca-Cola Lakewood Amphitheatre

At the Lakewood exit of I-75/85, 3¹/₂ miles south of downtown. ☎ **404/627-9704.** Take I-75 or I-85 south to Lakewood Frwy. exit (88E or 88W) and follow the signs. Free parking. MARTA: Lakewood/Fort McPherson (shuttle buses take patrons to and from the station).

The $15 million Lakewood Amphitheatre accommodates 19,000—7,000 reserved seats plus a sloping lawn that holds an additional 12,000. Needless to say, this is a vast facility used for major shows. Eric Clapton, Elton John, and Aerosmith have all performed here. In addition, the amphitheater hosts music festivals such as Lollapalooza and Reggae Sunsplash. There are umbrellaed picnic tables on the grounds, and though you can't bring in food or drink, a wide variety of refreshments are available, including beer, champagne, fruit and cheese, sandwiches, pizza, and of course Coca-Cola.

Fox Theatre

660 Peachtree St. NE (at Ponce de Leon Ave.). ☎ **404/881-2100** for information or 404/817-8700 to charge tickets. Ballet tickets $8–$40. Many paid parking lots nearby. MARTA: North Avenue.

Built in 1927, when movie theaters were conceived along lavish lines, the Fox is a Moorish-Egyptian extravaganza complete with arabesque arches, onion domes, and minarets. Its exotic interior reflects the Egytomania of that decade—a phenomenon resulting from archeologist Henry Carter's discovery of the treasure-laden tomb of King Tut. Throne chairs, scarab motifs, and hieroglyphics are seen throughout the theater, and the auditorium evokes a Middle Eastern courtyard under an azure sky. See Chapter 8 for details on the Fox's history and architecture, as well as information on tours.

Every year there's an October-to-April "Best of Broadway" season, featuring six major New York shows. It's followed by a summer Broadway series.

The Fox is home to the **Atlanta Opera** (see above) and the **Atlanta Ballet** (☎ **404/873-5811** for information), the oldest continually operating ballet company in the U.S. It presents four productions each fall-through-spring season, always including George Balanchine's *The Nutcracker* every December.

In addition, a wide spectrum of headliners plays the Fox, along with diverse entertainment ranging from ice skating to fashion shows to closed-circuit coverage of boxing matches.

Variety Playhouse

1099 Euclid Ave. (near Washita St.). ☎ **404/521-1786** for information. Parking lot on Euclid Ave. near Colquitt Ave., charging $2 a night.

Built in the 1930s as a neighborhood movie theater, the Variety today offers an eclectic array of performances, from folk rock to jazz. There are also frequent album-release parties here. It's definitely worth checking out.

2 The Club & Bar Scene

Nightclubs come and go, so it's always a good idea to call ahead. As we go to press, these are the major venues for varied nighttime revels. Most clubs are open until 2, 3, or even 4am.

DANCE CLUBS

Johnny's Hideaway

3771 Roswell Rd. (two blocks north of Piedmont Rd.). ☎ **404/233-8026.** No cover, but there's a two-drink minimum (at tables only) after 8pm nightly. Free self and valet parking.

Johnny's has been one of Atlanta's top night spots for over a decade. It's not glamorous, but the regular folks who frequent the club always seem to be having a super time. Ebullient host Johnny Esposito, always on hand to greet his guests, is a well-known Atlanta character. The music is primarily big-band era to '50s/'60s oldies, and so is the crowd. Tunes progress through the decades as the night wears on, but the music is always mellow.

This is a place for serious dancing, and most of the clientele can execute a pretty proficient two-step or tango. And though it's unpretentious, there are celebrities who hang out here when in town (Tommy LaSorda, Arnold Palmer, Steve Martin, Robert Duvall, Jake La Motta, and burlesque queen Tempest Storm). A silver ball rotates over the dance floor, and you're likely to see Glenn Miller on the video monitors. A reasonably priced menu lists items ranging from deli sandwiches to snack fare such as nachos and buffalo wings to steak and prime-rib main courses. Sunday at 6pm you can have a free spaghetti dinner. Special events here include Johnny's Tomato talent contests (about 1,500 women in Atlanta carry cards identifying them as "Johnny's Tomatoes") and occasional live oldies concerts featuring groups like The Four Freshmen. Dress is casual.

Masquerade

695 North Ave. NE (just east of Boulevard). ☎ **404/577-8178.** Cover $5 in Hell and Purgatory ($8 for ages 18–20), $2–$20 (depending on the performer) in Heaven; Music Park tickets vary with the performer. Parking $3–$5.

Housed in a century-old stone-walled Romanesque building—a former excelsior factory—Masquerade looks like the Bastille. Its interior, divided into three main areas, is adorned with factory remnants.

Downstairs, a bar called **Purgatory**—under a lofty corrugated-tin ceiling with rough-hewn wood beams and exposed pipes—offers music videos, pool tables, pinball, video games, and a photo machine. Across the way, in **Hell**—a dark and dank stone-walled setting adorned with hanging chains—Wednesday is Club Fetish night (S&M), Thursday the music is '80s, Friday (Bliss Night) a DJ plays alternative dance music, and Saturday is Cyber Nation Night featuring techno and high-energy music. Club-employed dancers perform on stages. Ascend the stairs to **Heaven** (not my conception, frankly), its walls painted blue with fluffy clouds; here live local and national acts perform (the latter have included Meat Loaf, Iggy Pop, Cheap Trick, Psychedelic Furs, David Lee Roth, Steel Pulse, and Veruca Salt). In addition to these interior spaces there's a 4,000-seat outdoor **Music Park** behind the club, where bands such as Porno for Pyro, The Connells, The KMFDM, The Cranberrys & Weezer, and 311 perform April through October (tickets available via Ticketmaster, **404/249-6400**). If you want to get away from the action, you can retreat to an al fresco bar with a tree-shaded wooden deck enclosed by a picket fence.

Rupert's

3330 Piedmont Rd. (just north of Peachtree Rd. in the Peachtree Crossing Shopping Center). ☎ **404/266-9866** or 404/266-9834. Cover $7 Fri–Sat; Tues $5 for women, $7 for men; Wed cover varies with performer; $4 Thurs. No cover if you arrive before 8pm. Valet parking $2, but you can park in the shopping center lot free if you wish.

One of Atlanta's most popular clubs is Rupert's, a high-energy, live-music venue with state-of-the-art sound and lighting systems. Its interior is agleam with mahogany paneling, silk wall coverings, mirrored columns, brass rails, and art deco lighting fixtures. The clientele is upscale/mainstream and attractively attired. There's a top-flight show every night—a nine-piece band and five versatile vocalists performing everything from Motown to top-40 tunes, from blues to funk—with a DJ filling in between sets. Many singers who perform here have a big local following.

The dance floor is right in front of the stage, and there are five bars downstairs. Rupert's has a pretty good visiting celebrity quotient. Rod Stewart, Alec Baldwin and Kim Basinger, Cher, Jon Secada (who took the stage), Eddie Murphy, and JFK, Jr., are among those who've partied here while in Atlanta. And the club is also popular with local and visiting athletes. A large $2 buffet is served Tuesday and Friday from 5:30 to 8pm. Big-name acts often appear Wednesday nights (call ahead). The club is closed on Sunday and Monday, and you should call ahead, since it's sometimes closed for private parties.

Tongue & Groove

3055 Peachtree Rd. (between E. Paces Ferry Rd. and Buckhead Ave.). ☎ **404/261-2325**. Cover $7 Wed–Sat, $5 Tues and Sun. Parking $5 at the lot at Buckhead Ave. and Bolling Way.

One of Atlanta's most elegant clubs, Tongue & Groove attracts a chic upscale crowd. You might see some of the Atlanta Braves (David Justice, Mark Lemke, Fred McGriff) here, along with other top athletes and celebrities. And major companies frequently celebrate new CD releases at T & G parties. The spacious interior (5,000 square feet) is on the plush side, with glossy oak floors, lofty ceilings, ultrasuede furnishings, and walls discreetly dotted with video monitors and hung with Len Prince's 1940s-Hollywood–style glamour photos of models and starlets (Beverly Johnson, Drew Barrymore, and others). Tuesday nights there's jazz and lounge music through 10pm, house music thereafter; Wednesday is Latin Night drawing a good crossover crowd; Thursday is basically a members-only/private party night, but if you look snazzy you might get in (it's worth a try if you want to party with athletes and models); Friday live jazz bands play during Happy Hour (5:30 to 8pm), followed by light jazz through 10pm and an '80s and '90s dance format until closing; Saturday features '70s disco; Sunday you'll dance to top-40 tunes. In addition to the dance floor, entertainments include On-Line America computer games. You can purchase sushi and quality cigars on the premises, and the bar offers a wide selection of fine wines and champagnes as well as almost every imaginable kind of premium liquor. Jackets are required for men Thursday through Saturday, and sports shoes are always verboten; you must be 21 to get in. Closed Mondays.

Note: Especially on Friday and Saturday nights, the Buckhead streets surrounding T & G are mobbed with revelers, and numerous nightspots in the area make this an ideal base for club-hopping.

✪ Velvet

89 Park Place (at John Wesley Dobbs Ave.). ☎ **404/681-9936.** Cover $3 Mon, $6 Wed, $7 Thurs, $5 Fri, $5 Sat before midnight ($7 after midnight); Sun $7 for women, $10 for men. Parking $4–$5. MARTA: Peachtree Center.

One of the hottest places to dance in Atlanta, Velvet has been featured in every national publication from *Interview* to *Details*. Many pop icons have partied here—RuPaul, Depeche Mode, U2, sports stars David Justice and Dominick Williams, even Madonna. It's outré/upscale interior displays bizarrely unrelated wall paintings—a cartoon fox, a vast eyeball, a moonscape, a steer, and a sun with teeth. The back room houses a big dance floor enhanced by high-tech lighting effects, and there's a VIP/private-party room upstairs. Monday night is Boy Brigade (the crowd is predominantly gay men); Wednesday a DJ plays house music; Thursday soul, hip-hop, and fashion shows are featured; top regional alternative bands play Friday nights, followed by progressive house music with a DJ; Sunday night is the wildly popular "Disco Hell" (wear your bell-bottoms). Pizza is available. Closed Tuesdays.

JAZZ CLUBS

✪ Dante's Down the Hatch

3380 Peachtree Rd. NE (across the street from the Lenox Square Mall). ☎ **404/266-1600.** Cover $5 for seating on the jazz ship, free on the wharf. MARTA: Lenox.

This wonderful jazz supper club is the realm of Dante Stephensen, a bona fide Atlanta character and former Aspen ski bum who makes his home in a posh private railroad car that was designed for the Woolworth family in the 1920s. He mans the decks of this well-rigged schooner, a fantasy 18th-century ship (actually afloat in murky waters) in a colorful seaport village. His aim was not to erect an exact replica but to create the period seagoing setting of everyone's imagination. It's a mix of antiques and nautical kitsch—200-year-old handstitched sails, oak paneling from English banks, pirate and sea captain mannequins, beveled-glass doors, 1892 leaded-glass panels from Lloyd's of London, centuries-old ship's lanterns and bells, Polish ship figureheads. Fish netting forms a canopy over the lower deck. There are many intimate seating areas—a velvet-curtained "bordello," a lighthouse, an English mahogany elevator, and a sail loft among them. Amber streetlamps and candlelight enhance the cozy ambience. The most romantic seating is in semienclosed private booths on the lower deck where the talented Paul Mitchell Trio plays traditional jazz. Earlier in the evening, classical folk guitarists perform on the "wharf," and weekend nights a solo pianist plays on the ship prior to the show.

Plan to have dinner during the show. Delicious cheese, Mandarin Chinese (beef, chicken, pork, and shrimp), and chocolate fondues are featured. Cheese platters and Chinese dumplings are additional specialties. And for dessert, there's chocolate fudge cake served hot. Main courses, all including a large and tasty salad, are $10.75 to $24. An extensive wine list is reasonably priced. Reservations are suggested.

✪ Yin Yang Café

64 Third St. NE (between Spring St. and I-75/85 at Georgia Tech). ☎ **404/607-0682.** Cover $3–$5 Thurs–Sun. MARTA: North Avenue.

This hip and happening jazz venue is comfortable, casual, and candlelit, with exposed brick walls used to display changing art exhibitions. There's a pool table, and some couches in the back room provide a funky conversation area. The crowd—of all ages—is most definitively not mainstream. Tuesday and Wednesday are coffeehouse nights (hang out and listen to recorded jazz). There's live music the rest of the week—acid jazz on Thursdays, straight-ahead traditional sounds on Fridays, and a mellow but groovy mix on Saturdays (acid jazz, funk, soul, a little hip-hop). Sundays feature Naked Jazz Jam Sessions with local and visiting musicians. A full menu lists items such as spicy jerk chicken salad; a sandwich stuffed with roasted veggies, feta cheese, and portabello mushroom; and linguine with red wine marinara, fresh garlic, and basil. At this writing only wine and beer are offered, with more than a dozen premium wines offered by the glass; a full bar is in the works. Closed Mondays.

A COMEDY CLUB

Punchline Comedy Club

280 Hildebrand Dr. NE (off Roswell Rd. in the Balconies Shopping Center), Sandy Springs. ☎ **404/252-5233.** Cover $7 Tues–Thurs and Sun, $10 Fri, $12 Sat (occasionally more for big names). Free parking.

This popular suburban comedy club, about a 40-minute drive from downtown, features three comedians nightly in each show—two leadins and a headliner. The setting is casual. The club has a rustic knotty-pine-paneled interior, its walls plastered with photographs of famous comics. You don't need to dress up. Performers are pros on the national comedy-club circuit—the comedians you see on Leno and Letterman—except on Tuesday (open-mike night) when the regular show is followed by amateur wannabes (you can be one of them, if you sign up by 7pm). Doors open an hour before show time. Reasonably priced food—steak and cheese sandwiches, burgers, char-grilled chicken, potato skins, quesadillas—is available, along with drinks. Thursday and early Friday shows are smoke-free. Though you can buy tickets at the club, they often sell out, so it's best to reserve by phone using a major credit card. Seating is first-come, first-served; arrive early. You must be 21 to get in. Tuesday through Thursday shows are at 8:30pm, Friday and Saturday at 8 and 10:30pm, Sunday at 8pm. But hours may vary; call ahead to check.

KENNY'S ALLEY IN UNDERGROUND ATLANTA

Since so many nightclubs offering varying entertainment formats are grouped conveniently at Underground Atlanta, Kenny's Alley club-hopping is very popular. See also Damon's Clubhouse, below, another Underground nightspot.

✪ Dante's Down the Hatch

Kenny's Alley. ☎ **404/577-1800.** Cover $1 for folk music on the wharf, $5 for jazz on the ship. MARTA: Five Points.

This is the original Dante's, the prototype for the Buckhead branch described in detail above. To enter, you literally go down a hatchway similar to any ship's descent to lower decks, except that its walls are lined with photographs of celebrity guests—Bill Cosby, Jimmy Carter, Rod Stewart, Count Basie, and others.

Owner Dante Stephensen earns kudos for highlighting the historic sites within his club. A sign informs visitors, for instance, that an exposed wall of the hatchway staircase is from the 1850s Planter Hotel and is the actual site of the hospital depicted in *Gone With the Wind.* An 1810 well on the premises was the water source for Atlanta's first fire department, and a steam engine on view powered the Frank E. Block Candy Company from 1868 to 1888. Like the Buckhead club, this is a fantasy ship moored in crocodile-infested waters (live crocs swim in the moat). And there's plenty of nautical ambience—oak-plank floors, ship's ropes, steering wheels, and more. A singer and guitar player entertain on the "wharf," while the Brothers Three offer progressive jazz Monday and Tuesday, and the John Robertson Trio does the same Wednesday through Sunday. Sometimes well-known artists come in and jam with the band. Fondue dinners are featured (see details in Buckhead listing).

Fat Tuesday

Kenny's Alley. ☎ **404/523-7404.** No cover. MARTA: Five Points.

This New Orleans–concept club has a bar similar to a Mardi Gras float, but with an Atlanta twist—it's adorned with busts of Rhett and Scarlett. Special machines behind the bar mix over 20 flavors of frozen daiquiris—margarita, peach colada (that's mixed with peaches, rum, ice cream, and coconut cream), white Russian, and more—and you can sample an ounce of any flavor on the house. Po' boy sandwiches are also available. Rock and top-40 tapes are played at an ears-plitting level. IDs are checked at the door: You have to be 21.

Teddy's Live Entertainment & Restaurant

Kenny's Alley. ☎ **404/653-9999.** Cover $8 Fri–Sat, $5 Sun–Thurs. MARTA: Five Points.

This immense club—with bars at either end, gold records lining the walls, and the requisite high-tech lighting system over the dance floor—offers live music (local and national artists) Wednesday through Sunday nights. Recent performers have included Joe Sample, Norman Conners, Randy Crawford, Jennifer Holiday, Danny Lernman, George Clinton, and Michael Henderson. And sometimes major record companies showcase new artists here. Tuesday is karaoke night, Wednesdays blues groups are featured, Thursdays Caribbean bands perform, Fridays and Saturdays local and national jazz musicians take the stage, Sunday nights there are jazz jam sessions. The format is subject to change; call ahead. You must be 21 to get in. A full menu offers prime rib, steaks, and seafood, in addition to lighter fare—burgers, sandwiches, chicken tenders, and salads. Every Sunday Teddy's hosts a jazz/gospel buffet brunch from 11:30am to 4pm.

A MIXED BAG

Red Light Cafe

533 Amsterdam Ave. (between Monroe Dr. and Piedmont Park). ☎ **404/874-7828.** Cover $2–$3. Free parking.

A classic San Francisco–style coffeehouse, the cavernous Red Light Cafe has a funky red-walled, high-ceilinged interior with a mix of tables and some worn but comfy sofas in the back room. One gallery-white wall, illuminated by track lighting, is used to display changing art exhibitions. You can also access the Internet here (E-mail address is Redlight &mindspring.com), or sit outside sipping port or beer (microbrewery, imported, or draft) in a flower-bordered garden. No hard liquor is served. A menu offers sandwiches (such as roast turkey breast with cranberries and mayo), salads, and snack fare. Thursday and Saturday nights improvisational comedy groups perform at 8pm; acoustic-oriented live bands play from 10pm to midnight Wednesday, Friday, and Saturday; and there's live contemporary jazz on Sunday. There are also poetry readings on Wednesday nights. Call to find out what's on. Closed Monday.

Star Community Bar

437 Moreland Ave. NE (between Euclid and Mansfield aves.). ☎ **404/681-9081.** Cover $3–$7. Free parking in a lot behind the club.

Housed in a former bank, this funky and cavernous club features the "GraceVault"—a small shrine filled with Elvis posters, an all-Elvis jukebox, Elvis clocks and other memorabilia, as well as posters of Elvez, "the Spanish Elvis" who performs here once a year and claims to be the illegitimate son of Elvis and Charo! You can even light candles to the King here. Primarily a Little Five Points neighborhood hangout—popularly known as Star Bar—this is a comfortable, low-key kind of place, with Christmas-tree lights strung over the bar, a mirror ball overhead, and walls hung with mounted hunting trophies, fight posters, and photos of music legends like B. B. King and Hank Williams. Live music Tuesday through Sunday nights runs the gamut from rockabilly to rock 'n' roll, blues, and R&B. Most of the performers are local and regional, but occasionally bigger names play here as well (e.g., Dave Alvin, Ronnie Dawson, the Beet Farmers, Swimming Pool Cues, and Bruce Hampton). There's a full bar, and light fare is available—pizza, gumbo, and chili supplemented Monday and Wednesday nights by Mexican entrées. Some people dance, though there's no real dance floor. Poetry-reading sessions called *Howl* take place the first Sunday night of every month. You must be 21 to get in.

SPORTS BARS

Champions

At the Marriott Marquis, 265 Peachtree Center Ave. (between Baker and Harris sts.). ☎ **404/586-6017.** MARTA: Peachtree Center.

Champions is the quintessential sports bar. It's decorated with neon beer signs and a hodgepodge of athletically themed paraphernalia and memorabilia—a baseball autographed by Willie Mays, a 1962 Patterson-Liston fight poster, Duke Snider's baseball mitt, and more. The circular oak bar is plastered with thousands of baseball cards under a laminated surface, and 25 TV monitors, plus two large screens, air nonstop sporting events. (In those rare times when no game is on, they replay highlights.) But there's more to do than sit with your eyes glued to a TV set. You can test your skills on sports video games, play Full Court Frenzy (a coin-op basketball game), or shoot pool. There are frequent promotions involving sports celebrities; they tend to stop in when in town. The menu features chili, nachos, salads, pastas, and burgers. Men outnumber women about five to one.

Damon's Clubhouse

76 Wall St. (near the Esplanade Fountains, above ground at Underground Atlanta). ☎ **404/659-RIBS.** MARTA: Five Points.

This simpatico sports bar at Underground is lots of fun. Out front, on a brick patio shaded by maples, jazz artists occasionally perform on weekend nights. Inside, the action centers on the comfortable Clubhouse, its walls hung with sporting paraphernalia. Windows are attractively shaded by Bermuda shutters, a kayak is suspended from the ceiling, and neon signage includes little tomahawks in honor of the Braves. Big roomy booths all provide great views of five large-screen TVs, on four of which a variety of sporting events are aired. The fifth monitor broadcasts an ongoing trivia game. Ask your server for a push-button set-up, and you can compete for prizes (I won a T-shirt and a $35 gift certificate good for meals here!). Entry is free. A full menu features barbecued chicken, shrimp, and ribs, along with steaks, prime rib, and seafood. Other areas include the more sedate garden room under a beamed cathedral ceiling and a convivial oak-paneled bar. Atlanta sports teams often party here.

Note: Damon's runs a free round-trip shuttle bus to and from Friday Braves games.

GAY/ALTERNATIVE LIFESTYLE

Monday night is gay night at Velvet, listed above.

The Otherside

1924 Piedmont Rd. (just north of Cheshire Bridge Rd.). ☎ **404/875-5238.** Cover $4 Wed and Fri–Sat, $3 Sun (if a band is booked, otherwise $1), free Tues and Thurs. Valet parking $3.

A converted Steak & Ale location, the Otherside retains mementoes of its previous incarnation including Tudor woodwork, cozy amber lighting, and five working fireplaces. Though many people think of it as a lesbian bar, a transexual manager describes the clientele as "gay and straight, black and white, bi and tri, pre- and post-op." I think of it as a relaxed, slightly unhinged place to hang out and dance, where conversation is provocatively unpredictable. There are several appealing rooms. The Key Club, with sofas and a working stone fireplace, has billiards, video games, and a large-screen TV that airs videos appropriate to the evening's entertainment—for instance rodeo footage on a country music night, Broadway movies during show-tune sing-alongs. Live shows take place on the Main Floor. The Hitching Post area offers pool tables, foosball, and country music; it adjoins a patio with umbrella tables under the trees. Sundays the Otherside offers show-tune sing-alongs in the Key Club from 7pm to midnight and dancing to live salsa bands and salsa DJs on the Main Floor from 8pm to 2am. Tuesdays and Thursdays a DJ plays pop and country music, and there's free dance instruction between 8 and 9pm. Wednesdays female impersonators perform at 8 and 10pm, followed by a DJ playing hip-hop, house, and Miami base music. Friday nights there's pop and country on the Main Floor through 10pm, house and dance music till the end of the evening with a break for the Amber Richards Show (female impersonation/comedy) from 11 to 11:30pm; country only in the Hitching Post area (with advanced line-dancing lessons between 9 and 10pm); and live entertainment (acoustic guitar players, pianists, vocalists, etc.) in the Key Club. Saturday's format is almost identical to Friday's, except that house music replaces pop and country on the Main Floor and additional live entertainment during an early show (8 to 9pm) includes male and female strippers and female impersonators. Closed Mondays.

3 More Entertainment

DINNER THEATER

Agatha's Mystery Dinner Theatre

693 Peachtree St. (at 3rd St.). ☎ **404/875-1610.** $39–$45 per person for the show and a five-course dinner including wine, tax, and tip. Paid parking garage three doors south. MARTA: North Avenue.

Thespians manqué and Poirot aficionados: Here's a unique night on the town made to order for you. Agatha's presents comic mystery dramas, with everyone in the audience taking a small role in the play. The action takes place in the dining room during a five-course meal, including a buffet of hot hors d'oeuvres, soup, salad, a choice of five main courses, dessert, wine, and coffee.

When you sit down, you'll be given your lines or instructions. Many roles require finding and collaborating with other members of your performance group. The night I was here, I had to locate other "monkeys" in the room, compose a song with them, and perform it. Don't be nervous about it. Everyone's an amateur, and it's impossible to mess up. In most roles, you're part of a large group. Is it corny? You bet. But it's also an unbelievable amount of fun. Two talented professional actors—who are also the script writers—keep things moving along smoothly, and sometimes they're upstaged by would-be Barrymores in the audience. New shows come on every 12 weeks. Use your little gray cells; all evidence points to the advisability of an evening at Agatha's. Shows are at 7:30pm most nights, 7pm on Sundays. Reservations are essential.

FILM & VIDEO

The IMAGE Film/Video Center, 75 Bennett St. NW, off Peachtree Road between Collier Road and Colonial Homes Drive (☎ 404/ 352-4225), offers regular screenings of work by the nation's most important independent media artists. Screenings might include animation programs (such as a showcase of works by Will Vinton of California Raisin fame), a gay and lesbian film festival, politically themed films and videos, or works of southern media artists. A wide gamut is covered, ranging from existentialist works to Dr. Seuss stories. IMAGE also sponsors numerous lectures and workshops related to film and video on subjects such as "An Introduction to Computer Graphics," "Beginning Screenwriting," and "VCR and Camcorder Basics." And, of course, there's the film festival in June (for details, see "Calendar of Events" in Chapter 3). Most films are $5, $4 for students and seniors.

A COFFEEHOUSE

Virginia's Koffie & Thee Café
1243 Virginia Ave. (between Briarcliff and Rosedale rds.). ☎ **404/875-4453.**

This dreamy candlelit Virginia-Highland café is a rather unconventional choice for a nightlife chapter, but I include it because it suits a certain mood. It's a peaceful place to while away an evening over convivial conversation with a pleasing backdrop of récherché recorded music (mellow jazz, blues, Edith Piaf, whatever). Inside, exposed brick and yellow stucco walls display changing art and photography exhibitions, and racks are filled with interesting books and magazines (including European publications) for your perusal. Gaslight-style lighting fixtures and swagged red velvet draperies over the bar add a note of funky elegance. But weather permitting, the place to be is the patio—a secret garden with seating amid lush greenery under a bamboo-twig awning. No liquor is served, but there are dozens of varieties of coffee and tea to choose from, not to mention ice cream sodas, hot chocolate with marshmallows, and Thai iced tea. Food items range from yogurt with granola to gado gado (a warm Indonesian salad) as well as hefty wedges of fresh-baked pies and cakes. Open nightly till 10 or 11pm.

Index

Now Save Money on All Your Travels by Joining

Frommer's
T R A V E L   B O O K   C L U B

The Advantages of Membership:

1. Your choice of any **TWO FREE BOOKS.**

2. Your own subscription to the **TRIPS & TRAVEL** quarterly newsletter, where you'll discover the best buys in travel, the hottest vacation spots, the latest travel trends, world-class events and festivals, and much more.

3. A **30% DISCOUNT** on any additional books you order through the club.

4. **DOMESTIC TRIP-ROUTING KITS** (available for a small additional fee). We'll send you a detailed map highlighting the most direct or scenic route to your destination, anywhere in North America.

Here's all you have to do to join:

Send in your annual membership fee of $25.00 ($35.00 Canada/Foreign) with your name, address, and selections on the form below. Or call 815/734-1104 to use your credit card.

Send all orders to:

FROMMER'S TRAVEL BOOK CLUB
P.O. Box 473 • Mt. Morris, IL 61054-0473 • ☎ 815/734-1104

YES! I want to take advantage of this opportunity to join Frommer's Travel Book Club.

[ ] My check for $25.00 ($35.00 for Canadian or foreign orders) is enclosed.
   All orders must be prepaid in U.S. funds only. Please make checks payable to Frommer's Travel Book Club.
[ ] Please charge my credit card: [ ] Visa or [ ] Mastercard

   Credit card number: _____

   Expiration date: ___ / ___ / ___

   Signature: _____

   Or call 815/734-1104 to use your credit card by phone.

Name: _____

Address: _____

City: _____ State: _____ Zip code: _____

Phone number (in case we have a question regarding your order): _____

Please indicate your choices for TWO FREE books (*see following pages*):

   Book 1 - Code: _____   Title: _____

   Book 2 - Code: _____   Title: _____

For information on ordering additional titles, see your first issue of the *Trips & Travel* newsletter.

Allow 4–6 weeks for delivery for all items. Prices of books, membership fee, and publication dates are subject to change without notice. All orders are subject to acceptance and availability.   AC1

The following Frommer's guides are available from your favorite bookstore, or you can use the order form on the preceding page to request them as part of your membership in Frommer's Travel Book Club.

FROMMER'S COMPLETE TRAVEL GUIDES

(Comprehensive guides to sightseeing, dining and accommodations, with selections in all price ranges—from deluxe to budget)

FROMMER'S $-A-DAY GUIDES

(Dream Vacations at Down-to-Earth Prices)

FROMMER'S SPECIAL-INTEREST TITLES

Arthur Frommer's Branson!	P107	Frommer's Where to	
Arthur Frommer's New World		Stay U.S.A., 11th Ed.	P102
of Travel (avail. 11/95)	P112	National Park Guide, 29th Ed.	P106
Frommer's Caribbean		USA Today Golf	
Hideaways (avail. 9/95)	P110	Tournament Guide	P113
Frommer's America's 100		USA Today Minor League	
Best-Loved State Parks	P109	Baseball Book	P111

FROMMER'S BEST BEACH VACATIONS

(The top places to sun, stroll, shop, stay, play, party, and swim—with each beach rated for beauty, swimming, sand, and amenities)

California (avail. 10/95)	G100	Hawaii (avail. 10/95)	G102
Florida (avail. 10/95)	G101		

FROMMER'S BED & BREAKFAST GUIDES

(Selective guides with four-color photos and full descriptions of the best inns in each region)

California	B100	Hawaii	B105
Caribbean	B101	Pacific Northwest	B106
East Coast	B102	Rockies	B107
Eastern United States	B103	Southwest	B108
Great American Cities	B104		

FROMMER'S IRREVERENT GUIDES

(Wickedly honest guides for sophisticated travelers and those who want to be)

Chicago (avail. 11/95)	I100	New Orleans (avail. 11/95)	I103
London (avail. 11/95)	I101	San Francisco (avail. 11/95)	I104
Manhattan (avail. 11/95)	I102	Virgin Islands (avail. 11/95)	I105

FROMMER'S DRIVING TOURS

(Four-color photos and detailed maps outlining spectacular scenic driving routes)

Australia	Y100	Italy	Y108
Austria	Y101	Mexico	Y109
Britain	Y102	Scandinavia	Y110
Canada	Y103	Scotland	Y111
Florida	Y104	Spain	Y112
France	Y105	Switzerland	Y113
Germany	Y106	U.S.A.	Y114
Ireland	Y107		

FROMMER'S BORN TO SHOP

(The ultimate travel guides for discriminating shoppers—from cut-rate to couture)

Hong Kong (avail. 11/95)	Z100	London (avail. 11/95)	Z101